LEGAL TRANSPLANTS IN EAST ASIA AND OCEANIA

This volume provides a unique overview of methodologies that are conducive to a successful legal transplant in East Asia and Oceania. Each chapter is drafted by a scholar who holds direct professional experience on the legal transplant considered and has a distinctive insight into the pragmatic difficulties related to grafting an alien institution into a legal tradition. The range of transplants includes the implementation of contractual obligations, the regulation of commercial investments, and the protection of the environment. The majority of recent legal reforms in these geographical areas have aimed at improving national economic performance and fostering trade, and have been directly inspired by European and North American institutional experiences. There is also, however, a growing tendency to couple economic reforms, geared to attract foreign investment, with constitutional reforms that improve the protection of individual rights, the environment and the rule of law.

Dr Vito Breda is the research leader of the International and Comparative Law Group at the University of Southern Queensland.

Previously he was MacCormick Fellow at the Law School of the University of Edinburgh, Visiting Fellow at the Center for European Studies at the A.N.U. and Lecturer in Law at Cardiff University. Vito is the sole author of *Constitutional Law and Regionalism* (2018) and also wrote *The Objectivity of Judicial Decisions* (2017). He was the co-editor with Lidia Rodack of *Diverse Narratives of Legal Objectivity* (2016).

Legal Transplants in East Asia and Oceania

Edited by
VITO BREDA
University of Southern Queensland

CAMBRIDGE
UNIVERSITY PRESS

CAMBRIDGE
UNIVERSITY PRESS

University Printing House, Cambridge CB2 8BS, United Kingdom

One Liberty Plaza, 20th Floor, New York, NY 10006, USA

477 Williamstown Road, Port Melbourne, VIC 3207, Australia

314-321, 3rd Floor, Plot 3, Splendor Forum, Jasola District Centre, New Delhi - 110025, India

79 Anson Road, #06-04/06, Singapore 079906

Cambridge University Press is part of the University of Cambridge.

It furthers the University's mission by disseminating knowledge in the pursuit of education, learning and research at the highest international levels of excellence.

www.cambridge.org
Information on this title: www.cambridge.org/9781009001830
DOI: 10.1017/9781108605991

First published 2019
First paperback edition 2021

A catalogue record for this publication is available from the British Library

ISBN 978-1-108-47529-7 Hardback
ISBN 978-1-009-00183-0 Paperback

To the memory of Ottavio

Contents

Figures

Tables

Contributors

Vito Breda is Senior Lecturer at the School of Law and Justice at the University of Southern Queensland and Professor in Comparative Law (Tier II- National Evaluation Rome)

Colin Campbell is Senior Lecturer in Law at Monash University (Faculty of Law)

Jennifer Corrin is Professor of Law and Director of Comparative Law, Centre for Public, International and Comparative Law at TC Beirne School of Law at The University of Queensland

Anthony Gray is Professor of Law at the School of Law and Justice at the University of Southern Queensland

Benjamen Gussen is Lecturer in Law at the Swinburne Law School

Andrew Harding is Professor of Law at the National University of Singapore

Michihiro Kaino is Professor of Law at Doshisha University

Jonathan Liljeblad is Senior Lecturer at the Australia National University (ANU) School of Law

Sophia O'Brien is Lecturer in Law at University of the Sunshine Coast Law School

Hoong Phun (H. P.) Lee was Sir John Latham Professor of Law (1995–2014) and is Emeritus Professor in Law at Monash University (Faculty of Law)

Drossos Stamboulakis is Lecturer in Law at University of the Sunshine Coast Law School

Erika Techera is Professor of Law at the University of Western Australia Law School and University of Western Australia Oceans Institute

Tiziana Torresi is Lecturer in Politics at Politics and International Relations the University of Adelaide

Jessica Viven-Wilksch is Lecturer in Law at the Adelaide Law School at the University of Adelaide

Acknowledgements

This edited collection book would not have been possible without the generous sponsorship of the University of Southern Queensland. I also owe thanks to: Anthony Gray, Jennifer Corrin for her support as the Director of Comparative Law; Centre for Public, International and Comparative Law at The University of Queensland and the staff of the Australian National University Centre for European Studies for their continuous backing. This has been a long project, and I am deeply grateful to my publisher, all the anonymous peer reviewers, Cambridge University Press, and its truly wonderful staff for their help, kindness and, above all, patience. Finally, I would like to thank Stefania Morandini for patiently and diligently reading my work. Without her, this project would never have been completed.

Table of Cases

Estate of James Sholu, Re [1932] 11 NLR 37
Estate of Lydia Keith and Windy Keith *v.* Vanuatu Internak Air Services Ltd (Vanair) [2006] VUSC 61
Estate of Victor Eoaeo, Re [1999] SBHC 8
First Energy (UK) Ltd *v.* Hungarian International Bank Ltd [1993] 2 Lloyd's Rep 194 (CA)
Forestal Guarani SA *v.* Daros International United States Court of Appeals for the Third Circuit No. 08–4488 [2010]
Fothergill *v.* Monarch Airlines Ltd [1981] AC 251
Fresha Exports Ltd *v.* Tonga Co-operative Federation Ltd [2010] TongaLawRp 31
G *v.* L [1990] 2 Van LR 486
GDH Ltd *v.* Creditor Co Ltd [2008] HCA 1462/2006
Globe Motors Inc *v.* TRW Lucas Varity Electric Steering Ltd [2016] EWCA Civ 396
Gorce v. Miller [2003] TongaLawRp 4
Great Woods Ltd *v.* Springhill Ltd [2012] SBCA 14
Hain, Re [2008] SBHC 112
Halapua *v.* Tonga [2004] TOCA 5
Harrisen *v.* Holloway (No. 2) [1984] 1 Van LR 147
Harry *v.* Kalena Timber Co [1999] SBHC 58
Harry *v.* Kalena Timber Co [2001] 3 LRC 24
HIH Casualty and General Insurance Ltd *v.* Chase Manhattan Bank [2003] UKHL 6
Hospital Products Ltd *v.* United States Surgical Corporation [1984] 156 CLR 41
HSBC International Trust Services (Singapore) Ltd (Trustee of Starhill Global Real Estate Investment Trust) *v.* Toshin Development Singapore Pty Ltd [2012] SGCA 48
Horkulak *v.* Cantor Fitzgerald International [2004] EWCA Civ 1287 (CA)
Hughes Aircraft Systems International *v.* Airservices Australia [1997] FCA 558
Hyundai Engineering and Construction Co Ltd *v.* Vigour Ltd [2005] 3 HKLRD 723 (CA)
Indian Printing and Publishing Co *v.* Police [1932] 3 FLR 142
Indulge Food Pte Ltd *v.* Torubi Marashi Bahram [2010] 2 SLR 540 (HC)
Interfoto Picture Library Ltd *v.* Stilletto Visual Programmes Ltd [1989] 1 QB 433
Iosefo *v.* Tuvalu Red Cross [2012] TVHC 9

Isaac *v*. Kadir [1962] 9 FLR 152
JML Direct Ltd *v*. Freesat UK Ltd [2010] EWCA Civ 34 (CA)
Joli *v*. Joli [2003] VUCA 27
K *v*. T [1985/86] SILR 49
Kapiel *v*. Jenkinson [2002] VUSC 20
Kasa *v*. Biku [2001] LRC 133
KHY Co (SI) *v*. Ling Kun Xiang [1988–1989] SILR 63
Kingdom of Tonga *v*. Save [1993] TOSC 7
Korean Enterprises Ltd *v*. Shell Co (Pacific Islands) Ltd [2002] SBCA 1
M *v*. P [1988] 1 Van LR 333
Mahlon *v*. Mahlon [1984] SILR 86
Matter of the Constitution of Tuvalu and of the Laws of Tuvalu Act 1987, Re the (Unreported, High Court, Tuvalu, Donne CJ, 1989)
McCluskey *v*. Attorney General [1993] SBHC 88
Marcus Clark & Co Ltd *v*. Commonwealth [1952] 87 CLR 177
McCulloch *v*. Maryland 7 US 316 [1819]
McCloy *v*. NSW [2015] HCA 34
Mellish *v*. Motteux [1792] Peake 156; 170 ER 113
Messner *v*. Kruuger [2009] C489/07
Metropolitan Borough Council *v*. Secretary of State for Business, Innovation and Skills [2015] UKSC 6
Milirrpum *v*. Nabalco Pty Ltd (1971) 17 FLR 141
Mineralogy Pty Ltd *v*. Sino Iron (No 6) [2015] FCA 825
Minister for Aboriginal Affairs *v*. Peko-Wallsend [1986] 162 CLR 24
Minister for Immigration and Citizenship *v*. Li 362 [2013] 249 CLR 332, 362 [63]
Minister for Resources *v*. Dover Fisheries Pty Ltd [1993] 116 ALR 54
Miria, Re [2007] SBHC 138
Molaisuva *v*. MV Francis Gerena [2013] SBHC 59
Monde Petroleum SA *v*. Western Zagros Ltd [2016] EWHC 1472 (Comm)
Monis *v*. The Queen [2013] 249 CLR 92
MSC Mediterranean Shipping Co SA *v*. Cottomex Anstalt [2016] EWCA Civ 789
Mulholland *v*. Australian Electoral Commission [2004] 220 CLR 181
Myers *v*. Kestrel Acquisitions Ltd [2015] EWHC 916 (Ch)
Nationwide News Pty Ltd *v*. Wills [1992] HCA 46; [1992] 177 CLR 1
Naylor *v*. Foundas [2004] VUCA 26
Ng Giap Hon *v*. Westcomb Securities Pty Ltd [2009] 3 SLR (R) 518
Nyali Ltd *v*. Attorney-General [1956] 1 QB 1

Table of Statutes

Abbreviations

ASEAN	Association of Southeast Asian Nations
(C)	constitution
CLOUT	UNCITRAL Texts project
CBD	Convention on Biological Diversity
CTH	Commonwealth
D_i	constitutional design for constitution
(e)	efficiency
EEZ	Territorial Sea and Exclusive Economic Zone
FLR	Fiji Law Reports
FSM	Federated States of Micronesia
GCC	Gulf Cooperation Council.
IBA	International Bar Association
IBAHRI	IBA Human Rights Initiative
ICAC	Independent Commission Against Corruption
ILAM	Independent Lawyers' Association of Myanmar
IMTFE	International Military Tribunal for the Far East
IUCN	International Union for Conservation of Nature: Guidelines for Applying Protected Area Management Categories
KIHC	Kiribati High Court
NRSC	Nauru Supreme Court
MPA	marine protected area
MRT	Migration Review Tribunal
NGO	non-governmental organization
NSW	New South Wales
NZ	New Zealand
PC	Privy Council
PECL	Principles of European Contract Law

POGG	peace, order, and good government
PNCA	Pitcairn Court of Appeal
PNSC	Pitcairn Supreme Court
Qld	Queensland
SICA	Solomon Islands Court of Appeal
SIHC	Solomon Islands High Court
SI	Solomon Islands
SICC	Singapore International Commercial Court
SILR	Solomon Islands Law Reports
τ 1	vertical separation of power
τ 2	horizontal overlap of powers
τ (i)	constitutional characteristics
τ Offspring	vertical overlap of powers
TongaLawRp	Tongan Law Reports
TOSC	Tonga Supreme Court
TRA	Trades Recognition Australia
TVHC	Tuvalu High Court
UNCITRAL	United Nations Commission on International Trade Law
UNHRC	United Nations Human Rights Council
UNILEX	Database of international case law and bibliography on the UN Sales Convention (CISG) and the UNIDROIT Principles
UNIDROIT	International Institute for the Unification of Private Law
UK	United Kingdom
Van LR	Vanuatu Law Reports
VUCA	Vanuatu Court of Appeal

Introduction

Vito Breda

This collection of essays discusses the processes and the effects of legal transplants in a sample of legal systems located in the East Asian and Oceania regions. In particular, this book reports on a selection of the latest legal reforms that are currently reshaping institutional relations, individual rights and the protection of the environment in, among others, China, Singapore, Japan, Hong Kong, Thailand, Myanmar, Australia, and a series of Pacific nations. Most of these reforms were inspired by European and North American institutional experiences; others were derived from recent economic developments imposed by international obligations, or by an increased awareness of global environmental implications of unbridled industrial policies.

Three decades ago, a series of legal reforms in the People's Republic of China prepared the conditions for formidable East Asian economic growth. The development has not been without costs. The unbridled development has proceeded, sometimes, without considering safeguards for investors, workers, the environment, or individual rights. There are, however, indications that legal systems in the regions are preparing for a new wave of legal reforms. The aim of this Volume is twofold. Firstly, it reports on the latest phase of development in the institutional structures of the regions aimed at increasing trust among international traders, the judicial procedures aimed at the resolution of disputes, the management of environmental issues and the protection of rights. For instance, Anthony Gray's chapter discusses the recent development of the doctrine of good faith in contractual relations. Examples are taken from Chinese, Hong Kong, Singaporean and Australian contract law. Colin Campbell and H. P. Lee instead focus on the cross-fertilization of the concept of proportionality between European final appellate jurisdictions and Australia. The current developments are, according to Campbell and Lee, inspired by the jurisprudences of the Court of Justice of the European Union and the

European Court of Human Rights, and the German Constitutional Court's jurisprudence.

Secondly, *Legal Transplants in East Asia and Oceania* delivers accounts of a cluster of epistemic methods that have been developed in different legal systems to implement overseas-inspired institutional reforms. The collection of essays, in particular, tests the correlation between foreign-inspired legal reforms and expected (and unexpected) cultural changes. In the late eighties, the transplant of capitalist principles such as labour and management meritocracy, and competition, into the Chinese legal system delivered, it is reasonable to suggest, the expected economic surplus in the Chinese economy.[1] One could be forgiven for considering the grafting of legal axioms of the market economy onto a socialist society as a success, but the multiplicity of factors that distinguish a modern cross-fertilization of legal, institutional, and economic principles cannot easily be measured. Harding's chapter directly engages with the debate over measuring the success of legal transplants. Perhaps one of the most lucid examples of complexity and the unforeseen effect of legal transplants in South East Asian legal transplants considered in this collection of essays is the case of the grafting of English trust law into Chinese law. Harding noted that China's ruling party actively sought to transplant the English and Welsh trust law into its own legal system. The assumption was that institutions such as the English and Welsh trust law might foster a controlled development of a *quasi*-capitalist legal economy. The results of the reform were probably unforeseen. The case of the unexpected institutional structure of the English–Chinese trust transplant might attract a sceptical view on the benefits – even the conceptual significance – of the idea of transplanting complex legal devices. However, the aims of legal transplants are, it is reasonable to suggest, not to create hollow institutions, nor to translate rules mechanically into a recipient system. Rather, the aim of the majority of the East Asian and Oceania legal transplants is, within the limits of reasonableness related to the assessment of any legal reforms, to alter human conduct in a way that increases prosperity and, sometimes, protects rights. From this perspective, the English–Chinese trust law might have achieved, albeit with a supernumerary of foreign references, its aim, or merely just a quick reprieve before another inevitable institutional reform.

In discussing the farrago of rules associated with the English–Chinese trust law, it might be important to mention that Harding's narrative, as with all the

[1] For an analysis of the political background that led to the establishment of many of the recent Chinese reforms see, for instance: F. Fukuyama, *Political Order and Political Decay: From the Industrial Revolution to the Globalisation of Democracy* (Profile Books, 2014) 342–64.

analyses provided in this collection, required an assessment of the probability of the connection and the reasonableness of deductive analyses. To enhance the reader's experience, reasoned effort was made to reduce the extent of tropes that manifest such uncertainty. Thus, tiresome indicators of underlying cognitive processes such as 'in all probability' or 'it appears likely' were omitted whenever possible, yet readers should assume that such cognitive processes were carried out.

It could be argued, and again Harding points out the relative futility of such an exercise, that Chinese equity law has very little in common with the English legal system, and thus, the transplants failed. This would be a persuasive narrative if the aims of the legal reform were to replicate the laws of England in China. However, the example mentioned in Harding's chapter is only one of the many institutional experiences that, in the past three decades, took place in East Asia and Oceania. These new – in terms of comparison to their colonial predecessors – waves of legal transplants are designed to 'fit' into a pre-existing culture. Myanmar, for instance, has recently begun to establish institutions that allow a free flow of ideas and capital. Myanmar is, by way of comparison to China, not a socialist political system. Recent reforms are seeking to balance aspirations for the economic development of a new democracy with safeguarding the stability linked to a pre-existing system of governance. In discussing Myanmar's intention to reform the national bar association in a way that guarantees a level of independence from government, Jonathan Liljeblad's chapter explains the complex mechanisms and the effects that such an aim might have on pre-existing legal cultures.

More generally, Liljeblad's analysis of the reform of the legal profession hints at the lexical inadequacy of the term 'legal transplants'. The term is, it would be reasonable to suggest, misleading. There is, in relation to law, no horticultural or clinical term for such a transplant. Foreign-inspired legal reforms discussed in this book are often elements of wide-ranging socioeconomic policies aimed at fostering specific aims. It is for this reason that *Legal Transplants in East Asia and Oceania* seeks to capture a sample of the methodologies, rather than defining an archetypical model for the implementation of foreign law.

Colin Campbell and H. P. Lee, for instance, explain how the High Court of Australia developed, or is in the process of developing, its own concept of proportionality inspired by the British common law. The term 'proportionality' is a general concept associated in Europe and in the British legal systems with a judicial cognitive process. The court refers to proportionality in instances in which it is asked to qualify and balance, for instance, conflicts between rights. A decision that balances a conflict between rights and freedom (such as the right to privacy and the freedom of a free press) has general implications and so, Lee and Campbell noted, Australian jurisprudence has been cautious. This point is delicate, so I must be precise. The aim of the collection is not to suggest that legal transplants are risky. Rather, essays such as the ones by Lee and Campbell show that legal transplants are part of a communal learning experience designed to meet the specific demands of a legal culture. Consequently, the collection includes, for instance, an evaluation of legal transplants such as those that resulted in the decolonization in the Pacific regions. Jennifer Corrin discusses the risks associated with the introduction of General Application Statutes in the Pacific islands. However, the majority of the essays included in this endeavour show that legal transplants must fit.

Legal transplants, even during times of colonial exploitation, have seldom been a 'cut-and-copy job'. Corrin, in her chapter, explains how English law was adapted to fit the specific cultural requirements of the British colonies in the Pacific region. The overall exploitative and military strategic aims of colonial transplants, from the outset, outweighed cultural sensibilities. The recent reforms of East Asian legal systems have, Harding suggests, little in common with those colonial experiences. The aims of the new reforms inspired by overseas experiences are, by way of comparison to imperial strategic predecessors, to enhance the commonwealth of the community and to establish a commercial and cultural exchange with an alien system.

Often the migration of legal concepts aimed at enhancing the problem-solving capabilities of a legal system do happen without political prescience. In his contribution to this collection, Drossos Stamboulakis shows how judges and legal professionals working in modern legal systems interpret legal norms based on a series of historically inherited epistemic practices. These practices are perceived by the professional community, for multifarious reasons, as scientifically objective *sic*. The existence of cultural variations in judicial practices is a platitudinous concept and Legrand derives from it an argument against the benefits, perhaps even the reason for the existence of the idea of legal transplants. This deduction is not only contrafactual, as modern legal systems are and, from a historical perspective, have always been inspired by foreign material; but is also epistemically unpersuasive. Most legal systems are the result of multiple layers of legal transplants, which, in many legal systems, commenced with the grafting of Roman law onto local customs. Such a multi-layered system might be due to the competitive nature of litigation (it is expected that the legal counsel will use all legal narratives to support the client's claim) or because the majority of judges do perceive the court system as an imperfect truth-finding device that needs constant tuning.

Independently from this reasoning, there is compelling evidence that legal transplants do occur, and foreign-inspired reforms are changing the legal landscape of East Asia and Oceania. There is, for instance, a long-established cooperation and sharing of training resources between European and Chinese universities. The list of activities of the Sino-German Legal Cooperation Programme is one of the many examples of a long-term exchange of legal expertise between Europe and China, which commenced with the German- (and Japanese-) inspired reform of the Chinese Civil Code. The combination of new training with the consistent development experienced in the regions has also inspired, according to a recent collection titled *Law and Economics with Chinese Characteristics: Institutions for Promoting Development in the Twenty-First Century* edited by David Kennedy and Joseph E. Stiglitz, other developing nations.[2]

Again, *Legal Transplants in East Asia and Oceania* will not seek to provide a comprehensive analysis of the legal transplants in a rather large and culturally diverse area of the world. Given the current dynamic nature of the legal systems of East Asia, a book that focuses on describing legal reforms would merely bring a transient benefit to its readership. The descriptive analyses in this Volume will instead inform the readership of the gamut of methods used to implement legal transplants. The range of essays focuses on, for instance, the methods employed in comparative studies (such as the analysis of the cross-fertilization of judicial practices and how to pilot legal reforms inspired by overseas laws).

Thematically, the Volume is divided into three sections. In the first part, contributors discuss the methods (in theory and practice) of modern legal transplants in East Asia and the Pacific. This part includes a critical assessment of imperialistic, so to speak, legal transplants. The second part focuses on legal transplants that seek to increase trade. The third part relating to reforms focuses on environmental protection, and more generally, on the protection of individual rights.

In the first part of this collection, Professor Andrew Harding's chapter describes, by referring to the recent Chinese, Singaporean and Myanmar experiences, the distinctive elements of East Asian legal transplants. The chapter, titled 'The Legal Transplants Debate: Getting beyond the Impasse?' provides a critical overview of the Eurocentric (and mostly hollow) polemic over the role of transplants in modern legal studies. The main

2 D. Kennedy and J. E. Stiglitz (eds.), *Law and Economics with Chinese Characteristics: Institutions for Promoting Development in the Twenty-First Century* (Oxford University Press, 2013).

contention in Harding's chapter is that legal transplants, once the stakeholders have been 'informed' of the ways of the donor legal system, are designed and carefully managed by the receiving legal system. The essay is rich with examples taken from Harding's direct experience as a law teacher in Singapore and as a comparative constitutional law expert.

The breath and the depth of Harding's evaluation sets the theme of the collection. A legal transplant, that is the key contribution of his rich essay, must be 'fit for purpose'. Thus, a foreign-inspired reform must be socially integrated, or at the very least, it must prepare the conditions for its progressive legal and sociological acceptance. It should (short of when a state has the desire to mimic a legal reform to obtain the financial support of international organizations) also facilitate the achievement of a specific aim.

The first test of Harding's contention is in Jennifer Corrin's essay in which she appraises a sample of controversial legal transplants. The paper is titled 'Transplant Shock: the Hazards of Introducing Statutes of General Application' and provides an example of the lingering negative effects of colonial Eurocentric legal transplants. Corrin moves the centre of attention of the collection squarely onto the Pacific region, where she reviews the effect of 'statutes of general application' in, among others, Fiji and the Solomon Islands' legal systems. Statutes of general application graft foreign legal material onto a national legal system. Statutes of general application are typically adopted to prevent a legislative lacuna during the decolonization process, but often, as is the case of the Solomon Islands, their effect lingers on. Reliance on foreign legal expertise and the related case law brings obvious pragmatic advantages but, as Corrin points out, it also increases the level of uncertainty. In areas such as family law, for instance, English jurisprudence has followed (dynamically) the distinctive societal changes of English secular society. It is relatively safe to say that religious attitudes in the Pacific have not followed the path set in England and Wales.

Michihiro Kaino's chapter instead engages the role of legal transplants as a part of social-engineering endeavours. Japan's institutional history is considered, by, for instance, Fukuyama, as the reference point of current economic development in East Asia. Kaino, in his chapter titled 'Bentham's Theory of Legal Transplants and His Influence in Japan', discusses the complex debates and the subsequent adjustments which prepared the route for the modernization process of Japan's legal system. It is reasonable to suggest that the Japanese eighteenth-century process of rapid industrialization, the early twentiethcentury disastrous flirtation with militarism and the present flourishing democracy have all been inspired by European and North American legal institutions. The connection between European and Japanese legal cultures has been discussed elsewhere, yet Kaino's chapter is revealing because it focuses on the historical narratives that prepared legal transplants in the Japanese legal landscape.

For instance, Bentham's idea of codification was, as Kaino explains, not accepted in Japan. European family law has been perceived as particularly at odds with Japanese culture, but Kaino's contribution to this collection is conceptual. It is, he argues, the dialectical interaction between national aspirations, embedded cultural assumptions and foreign institutions that tilts a legal system towards a specific goal.

The debate over reforms that aim at increasing efficiency is also discussed by Benjamen Gussen's essay. Gussen, by drawing from his experience as an engineer, drafts a complex narrative that focuses on the comparison between the Australian, American, and Canadian federal systems. The Australian Constitution is, Gussen points out, one of the examples of a legal transplant grafted onto a decolonization process. The Federal Constitution was largely inspired by America's constitutional experience that developed a two-tier state/federal sovereignty, but the jurisprudential interpretation of the text was left to judges who were trained in a British, and distinctively English and Welsh, public tradition. Gussen points out the negative implications in economic terms and the potential solutions to dealing with an uncoordinated legal transplant. In this intricate analysis, he suggests an alternative to Harding's analysis of modern legal transplants in East Asia.

The second part of *Legal Transplants in East Asia and Oceania* discusses legal reforms aimed at increasing trade and national economic efficiency. The shift is both methodological and thematic. The first chapter of this section is authored by Anthony Gray and it focuses on the cross-border fertilization of the principle of contractual good faith. Good faith is often perceived in codified European legal systems as a cornerstone of contractual relations.

In civil law systems, the concept defines, via the implementation of the jurisprudence of the 'mistake', the set of criteria necessary for the completion of a contract. In common-law jurisdictions, the idea of good faith in a contract has not travelled well. *Baird Textile Holdings Ltd* v. *Marks & Spencer plc* is the leading case in English and Welsh law. Yet, Gray shows in his rich chapter that Singapore and Hong Kong, as well as Australia and New Zealand, have all been reluctant to accept the role of the concept of good faith in contractual relations. The chapter is aptly titled 'The Incomplete Legal Transplant: Good Faith and the Common Law.' The difficulties of expanding the role of good faith in East Asian and Oceanic common-law jurisdictions are analyzed in detail and Gray shows that a more expansive role of the concept might serve both the aim of increasing economic efficiency and the coherence of common law jurisdictions. Again, the resistance to adopt a legal concept does not prove, as Kaino persuasively argued, the infeasibility of a legal transplant. Rather, it shows the effects of idiosyncratic assumptions and the potential benefits that a foreign-inspired reform might have had.

The resistance to change a legal system, as introduced by Gray, is also discussed in Jessica Viven-Wilksch. The aim of her essay is to evaluate the transplant of the UNIDROIT Principles of Commercial Contracts and the Convention on the International Sale of Goods in Australia. The chapter is titled: 'How Long Is Too Long to Determine the Success of a Legal Transplant? International Doctrines and Contract Law in Oceania'. There is, Viven-Wilksch argues, a dichotomy between the formal and substantive implementation of, for instance, UNIDROIT Principles in Australian law. The lack of jurisprudential implementation has, among other pernicious effects, a negative impact on international trade for Australia. The conditions for a transplant of the UNIDROIT Principles in Australia, Viven-Wilksch persuasively argued, have been well prepared and the recipient legal system should increase the speed of adoption.

As mentioned earlier, Campbell's and Lee's contribution analyses the Australian High Court's development of the concept of proportionality inspired by English and Welsh law jurisprudence. The concept of proportionality has been in the daily diet of the jurisprudence of the final appellate of European national and international jurisdictions. The European Court of Justice, European Court of Human Rights, the UK Supreme Court and the German Constitutional Court have all referred to it. However, the argument defended in this technical analysis is that a distinctive English and Welsh idea of proportionality is 'trickling into' several areas of Australian law. High Court judges do refer to the concept of proportionality as elaborated by Law Ladies and Lords in Britain. Again, Australian jurisdiction appears, in Campbell's and Lee's analysis, and by way of comparison to other common-law systems, extremely cautious.

The distinctive Australian – at least in the examples considered in this collection – resistance towards the adoption of foreign law is made more evident in the conclusive chapter of this section on trade and economic efficiency. Stamboulakis's essay focuses on the procedures of the Singapore International Commercial Court. The debate over the procedural distinctiveness of the Singapore International Commercial Court is a proxy for the debate over the acceptance of alien legal material in home jurisdictions. Stamboulakis argues, in a nutshell, that the Singapore International Commercial Court is currently positioning itself as the court of choice for international disputes in the Asia and Pacific regions.

Stamboulakis's essay on protecting contractual commercial relations provides the springboard for the last section of this collection in which legal transplants protect individual rights and the environment. The development of trade and the promotion of private initiatives might have been, among others, two of the driving elements of the economic renaissance of East Asia and the Pacific regions. Yet, there is an increased awareness of the detrimental effects of exploitative industrial policies. The third part of this Volume focuses on legal transplants aimed at protecting rights and the environment. The aims of these foreign-inspired legal reforms are to increase the commonwealth and to reduce the gap between the quality of life between Western-style democracies and East Asian legal systems. Again, the dilemma that contributors were asked to engage with was whether the implementation of international commitments was *in practice and in theory* fitting of a distinctive legal culture.

The part opens with Erika Techera's essay on the protection of the marine environment. More specifically, in her essay titled 'Shark Sanctuaries As Vehicles for Transplanting Conservation Tools in Disparate Legal Jurisdictions', Techera shows the clearest example of a direct correlation between social attitudes, legal transplants and, in this case, international environmental policies. As is the case for the industrialization of North America and Europe, the economic development of East Asia had, it is reasonable to suggest, a detrimental effect on the marine environment. The detrimental effects on EU fisheries due to increased demand is well known, but the depletion of shark populations has been particularly associated with East Asian cultural practices. Techera does not dwell on that. Her essay focuses instead on testing the cultural interdependencies that facilitated (or hindered) the establishment of marine sanctuaries aimed, among other aspects, at the protection of a depleting shark population. This process has been defined by borrowing legal concepts and by legal transplants. One of the most interesting observations in Techera's essay is that Pacific nations that are heavily dependent on sea resources but where shark protection is linked to animist beliefs tend to be willing recipients of environmental policies. This is the case even if such policies might have, by way of comparison to other more industrialized and wealthier nations, a substantial burden on individual and national prosperity.

Sophia O'Brien's chapter continues the analysis of the protection of rights by focusing on the general development of a human rights culture in East Asia. The essay discusses the increased level of accountability expected from perpetrators of crimes against humanity. In her paper titled 'Global Norms; Local Resistance: Addressing Impunity in Japan and Beyond', she provides an analysis of the establishment of a multifaceted human rights culture in the

East Asian legal system by considering the Japanese legal system. In East Asia, human rights are still perceived as a mildly elaborate manifestation of cultural imperialism or, in the case of Australia, as an unnecessary set of legal devices in a common-law tradition. By considering the processes put in place by successive governments, O'Brien makes a cogent case for the expansion of institutional accountability. The analysis again shows what Harding would describe as a tension between what is perceived as culturally appropriate and the legalist implementation of foreign law.

Tiziana Torresi's chapter discusses the potential benefits, rather than the limits, of inserting foreign legislation into East Asian legal systems. This essay is, compared to O'Brien's contribution, a theoretical analysis of the beneficial effects of allocating a series of rights, *à la* citizenship of the European Union so to speak, to East Asian immigrants. The set of rights included in the citizenship of the European Union were introduced as one of the many measures to ensure peace and stability in Europe. In the 1950s, European leaders actively signed a series of international agreements which, for instance, opened the markets for coal, steel and, later, atomic energy. An open market, it was surmized, would discourage European member states from seeking military expansion at the expense of neighbouring countries. The opening of the human capital market arrived later but it was one of the policies that ensured, it could be reasonably argued, peace and prosperity in the region. Torresi's chapter focused on the effect that an analogous allocation of a set of rights to East Asian immigrants might have in the region. Again, the chapter includes an evaluation of the cultural limits of such a courageous transplant.

PART I

1

The Legal Transplants Debate: Getting Beyond the Impasse?

Andrew Harding

I WATSON/LEGRAND AND OTHER BINARIES

The debate about legal transplants is very well known.[1] Unfortunately that debate, while familiar, or at least familiarly confusing to many, has become trapped in a number of rather fixed binaries. It appears to have failed to achieve either resolution or forward movement. And this is in spite of a number of laudable attempts to untie the knot. These binaries may be stated briefly as follows:

1. Legal transplants are said to be either possible or impossible (but does this mean logically or just in practice?)
2. They are fundamentally either related or unrelated to society and 'culture'.
3. They are only possible in private, not public, law; or they are possible in both. (This issue I do not explore here.)
4. What counts as success? It is possible/ impossible to say, or there is no such thing.

Unfortunately much of this debate centres on, and commences with, the views of Alan Watson and Pierre Legrand. I say 'unfortunately' not out of disrespect (in fact I will go on to state what we owe to both of these scholars), but because, to judge by the lists of their publications at least,[2] neither of them

[1] For good summaries of the debate, see W. Ewald, 'Comparative Jurisprudence (II): the Logic of Legal Transplants', *American Journal of Comparative Law* 43 (1995), 489; and, for a comparative commercial law scholar's views, N. Foster, 'Transmigration and Transferability of Commercial Law in a Globalized World', ch. 4 of A. Harding and E. Örücü (eds.), *Comparative Law in the 21st Century* (Kluwer Law International, 2001).

[2] For Alan Watson see www.law.ed.ac.uk/people/alanwatson; his work is directed mainly to EU law and legal history. For a conspectus of Legrand's work, see www.sandiego.edu/law/faculty/recent-scholarship.php?ID=639.

appears to have any real interest in legal transplantation as a phenomenon relevant to the law in any area or areas of the world where attempts are being made to reform and develop the legal system. Their concerns are not with the development of law as a project but rather with legal theory. Watson is a legal historian concerned mainly with the 'reception' of Roman law in Europe and with European or civil law more generally,[3] while Legrand is a legal theorist with an interest in comparative law. It might seem unlikely that these scholars, whomever is right (and in my view they are both wrong in important respects on the issue of legal transplants), having very little experience of these issues across the world, would have any convincing judgement to offer. Indeed, one supposes that such judgement would have to be based on research that is both deeply considered and broadly based. Reference to research of this kind is missing in their work.

In Legrand's case, if he is correct in saying, as he does, that legal transplantation is logically impossible,[4] he could of course be excused from investigating the empirical truth of his assertion, because on his thesis facts would be completely irrelevant. Nonetheless, we could, I think, reasonably demand in return that he provide an explanation of what exactly it is that thousands of law reformers are doing when they perform the task the rest of us are inclined to call (even if inaccurately as Legrand avers) 'legal transplantation'. They are patently engaged in doing *something*, whatever name we choose to give to it. We cannot simply deny that an industry exists in which many billions of dollars are spent, even if we wish it did not, or we believe its premises to be misguided or perhaps even dangerous.[5] The debate on both sides makes very large claims indeed without, apparently, there being any obligation on either scholar to check whether these claims are in fact true in what (to use a neutral term, and in the absence of any other likely candidate) I will call 'the real world of legal diffusion'.[6] Empirical inquiry is just not on the agenda of either of these scholars, and they have no pretence of engaging in socio-legal research of a kind that would furnish some answers to the important questions about legal transplants. Now, admittedly it would be difficult even to design let alone execute a research project on legal transplantation in the real world of legal

3 He has however advised on the drafting of a civil code for Armenia: see above n. 2.

4 P. Legrand, 'The impossibility of "legal transplants"', *Maastricht Journal of European and Comparative Law* 4 (1997), 111.

5 For discussion of legal transplants in relation to legal technical assistance, see J. Arnscheidt, B. Van Rooij, and J. M. Otto (eds.), *Lawmaking for Development: Explorations into Theory and Practice of International Legislative Projects* (Leiden University Press, 2008).

6 W. Twining, 'Diffusion of law: A global perspective', ch. 9 of W. Twining, *General Jurisprudence: Understanding Law from a Global Perspective* (Cambridge University Press, 2004).

diffusion that would definitively answer the questions posed by this debate, given the potential breadth and complexity of such a project. This difficulty should encourage us to be modest and provisional, rather than sweeping and definitive, about our conclusions. The latter does not describe the work of either Watson or Legrand.

As a teacher who has taught classes on legal transplants for many years, I can affirm that it is quite obvious to most students in my classes (currently second year undergraduate LLB students at the National University of Singapore) that Watson and Legrand do not actually address the same issues, and that their disagreements are largely about the use of words rather than the use of law. It takes most of my students about two or three hours of familiarity with the literature (i.e. the time taken to absorb two or three representative pieces) to realize that this is so. Unfortunately the sterile nature of the debate about legal transplants gives the impression that the debate is over because it has reached an impasse. We are right to move on from the Watson-Legrand binary,[7] but we are not right to conclude that the debate is therefore over. Indeed in many ways it seems to me the debate has not even been properly joined, because it has largely proceeded on the basis of false premises and irrelevant concerns, and a kind of disengagement with the real world of legal diffusion that I find, frankly, quite astonishing. I say 'largely' because I believe there are in fact some very useful things to be learned from the legal transplants debate and indeed from both scholars; so before we move forward let me indicate in what ways we have profited from this titanic, if unfortunate, clash, as well as the ways in which this clash propels us to other issues or approaches. Following that I will critique the binaries listed above, drawing on Asian experiences. I do so partly because I know more about law in Asia than in other regions, and partly because I wish to demonstrate quite concretely with examples (as does Foster, using the concept of universal security in England, France and Quebec[8]) just how far the debate has been drawn away from the real world of legal diffusion. Asian experience could also help us test the universality of relevant propositions. Given the space limitations I am not able to be thorough in this task, and will make use of examples rather than macro-comparative research.

Legrand claims that Watson does not consider 'sociological, economic, political, historical, cultural, epistemological or ethical'[9] realities; but at the

7 See, further, Foster (n. 1); and G. Teubner, 'Legal Irritants: Good Faith in British Law or How Unifying Law Ends Up in New Divergences', *Modern Law Review* 61 (1998), 11.

8 Above, n. 1.

9 Legrand (n. 4), 122.

same time adduces no evidence of this kind himself to support his ideas; he merely makes assertions. Watson similarly makes use of very little evidence other than the reception of Roman law in medieval Europe. Both approaches seem as far from the real world of legal diffusion as they could possibly be.

II THE WATSON/LEGRAND DEBATE: POSITIVE AND NEGATIVE CONTRIBUTIONS

Watson informs us (I believe he is right here) that law can in principle be detached from the social, political, and economic conditions of the society in which it originates. We call this the 'donor' society, the 'donee' being the receiving society; but the generosity of such transfers is not terribly apparent. Moreover, he says that legal transplantation is the primary means of legal change.[10] His work created controversy because he denied that law is a mirror of society. Using his own example, it is of no interest for legal transplantation purposes (although it is extremely interesting from other points of view) to know how law operated in the Roman empire – let us say in Constantinople at the time of Justinian and the formulation of the *corpus juris civilis*. Indeed at the time of the great reception of Roman civil law in Europe (Watson's prime example[11]) we knew nothing about this, and probably cared even less; even now we know relatively little about the real world of Roman law.[12] One can of course imagine the *plebs Romana* reacting cynically to the tendency of their leaders to praise their ancient law and see it as defining them separately from the rest of juridically impoverished humanity. However, this is something we are right not to worry about.

Based on legal experience in South East Asia (SE Asia), which is my own area of interest, it seems to me quite correct both to say that law is not a mirror of society and that legal transplantation is the primary mode of legal change. In that region there is a plurality of laws but almost all were transplanted by some means or other from elsewhere. The issue of the law-and-society gap is not simply a matter of defective enforcement of law; it is also a matter of societal fit. The existence of such a gap is hardly surprising when most of the law in that region is derived from civil law or common law, both of which were

10 A. Watson, *Legal Transplants: An Approach to Comparative Law* 2nd edn (University of Georgia Press, 1993), ch. 2.

11 Ibid., ch. 1; and see A. Watson, 'Legal Transplants and European Private Law', 4.4 *Electronic Journal of Comparative Law* (December 2000), www.ejcl.org/ejcl/44/44-2.html (accessed 25 May 2017).

12 See, however, P. Du Plessis, C. Ando, and K. Tuori (eds.), *The Oxford Handbook of Roman Law and Society* (Oxford University Press, 2016).

developed in Europe and largely imposed (except for Thailand) by colonial governments.[13] This rather obvious issue leads me to think that law is indeed not entirely a mirror of society. On this point Watson is right. But the gap also alerts us to the problems we undoubtedly find when law is transplanted. Watson claims that he never said legal transplantation was easy. In fact he does say that, leading us to think, with Ewald, that there is a 'strong' Watson and a 'weak' Watson.[14] However that may be, we should in legal transplantation pay attention to the obvious fact that legal transplants encounter problems of 'fit' of the kind to which Legrand draws our attention.

It could of course be argued that what we should be paying attention to is not law as set out in the books, but the lived reality of law, which especially in legal-transplant areas like SE Asia will differ very much from law in the books. This calls into question our definition of law. It makes little sense to me to define law in terms of lived experience or cultural factors, and so on. This is not because such lived experience is illusory or irrelevant (far from it), but because reasonable use of language demands it. If law is defined in such a way, then the statement, 'the law does not reflect society's lived experience of law' would be quite incoherent, equivalent to saying 'the law does not reflect itself'. So I wish to insist that there is indeed a gap between law and society, and that law does not always mirror, or variably mirrors, society. This does not entail the impossibility of legal transplants, either logically or practically. Nor does it mean defining law in a way that folds into it a number of non-legal factors. The fact that I use the term 'non-legal' here (I suggest neither controversially nor vaguely) rather proves my point about the use of language. Here of course we are close to entering another problematical debate –one concerning legal pluralism – but that will have to be left on one side.[15]

One other issue to which the legal transplants debate therefore alerts us is the indeterminacy of the words 'law' and 'legal', at least as used by legal scholars. In this sense the debate contributes to understanding of 'law', even if not of legal transplantation as such. We might wish to see 'law' as a collection of ideas or socially inflected norms, not necessarily just as a collection of rules (although I think most people see law as precisely a set of rules, as I have hinted

13 I have set the argument out in full in A. Harding, 'Comparative Law and Legal Transplantation in South East Asia: Making Sense of the "Nomic Din"', ch. 9 of D. Nelken and J. Feest (ed.), *Adapting Legal Cultures* (Hart Publishing, 2001); see also A. Harding, 'Legal traditions of Southeast Asia', in J. D. Wright (editor-in-chief), *International Encyclopedia of the Social & Behavioral Sciences*, 2nd edn, vol. 13 (Elsevier, 2015), 812.

14 Ewald (n. 1), 491.

15 B. Tamanaha, 'Understanding Legal Pluralism: From Past to Present, Global to Local' *Sydney Law Review* 30 (2007), 375.

in the last paragraph, and they are not in essence wrong to do so). Legrand shows us that even the notion of a 'rule' is indeterminate, whereas Watson appears to think the meanings of the words 'law' and 'rule' are obvious. What we learn from Legrand is that a rule carries along with it a good deal of interpretive baggage, and indeed he goes further to say it is meaningless without that baggage. He sees law as a combination of propositional statements and their culture-specific meanings.[16]

> Let us then examine Legrand's idea a little further. Are rules really always subject to culture-specific meaning? For example, a rule that says a person can marry only on attaining the age of 18 – is there really any room for such culture-specific meaning?

Now of course it may be argued that words such as 'can', 'marry' and 'age' may have such meanings and, if we stretch our imaginations beyond what is reasonable, I suppose these might differ somewhat from one society to another. But what would be relevant to our inquiry is simply the legal meaning. Legal meanings are, obviously, not always completely clear, nor are they always taken seriously or complied with; but they are not unclear in the sense that they differ from ordinary usage. Let us consider an example.

If for example, we found, as is indeed often the case, that couples in Singapore go through a customary marriage ceremony long after they have registered the marriage officially (which they might do in order, for example, to gain an advantage in the public housing queue),[17] the fact that their wedding banquet guests at the ceremony congratulated them on being 'married' would not alter the fact that they were actually already married. A guest might of course be quite aware of this, but would be using the word 'married' in a special (sociological or cultural) sense. If the happy couple were told that Legrand says they were not married, because the rule needs to have some baggage attached to it before we can understand it, they might fear losing their place in the queue; but they would fear this outcome for no good reason – they are married.

The legal meaning of marriage would only be unclear if there was legal doubt as to whether observance of custom or official registration was the legally salient event; or if one of the partners were Muslim, a different rule might be applicable. What society thinks or unconsciously assumes may be interesting sociologically or psychologically, but it would actually be legally

[16] Legrand (n. 4), 114.

[17] C. Tan, 'We Are Registered: Actual Processes and the Law of Marriage in Singapore', *International Journal of Law, Policy and the Family* 13 (1999), 1.

and practically irrelevant. If this is not so, then why do clients see lawyers in order to ascertain the meanings of rules affecting them? Imagine if a young woman seeking to marry her fiancé faced a problem of having lost her birth certificate. Her lawyer should, on Legrand's hypothesis, advise her as follows: 'Never mind the lack of proof that you are 18; we can always get a sociolinguist carry out a survey to discover how the language in question is interpreted sociologically, and then you can go through a culturally informed wedding ceremony in which your adulthood is part of the deal. The rule, you see, is in itself meaningless.' A court may well not be impressed by this, and the client, I suggest, should not pay for the advice rendered.

We can of course also question, when we say 'culture-specific meaning', what this term actually means. Whose culture and how specific? Would the sociolinguist in my example actually be able to carry out the relevant survey even if it were relevant? Where should he or she start and when would the answer truly have been found?

Watson, on the other hand, defines law as consisting of 'bare propositional statements'[18], which on Legrand's view cannot survive their removal to another society. This is the 'borrowing of a bare string of words ... a rhetorical strategy involving the ordinary act of repetition'.[19] For me this insight of Legrand can be taken along with the work of Rodolfo Sacco[20] on legal formants. It helps us understand the complex relationship between law and society, and in practice it is a forceful reminder of the fact that legal transplantation is never easy; it does not, however, lead to the conclusion that it is impossible. Nor does it lead to the conclusion that law is not, indeed, a series of bare propositional statements. Watson replies to Legrand that he never said that legal transplantation was easy;[21] and that he agrees that once a rule is transplanted its *effect* is changed by the new context in which it finds itself.[22] And despite Legrand's contempt for bare strings of words, it seems a perverse use of language to say that, if such a bare string of words finds itself on somebody else's statute book, then it is simply not law. The issue is actually *not whether it is law, but whether it is good law*.

18 Legrand (n. 4), 113.

19 Ibid., 121.

20 R. Sacco, 'Legal Formants: a Dynamic Approach to Comparative Law', *American Journal of Comparative Law* 39 (1) (1991), 343.

21 Actually he did: Watson (n. 10), 95–6.

22 Watson (n. 11) [note: no pinpoint reference provided since it is an electronic journal with no page numbers].

III WHAT IS IT WE TRANSPLANT WHEN WE 'TRANSPLANT LAW'?

The word 'law' in English translates rather uncertainly or ambiguously into most other languages. Asian languages, for example, tend to have different words indicating the different things we subsume into 'law'.[23] To this extent 'law' is indeterminate in some contexts, and may explain some of the confusion we encounter in this debate. It catches too much. In many legal-transplant situations the 'law' that is being transplanted is likely in fact to be just an idea of a law, where the institutional and interpretive baggage that Legrand finds so problematical in practice (and indeed in logic) has been stripped away. Here we can see 'law' or 'legal' as relating to a mere idea; we should in fact find another word to indicate this, because in my view it is probably at least as common as transplanting a statute or a legal rule as such, narrowly defined in the way I have set out above. The notion of a legal idea is helpful in explaining how law can be transplanted. It needs to be separated from its context, which (I agree with Watson) can be achieved easily. The problem is how to fit it into its new context. Largely in practice we are talking about the transplantation of a legal idea, not a law as such. To that extent Legrand's objections are irrelevant in practice.

To give an example of this, many societies have adopted law reflecting, say, regressive taxation, constitutional review of legislation, insanity as a defence to a criminal charge, the inability of a vendor with a defective title to pass on a good title to goods, or the legal recognition of same-sex marriages. Asking where this 'law' came from might seem to the legislator a rather odd question. She might well reply, 'Why should it matter? It is just an idea (maybe even an obvious one) that we took and used to our advantage.' Equally she might, I suppose, reply 'I don't recall, it doesn't matter', or 'Queensland', or 'utilitarianism', or 'international law'. She might even, I suppose, reply that Japanese law was carefully examined to see if it worked well in practice. So – yes there are plenty of cases where a body of law is regarded as authoritative, comprehensive, and tested by evident utility in a given society; my point is that there are also plenty of cases where nothing like that is true, and, as far as I can see, the increased sophistication of the process we call 'transplantation' may lead us to think that it is not actually properly called 'transplantation' at all: it is more like paying attention to the global white noise of law. There is indeed a lot of it about to listen to these days; but little of it can be investigated sociologically to discover whether it is useful noise. We just make rough

[23] In Malay/Indonesian, for example, 'law', according to the context, can be translated as '*hukum*' (as in law and order), '*undang-undang*' (as in to obey the law), or '*keadilan*' (as in court of law).

assumptions that in general do not take account of the legal 'fit' in the donor society, partly because we do not have the information and partly because it would probably be irrelevant.

It is of course then a difficulty to know when there is a true transplant. Given that the outcome in terms of law in the donee system is likely not to resemble precisely the law of the donor system, even in a strong case, at what point on the spectrum between law-as-an-idea and law-as-specific-statutory-provisions do we apply the term 'legal transplant'? This is not, it seems, terribly clear. For this reason we might want to abandon the term 'legal transplant'. I will suggest some changes in usage later in this essay.

On the issue of culture, the case of international law that Watson also discusses is a good case in point.[24] Much legal reform is derived these days from international law or an obligation to comply with it – from what jurisdiction is such law being transplanted and what is the Legrand-style baggage that such law carries along? On the contrary, in such a case law is at its most abstract and we do not need to examine the 'culture' or the 'society' that 'has' international law to discover either the secret of its success or its authority (if it has either); this is because essentially no such thing exists. Indeed international lawyers might fairly be accused of caring little for the practical problems encountered by legal transplantation: law here is simply an obligation you have agreed to fulfil, and that is the end of the matter.

Let me also adduce another example from China, which seems to me somewhat more typical in the Asian context than the examples in the literature.

Lacking the device common lawyers call a trust, which is absent from the civil law as transplanted to China, China adopted this common-law device, itself part of that curious type of law that common lawyers call 'equity'. It is hard to find anything less promising as a potential legal transplant, even given the evident utility of the trust in common-law systems as a legal device for the holding of property. Since China has a civil-law system, the trust – adapted to Chinese law and society – was pragmatically grafted onto its legal system by a statute. The result was something different from both common law and civil law (Teubner, the coiner of the term 'legal irritant',[25] would be pleased with this example, I think). According to Chinese judgement (and I suppose, Watson's too) this is a 'successful' transplant; according to Legrand this is not even a transplant at all. The real issue, irrespective of the correct terminology to describe what happened in this case, is whether such a process results in

[24] Watson (n. 11).

[25] Teubner (n. 7).

law that we may plausibly judge to be effective or useful. If the case proves anything, it proves that a broad range of legal ideas can be transplanted, but that some skill or imagination is required to translate them into a comprehensible and functional vernacular. We should bear in mind here that questions of fit are seen in the context of Asian development in a totally different way from the assumption of legal theorists. Often the entire purpose of legal change is to change society's behaviour, not to find the best societal fit. One can imagine a law reformer castigating a foreign legal consultant along the lines that he was not invited there to advise on how to transplant law without disturbing anything, because otherwise it will be difficult. Note that the Chinese law reformers did not feel a need to understand the evolution of medieval English equity before moving forward with reform. They merely had to understand what China needs at the present time, and the legal concepts used in their own law. Neither of these things proved exceptionally difficult in the event.[26] In discussing this I do not see the need to decide whether this is or is not a legal transplant.

Having said that, it is, I think, however a mistake to extend Watson's argument too far and say that law is somehow always detached from societal conditions in the *donee* society too. Watson's mistake is alleged to be that of regarding law as simply a piece of technology, safeguarded by the inherent conservatism of a legal tradition fiercely maintained by the legal profession.[27] To use Kahn-Freund's analogy, law (or as I would have it, a legal idea) is being regarded by Watson – the critique might go – as being like a carburettor rather than a kidney.[28] To use a more contemporary analogy, I do not find anyone arguing that the mobile phone is inconsistent with some group's cultural values, and that they should therefore reject its use (perhaps the Amish in the United States are a narrow exception). Some law is indeed analogous to a mobile phone, but other kinds of law are more akin to K-pop. Both have spread across the world, but just as jihadists use mobile phones, I seriously doubt if they tune in to K-pop. One is technology, the other is culture. The same is I think true of law: some law has a potentially complex relation to culture (e.g. rules concerning the age at which one can marry) and some law potentially does not (e.g. rules concerning the validity of a will). For this reason some laws are easy to transplant and others are not. Laws introducing a 'modern' marriage system in SE Asian countries such as

26 S. Tensmeyer, 'Modernising Chinese Trust Law', *New York University Law Review* 90 (2015), 710.

27 Watson (n. 10), 27.

28 O. Kahn-Freund, 'Uses and Misuses of Comparative Law', *Modern Law Review* 37 (1974), 1.

Malaysia and Indonesia have encountered a difficult choice. With regard to the validity of customary marriages concluded after the change in the law, does the need for legal certainty outweigh the need not to invalidate customary marriages on a socially disruptive scale?[29] Similarly it has been seen that a laudable attempt to create registration of land titles in Cambodia has led directly to instances of abusive land-grabbing in areas deliberately excluded from the project. The problem, let me emphasize, is not one of not being clear what the law is; it is a problem of the effects of legal change. The cultural point (do Cambodians actually, culturally, understand land registration?) seems curiously irrelevant; they understood land registration all too well when they saw their land and houses unjustly taken away just because they lived on a lake.[30]

> Watson does concede that donee societies look at foreign law carefully when legislating in order to ensure so far as possible an effective transplant.[31] The crafting of Singapore's Personal Data Protection Act, for example, was influenced by the data protection laws of Canada, Hong Kong, and New Zealand in order to 'develop the most suitable model for Singapore'.[32] (We can seriously ask if this is a legal transplant – if so, from which garden was this law transplanted? Does it really matter?) Another example from South East Asia is the French Civil Code of 1931, which as a result of French colonialism operated in Vietnam until 1950. This Code has been continually reinterpreted to suit 'guiding principles' and new governmental policies.[33] The process of adaptation of a law may go on long after the law has been transplanted. This makes it very difficult to talk of success and failure. What looks like short-term failure may turn out to be a success in the longer term. Equally short-term success may turn out badly in the longer term; although longevity must surely be one of the relevant criteria, however we define success. Thus we may well find in the real world of legal diffusion that there is a series of legislative initiatives; but when and in relation to what do

29 See, e.g., I. Jauhari, 'The Role of Government in Regulating Marriage Administration System in Indonesia', *International Journal of Humanities and Social Science* 5 (1) (2015), 162.

30 L. Trzcinski and F. Upham 'Creating law from the Ground Up: Land Law in Post-Conflict Cambodia', *Asian Journal of Law and Society* 1 (1) (2014), 55.

31 Watson (n. 4), 99. In China and Vietnam there is a law on Legislation which, contrary to many perceptions of legal transplantation, requires as a matter of law that the government carry out careful processes of scrutiny and even socio-legal inquiry before legislating. This is aimed at legal transplantation. Few legislative initiatives have never been tried anywhere else.

32 *Parliamentary Debates Singapore: Official Report*, vol. 89 (15 October 2012) (Associate Professor Dr Yaacob Ibrahim). I am grateful to one of my students in anonymous work for this information and citation.

33 P. Nicholson, *Borrowing Court Systems: The Experience of Socialist Vietnam* (Brill, 2007), 38.

we judge success? Even Watson allows that law is 'the fruit of human experience'.[34] We muddle through these exercises more often than not, and human experience does not necessarily aggregate in our favour.

Here again, though, there is something to be learned from Watson. To the extent that law can be seen as technical (Mattei helpfully calls this 'professional lawyers' law' as opposed to 'the law of politics' or 'traditional law'[35]) it might well be more easily transplanted. We would not, for example, think of discussing the transplantation of customary law, because we see it is virtually impossible, apart from the transplanting of customary law via migrant populations (here it is strictly a population, not law, that is being transplanted). Conversely, the index-linked pension, for example, seems so easily transplanted that we may not even think of using the term 'transplant' in such a context – these innovations are obviously fair and useful pieces of social-engineering-style legal technology. The mistake is to think that what are good laws for one society are always good laws for another. We may think this error is obvious, but Bentham believed that they were, and many international agencies still proceed as if he were right. This has been the real lesson of legal transplants, and it is not clear that the lesson has been learned even now.[36] If Legrand has encouraged us to think along these lines, then we should agree.

IV SUCCESS AND FAILURE: TREATING THESE TWO IMPOSTERS JUST THE SAME?

The trick of successful legal transplantation is, I have argued, to understand very precisely how a law *would operate* in the donee society, not how it operates practically in the donor society. The latter information may well be useful in some cases, but is not a universally mandatory requirement. If it were, legal reform would be almost impossible to achieve, and we would waste a lot of time on quite irrelevant inquiries. I would of course concede that knowledge of why a law operates effectively in the donor society might be helpful, but that is a contingent factor. To illustrate this, legal reformers in Thailand adopted the civil code, adapted from France and Germany (completed in 1935), because those systems were authoritative in terms of 'modern' law that they were seeking; and because the Japanese had been there first and did not see

34 Watson (n. 10), 100.

35 U Mattei, 'Three Patterns of Law: Taxonomy and Change in the World's Legal Systems', *American Journal of Comparative Law* 45 (1) (1997), 5.

36 A Harding, 'Law and Development in Its Burmese Moment: Legal Reform in an Emerging Democracy', ch. 20 of T. Lindsey and M. Crouch (eds.), *Law, Society and Transition in Myanmar* (Hart Publishing, 2014).

that having an Asian society was a hindrance (nor in fact did China, which did the same as Thailand in 1930).[37] None of these factors was capable of being rigorously assessed. Yet the transplant seems to have worked in the sense that there is no obvious lack of fit eight decades on; at least there has been no rejection. As we have seen the same is largely true in Vietnam despite the colonial origins of civil law there.

A law that works badly in one society might work very well in another; the conditions for success may be more favourable. On the other hand a practically problematical law is rather unlikely to become a candidate for transplantation in the first place. It would lack authority. The same applies over time in the same society: an effective law may become ineffective due to change of circumstances, for example, and an ineffective law effective due to superior enforcement. But the real emphasis should be on the *donee* society not the donor society. Legislators seek in vain the silver bullet that makes a good law successful in the donor society.

The least knowledge of legal technical assistance (what an interesting phrase that is – is legal assistance always technical or is that a way of avoiding real issues of political or moral weight, or of cultural specificity?) will indicate that the main problem is indeed the dire and persistent tendency to transplant law without due regard to its appropriateness in the given societal context. To this extent Legrand is clearly right in drawing attention to the link between law and society ('weak' Watson agrees with Legrand here, 'strong' Watson does not[38]). To call this process a logical impossibility is however rather like calling the black swan a logical impossibility, as indeed it once was, before in the late seventeenth century Australian experience forced a redefinition of 'swan' in terms of evolution not colour: if the black 'swan' is not a swan at all, then what on earth is it? (This was for European benefit: Australian aboriginal people had observed black swans for about 40,000 years, so they had no problem with the idea of a black swan).[39] Far from isolated instances we have thousands of equivalents of black swans in the real world of legal diffusion. I do not see in Legrand's work any recognition of legal diffusion that takes place, via the best processes of which we are capable, addressing common problems having a narrow range of possible legal solutions. Again, Watson is correct; for a given problem the scope for original solutions is really quite limited: almost everything has been tried before. To this extent Legrand's work makes us think

37 A. Harding, 'The Eclipse of the Astrologers: King Mongkut, His Successors, and the Reformation of Law in Thailand', ch. 10 of P. Nicholson and S. Biddulph (eds.), *Examining Practice, Interrogating Theory: Comparative Legal Studies in Asia* (Brill, 2008).

38 Ewald (n. 14).

39 N. N. Taleb, *The Black Swan: The Impact of the Highly Improbable* (Random House, 2007).

more carefully about the true nature of law; but it is not useful in any important respect – it does not solve any problems. Indeed the lesson of legal diffusion is quite the opposite of Legrand's message: we can strip a law or a rule of its Legrand-baggage and by doing so we are more likely to achieve clarity and perhaps even an effective transplant.

It should be apparent at this point that the legal transplant debate is largely and unhelpfully about the correct use of terminology; it does not really assist us in understanding legal diffusion, especially in areas like Asia and Africa, which have seen a great deal of what is still called 'legal transplantation'. Clifford Geertz quipped that SE Asia has every kind of law except African law and Eskimo law, almost all kinds being transplanted from elsewhere (pure Watson); but he also described law as 'local knowledge' (pure Legrand). How 'global doctrine' (law as a set of general legal ideas abstracted from the lived experience of law) becomes 'local knowledge' (law as ingested normative ideas applicable, effective, and accurate in a given society) should be the focus of scholarly effort at this crucial interface.[40] Law cannot be understood properly except in its context,[41] but that very context, in most societies at least, needs to address the way in which foreign laws influence or provide solutions to local problems. We know too little about these processes. Shutting one's eyes to such things occurring, or denying that they are transplants, avoids what seems to me to be the central issue.

V THE TERMINOLOGY OF TRANSPLANTS

I have avoided thus far being entirely clear about terminology, but in failing to define my own use of terms clearly I have perhaps illustrated how confusing the debate has become. I have indicated, however, that we lack rigour in our use of virtually all of the terms involved, and it might be useful to start over again.

Let us start with 'legal transplants'. This needs renovation on two grounds. First, it catches too much; and secondly, it is a misleading metaphor.[42] Adopting Roman law in medieval Europe is very different, for example, from adopting, say, a new law on environmental management in Malaysia. 'Legal transplantation' seems to try to deal with everything from the Great

40 A. Harding, 'Global Doctrine and Local Knowledge: Law in South East Asia', *International and Comparative Law Quarterly* 51 (1) (2002), 35.

41 R. Cotterrell, 'Why Must Legal Ideas Be Interpreted Sociologically?', *Journal of Law and Society* 25 (2) (1998), 171.

42 D. Nelken, 'Legal Transplants and Beyond: Of Disciplines and Metaphors', ch. 2 of A. Harding and E. Örücü (eds.), *Comparative Law in the 21st Century* (Kluwer Law International, 2001).

Reception to the diffusion of common law in the British Empire, to the High Court of Australia following a decision from New Zealand. We need to break all this down into distinct ideas and areas, or even modes or agents of operation. That is a task too large to undertake here, but we could, for example, distinguish the adoption of a legal idea, that is just part of the corpus of legal understanding and experience, from the wholesale incorporation of a regulatory statute, or the adoption of a doctrinal principle that has appealed to courts in other jurisdictions.

The idea of a transplant carries images of something growing in its own soil, and then removed by an Olympian gardener to someone else's garden, where it might grow or fail to grow. This is not of course in general how legal diffusion takes place. Law is not a garden, nor are horticultural metaphors really helpful. What we call legal transplantation involves many types of legal project instituted for many different reasons by many different actors using many legal sources. We look to other jurisdictions for solutions, or at least types of solution, because we are chary of absolute innovation. The details of the law that is ultimately enacted will typically vary considerably, because laws tend to attach to institutional settings, procedural preferences, and constitutional constraints, for example. Whether these contingencies will prove obstacles to transplantation depends on the degree of specificity sought and the extent to which the law in question is organically connected. That a statute with all its Legrand-baggage cannot easily be successfully transplanted to another society is in general fairly obvious. Nonetheless there are I think plenty of examples of this happening. In Vietnam the Law on Legislation assumes that careful canvassing of foreign legal experience is de rigueur when drafting legislation.[43] This indicates that the Vietnamese legislator both believes that law can be transplanted, and that whatever varieties exist should be examined carefully.

I would suggest that we confine 'legal transplantation' to the imperial transplanting of law to colonies, and that 'legal mimesis' or copying captures better what happens in twenty-first century law-reform processes, where we are looking at ideas from elsewhere. 'Legal reception' should be confined to the Great Reception of Roman law, and possibly to statutes which use the phrase 'on the topic x the law of y shall be received into jurisdiction z';[44] in this latter instance there is usually a problem defining what circumstances or what

[43] Speech of Hoang The Lien, Vice-Minister for Justice, Vietnam, 'Reforming the Law-Making Process', *Vietnam Law Magazine*, 22 June 2007, http://vietnamlawmagazine.vn/reforming-the-lawmaking-process-3279.html accessed 25 May 2017.

[44] A. Phang, 'The Reception of English Law in Singapore: Problems and Proposed Solutions', *Singapore Academy of Law Journal* 2 (1990), 20.

degree or scope of applicability is being envisaged, but 'reception' merely echoes the term the legislator has decided to use, and is therefore defensible. I do not, for lack of space, continue to discuss what we mean by 'legal' or 'law' in the circumstances I have just adumbrated. But I do think that we need to have a flexible notion of law in order to capture a range of possible approaches in practice. One might, for example, adopt an institution without formal resort to enacting a statutory basis for it, in order to see how it might work before formalizing the position.[45]

Another binary to get beyond (but I have no clear idea how) is the idea of successful/ unsuccessful transplantation. I have used the word 'effective' in what I have stated above, but although preferable that does not avoid the problem, which is that we have no criteria to apply in deciding whether a law is successful or effective. Do we judge by the objectives of those promoting the legal change? If so, over what period of time? What if, as is typical, a legal change is largely accepted, but fails in the short-to-medium term to deliver to a substantial extent what was desired, and leads to other problems which are being addressed by further proposals for legal change? Or what if it appears to work in the sense of being complied with, but at much greater economic, social or political cost than was anticipated? Or as in the Cambodian case, it has some unforeseen catastrophic effects, but was doubtless a good idea in the first place? It is hard to draw any conclusions. Indeed we usually have no solid socio-legal data from which we could even in principle draw such conclusions.

But we can still try. In relation to constitutional review, for example, Alec Stone Sweet has set out three benchmarks as a good general indicator: 'constitutional review can be said to be effective to the extent that the important constitutional disputes arising in a polity are brought to the [constitutional court] on a regular basis, that the judges who resolve these disputes give reasons for their findings, and that those who are governed by the constitutional law accept that the court's rulings have some precedential effect'.[46] One might add that they should routinely accept the court's rulings per se, and act upon them. These markers merely of course describe a system that functions in terms understood in Western legal thinking. Whether in the larger picture a court innovation is effective might depend on a wider range of inquiry. H. P. Lee points out, for example, that the special court for trying cases against

[45] For an example of this (Myanmar's Human Rights Commission), see C. Renshaw, 'Human Rights under the New Regime', ch. 11 of A. Harding and K. K. Oo (eds.), *Constitutionalism and Legal Change in Myanmar* (Hart Publishing, 2017).

[46] A. Stone Sweet, 'Constitutional Courts', in M. Rosenfeld and A. Sajo (eds.), *The Oxford Handbook of Comparative Constitutional Law* (Oxford University Press, 2012), 825.

traditional rulers in Malaysia has been successful *because of rather than despite* the small number of cases brought before it; on Stone Sweet's test this court might be seen as a failure.[47] Disputes concerning rulers' behaviour are usually not settled in the special court, and persons affected might well be fearful of bringing a case at all; but the threat of such a process appears to have improved the behaviour of the royal families, which was the purpose of the innovation. It is a toss-up whether this is what we would call a successful innovation. It is also not very obviously any kind of a legal transplant, except insofar as one might see it as a transplant from the ordinary court system, resembling that system in almost every respect. Law reform, with its highly eclectic approach and wide range of inspirations, is not in any sense a science at this juncture.

We know that new law never fits society completely. If it did it would have become law long before it was adopted, or would not have been strictly necessary. Often law is adopted precisely because it does not fit society – the objective being to change society, not to reflect it. The fact is that in the mirror analogy some laws mirror what society does, while others are designed to engineer what society wants to achieve by legal change. In practice most statute laws are probably somewhat muddily incoherent compromises between these two objectives, moulded by vested interest, political ambition, and bureaucratic caution. They derive legitimacy from the process of enactment but are not even designed to fulfil precisely the intention of their promoters. (I am indeed somewhat mystified by the idea that the intention of those promoting a statute that has been amended several times, as statutes typically are, should have their intention promoted to the level of a legal principle.) The legitimacy to which I refer is often achieved by compromising the objective, not by fulfilling it to the letter. Legislation is after all an art of the possible. But hopefully we have finally learned that societal fit or at least impact is something we need to understand rather deeply before we legislate. I am therefore unsure that we could decide on appropriate standards for judging success or effectiveness in law reform other than to judge by the intention of the legislator if indeed such intention can be identified. But we also need to understand that the binary of law and society is also to some extent misleading. Legal change is not an art of designing the best fit, as if we are tailors making comfortable clothing. To this extent Teubner's 'legal irritants' is probably a more accurate term than most to describe what happens.

Let me adduce here, to illustrate the complexity of the issue of legal transplantation, the example of Singapore's Maintenance of Parents Act

[47] H. P. Lee, 'Malaysian Royalty and the Special Court', ch. 15 of A. Harding and P. Nicholson (eds.), *New Courts in Asia* (Routledge, 2010).

1993. This law was presented as *reflecting* society's fundamental value of filial piety by ensuring that children provide for their indigent parents. But to the extent that they did not do so, it was also attempt to *change* the culture, with legal proceedings before a tribunal as the sanction. The use of Confucianism to justify the law was controversial; Confucianism encourages filial piety but is also very hostile to lawsuits, especially between children and their parents. Some saw the measure as simply offloading responsibility for the aged onto the population, which was seen, variously, as a good and as a bad thing, according to one's view of the role of the state. In the end, it is hard to say whether such a law was effective.[48] We would have to conduct research to see if the purpose had been fulfilled. But there lies the problem: what purpose should we start by identifying? Do we look for a decline in the number of uncared-for parents? Or an increase in filial piety (judged how, exactly)? Or do we look at the number of cases successfully resolved by the tribunal? It is also hard to say if it was a legal transplant, because we do not have a clear definition of a legal transplant. Suffice it to say that as an idea it was in evidence in other jurisdictions, and in turn it may well have influenced jurisdictions such as China that have adopted filial piety laws.[49] I doubt that these instances are ones in which the legislator has discovered anything about the success or failure of the Singapore statute. It is probably assumed to be authoritative because statutory innovations in Singapore tend to be effective due to rigorous enforcement.[50]

Seen in this light we might revisit the work of Teubner, who coined the term 'legal irritant' to replace 'legal transplant'. In Teubner's theory new law derived from elsewhere irritates the receiving system, creating a debate that settles the irritation, often with new outcomes. It is a classic case of thesis, antithesis and synthesis. This approach explains much about these processes and is more in line with our experience of legal diffusion, as I think several papers in this conference suggest. I find it hard, however, to think of this as an overarching theory of what happens in law reform. As with other writing in this area, it is not based on empirical research, but relies on a single, rather doctrinal, example – the adoption of good faith in English contract law. But not all of these exercises actually involve irritation.

48 W. C. Chan, 'The Duty to Support an Aged Parent in Singapore' *Pacific Rim Law and Policy Journal* 13 (3) (2004), 547.

49 *Law of the People's Republic of China on the Protection of the Rights and Interests of Elderly People*, 2013, www.china.org.cn/english/government/207404.htm accessed 24 May 2017.

50 See, e.g., K. Y. L. Tan, 'Defaming Politicians, Scandalising the Courts: A Look at Recent Developments in Singapore', ch. 5 of A. T. Kenyon, T. Marjoribanks and A. Whiting (eds.), *Democracy, Media and Law in Malaysia and Singapore: A Space for Speech* (Routledge, 2014).

VI CONCLUSION

Finally let me revisit the binaries set out at the beginning of this discussion. I conclude as follows:

i) Legal transplants are possible both logically and practically, although the process is not easy.
ii) They are fundamentally related to the society of the donee but not necessarily that of the donor.
iii) They are possible in private and in public law. This issue is not elaborated here, but a scan of the examples used does not indicate a distinction in principle between private and public law.
iv) Success is hard to assess, but legal change is not for that reason impossible to achieve or dangerous to undertake.

By way of conclusion, I think the idea of legal transplantation needs to be broken down into distinct types of legal activity, and we need to study how these work in practice across the world. We need more understanding of these processes, how to assess their impact, and how to improve them. In doing so, I wish to insist, we do live in a world of legal connectivity in which we share common problems which can only be addressed by a limited range of solutions which are unlikely not to have been tried before. As Watson argues, transplantation in all its forms is still the main way in which law changes. But I the final analysis, both Watson and Legrand seem to approach the starting line, in different stadia, claiming to have won a race that has not quite yet begun.

VII BIBLIOGRAPHY

Cotterrell, R., 'Why Must Legal Ideas Be Interpreted Sociologically?', *Journal of Law and Society* 25, no. 2 (1998), 171–92.

Crouch, M. and Lindsey, T. (eds.), 'Law and Development in Its Burmese Moment: Legal Reform in an Emerging Democracy' in *Law, Society and Transition in Myanmar* (2014), 280–94. http://dx.doi.org/10.5040/9781474201650.

(eds.), *Law, Society and Transition in Myanmar* (2014). http://dx.doi.org/10.5040/9781474201650.

du Plessis, P. J., Ando, C., and Tuori, K. (eds.), *The Oxford Handbook of Roman Law and Society Oxford Handbooks* (Oxford University Press, 2016).

Ewald, W., 'Comparative Jurisprudence (II): The Logic of Legal Transplants', *American Journal of Comparative Law* 43, no. 4 (1995), 489–510.

Foster, N., 'Transmigration and Transferability of Commercial Law in a Globalized World' in *Comparative Law in the 21st Century*, Harding, A. and Örücü, E. (eds.), (Kluwer Law International, 2002).

Harding, A., 'Global Doctrine and Local Knowledge: Law in South East Asia', *International & Comparative Law Quarterly* 51, no. 1 (January 2002), 35–53.

and Nicholson, P., *New Courts in Asia* (Routledge, 2010).

and Örücü, E. (eds.) *Comparative Law in the 21st Century* (Kluwer Law International, 2002).

Hoang T. L., Vice-Minister for Justice, Vietnam, 'Reforming the Law-Making Process', *Vietnam Law Magazine*, 22 June 2007, http://vietnamlawmagazine.vn/reforming-the-lawmaking-process-3279.html accessed 25 May 2017.

Otto, J. M., van Rooij B., and Arnscheidt J., *Lawmaking for Development: Explorations into the Theory and Practice of International Legislative Projects* (Leiden University Press, 2008).

Jauhari, I., 'The Role of Government in Regulating Marriage Administration System in Indonesia' *International Journal of Humanities and Social Science* 5, no. 1 (2015), 11.

Kahn-Freund, O., 'On Uses and Misuses of Comparative Law', *Modern Law Review* 37, no. 1 (1 January, 1974), 1–27.

Kenyon, A., Marjoribanks, T., and Whiting, A. (eds.), 1st edn, *Democracy, Media and Law in Malaysia and Singapore: A Space for Speech* (Routledge, 2016).

Law of the People's Republic of China on the Protection of the Rights and Interests of Elderly People, 2013, available at: www.china.org.cn/english/government/207404.htm accessed 24 May 2017.

Lee, H. P., 'Malaysian Royalty and the Special Court' in *New Courts in Asia*, Harding, A. and Nicholson, P. (eds.) (Routledge, 2010) 240–56.

Legrand, P., 'Legal Transplants and European Private Law', vol. 4.4, *Electronic Journal of Comparative Law* 4, no. 4 .

'The Impossibility of 'Legal Transplants', *Maastricht Journal of European and Comparative Law* 4, no. 2 (1 June, 1997), 111–24.

Mattei, U., 'Three Patterns of Law: Taxonomy and Change in the World's Legal Systems', *The American Journal of Comparative Law* 45, no. 1 (1997), 5–44.

Nicholson, P., *Borrowing Court Systems: The Experience of Socialist Vietnam* (Brill Nijhoff, 2007).

and Biddulph, S. (eds.), *Examining Practice, Interrogating Theory: Comparative Legal Studies in Asia* (Martinus Nijhoff, 2008).

Biddulph, S. and Harding, A. (eds.), 'The Eclipse of the Astrologers: King Mongkut, His Successors, and the Reformation of Law in Thailand' in *Examining Practice, Interrogating Theory: Comparative Legal Studies in Asia* (Martinus Nijhoff, 2008).

Phang Boon Leong, A., 'Reception of English Law in Singapore: Problems and Proposed Solutions', *Singapore Academy of Law Journal* no. 1 (1990), 20.

Renshaw, C. 'Human Rights under the New Regime' in *Constitutionalism and Legal Change in Myanmar*, Harding, A. and Oo, K. K. (eds.) (Hart Publishing, 2017) 146–62.

Stone Sweet, A., 'Constitutional Courts' in *The Oxford Handbook of Comparative Constitutional Law*, Rosenfeld, M. and Sajó, A. (eds.) (Oxford University Press, 2012).

Tamanaha, B., 'Understanding Legal Pluralism: Past to Present, Local to Global' *Sydney Law Review* 30 (2007),375.

Tan, C., 'We Are Registered': Actual Processes and the Law of Marriage in Singapore', *International Journal of Law, Policy and the Family* 13, no. 1 (April 1, 1999), 1–32.
Tan, K. 'Defaming Politicians, Scandalising the Courts: A Look at Recent Developments in Singapore' in *Democracy, Media and Law in Malaysia and Singapore: A Space for Speech*, Kenyon, A. T., Marjoribanks, T., and Whiting, A. (eds.) 1st edn (Routledge, 2016).
Tensmeyer, S., 'Modernizing Chinese Trust Law', *New York University Law Review* 90 (2015), 710.
Teubner, G., 'Legal Irritants: Good Faith in British Law or How Unifying Law Ends up in New Divergences', *Modern Law Review* 61, no. 1 (1998), 11–32.
Trzcinski, L. M. and Upham, F. K., 'Creating Law from the Ground Up: Land Law in Post-Conflict Cambodia' *Asian Journal of Law and Society* 1, no. 1 (May 2014), 55–77.
Twining, W., *General Jurisprudence Understanding Law from a Global Perspective* (Cambridge University Press, 2004).
Watson, A., *Legal Transplants: An Approach to Comparative Law* (University of Georgia Press, 1993).
Wright, J. (ed.), *International Encyclopedia of the Social & Behavioral Sciences* 2nd edn (Elsevier, 2015).

2

Transplant Shock: the Hazards of Introducing Statutes of General Application

Jennifer Corrin

I INTRODUCTION

The term 'legal transplants' is usually taken to refer to laws made by the legislature of one country (the 'enacting country') which are then either applied or extended by that legislature to be in force in a second country, or which are adopted by the legislature of the second country (the 'receiving country') to be in force there.[1] These transplanted laws, sometimes referred to as 'introduced laws', might be constituted by a whole Act or just a part or even a single section of it. The term is also broad enough to cover the transplant of whole legal systems, as sometimes happened as a consequence of colonisation. In the case of transplanted common law, legal transplants may include precedents, and again; this might be individual principles or concepts, such as the trust,[2] or whole areas of common law, such a tort or contract. In addition to substantive laws, adjectival laws and the institutions in which they operate may also be transplanted, that is, a system of courts or tribunals and the rules of evidence and procedure.

Unlike Andrew Harding's chapter, the discussion here is not concerned primarily with the substance of legal transplants, but with the mechanism used to transplant legislation. Legislation may be applied or adopted by reference to a specific Act. Alternatively, the application or adoption may be more general. It is this more general method of legislative transplant, which employs a phrase such as 'statutes of general application' to incorporate the foreign law, on which this chapter focusses. Whilst it has been alleged that this formula does

[1] This is a simplistic depiction of the transplant process, which in practice is often more complex. See further W. Twining, 'Diffusion of Law: A Global Perspective', *Journal of Legal Pluralism* 49 (2004), 1.

[2] Harding, in Chapter 1 of this Volume, discussed the adoption of the trust in China by statute. In the Pacific it has been transplanted both through legislation and case law.

not give rise to 'serious trouble',[3] this chapter argues against this proposition. Just as the transfer of trees and shrubs without due consideration of the associated stresses may result in their failure to root well, a condition known as transplant shock, problems arise from using this method of transplant. The chapter commences by looking briefly at the advantages and disadvantages of transplanted legislation generally. It then moves on to discuss the conflicting interpretations of the phrase 'statutes of general application' and examines the issues surrounding the definition and operation of this particular process of transplantation. Examples from the Pacific Islands are drawn on to give context to this discussion and to illustrate some of the problems that arise from this method of introduction. However, it should be borne in mind that this means of transplanting legislation is not restricted to the Pacific, having been used by the United Kingdom and its administrating dominions as a device to introduce statute law in many former colonies.[4]

II ADVANTAGES AND DISADVANTAGES OF TRANSPLANTS

The debate about legal transplants is, as stated at the outset in Harding's chapter, very well known. In this chapter it is taken as read that Legrand is incorrect in his assertion that legal transplantation is logically impossible. Certainly, in the 'real world of legal diffusion', as Harding puts it, legal transplants underpin state legal systems in most Pacific Island. The main advantage of transplanted legislation is that the laws in question have already been drafted and have been scrutinized in the enacting country during the legislative process. Where legal resources in the receiving country are limited and, for example, experienced legislative drafters are not available, a ready-made Act may be a much swifter way of introducing a law. Also, if the legislation has been in force in another country, it will have been tried and tested there and any problems should have been ironed out. From the perspective of the country in which the legislation originates, the transplanting process allows that country to exert influence over the legal system of the overseas country, often a former colony. It also means that the legal systems of the two countries are compatible, which can be an advantage, for example, in relation to trade.

The main disadvantage of transplanted legislation, and the pitfall to which this chapter will give some consideration, is that the legislation is not autochthonous and may not be completely compatible with the context into which

[3] Sir Kenneth Roberts-Wray, *Commonwealth and Colonial Law* (Stevens and Sons, 1966) 545.

[4] Roberts-Wray (n. 3), 549.

it is introduced. Whilst agreeing with Watson that law is not entirely a mirror of society,[5] there is no doubt that, as Harding notes, we should 'pay attention to the obvious fact that legal transplants encounter problems of "fit"'. As will be discussed in this chapter, failure to do so may give rise to unforeseen problems. It has been argued by Kahn-Freund that the success of transplant depends on the type of law involved, with public laws being the least likely to succeed due to their cultural specificity.[6] As discussed below, these are the very laws most likely to qualify as of general application.[7] Transplants may also be objectionable from the point of view of sovereignty, giving the appearance, and perhaps – on occasion – the reality, of dominance by the originating country. Of course, none of these objections applies in the case of laws selected from other countries after careful examination of and testing for legal 'fit' in the receiving country, but as Harding notes, a more sophisticated process such as this may 'not actually properly [be] called "transplantation" at all'.

III RECEPTION RULES

According to the established common-law rules, in countries ceded to the Crown, such as Fiji, the law in force at the time of cession remains in force until altered by the Sovereign.[8] Whether this rule applied to Protectorates, such as Solomon Islands, or Protected States, such as Tonga, is unclear, but in practice, this seems to have been taken to be the case.[9] In settled colonies, British settlers take with them English law as their 'birthright'. However, the question of whether a country is 'desert and uncultivated',[10] uninhabited, or peopled by 'uncivilized inhabitants in a primitive state of society'[11] with no settled law and may thus be claimed by right of occupancy, is often a matter of debate.[12] In any event, the necessity of relying on the common-law rules was forestalled in the South Pacific by specific enactments, applying English 'Acts of general application'. This phrase was used by the British Government to refer to a whole body of legislation that was introduced into British

5 A. Watson, *Legal Transplants: An Approach to Comparative Law* 2nd edn (University of Georgia Press, 1993) ch. 2.

6 O. Kahn-Freund, 'Uses and Misuses of Comparative Law', *Modern Law Review* 37 (1974) 1, 5–6.

7 See, e.g., *Indian Printing and Publishing Co* v. *Police* (1932) 3 FLR 142.

8 See the authorities set out in Roberts-Wray (n. 3), ch. 222, n. 32.

9 Ibid., 543.

10 Blackstone, *Commentaries on the Laws of England* (vol. 1, 1765) 107.

11 *Milirrpum* v. *Nabalco Pty Ltd* (1971) 17 FLR 141, 201.

12 See, e.g., Australian Law Reform Commission, 'Recognition of Aboriginal Customary Laws' (Report 31), 1986, 64.

dependencies.[13] This introduction was part of the process of colonisation and protection in the Pacific. Whilst the policy in the Pacific was to preserve customary laws, English laws were introduced on the basis that 'the customs of an unsophisticated community cannot cover the whole field of the law of a highly developed country, especially in that large area of jurisprudence gathered under the generic term "commercial law"'.[14]

Examples of a typical reception rule can be found in the former colony of Fiji, where 'the statutes of general application which were in force in England' on 2 January 1875 were introduced.[15] Similarly, in the former British colony of Gilbert and Ellice Islands (now Kiribati and Tuvalu) and the former British Solomon Islands Protectorate (now Solomon Islands), 'the statutes of general application in force in England' on 1 January 1961 were introduced.[16] In the New Hebrides (now Vanuatu), which prior to independence was under the joint control of England and France 'the statutes of general application in force in England' on 1 January 1976 were introduced.[17] Similarly, in Nauru, it was provided that 'the statutes of general application ... in force in England' on 31 January 1968 were to be in force.[18] In Tonga, 'statutes of general application in England at the date on which this Act shall come into force' were adopted.[19] That date was 18 October 1966, but in 1983, the date-defining words were deleted,[20] leaving Tonga with Acts of general application whenever passed, in force. These reception rules also contained a proviso that statutes of general application were only to be applied 'so far as circumstances admit'[21] or some similarly worded limitation.[22] This proviso is discussed further below.

Since independence, Pacific countries have had their own parliaments to pass legislation. However, to fill the void until enactment of local laws, introduced legislation was kept in force until repealed, expressly or by implication, by the local parliament.[23] This perpetuated the relevance of the phrase

13 Roberts-Wray (n. 3), 545.
14 Roberts-Wray (n. 3), 535–6.
15 Supreme Court Ordinance 1875 (UK), s. 35.
16 Western Pacific (Courts) Order 1961 (UK), s. 15, replacing Pacific Order in Council 1893 (UK), s. 20.
17 High Court of New Hebrides Regulation 1976, s. 3, repealing Western Pacific (Courts) Order 1961 (UK), s. 15 for New Hebrides.
18 Custom and Adopted Laws Act 1971 (Nauru), s. 4(1).
19 Civil Law Act 1966 (Tonga), s. 3, replacing Pacific Order in Council 1893 (UK), s. 20.
20 Act 12 1983 (Tonga).
21 Pacific Order in Council 1893 (UK); Western Pacific (Courts) Order 1961 (UK).
22 For example, in New Zealand dependencies the phrase, 'inapplicable to the circumstances of' the receiving country was used: e.g. Cook Islands Act 1915 (NZ), s. 615.
23 See, e.g., Constitution of Vanuatu 1980, art. 95(2).

'statutes of general application'. Only three Pacific countries have enacted a wholesale repeal of Acts of general application. The first to do so was Tokelau, which repealed all introduced English legislation in 1997.[24] This was followed by Tonga, which passed the Civil Law Amendment Act in 2003. This had unwanted consequences, leaving a vacuum in certain areas. For example, Tonga had relied on England for its bankruptcy laws,[25] admiralty laws,[26] provisions allowing distribution of property on divorce,[27] and miscellaneous other laws.[28] The third country was Niue, which repealed all English legislation in 2004.[29]

In Samoa, parliament has been active in replacing introduced legislation and there are currently no British Acts of Parliament in force, although three New Zealand Acts: the Bankruptcy Act 1908, the Property Law Act 1952, and parts of the Samoa Act 1921 (ss. 360 and 362) remain in force.[30]

In many of the other Pacific countries, 'general application' remains one of the factors determining whether an English Act is in force. However, while Roberts Wray asserted that, 'it has not given the Courts serious trouble',[31] and this opinion has been accepted by the Privy Council,[32] this is not a unanimous view.[33] Sir Anthony Allott stated, in the context of British African territories, that, 'seldom has a phrase given rise to so much difficulty, or been interpreted in so many different senses by the judges'.[34] Sir Alison Russell, in his guide for drafters in British colonial territories, also expressed dissatisfaction with the phrase, considering that it, 'is by no means clear when an Act is or is not a statute of general application. In a sense every statute is a statute of general

24 Repeal of Laws Rules 1997 (Tokelau). Some New Zealand Acts remain in force: Application of New Zealand Law Rules 2004.

25 On the passing of the Civil Law Act Amendment Act 2003 (Tonga), the Insolvency Act 1986 (UK) ceased to apply: see *Pasili* v. *Tonga Development Bank* [2004] TongaLawRp 27; *Fresha Exports Ltd* v. *Tonga Co-operative Federation Ltd* [2010] TongaLawRp 31 [9].

26 'Tonga Laws Are There to Protect the People Who Have No Power' *Matangi Tonga*, 2004 www.matangitonga.to/home/ward/htm accessed 21 July 2004.

27 On the passing of the Civil Law Act Amendment Act 2003 (Tonga), the Matrimonial Causes Act 1973 (UK) ceased to apply: *Halapua* v. *Tonga* [2004] TOCA 5. This case and most of the other unreported cases cited in this article can be accessed via www.pacLII.org.

28 For example, the Charging Order Act 1979 (UK): see *Australia and New Zealand Banking Group Ltd* v. *Naufahu* [2011] TOSC 2.

29 Interpretation Act 2004 (Niue), s. 37(4).

30 See notes to the Reprint of Statutes Act, 1972 in Revised Statutes of Samoa, 1977.

31 Roberts-Wray (n. 3), 545.

32 [2007] 2 AC 400 (PC) [12].

33 From her time in practice in Solomon Islands between 1987 and 1996, the author experienced the difficulty of advising clients as to their legal position with any certainty where United Kingdom legislation had some potential bearing on the case.

34 A. Allott *New Essays in African Law* (Butterworths, 1970) 48.

application and in a sense every statute is a statute of special application.'[35] The following section of this chapter explores the meaning of the phrase in more depth.

IV DEFINITION OF 'STATUTES OF GENERAL APPLICATION'?

The phrase 'statutes of general application' is not defined in any of the laws which introduce these Acts in the Pacific, nor would it seem in any other legislation. Roberts-Wray, in his seminal work, *Commonwealth and Colonial Law*, stated:[36]

> The expression 'statutes of general application' is usually regarded as descriptive of Acts of Parliament which are of general relevance to the conditions of other countries and, in particular, not based upon politics or circumstances peculiar to England.

The phrase has received some judicial consideration in the Pacific region, having been considered by courts in Fiji,[37] Solomon Islands,[38] Tonga,[39] Tuvalu[40] and Vanuatu,[41] and, most recently, by the Privy Council in an appeal from Pitcairn Island.[42] However, as mentioned above, the decisions have not always been consistent. Neither do they explore directly what Harding refers to as the 'law-and-society gap', in the sense of societal fit, as a possible factor in determination of 'general application'.

In the Fijian case of *Indian Printing and Publishing Co* v. *Police*[43] a case decided before Fiji became independent, the question was whether the Obscene Publications Act 1857 (UK) was in force in Fiji.[44] Counsel for the appellant argued that the statute was a 'police law' and as such it was purely local in character and effect and had no application in Fiji unless re-enacted

35 Sir Alison Russell, *Legislative Drafting and Forms* 4th edn (Butterworth and Co, 1938) 20–1.
36 Roberts-Wray (n. 3), 556.
37 *Indian Printing and Publishing Co* v. *Police* (1932) 3 FLR 142.
38 *R* v. *Ngena* [1983] SILR 1; *Re Miria* [2007] SBHC 138.
39 *Tu'itavake* v. *Porter* [1989] TongaLawRp 14; *Teta Ltd* v. *Ulrich Ltd* [1981–1988] TongaLawRp 127.
40 *Re the Matter of the Constitution of Tuvalu and of the Laws of Tuvalu Act* 1987 (Unreported, High Court, Tuvalu, Donne CJ, 1989).
41 *Harrisen* v. *Holloway (No. 2)* (1984) 1 Van LR 147.
42 *Christian* v. R [2007] 2 AC 400 (PC). For further discussion of the complex issues faced by the Privy Council see S. Farran, 'The "Re-Colonising" of Pitcairn', *Victoria University of Wellington Law Review* 38 (3) (2007), 435.
43 (1932) 3 FLR 142.
44 Such offences are now dealt with by the Crimes Decree 2009 (Fiji), s. 377.

by the local legislature. It was held that the phrase 'statutes of general application' was:

> used in the sense of denoting a Statute binding upon all His Majesty's subjects in England at the relevant date. [It was] used to distinguish between public statutes not necessarily binding upon all the population, eg the Companies Act or the Friendly Societies Act on the one hand and the public statutes which on the other hand are binding upon everyone eg, the Offenses against the Person Act or similar legislation.

The Chief Justice referred to the division of English statutes under separate headings (presumably Public General Acts and Private Acts), dating from May 1801. He also cited *Rex* v. *London County Council*[45] where Bowen LJ had said, 'Now a general act prima facie is that which applies to the whole community. In the natural meaning of the term it means an Act of Parliament which is unlimited both in its area and as regards the individual in its effect.' The Chief Justice also noted the distinction drawn by Bowen LJ between Acts which dealt with the administration of justice and personal or local Acts, the former being 'not limited in the true sense either as regards place or persons.' However, His Lordship went on to say that, even without such authority, he was prepared to hold that an Act which dealt or purported 'to deal with protection of the public from a nuisance or crime committed by an individual member thereof is an Act of general application'.

In the Solomon Islands case of *R* v. *Ngena*,[46] the Chief Justice defined a statute of general application as, 'one that regulates conduct or conditions which exist among humanity generally, and in a way applicable to humanity generally', as distinct from a statute that is 'restricted to regulating conduct or conditions peculiar to or in a way applicable only to persons, activities or institutions in the United Kingdom'.

In that case, it was held that the Homicide Act 1957 (UK) was of general application, but did not apply in Solomon Islands as the Penal Code Cap 26 (SI) covered the field. *R* v. *Ngena*[47] was followed in *Re Miria*,[48] where Palmer CJ held that the Adoption Act 1958 (UK) was an Act of general application. Palmer CJ added his own refinement, restricting an Act of general application to one that 'deals with a subject matter which has general relevance not merely to the situation or conditions in Solomon Islands but anywhere in the world'.[49]

45 (1893) 2 QB 454.
46 [1983] SILR 1.
47 *R* v. *Ngena* [1983] SILR 1, 6.
48 [2007] SBHC 138.
49 *Re Miria* [2007] SBHC 138, 2.

The definition in *R* v. *Ngena* was also approved in *Emmett* v. *Emmett*.[50] Outside Solomon Islands, it was endorsed by the High Court of Tuvalu in *Re the Matter of the Constitution of Tuvalu and of the Laws of Tuvalu Act 1987*.[51]

However, in *Mahlon* v. *Mahlon*[52] the High Court of Solomon Islands, constituted by a Commissioner, rather than the Chief Justice, took a different approach, when considering the Marriage Act 1949 (UK). Commissioner Freeman held that as the Act laid down a complicated statutory framework it was not an Act of general application. A similar approach was taken in Vanuatu in *Harrisen* v. *Holloway (No. 2)*.[53] Like the High Court in *Mahlon* v. *Mahlon*, the Supreme Court appears to have thought the surrounding framework to be a pivotal consideration. It was held that the Police Act 1964 (UK) was not an Act of general application due to the differences in the way the various police forces in England and the single force in Vanuatu were set up, including the different modes of control and payment. Thus, the Court appeared to be of the view that to be an Act of general application, the subject matter of the Act must operate in the same way in Vanuatu and in England. This seems to be at odds with older Canadian authority to the effect that inapplicable machinery or procedural provisions may be excluded without prejudicing the remainder of the statute.[54] The fact that Vanuatu was a republic, and the fact that Crown immunity did not apply were also thought to be relevant. In fact, it is arguable that these factors are more relevant to the question of whether the Act is suitable to the circumstances of the country (discussed further below) than whether it is an Act of general application, although the two questions are closely related.

Another point that has been debated in the courts of Solomon Islands is whether the fact that an Act applies only in England (and possibly Wales), but not in Scotland prevents it being of general application. The reason why this point has been argued in Solomon Islands may be that, since independence, there is a distinction between the reception rule in that country, which now refers to 'United Kingdom' statutes of general application,[55] and rules in other Pacific countries which still refer to 'English' statutes.[56] There seems little

50 [2009] SBHC 29.

51 (Unreported, High Court, Tuvalu, Donne CJ, 1989).

52 [1984] SILR 86, 87–8.

53 (1984) 1 Van LR 147.

54 *Sheppard* v. *Sheppard* (1908) BCR 486; *R* v. *Hall* [1941] 2 WWR 245.

55 Constitution of Solomon Islands 1978, Sch 3, para. 1.

56 The position in Kiribati is unclear as the Kiribati Independence Order 1979 s. 5 continues in force existing laws which includes statutes in force in England, but then refers to Acts of Parliament of the United Kingdom when dealing with construction.

doubt that reception rules introducing 'English' statutes would be of general application whether or not they apply in Scotland.[57] The parliament of England ceased to exist in 1707 when the Act of Union merged it with the parliament of Scotland, and it finally became the parliament of the United Kingdom in 1801,[58] before any of these reception rules were framed. It would seem therefore that there is little significance in the change of wording introduced by Solomon Islands Constitution. However, in the Solomon Islands' case of *Mahlon* v. *Mahlon*[59] Commissioner Freeman referred to the fact that the Marriage Act applied only to England, and not even for the most part to Wales, and regarded this as enough to prevent it from being an Act of general application. More recently, the Court of Appeal of Solomon Islands took a contrary view. In *Harry* v. *Kalena Timber Co*,[60] it was held that although the Law of Property Act 1925 (UK) did not apply in Scotland, 'it none the less remains an Act of the United Kingdom of general application'. The court held that they had no doubt on this, citing with approval the view expressed by the West African Court of Appeal that 'the expression "of general application" refers primarily to the subject matter of the statute rather than its geographical ambit'.[61] The Court of Appeal also referred to the statement of Roberts-Wray that 'The view, adopted by Courts in Nigeria, that a statute is not one of general application if it does not extend to Scotland and Ireland is even more out of line, for it is only the law of England that is imported.'[62]

In 2007, the operation of Acts of general application received international attention due to the case of *Christian* v. *R*[63], a case on appeal from the Pitcairn Court of Appeal.[64] There, the meaning of the phrase[65] was considered by the Privy Council. It was submitted for the defendants that the phrase was too imprecise to incorporate the Sexual Offences Act 1956 (UK) as part of the law of Pitcairn. In concluding that this was a statute 'of general application', the Privy Council drew on the work of Sir Roberts-Wray, and was of the view that:

57 Cf *Faleatau* v. *'Akau'ola* [1997] TongaLawRp 185, 189, where it was held that the Inheritance (Provision for Family and Dependants) Act 1975 (UK) was not an Act of general application, as it only to the estates of persons dying in England and Wales.

58 After the merger of the previous Kingdoms of Great Britain and Ireland: Act of Union 1880. See also Royal and Parliamentary Titles Act 1927, inserting the word 'Northern'.

59 [1984] SILR 86, 87–8.

60 [2001] 3 LRC 24.

61 *Young* v. *Abina* (1940) 6 WACA 180, 184, rejecting the conclusion reached in *Re Estate of James Sholu* (1932) 11 NLR 37, and holding that the Land Transfer Act 1897 (UK) applied in Nigeria.

62 Roberts-Wray (n. 3), 556.

63 [2007] 2 AC 400 (PC).

64 *Christian* v. *R (No. 2)* [2006] PNCA 1 (2 March 2006).

65 Applied by Judicature Ordinance 1970 (UK), s. 14.

this language has been used in legislation for British overseas possessions for many years without causing any difficulty. As Sir Kenneth Roberts-Wray said in his book on *Commonwealth and Colonial Law* (1966), at p. 545:

'It has been in use for many decades, it has been the subject of judicial interpretation, it does not appear to have given the courts serious trouble, and it has much the same effect as the common law rule. So a change of formula may do more harm than good.'[66]

More recently, the meaning of 'statutes of general application was again discussed in Pitcairn in *Warren* v. *Queen*.[67] The question raised was whether the Bill of Rights 1688 (UK) was of general application. Adopting the approach of the Privy Council in *Christian* v. *R* and, again, citing the words of Sir Kenneth Roberts-Wray, the Court concluded that it was. Roberts-Wray's definition has also been adopted in Tonga, where the Supreme Court held in *Tu'itavake* v. *Porter*,[68] that the State Immunity Act 1978 (UK) was a statute of general application.

The lack of a precise definition, as discussed above, raises a number of questions regarding the application of the phrase in practice including the following:

Is Subsidiary Legislation Included?

It is unclear whether the word 'statutes' includes subsidiary legislation. It seems logical that legislation would carry with it the subsidiary legislation made under its authority. This was certainly the view of the Court of Appeal of Pitcairn in *R* v. *Seven Named Accused*,[69] where it was held that it was 'reasonably clear that the British Settlements Acts, being statutes of general application and in force in England, are in force in Pitcairn and form part of its law. It would follow that subsidiary legislation based on those Acts also forms part of Pitcairn law.'[70]

May Part of a Statute Be of General Application?

There are two situations where it may be vital to know whether part of an Act can qualify as a statute 'of general application'. The first is where part of an introduced Act is inapplicable to the circumstances of the receiving country.

66 [2007] 2 AC 400 (PC) [12].
67 [2014] PNSC 1.
68 [1989] TongaLawRp 14. See also *Teta Ltd* v. *Ulrich Ltd* [1981–1988] TongaLawRp 127.
69 [2004] PNCA 1 [32].
70 Ibid.

As discussed below, in addition to being of general application, an Act must not be inapplicable to the circumstances of the receiving country if it is to apply. If part of an Act is inapplicable, may the balance of the legislation be applied? This question does not appear to have been considered by a Pacific court. The second situation where it is vital to know whether part of a received Act may be of general application is where a country has passed legislation of its own on a topic, but it does not mention a particular matter which is provided for in the received Act. If the received Act is expressly repealed in toto, that will be the end of the matter, but if it is not, can an Act retain its character of 'general applicability' if parts have been repealed. Again, this has not been specifically considered by the court. The term 'statute of general application' appears on its face to refer to the statute as a whole. However, it would seem from decisions of the court which have permitted parts of Acts of general application to apply if the local Act does not cover the field, that this is not the case. In Solomon Islands[71] for example, in *Korean Enterprises Ltd* v. *Shell Company (Pacific Islands) Ltd*,[72] the Court of Appeal of Solomon Islands, whilst ultimately concluding that the Land and Titles Act covered the field on acquisition by prescription of easements and profits, seemed to have no difficulty in holding that a single section (s. 2) of the Prescription Act 1832 (UK) was included in the phrase 'Act of general application'.

Similarly, in Vanuatu, the Court of Appeal held in *Joli* v. *Joli*[73] that the broad provisions of the Matrimonial Causes Act[74] of Vanuatu authorising the court to order payments of weekly, monthly or annual sums of for maintenance and support of a wife, did not prevent the operation of s. 24 of the Matrimonial Causes Act 1973 (UK), which made provision for the adjustment of property interests on divorce.

However, in *R* v. *Ngena*[75] the court concluded that where a local Act covered the same area of human activity, an Act of general application would not take effect as part of the law. The Chief Justice held:

> The Homicide Act as in force on 1st January 1961 covers with some differences, the same areas of human activity and the regulation of them. It is clearly in my judgment an Act which must be 'subject to' the Penal Code. In the context of a comprehensive Act of Solomon Islands existing in the same field as an Act of the United Kingdom I take the view that the provisions

[71] *Harry* v. *Kalena Timber Co* [2001] 3 LRC 24; *Korean Enterprises Ltd* v. *Shell Co (Pacific Islands) Ltd* [2002] SBCA 1; *Emmett* v. *Emmett* [2009] SBHC 29.

[72] [2002] SBCA 1.

[73] [2003] VUCA 27.

[74] Cap 192 (Vanuatu).

[75] [1983] SILR 1.

of the Solomon Islands Act not only take precedence where there is a conflict but also that, in order to give the words 'subject to' any real meaning, the existence of the Solomon Island Act must prevent the provisions of the United Kingdom Act taking effect as part of the law of Solomon Islands even where there is no conflict.

His Lordship's words seem to dictate again the kind of cherry picking engaged in in *Korean Enterprises Ltd* v. *Shell Company (Pacific Islands) Ltd* and *Joli* v. *Joli*.

Are Acts Ratifying International Conventions Included?

In Tonga, it was stated in *Gorce* v. *Miller*[76] that an English statute which ratified an international convention (in that case, the Child Abduction and Custody Act 1985 (UK)) to which Tonga was not a party would not qualify as an Act of general application. As mentioned above, since the passing of the Civil Law Amendment Act in 2003, the question has been academic in Tonga. In other countries of the region, the courts do not appear to have been called on to consider whether an English statute ratifying a convention could be used as a back door means of endorsement or to give domestic force to a convention.

V LIMITATIONS ON STATUTES OF GENERAL APPLICATION

Apart from being of general application, introduced statutes are generally subject to important limitations. The most common limitations imposed by reception rules will now be discussed.

Cut-Off Dates

As mentioned above, most receiving countries introduce statutes in force in the enacting country at a specific date, often referred to as 'the cut-off date'. Any changes made by parliament in the enacting country after that date will not be part of the law of the receiving country. Cut-off dates differ from country to country and range from 2 January 1875 in Fiji[77] to 1 January 1976 in Vanuatu.[78] These cut-off dates mean that Pacific countries cannot take advantage of more recent reforms of the law in the United Kingdom and, until

76 [2003] TongaLawRp 4.
77 Supreme Court Ordinance 1875 (UK), s. 35.
78 High Court of New Hebrides Regulation 1976, s. 3.

action is taken locally, they are burdened with antiquated legislation which is out of touch with social mores.[79]

Applicability to Local Circumstances

The second common limitation on statutes of general application is, as mentioned above, that they are stated to be in force only in so far as they are not 'inapplicable to the circumstances of' or 'so far as circumstances admit' in the receiving country.[80] The question then arises whether inapplicability to local circumstances will prevent an Act being of general application in the first place. However, although there is certainly some overlap – as lack of generality makes it less likely that a statute will be appropriate and vice versa – these do seem to be distinct questions. Of course, much depends on the interpretation of 'general application'. If the *Ngena* approach is taken and it is viewed as a question of whether the statute in question 'regulates conduct or conditions which exist among humanity generally, and in a way applicable to humanity generally', then the applicability of local circumstances would seem to be easier to separate from the question of whether an Act is or is not of general application.

In practice, the case law seems to show that the questions have been conflated. In a number of regional decisions, including *Mahlon* v. *Mahlon*[81] and *Harrisen* v. *Holloway (No. 2)*,[82] the courts have found the lack of a suitable framework in which the Act may operate to be a pivotal consideration in deciding if it is of general application. The reference in Roberts-Wray's definition to Acts 'of general relevance to the conditions of other countries' and not based on 'circumstances peculiar to England' gives some support for this approach.

However, in *Balesaga* v. *Balesaga*[83] a clear line was drawn between these two considerations. In that case, the judge was satisfied that the Matrimonial Causes Act 1950 (UK) was a statute of general application. However, he found difficulty with the fact that its full implementation called for the availability of a Queen's Proctor and an Attorney-General, officers who were non-existent in Vanuatu (then the New Hebrides). On appeal the Court of Appeal approved of the separation of these two

79 See, e.g., notes on Evidence (Amendment) Bill 2016 (Tonga).

80 Solomon Islands is a notable exception: see *R* v. *Ngena* [1983] SBHC 1.

81 [1984] SILR 86.

82 (1984) 1 Van LR 147.

83 [1970] FLR 18.

questions and held that once it was established that the Matrimonial Causes Act 1950 was an Act of general application, the lack of a Queen's Proctor and Attorney-General were not factors of such moment as to render the Act inapplicable.

Similarly, and more recently, the two considerations were considered separately by the Privy Council in *Christian* v. *R*,[84] referred to above. Whilst counsel's question as to what was meant by a statute of general application was grouped with his assertion that 'there could be much dispute over whether "local circumstances" made it appropriate for the law to apply',[85] Lord Hoffman drew on different authorities in support of his approach. Whilst Roberts-Wray's definition was used to assist in answering the question of whether the Act was of general application, an English Court of Appeal's decision was used to dispose of the question of whether it was appropriate to local circumstances. It was held that:

> Similar language was considered by the Court of Appeal in *Nyali Ltd v Attorney-General* [1956] 1 QB 1, where Denning LJ said (at p. 17) that the task of making qualifications to English law to suit the circumstances of overseas territories called for wisdom on the part of their judges. But he described it (at p. 16) as a 'wise provision' and did not suggest that it was incapable of application. Their Lordships think that there can be no doubt that the 1956 Act is an act of general application and that there are no local circumstances which make it inappropriate to apply the provisions about rape, indecent assault and incest.[86]

The point was expanded upon in the judgment of Lord Hope, who also looked first at the question of whether the Sexual Offences Act was an Act of general application and, having concluded that it was, went on to give separate consideration to the qualification 'that the law thus imported was to be in force only so far as "local circumstances" permit', which he regarded as the more problematic question.[87]

Similarly, in *Warren* v. *Queen*[88] the Supreme Court of Pitcairn saw a clear distinction between the issues of 'whether (a), the Bill of Rights 1688 is a statute of "general application",' and 'whether (b), there are "local circumstances" which do not permit such application'.

84 [2007] 2 AC 400 (PC).
85 Ibid., [12].
86 Ibid., [13].
87 Ibid., [77], [78].
88 [2014] PNSC 1.

VI OTHER ISSUES

Apart from uncertainties regarding the definition and limitations on statutes of general application, there are other questions regarding these statutes, which include the following:

Hierarchical Position and Compatibility with Customary Law

Consideration of the requirement of general application and the overlapping question of what constitutes inapplicability to local circumstances leads into the more specific question, that is, whether incompatibility with customary laws prevents a statute being of general application or renders it inapplicable to local circumstances. Whilst Harding leaves to one side the 'problematic debate' concerning legal pluralism, pluralism as a social fact[89] cannot be overlooked in the discussion of legal transplants in Pacific Islands. The hierarchy set up by regional constitutions generally places statute law above customary law. However, this does not answer the question raised here; rather it gives rise to two preliminary questions. First, do these superior statutes include introduced legislation, and more specifically, statutes of general application, or only Acts of the local parliament. Secondly, if they do include introduced legislation, are such statutes excluded if they conflict with customary laws on the basis that they are inapplicable to local circumstances. From the case analysis conducted above, it would appear that the existence of customary law, even if in conflict with the statute in question, has not been considered to be relevant to the question of general applicability. However, it would appear to be relevant to the related question of applicability to local circumstances.

With regard the first question, this has been considered by the High Court of Solomon Islands. In both *R* v. *Ngena*[90] and *K* v. *T*[91] the High Court held that the term 'Act of Parliament', as defined in the part of the Constitution dealing with the hierarchy of laws,[92] means an 'Act of Parliament of Solomon Islands',[93] and does not include an 'Act of Parliament of the United Kingdom'.[94] This means that customary law is not placed below an Act of

89 For an explanation of social fact legal pluralism see W. Twining, 'Normative and Legal Pluralism: A Global Perspective', *Duke Journal of Comparative & International Law* 20 (2010), 473, 488–9.

90 [1983] SILR 1.

91 [1985–86] SILR 49.

92 Constitution of Solomon Islands 1978, Sch. 3.

93 *R* v. *Ngena* [1983] SILR 1 refer to 'Act of the National Parliament of Solomon Islands'.

94 *K* v. *T* [1985–86] SILR 49.

> general application.[95] Rather, in *K* v. *T*,[96] it seems to have been suggested that statutes of general application and customary laws rank equally as sources of law and that public policy may be a determining factor in deciding which to apply. This principle was more explicitly stated in *Harry* v. *Kalena Timber Co*,[97] where Muria CJ said that the provisions of the Trustee Act 1925 (UK) could not be applied across the board in customary land related disputes,' lest we may be placing one source of law, i.e. an Act of UK Parliament of general application, above another source, i.e. customary law which is an equal source of law in this country.' Other regional courts do not appear to have considered this question and the answer depends to some extent on the wording of the provision establishing the hierarchy of laws.

With regard to the second question, the existence of customary laws is obviously a local circumstance which has a profound effect on the application of English law. According to Roberts-Wray, 'where a case is more suitably determined in accordance with customary law, English law will be excluded under the rule that it is to be applied only so far a local circumstances permit'.[98] Since independence, the argument that Acts conflicting with customary laws should not be applied gains force in South Pacific jurisdictions from the fact that most give state recognition to customary laws, obliging the courts to take it into account, often in preference to common law.[99] Many of these countries also emphasize the importance of customary laws in constitutional preambles. For example, the Constitution of Kiribati refers to 'faith in the enduring value of our traditions and heritage' and pledges to 'continue to cherish and uphold the customs and traditions of Kiribati'. This question only appears to have been expressly discussed in one Pacific case. In *Kasa* v. *Biku*,[100] it was held that the Trustee Act 1925 (UK), which had been previously recognized by Solomon Islands' courts as an Act of general application, was inappropriate to Solomon Islands circumstances in that it was not in accord with customary practices governing ownership and disposition of customary land. This finds some support in *Harry* v. *Kalena Timber Co*,[101] where, as mentioned above, Muria CJ said that the provisions of the Trustee

95 Constitution of Solomon Islands 1978, Sch 3, para. 3(2).

96 [1985–86] SILR 49.

97 [1999] SBHC 58. This decision was upheld on appeal, but with no direct discussion on this point: *Harry* v. *Kalena Timber Co* [2001] 3 LRC 24.

98 Roberts-Wray (n. 3), 556.

99 See, e.g., Constitution of Solomon Islands 1978 Sch. 3, para. 2(1)(c).

100 [2001] LRC 133.

101 [1999] SBHC 58. This decision was upheld on appeal, but with no direct discussion on this point: *Harry* v. *Kalena Timber Co* [2001] 3 LRC 24.

Act 1925 (UK) would not necessarily apply in customary land disputes, as the position of tribal representatives were closely linked to customary land rights.

In *Joli* v. *Joli*,[102] the Vanuatu Court of Appeal, in considering whether certain sections of the Matrimonial Causes Act 1973 (UK) were to be imported into Vanuatu law, observed that Article 95 (2) of the Constitution provided that English and French laws were to apply 'wherever possible taking due account of custom'. The court therefore felt it necessary to examine the relevant sections to decide whether they took sufficient account of custom to fulfil the requirement of Article 95(2). Having noted that it had not been suggested that the provisions of the 1973 Act were inconsistent with custom, and that the provisions allowed scope for particular customary factors to be taken into account, the Court concluded that the relevant sections were in force.

Apart from these rare examples, neither compatibility with customary law nor the broader issue of the 'law-and-society gap' referred to by Harding has been argued as rendering a transplanted statute inapplicable to local circumstances. Instead, South Pacific courts have tended to apply English Acts even when they conflict with customary laws. Thus, for example, in Solomon Islands, the Guardianship of Infants Act 1925 (UK) has been applied on numerous occasions,[103] even though it dictates that custody decisions be made in accordance with the best interests of the child,[104] which may conflict with customary norms driven by principles of patriarchy, giving a male parent or relative superior rights to those of the wife or widow. As mentioned above, *K* v. *T*[105] seems to suggest that statutes of general application and customary laws rank equally and that in cases of conflict public policy might be the determining factor. In that case the Guardianship of Infants Act prevailed.

A similar approach has been taken in Vanuatu where the Supreme Court stated in three child custody cases (*Toma* v. *Charley*,[106] *M* v. *P*[107] and G v. *L*[108]), that the welfare principle[109] applied, even if this was not in accordance with custom, which often favours the father or his relatives over the mother.[110]

102 [2003] VUCA 27.
103 See, e.g., *K* v. *T* [1985–86] SILR 49.
104 The court must 'regard the welfare of the infant as the first and paramount consideration': s. 1.
105 [1985–86] SILR 49.
106 (Unreported, Supreme Court, Vanuatu, 15 April 1985).
107 (1988) 1 Van LR 333.
108 (1990) 2 Van LR 486.
109 Guardianship of Minors Act 1971 (UK), s. 1, applying in Vanuatu as a statute of general application in force in England on 1 January 1976 (High Court of the New Hebrides Regulation 1976, s. 3) was not expressly referred to in these cases.
110 See, e.g., the evidence of customary law in *Sukutaona* v. *Houanihou* [1982] SILR 12; *Re B* [1983] SILR 223; *K* v. *T* [1985–86] SILR 49 (in this case the mother was claiming custody

Another context in which a statute of general application has conflicted with custom is adoption. The Adoption Act 1958 (UK), which applied in Solomon Islands until 2008, was drafted for use in the United Kingdom, and consequently made no reference to customary laws. It was not a good fit with local circumstances, which included the widespread and well-accepted practice of customary adoption, which is based on very different norms. In *Re Tiokobule Bero*[111] Brown J remarked, *obiter*, that customary adoption was more appropriate for Solomon Islands than adoption under the English Act. His Lordship suggested that customary adoption could be recognized through a Certificate of Recognition of Adoption. His Lordship set out various criteria to be satisfied before the granting of the Certificate, including that the adoption must have taken place in accordance with the custom of the child and the adoptive parents. Brown J appears to have garnered these ideas from Papua New Guinea.[112] However, Brown J's approach to statutes of general application was, later the same year, overturned by Chief Justice Palmer.[113] A further example of the courts' refusal to exclude the Adoption Act 1958 on the grounds that it conflicts with customary laws can be found in *Re Belo*[114] where the court refused to make an order based only on the existence of a prior customary adoption of the child by the applicant, insisting that the factors to be considered under the 1958 Act were the relevant principles. Similarly, in *R* v. *Takabea*[115] the defendant had been adopted under Kiribati custom by a citizen of Solomon Islands, and he argued that on such a basis he held Solomon Islands citizenship. The Court held that, in order for the adoption to be recognized, the defendant would need to commence proceedings for a formal adoption order under the Adoption Act 1958. The applicability of the Adoption Act 1958 as an Act of general application is now academic as Solomon Islands has brought its own local Act, the Adoption Act 2004, into force. Unfortunately, that Act does not reconcile the tensions between state and customary adoptions.[116]

against paternal relatives, the father of the children having died); *Sasango* v. *Beliga* [1987] SILR 91.

111 [2007] SBHC 94.

112 Section 54 of the Adoption of Children Act 1968 [Cap 275] provides that the Local Court may, on application by a party, grant a certificate that a customary adoption has been made or terminated.

113 *Re Miria* [2007] SBHC 138.

114 [2003] SBHC 84.

115 [1993] SBHC 81.

116 See further, J. Corrin and E. Foote, 'Failing to adopt a new approach: the law of adoption in Solomon Islands' in B. Atkin (ed.), *The International Survey of Family Law* (Jordan Publishing, 2014). The Adoption (Amendment) Act 2017 introduced safeguards to govern overseas adoptions.

Of course, all these decisions relate to children and could be justified by reference to the International Convention on the Rights of the Child,[117] to which all the Pacific countries under discussion are parties. The Convention provides that in all actions concerning children, 'the best interests of the child shall be a primary consideration'.[118] Although this obligation has only been incorporated into domestic law in Fiji[119] and Vanuatu,[120] in other regional countries it would have provided a policy reason for preferring the received law. However, this has not been raised in any of regional court; in fact there has been no direct discussion of the requirement that statutes of general application be applicable to local circumstances.

Is further Action Necessary to Bring Introduced Legislation into Force?

In most countries of the region, phrases such as 'in force' or 'part of the law' make it clear that introduced laws are automatically in force in the country to which they have been applied or in which they have been adopted. This point was endorsed in *Christian v. R (No. 2)*[121] where it was made clear that there is no need for any further legislative or judicial Act to bring statutes of general application into force. It was held:

> The observation in some academic writing to the effect that a particular law is not engrafted on to the law of the colony under this form of enactment until a legislative or a judicial pronouncement has been made, and which in principle would not have retrospective effect, was not advanced in any substantive way before us. We do no more than observe that such an approach would really be tantamount to denying the provision any efficacy and requiring the specific adoption of each and every law it is intended should apply before it could be applied. That would seem to be contrary to the plain words of subs (1).[122]

117 Convention on the Rights of the Child (adopted 20 November 1989, entered into force 2 September 1990) 1577 UNTS 3. The Convention came into force 2 September 1990. Solomon Islands acceded 10 April 1995; Tonga acceded 6 November 1995; Vanuatu ratified 7 July 1993; Kiribati acceded 11 December 1995; Fiji ratified 13 August 1993; Nauru acceded 27 July 1994; Niue acceded 20 December 1995; Tuvalu acceded 22 September 1995; Samoa ratified 29 November 1994; New Zealand (Cook Islands) acceded 6 April 1993.

118 Convention on the Rights of the Child, art. 3.1.

119 Family Law Act 2003 (Fiji), s. 26.

120 Convention on the Rights of the Child (Ratification) Act 1992 (Vanuatu).

121 [2006] PNCA 1 [50].

122 The Judicature Ordinance 1970 (Pitcairn), s. 14(1) provides that 'the statutes of general application as in force in and for England at the commencement of this Ordinance shall be in force in the Islands'.

However, in countries where the application of British legislation stemmed from s. 15 of the Western Pacific (Courts) Order 1961 (UK), the position was not so straightforward. That section states:

> the civil and criminal jurisdiction of the High Court shall, so far as circumstances admit, be exercised upon the principles of and in conformity with:
> (a) the statutes of general application in force in England on the first day of January 1961.

In *Re the Constitution of Tuvalu and the Laws of Tuvalu Act 1987*[123] Donne CJ pointed out that the application of statutes of general application was subject to limitations spelt out in the proviso to s. 15(1) including the requirement that the legislation must be permitted by the 'circumstances of Tuvalu'.[124] Accordingly, he held that English Acts did not have effect in Tuvalu until either expressly adopted by the Parliament of Tuvalu or declared to be in force by the court.

More recently, in *Iosefo* v. *Tuvalu Red Cross*,[125] however, a differently constituted High Court in Tuvalu took a different approach. Whilst agreeing with the historical development of the law set out in *Re the Constitution of Tuvalu and the Laws of Tuvalu Act 1987*, Ward CJ held that statutes of general application were part of the law irrespective of whether they had been expressly adopted by Parliament or applied by the court.[126] His Lordship pointed out that to 'read otherwise would mean that, after independence, Tuvalu would have no law covering those fields until and if the High Court ruled on the law'. Section 15 is no longer in force in the region, but this debate does illustrate the type of problem that can arise in relation to this transplanted legislation.

A Question of Fact or Law?

Is being a statute 'of general application' a matter of fact to be proved to the court, or is it a question of law, on which the court is free to inform itself? This question does not seem to have been considered by a court in the Pacific. In practice, courts do not usually require evidence to be adduced on this matter, and seems to operate on the basis that the question is one of judicial notice. Among the numerous examples of cases where English Acts have been applied without argument or evidence in support is *Isaac* v. *Kadir*[127] where the

123 (Unreported, High Court, Tuvalu, Donne CJ, 1989).
124 Ibid.
125 *Iosefo* v. *Tuvalu Red Cross* [2012] TVHC 9.
126 Ibid., [15]–[19].
127 (1962) 9 FLR 152.

Supreme Court of Fiji was prepared to assume that the Forfeiture Act 1870 (UK) was a statute of general application in force in that country. In Solomon Islands, examples include *Buchanan* v. *Wilikai*,[128] where the Partnership Act 1890 (UK) was applied;[129] *KHY Co (SI)* v. *Ling Kun Xiang*,[130] where the Debtors Act 1869 (UK) was applied; *Allardyce Lumber Co Ltd* v. *Attorney-General*,[131] where the Trustee Act 1925 (UK) was applied; and *Re Miria*,[132] where the Adoption Act 1958 (UK) was applied. Similarly, in Vanuatu, in *Clements* v. *The Hong Kong and Shanghai Banking Corporation*,[133] the Court of Appeal was satisfied that the English Bankruptcy Act 1914 was an Act of general application without requiring evidence to be adduced. In *Boe* v. *Thomas*,[134] the Fatal Accidents Act 1846 (UK) and the Law Reform (Miscellaneous Provisions) Act 1934 (UK) were applied. An example from Tuvalu is the case of *Iosefo* v. *Tuvalu Red Cross*,[135] where the Limitation Act 1939 (UK) was applied without evidence in support.

However, in S v. *Moti*,[136] the Supreme Court of Vanuatu suggested, *obiter*, that the application of a British Act was a matter to be proved. This case also dealt with the related question of who bears the burden of proof if evidence is required and the matter is disputed. In S v. *Moti*,[137] it was held that the onus lay on the party relying on the law:

> [Q]uite clearly, the onus is on the party who asserts that a British law is applicable in Vanuatu to prove to the satisfaction of the Court that the British law concerned is a British law in force or applied in the New Hebrides immediately before the 30th July 1980 (the day of Independence of Vanuatu) and Vanuatu Parliament does not provide otherwise.

However, this case was dealing primarily with British case law, and it goes against the preponderance of authority set out above. It seems that, in most cases, the courts are willing to apply English statutes without supporting evidence, and without giving reasons. This appears to support, albeit implicitly, the contention that there is a general presumption in favour of general

128 [1982] SILR 123.
129 *Buchanan* v. *Wilikai* [1982] SILR 123.
130 [1988–89] SILR 63.
131 [1988–89] SILR 78.
132 [2007] SBHC 138.
133 (1980) 1 Van LR 416.
134 (1987) 1 Van LR 293.
135 [2012] TVHC 9.
136 S v. *Moti* [1999] VUSC 38.
137 Ibid.

application, and that the onus of proof rests on a party trying to show inapplicability.[138]

Publication and Accessibility

Another issue is accessibility. Where legislation from another country is incorporated by general reference it may not be physically available in the receiving country, particularly if it is a small island state with limited resources. This has implications for the core rule of law principle that justice should be accessible. The issue received international attention in *Christian* v. *R*,[139] where, as mentioned above, the accused were prosecuted under the Sexual Offences Act 1956 (UK), which was contended to be an Act of general application. The defence argued that prosecution under an Act which had not been published locally was an abuse of process. As stated by the Supreme Court in that case, 'individuals and those advising them . . . should have access to [the law] in authentic form'[140] because 'a citizen, before committing himself to any course of action, should be able to know in advance what are the legal consequences that will flow from it'.[141] However, whilst accepting 'the fact that a law had not been published and could not reasonably have been known to exist [might] be a ground for staying a prosecution for contravention of that law as an abuse of process',[142] the Privy Council agreed with the Court of Appeal of Pitcairn that, as rape and various sexual offences were known locally to be criminal offences, the lack of local publication was irrelevant. In a separate, but ultimately concurring, judgment, Lord Hope – with whom Lord Woolf agreed – [143] expressed concern about this aspect of the case, stating:

> But it is one thing for this well-established method of legislating to be used in circumstances, such as in New South Wales or New Zealand, where ample

138 See, to the contrary, Roberts-Wray (n. 3), 555, where Sir Kenneth Roberts-Wray extracted from Canadian cases the principle that English statutes did not apply unless shown to be suitable as opposed to the common law, which applied unless shown to be unsuitable. However, he conceded that this might not be the case in a jurisdiction where common law and statute were given effect subject to exactly the same qualifications for local circumstances. Unfortunately, he did not go on to say what he considered the test would be in that case.

139 [2007] 2 AC 400 (PC).

140 *R* v. *Christian (No. 2)* [2005] LRC 245 [163], citing *R (on the application of L)* v. *Secretary of State for the Home Department* [2003] 1 All ER 1062, 1069.

141 *R* v. *Christian (No. 2)* [2005] LRC 245 [164], citing *Black-Clawson International Ltd* v. *Papierverke Waldhof-Aschafenburg AC* [1975] 1 All ER 810 at 836.

142 *Christian* v. *R* [2007] 2 AC 400 (PC) [24].

143 Ibid., [30].

> resources existed for finding out what the law was and for obtaining advice about it in case of doubt. It is quite another to use it in the circumstances of a tiny, remote and isolated community like Pitcairn, where at the relevant time these resources were entirely absent. As Lord Diplock observed in Fothergill v Monarch Airlines Ltd [1981] AC 251, 279, elementary justice requires that the rules by which the citizen is bound should be ascertainable by reference to sources that are accessible. In R v Rimmington [2005] UKHL 63; [2006] 1 AC 459, 482, para. 33 Lord Bingham of Cornhill said:
>
> 'There are two guiding principles: no one should be punished under a law unless it is sufficiently clear and certain to enable him to know what conduct is forbidden before he does it; and no one should be punished for any act which was not clearly and ascertainably punishable when the act was done.'
>
> The requirement of ascertainability is an essential component of the rule of law. But in the case of statutes of general application in force in England, as the Governor should have known, it was incapable of being met on Pitcairn.[144]

On the facts of this case, his Lordship overcame his misgivings by reference to the fact that the provisions of the English legislation did not create new crimes, but built on offences existing under the common law which, under well-established principles, the islanders had brought with them when they settled on Pitcairn, merely operating to prescribe the penalties that were to attach to these offences. Lord Hope distinguished the facts of *R* v. *Rimmington*,[145] on the basis that there the common-law crime of causing a public nuisance had been enlarged.

Whilst the Sexual Offences Act was upheld in *Christian* v. *R*, that legislation governed serious criminal offences. Such offences are likely to be well known. In other cases, and where legislation is not substantially repeating common-law principles, it remains the case that legislation introduced by general reference may be subject to objection on the grounds of lack of access to or knowledge of its terms. Accordingly, there is still uncertainty arising from the fact that there remains a large body of introduced law which is potentially invalid.

VII ACTS WHICH HAVE BEEN APPLIED AND PRECEDENT

Once an Act has been applied, this creates a precedent for the country in which this has occurred and provides persuasive authority for other countries in the region. In addition to decisions of courts based locally, as discussed

144 *Christian* v. *R* [2007] 2 AC 400 (PC) [81].
145 [2006] 1 AC 459.

above, the phrase has been considered by the Privy Council. Whilst appeals to the Privy Council have been abolished by most South Pacific nations, appeals are still allowed in Cook Islands, Niue, Kiribati, and Tuvalu. In the other countries of the region, whilst not binding, decisions of the Privy Council are still highly persuasive. Unfortunately, the Privy Council missed the opportunity presented by *R* v. *Christian* to set its stamp on the definition of 'general application' and, until a court has made a pronouncement, it is still often difficult to tell in advance whether a particular Act will qualify. In this context precedents are vitally important.

Acts of general application have been found to apply in a number of substantive areas. In spite of academic expressions of doubt,[146] this clearly includes criminal statutes.[147] Whilst it is impossible to provide a complete round-up of relevant decisions, a number of English statutes have been applied consistently throughout the region, in countries which do not or did not at the time of application have their own legislation in these areas. These include the following:

- Adoption Act 1958;[148]
- Bankruptcy Act 1914;[149]
- Debtors Act 1869;[150]
- Fatal Accidents Act 1976 (UK), or in countries with an earlier cut-off date, the Fatal Accidents Act of 1846–1959;[151]
- Guardianship of Infants Act 1925; Guardianship of Minors Act 1971 (discussed above);
- Law of Property Act 1925;[152]

146 T. Angelo and F. Wright, 'Pitcairn: Sunset on the Empire?', *New Zealand Law Journal* (2004) 431, 431–2.

147 *Christian* v. *R* [2007] 2 AC 400 (PC); *R* v. *Ngena* [1983] SBHC 1; *Indian Printing and Publishing Co* v. *The Police* (1932) 3 FLR 142, discussed above. See also *R* v. *De Baun* (1901) 3 WALR 1, applying the Lotteries Act 1698 (UK) and *Attorney General* v. *Edgely* (1888) 9 NSWR 157, applying the Gaming Act 1802 (UK).

148 *Re Miria* [2007] SBHC 138; *Watts* v. *Tetika* [2005] KIHC 62; *Re Tyson Togomiro* [2013] VUSC 178.

149 *McCluskey* v. *Attorney General* [1993] SBHC 88; *Clements* v. *Hong Kong and Shanghai Banking Corporation* [1988] VUCA 3; [1980–1994] Van LR 416. In Tonga, the more recent equivalent, the Insolvency Act 1986 (UK) applied prior to the passing of the Civil Law (Amendment) Act 2003.

150 *KHY Co (SI) Ltd* v. *Ling Kun Xiang* [1988/9] SILR 63; *Ramanlal & Sons Company Ltd* v. *Cater* [1999] TongaLawRp 45; *Naylor* v. *Foundas* [2004] VUCA 26, this Act also applies in Nauru by virtue of the Custom and Adopted Laws Act 1971 (Nauru).

151 *Boe* v. *Thomas* (1987) 1 Van LR 293; *Estate of Lydia Keith and Windy Keith* v. *Vanuatu Internak Air Services Ltd (Vanair)* [2006] VUSC 61.

152 See, e.g., *Harry* v. *Kalena Timber Company Limited* [2001] 3 LRC 24.

- Law Reform (Miscellaneous Provisions) Acts 1971 or in countries with an earlier cut-off date, the Law Reform (Miscellaneous Provisions) Acts 1934 and 1945;[153]
- Limitation Act 1939;[154]
- Law Reform (Contributory Negligence) Act 1945 UK;[155]
- Sale of Goods Act 1893,[156] or in Tonga, Sale of Goods Act 1979;[157]
- Trustee Act 1925.[158]

Other Acts which have been applied in some countries include:

- Administration of Justice Act 1956 (in Solomon Islands);[159]
- Administration of Estates Act, 1925 (in Solomon Islands);[160]
- Defamation Act 1952 (in Solomon Islands);[161]
- Evidence Act 1968 (in Vanuatu);[162]
- Obscene Publications Act 1857 (Fiji);[163]
- Partnership Act 1890;[164]
- Prescription Act 1832 (in Solomon Islands);[165]
- Sexual Offences Act 1956 (in Pitcairn).[166]

However, there have been instances where introduced legislation has been accepted in one country, but rejected in another. Where rejection is a result of the receiving country having its own legislation, no inconsistency arises.[167]

153 *Boe* v. *Thomas* (1987) 1 Van LR 293; *Estate of Lydia Keith and Windy Keith* v. *Vanuatu Internak Air Services Ltd (Vanair)* [2006] VUSC 61.

154 *Tiba* v. *Takabwebwe* [1996] KIHC 153 *Tamakin* v. *Ronphos* [2012] NRSC 9; *Bird* v. *Registrar of Titles* [1980–1981] SILR 47; *Iosefo* v. *Tuvalu Red Cross* [2012] TVHC 9.

155 See, e.g., *Kapiel* v. *Jenkinson* [2002] VUSC 20.

156 See *Great Woods Ltd* v. *Springhill Ltd* [2012] SBCA 14; *Quarter Enterprises Pty Ltd* v. *Allardyce Lumber Company Ltd* [2007] SBHC 118; *ANZ Bank (Vanuatu) Ltd* v. *Marchand* [2001] VUCA 2.

157 *Tu'iva* v. *Fifita* [1991] TongaLawRp 63. See also *Corbett* v. *Si'i Kae Ola Holding Co Ltd* [2006] TOSC 32.

158 *Allardyce Lumber Company Ltd* v. *Attorney-General* [1988–1989] SILR 78, but see *Kasa* v. *Biku* [2001] LRC 133.

159 *Shell Company* v. *Daoga No. 2* [2000) SBHC 39.

160 *Re Estate of Victor Eoaeo* [1999] SBHC 8; *Y Sato & Company Ltd* v. *Tiare* [1999] SBHC 8.

161 *Sikua* v. *Tradewinds Investment Company Ltd* [2010] SBHC 9 [9], *obiter*.

162 *Turala* v. *Republic of Vanuatu* [2013] VUCA 20 [12], [13].

163 *Indian Printing and Publishing Co* v. *The Police* (1932) 3 FLR 142.

164 *Buchanan* v. *Wilikai* [1982] SILR 123; *Molaisuva* v. *MV Francis Gerena* [2013] SBHC 59.

165 *Korean Enterprises Ltd* v. *Shell Company (Pacific Islands) Ltd* [2002] SBCA 1. However, the Prescription Act 1832 (UK), s. 2, was held not to apply, as the point was governed by the Land and Titles Act Cap 133 (SI).

166 *R* v. *Christian* [2007] 2 AC 400 (PC) [77].

167 See, e.g., *Kingdom of Tonga* v. *Save* [1993] TOSC 7, where the Limitation Act 1980 (UK) was held not to apply as the Fatal Accidents Act Cap 34 (Tonga) governed the limitation period.

However, there have been instances of differences of opinion as to whether legislation is 'of general application' or not. An example can be found in respect of the Limitation Act 1939 (UK), which has been found to be of general application in Kiribati, Nauru, Solomon Islands, and Tuvalu,[168] whereas the Limitation Act 1933 (UK) was held not to apply in Jamaica.[169] Whilst conflicting decisions may be the result of different circumstances prevailing in the countries in question, the consequence is that decisions from other Commonwealth countries cannot be relied upon to settle conclusively the question of whether an English Act is of general application.

There has also been at least one instance of inconsistent application within the same country. This occurred recently in Solomon Islands where the High Court held that the Adoption Act 1958, which until 2008, when the Adoption Act 2004 (SI) came into force, had formed the sole avenue for state adoption. Up until 2007, there had been at least four decisions of the High Court applying the 1958 Act,[170] although the rational for its qualification as an Act of general application was not specifically discussed. However, as mentioned above, in 2007 in *Re Tiokobule Bero*[171] Brown J refused to apply the Act on the basis that it was not an Act of general application. His Lordship stated that the Act was 'wholly irrelevant' to Solomon Islands and was applicable only to UK residents. His Honour based this conclusion primarily on the fact that the Act required reports and consents from authorities which only existed in the United Kingdom. While this approach draws some authority from *Mahlon* v. *Mahlon*,[172] as discussed above, it seems to confuse the question of general application with the question of inapplicability to local circumstances. The decision also conflicts with Brown J's own earlier decision in *Re Belo*,[173] where His Lordship applied the Adoption Act 1958 without question. Later the same year, in *Re Miria*,[174] Palmer CJ had the opportunity to put things back in place. He held emphatically that the 1958 Act was a statute of general application, applying the test used by the High Court in *R* v. *Ngena*.[175] Palmer CJ took

168 *Tiba* v. *Takabwebwe* [1996] KIHC 153; *Tamakin* v. *Ronphos* [2012] NRSC 9; *Bird* v. *Registrar of Titles* [1980–1981] SILR 47; *Iosefo* v. *Tuvalu Red Cross* [2012] TVHC 9.

169 *Pitt* v. *Lord Dacre* (1876) 3 Ch D 295.

170 *Re V* [1985–86] SILR 252; *Re Okini Manu* [1999] SBHC 74; *Re Stickel* [2001] SBHC 138; *Re Belo* [2003] SBHC 84.

171 [2007] SBHC 94.

172 [1984] SILR 86.

173 [2003] SBHC 84. His Lordship raised no objection to an application made under the 1958 Act, but refused to make an adoption order on the basis that it was a court's 'duty to be satisfied in relation to particular matters' under the legislation.

174 *Re Miria* [2007] SBHC 138. See also *Re Hain* [2008] SBHC 112.

175 [1983] SILR 1.

into account the fact that the Act applied to persons not normally resident in the UK, that it was not inappropriate to local circumstances and that it concerned matters which were of general relevance and not particular to the UK. As discussed above, the appropriateness of the Act to local circumstances is really a separate consideration. In any event, it is arguable that the introduced Adoption Act was not appropriate as it did not cater for customary adoptions.[176]

As mentioned above, conflicting decisions from different countries may result from the fact that circumstances prevailing in those countries differ. However, this cannot be the case where decisions within a country are conflicting.

VIII CONCLUSION

As Harding notes, the lack of empirical evidence and the fact that adaptation of law may continue after transplantation makes it difficult to talk in terms of success or failure of an introduced statute. However, that does not apply to discussion of the process of transplantation. In the case of the typical reception rule employed in the Pacific and throughout the Commonwealth, it has not been an unqualified success. The precise meaning of the phrase 'statutes of general application' remains unclear. The most commonly applied definition appears to be that penned by Sir Roberts-Wray, being 'Acts of Parliament which are of general relevance to the conditions of other countries and, in particular, not based upon politics or circumstances peculiar to England'.[177] As discussed above, this definition, and the competing, often inconsistent definitions put forward by Pacific courts, leave room for argument, and this has led to uncertainty. Surprisingly, with a few exceptions, legal counsel have shown little appetite for arguing the point. Principles which can be extracted from the various cases include the following:

- The term refers to public, rather than private Acts.[178]
- The term includes criminal laws.[179]
- The term refers primarily to the subject matter of the statute rather than its geographical reach.[180]

[176] See further Corrin and Foote (n. 116).

[177] Roberts-Wray (n. 3), 556.

[178] *Indian Printing and Publishing Co* v. *Police* (1932) 3 FLR 142.

[179] *Christian* v. R [2007] 2 AC 400 (PC) [14]; *Indian Printing and Publishing Co v Police* (1932) 3 FLR 142.

[180] *Harry* v. *Kalena Timber Co* [2001] 3 LRC 24.

- Acts ratifying International Conventions are not included.[181]
- Subsidiary legislation appears to be included.[182]
- Part of an Act may be applied.[183]
- Further action is not required to bring an Act of general application into force.[184]
- There appears to be a presumption in favour of an Act being of general application, and the onus of proof rests on a party trying to show that it is not.[185]

However, there are many questions remaining and the Pacific case law discussed above casts doubt on the current accuracy of Roberts-Wray's contention that the phrase '"statutes of general application" does not appear to have given the courts serious trouble'.[186] Notwithstanding, he may be correct that at this stage, 'a change of formula may do more harm than good'.[187] A better approach would be to patriate statute law in the Pacific. Reliance on introduced legislation, as opposed to legislation drafted specifically to meet the needs of Pacific peoples has a colonial flavour. In addition to being developed out of context, transplanted laws are imposed on pre-existing systems of custom and culture, with which they may be out of harmony. However, in countries other than Niue, Samoa, Tokelau and Tonga, action on this front appears to have stalled. For example, the 1995 reference to Solomon Islands Law Reform Commission to report on introduced Acts applying and make recommendations for reform has not progressed.[188] Whilst lack of resources will make recourse to models from other countries (redefined by Harding as 'legal mimesis', or 'copying') an attractive proposition for some time to come, rejection of the wholesale application of foreign legislation, frozen in time at a cut-off date determined by colonial history, is a necessary part of true independence.

As time goes on and more Pacific countries fill out their statute books with homegrown law, or, at least, 'borrowed' laws that have been individually examined for 'fit', statutes of general application will become gradually less relevant. In the meantime, whilst the courts are faced with some conflicting

181 *Gorce* v. *Miller* [2003] TongaLawRp 4.
182 *R* v. *Seven Named Accused* [2004] PNCA 1 [32].
183 *Joli* v. *Joli* [2003] VUCA 27.
184 *Christian* v. *R (No. 2)*, [2006] PNCA 1 [50].
185 *Clements* v. *The Hong Kong and Shanghai Banking Corporation* (1980) 1 Van LR 416.
186 Roberts-Wray (n. 3), 545.
187 Ibid.
188 Correspondence between the author and the Chair of Solomon Islands Law Reform Commission, 22 December 2017.

definitions, they also have an increasing body of precedent to call upon. However, where English statutes are relied on for the first time, courts must contend with the phrase on a case by case basis, perhaps concluding, like Roberts-Wray that '[i]f the phrase were offered as a novelty to a legislative draftsman today, he would disclaim responsibility for its consequences unless it were defined'.[189]

IX BIBLIOGRAPHY

'Tonga Laws Are There to Protect the People Who Have No Power', *Matangi Tonga*, 2004 www.matangitonga.to/home/ward/htm accessed 21 July 2004.

Notes on Evidence (Amendment) Bill 2016 (Tonga).

Notes to the Reprint of Statutes Act 1972 (Samoa) in: Revised Statutes of Samoa 1977

Allott, A., New Essays in African Law (Butterworths, 1970).

Angelo, T. and Wright, F., 'Pitcairn: Sunset on the Empire?', *New Zealand Law Journal* (2004), 431.

Australian Law Reform Commission, 'Recognition of Aboriginal Customary Laws' (Report 31, 1986).

Blackstone, Commentaries on the Laws of England vol. 1 (1765).

Corrin, J. and Foote, E., 'Failing to adopt a new approach: the law of adoption in Solomon Islands' in Atkin B. (ed.), *The International Survey of Family Law* (Jordan Publishing, 2014).

Farran, Sue, 'The "Re-Colonising" of Pitcairn', *Victoria University of Wellington Law Review* 38 (3) (2007), 435.

Kahn-Freund, O., 'Uses and Misuses of Comparative Law', *Modern Law Review* 37 (1974), 1.

Roberts-Wray, K., *Commonwealth and Colonial Law* (Stevens and Sons, 1966).

Russell, A., *Legislative Drafting and Forms* 4th edn (Butterworth and Co, 1938) 20–1.

Twining, W., 'Diffusion of Law: A Global Perspective', *Journal of Legal Pluralism* 49 (2004), 1.

Twining, W., 'Normative and Legal Pluralism: A Global Perspective', *Duke Journal of Comparative & International Law* 20 (2010), 473.

Watson, A., *Legal Transplants: An Approach to Comparative Law* 2nd edn (University of Georgia Press, 1993).

[189] Roberts-Wray (n. 3), 545.

3

Bentham's Theory of Legal Transplants and His Influence in Japan

Michihiro Kaino

I INTRODUCTION

Jeremy Bentham (1748–1832) is known as a pioneer of utilitarianism and legal positivism. It is less well known, however, that he aspired to be 'the legislator of the world'. He sought to invent complete codes of laws, known as 'Pannomion', which mainly comprised the Constitutional Code, the Civil Code, the Criminal Code and the Procedure Codes based on the principle of utility. Bentham also argued that, as human beings are sufficiently similar, his Pannomion, based on the 'abstract utility' induced by empirical generalizations about human psychology, could be introduced universally. He proposed that the United States, Russia, Spain, Portugal, Greece, and the countries in Latin America should adopt his Pannomion.

Bentham developed a theory of legal transplants in his article 'Place and Time' (written around 1780). Bentham was well aware that the natives would refuse his Pannomion due to their prejudicial biases or sensibilities. Thus, he tried to bring the actual utility experienced by the natives in line with the abstract utility through 'indirect legislations' such as freedom of the press and public discussion. On the other hand, Bentham also emphasized the importance of freedom of the press and public discussion in terms of security. In terms of abstract utility, Bentham argued that its most important component is security. Thus, in 'Securities against Misrule' (written from 1822 to 1823), where he developed his plan for constitutional reform in Tripoli, Bentham argued that the introduction of freedom of the press and public discussion, as well as his Pannomion, would bring security and defended this as universally desirable.

Bentham might have been too optimistic to think that if people were fully informed, they would free themselves of prejudice and adopt his Pannomion, which was, according to him, based on their 'true' interests. As we will see,

Bentham's theory of codification was given serious consideration in late nineteenth-century Japan. In the end, Bentham's Pannomion was not adopted in Japan or anywhere else in the world. However, Bentham's concept of security and his principle of utility depended not on (Western) values but on people's interests or pleasures. I will argue that Bentham's theory of legal transplants is still worthy of consideration in our age of value pluralism. I will also argue that Bentham's theory of codification provides a reasonable explanation for the development of Japanese legal history from the late nineteenth century to the present.

II BENTHAM'S THEORIES OF CODIFICATION AND LEGAL TRANSPLANTS

Bentham criticized common law and tried to abolish and replace it with his Pannomion. Bentham's criticisms of common law were developed in such works as *A Comment on the Commentaries* (written around 1775), in which he heavily criticized William Blackstone (1723–80). The work can be summarized as follows.[1]

The first defect of common law that he pointed out was the law's retroactive nature. In common law, the law and legal provisions were not the same thing, and because judgments were regarded solely as evidence in common law, judges could overthrow judgments that were contrary to reason. Thus, according to Bentham, people's rights and obligations in common law cannot be clarified until judgments are rendered. The other defect of common law that he noted was the law's excessive complexity. According to Bentham, common law was 'a labyrinth without a clue'. Bentham's famous metaphor, 'dog law', comes from the mystifying nature of common law.

In summary, Bentham rejected common law because of its uncertainty and obscurity. This rejection came from his conception of the role of law, which was to coordinate social interaction and guide people's behaviour effectively by securing their expectations. Bentham also thought that people's expectations or security could be accomplished only by introducing the definite rules of his Pannomion.

The concrete nature of the Pannomion can be clarified using 'A General View of A Complete Code of Laws', John Bowring's edition of Bentham's works[2] and 'First Lines of a proposed Code of Law for any Nation compleat

[1] J. Bentham, *A Comment on the Commentaries and a Fragment on Government*, ed. J. H. Burns and H. L. A. Hart (The Athlone Press, 1977).

[2] J. Bentham, 'A General View of a Complete Code of Laws', in J. Bowring (ed.), *The Works of Jeremy Bentham* (Russell and Russell, 1962) vol. 3. This work was first published in French in 1802.

and rationalized', in *Legislator of the World: Writings on Codification, Law and Education*, which includes Bentham's writings on codification and his letters trying to persuade politicians to adopt his codes. Firstly, regarding the composition, Bentham noted that the Pannomion mainly comprizes the Constitutional Code, the Civil Code, the Criminal Code and the Procedure Codes. In the Civil Code, the rights of person, property, condition and reputation, which are given their effect by the sanctions of the Criminal Code, are distributed to the people.[3] Some provisions of the Constitutional Code, having distributive character, are also sanctioned by the Criminal Code. Regarding the arrangement, Bentham argued in 'First Lines' that 'it is the Civil Code that applies more immediately to the common end in view –viz. the greatest happiness of the greatest number: with relation to the Civil Code, taking the mass of its arrangements for an intermediate end, the matter of the penal code is but a means'.[4] The reason for this statement may be the importance of expectation utility, or the security generated from the definition of social relations in the Civil Code.

Bentham also developed devices to secure people's legitimate expectations, and his ultimate philosophy was that 'everyman his own lawyer'. Firstly, as the maximisation of the notoriety of law is important for the security of expectation, Bentham divided the whole Pannomion into general and particular codes to make it easier to memorize. The general codes are codes for individuals, and codes such as the Constitutional Code, the Civil Code, the Criminal Code and the Procedure Codes are included in this category. On the other hand, the particular codes are for certain categories of people. Bentham thought that, by introducing particular codes, it would be possible to reduce the amount of legal matter which people have to bear in mind.[5] Bentham's next device was to accomplish an all-comprehensive division of offences. Of course, it is impossible to predict every offence, but as the classes of offences are clear, he thought it possible to respond to new offences so that expectations can be secured.[6] Lastly, Bentham proposed that each provision of the Pannomion should be accompanied by justifications. These justifications, Bentham thought, would secure people's expectations by making the provisions clear and restraining the deviations of judges and legislators.[7]

3 J. Bentham, *Legislator of the World: Writings on Codification, Law and Education*, ed. P. Schofield and J. Harris (Oxford University Press, 1998) 237.

4 Ibid.

5 Ibid., 8–10.

6 Ibid., 138.

7 Ibid. 249.

It is remarkable that Bentham's Pannomion was thought to be usable in any country if some adjustments were made according to the circumstances of that country. Bentham made every effort to persuade foreign officials to adopt his Pannomion.[8] First, he approached the United States. In 1811, he proposed to President Madison the adoption of his Civil and Criminal Codes, but this was declined in 1816. In 1814, he also approached the governor of Pennsylvania where some codification of the common law was underway. This proposal also did not succeed, because of the governor's indifference. Bentham thus changed his tactics and sent a circular to the governors of the United States. He received a reply from William Plummer, the governor of New Hampshire, who was an eager reformer of law. This proved to be disappointing as well, however, because of disagreement among the common lawyers who dominated the state parliament.[9]

Meanwhile, Bentham also tried to convince Russian authorities. Between 1813 and 1814, he wrote a letter to Alexander I of Russia asking for permission to draft a Criminal Code.[10] As Bentham was on bad terms with Gustav Rosenkampf, who was the head of the Commission of Codification for Russia, his interest moved, in time, from Russia to Poland. In Poland, Bentham believed that he had a better chance because he knew Adam Czartoryski, who had been expected to become the first viceroy of the restored kingdom of Poland. Between Bentham and Czartoryski, there was an agreement that Bentham would write the Constitutional, Civil and Criminal Codes for Poland.[11] However, a person of whom Bentham knew nothing was instead appointed as the viceroy, and so Bentham's interest in Poland gradually faded.

In the 1820s, many newly liberal countries emerged in Southern Europe and Latin America, and Bentham tried to make the most of this situation. Firstly, in 1820, he proposed the adoption of his Pannomion to the new Spanish government. He saw that the principle of utility was embodied in the new Spanish Constitution. Although nothing went ahead concerning adoption of the Pannomion, Bentham's theory became influential in Spain after it was widely introduced by Spanish scholars.[12] He was also deeply involved with the Greek interim government. Although the chances of introducing the Pannomion were not high in this country either, Bentham made

8 Regarding the following description generally, see P. Schofield, Editorial Introduction, in Bentham, *Legislator of the World* (n. 3) xi–lviii.

9 Bentham (n. 3) 5–43, 52–4, 323–4.

10 Ibid., 44–7.

11 Ibid., 108.

12 J. R. Dinwiddy, 'Bentham and the Early Nineteenth Century' *Bentham Newsletter* 8 (1984), 15, 20–1.

certain contributions to this new government, such as commenting on the new Greek Constitution and advising the minister of justice, Theodore Negris, who was trying to develop a civil code for Greece.[13] Bentham's plan to introduce his Pannomion also did not go well in Latin America either. He had some influence on the regulation of parliament in Buenos Aires, and he received a request from José del Valle to help draw up a Civil Code for Guatemala, but these were his only achievements there.[14] However, Bentham's *The Theory of Legislation* was used as a textbook in the universities of such countries as Chile, Columbia and New Granada.

When we consider Bentham's role as a legislator of the world, we cannot ignore what happened in Portugal. In 1821, he offered his Constitutional, Civil and Criminal Codes to the newly elected Portuguese government. Bentham had been thinking that, to embark on an effort to make the codes, there should be a formal and concrete offer because it required enormous hard work and commitment.[15] When the Portuguese parliament fully accepted his offer, he finally began drawing up his Pannomion. Unfortunately, the Portuguese government was overthrown in 1823 and only some parts of Bentham's Constitutional Codes were completed. However, it remains remarkable that there was quite a high possibility that a legal system, independent of Roman law and the common law, could have been introduced in nineteenth-century Europe.

José del Valle of Guatemala once called Bentham 'the legislator of the world (de legislador del mundo)'[16], a title which Bentham liked very much. Bentham argued that 'in comparison of the *universally-applying*, the extent of *the exclusively applying circumstances* will be found very inconsiderable'.[17] In fact, as we saw, he proposed to many countries that they should adopt his codes. Bentham's plan to be the legislator of the world may be criticized for his lack of consideration of the historical or social features of each country. However, he was certainly aware of the problems of cultural diversity suggested by Montesquieu (1689–1755). In 1811, in a letter to the US President James Madison, Bentham described himself as follows:

> Nor, if I may venture to say as much, would it be easy to find any person, more compleatly aware of the demand, presented by the nature of the case, for attention to those local exigencies; nor more compleatly in the habit of

13 Bentham (n. 3) 350–4.
14 Ibid., 370–1.
15 Ibid., 334.
16 Ibid., 370.
17 Ibid., 291 (emphasis in original).

looking over the field of law in this particular view. Of this disposition, and this habit, exemplifications of considerable amplitude may be seen, in the already mentioned work, which for these nine years, has been under the public eye.[18]

In the following section, I want to consider how Bentham thought about the problems of cultural diversity by discussing 'Place and Time', which is substantially identical to the work mentioned by Bentham in the extract above.[19] In section 2 of the work, Bentham began by considering the following question: 'by what principles are the variations necessary to be made in these laws (the best laws for England), in order to accommodate them to the circumstances of Bengal [as an example], the country into which they are to be transferred, to be determined'?[20] The answer Bentham gave was a very simple one, which is related to the 'circumstances influencing sensibility'.

As is well known, Bentham cited seven dimensions for calculating pains and pleasures. Of these, the most important are intensity, duration, certainty, and propinquity. Bentham thought that duration, certainty, and propinquity of pain or pleasure can be measured precisely. However, according to Bentham, intensity that 'reflects a particular person's response to a particular pleasure or pain' is subjective and cannot be measured precisely.[21] This is because 'in the same mind such and such causes of pain or pleasure will produce more pain or pleasure than such or such other causes of pain or pleasure: and this proportion will in different minds be different'.[22]

Bentham thought that biases or sensibilities are not only different among individuals but also different among communities. Bentham's ethics depended to some extent upon the responses to pleasures and pains of the relevant community. On the other hand, Bentham recognized the universality of human nature and human needs. In 'Place and Time', he denied that different countries have different catalogues of pleasures and pains by saying that 'in this point at least, human nature may be pronounced to be every where the same'.[23] According to Bentham, the difference does not lie in the pains and

18 Bentham (n. 3) 26. The work mentioned by Bentham is in *The Theory of Legislation* (1802). However, I will examine the work 'Place and Time' recently edited by Professors Schofield and Engelmann.

19 J. Bentham, ed. P. Schofield and S. Engelmann, 'Place and Time' in S. Engelmann (ed.), *Selected Writings: Jeremy Bentham* (Yale University Press, 2011) 152–219.

20 Ibid., 155.

21 T. Warke, 'Classical Utilitarianism and the Methodology of Determinate Choice in Economics and in Ethics', *Journal of Economic Methodology* 7 (3) (2000), 373, 377.

22 J. Bentham, *An Introduction to the Principles of Morals and Legislation*, ed. J. H. Burns and H. L. A. Hart (The Athlone Press, 1970) 51.

23 Bentham (n. 19) 155.

pleasures themselves, but in their causes. Bentham proceeds to argue that even the same individual event, which would produce pain or pleasure in one country, would not produce the same effect of the same sort, or not in equal degree, in another country.[24]

Therefore, in the catalogue of circumstances influencing sensibility, 'we shall find the sum total of the principles of which we are in search: the principles which, in our inquiry concerning the influence of place and time on matters of legislation, are to serve as a guide'.[25] The legislator should thus be provided with two tables to do the work required:

> Those of the first set would exhibit a number of particulars relative to the body of laws which has been pitched upon for a standard. [...] [T]hose of the other set will be: a general table of the circumstances influencing sensibility' [such as] 'tables or short accounts of the moral, religious, sympathetic and antipathetic biases of the people for whose use the alterations are to be made.[26]

In section 4 of 'Place and Time', titled 'Regard to be Paid to Subsisting Institutions', Bentham divided the influence of circumstances into two classes. According to Bentham:

> the first, consisting of those in which the influence of circumstance operating as a ground of variation is insurmountable: the other, consisting of those in which that influence is not necessarily and absolutely insurmountable. [...] In the former predicament stand all those cases in which the ground of variation is brought about by causes purely physical. [...] Of this nature are the circumstances of climate and texture of earth [...] Of the opposite nature come the circumstances of government, religion, and manners.[27]

With regard to the first class of the influence of circumstances, Bentham gave the example that a wound in a hot climate may be much more painful; that confinement in a hot country may result in significant pain and that drunken persons in the south may be more harmful than those in the north. Concerning the second class of the influence of circumstances, he gave the example that confinement of a Hindu may result in serious pain by excluding him from religious ceremonies; that the votary of every sect may receive a cruel wound from any discourse which reflects contempt for the object of his veneration; that imputations of homosexuality may be much more painful

24 Ibid.
25 Ibid.
26 Ibid., 155–7.
27 Ibid., 167.

in England than in ancient Greece (so that false claims of homosexuality must be punished more heavily in England) and that keeping wives in confinement may be reasonable in Mahometan countries.[28]

It is in his discussion of the second class that Bentham distanced himself from Montesquieu. The point of Montesquieu's theory may be that successful legislation must take empirically recognized sociological varieties into account, and Bentham clearly agreed with this. However, Bentham criticized Montesquieu for not distinguishing what *is* and what *ought* to be, by arguing that Montesquieu appears to have confounded the question of fact with the question of fitness. Bentham was fully aware that Montesquieu's idea of adjusting laws and institutions to fit given circumstances could and often did have an essentially conservative tendency.[29] Harding suggested an insightful distinction that laws which have potentially complex relations to the culture of the donee country are more difficult to transplant than those which do not.[30] Bentham seemed to have accepted this view, but he stressed that even those laws which have deep relations to the culture of the donee country should be replaced by better laws.

Thus, according to Bentham, biases of sensibilities caused by governments, religions, and customs are not insurmountable, and the maintenance of subsisting institutions is not justified a priori so that 'a bad form of government, a bad set of opinions on matters of religion, or a bad system of manners, may be changed into a better'.[31] What should legislators do, then? To answer this question, Bentham developed eight rules respecting the method of transplanting laws.

Of the eight rules, the following are important. That 'the clear utility of the law will be as its abstract utility, deduction made of the dissatisfaction and other inconvenience occasioned by it' is the fifth rule, which is complemented by the sixth rule, 'the *value* of dissatisfaction will be in the compound ratio of 1. The *multitude* of the persons dissatisfied; 2. The *intensity* of the dissatisfaction in each person; 3. The *duration* of the dissatisfaction on the part of each'. We should also note the seventh rule, which is that 'as a means of obviating dissatisfaction, indirect legislation should be preferred to direct: gentle means, to violent: example, instruction, and exhortation should precede or follow, or, if possible, stand in the place of law'.[32]

[28] Ibid., 158–9, 162, 165.

[29] J. H. Burns, 'Utilitarianism and Reform: Social Theory and Social Change, 1750–1800', *Utilitas* 1 (2) (1989). 211, 212–13.

[30] A. Harding, 'The Legal Transplants Debate: Getting beyond the Impasse?', Chapter 1 in this Volume.

[31] Bentham (n. 19) 167.

[32] Ibid., 174.

Here, I would like to mention Bentham's distinction between abstract and net utility. As aforementioned, Bentham distinguished the physical circumstances, which are unchangeable by the legislator, from the circumstances of government, religion and manners, which are not unchangeable. According to Quinn, Bentham also made a distinction between abstract and net utility. 'Abstract utility' relates to 'the pains and pleasures liable to be experienced by human agents as such, which are embodied in the empirical generalizations about human psychology'.[33] 'Net utility' is identical to 'clear utility' in the fifth rule of legal transplants. Bentham was aware that net utility would fluctuate with the introduction of his codes based on abstract utility according to the prejudicial biases or sensibilities of the natives reacting to his Pannomion. Thus, Bentham argued that to bring net utility in line with abstract utility, 'indirect legislations' were necessary, and the main components of indirect legislations were freedom of the press and public discussion.

Freedom of the press and public discussion had a critical role in Bentham's theory. Bentham thought that, through freedom of the press and public discussion, people would find their 'true interests' and would abandon laws which were at odds with the abstract utility embodied in his Pannomion. As Postema wrote, 'Bentham thought that human beings are sufficiently similar, when it comes to matters of public philosophy, that there will be a substantial core of converging interests, sufficient to constitute a robust universal interest'.[34] Harding rightly noted that Bentham thought that good laws for one society are always good for another.[35] However, it is important to bear in mind that Bentham's way of introducing good laws or laws based on abstract utility was very incremental.

III BENTHAM'S PANNOMION IN JAPAN'S MEIJI ERA (1868–1912)

As aforementioned, Bentham tried to become 'the legislator of the world' by encouraging officials of the United States, Russia, Spain, Portugal, Greece and the countries in Latin America to adopt his Pannomion. In Japan in the late nineteenth century, officials and legal scholars sought Bentham's works, along

33 M. Quinn, 'Popular Prejudices, Real Pains: What Is the Legislator to Do When the People Err in Assigning Mischief' in X. Zhai and M. Quinn (eds.), *Bentham's Theory of Law and Public Opinion* (Cambridge University Press, 2014) 77.

34 G. Postema, 'Interests, Universal and Particular: Bentham's Utilitarian Theory of Value', *Utilitas* 18 (2) (2006), 109, 130.

35 Harding, 'The Legal Transplants Debate: Getting beyond the Impasse?', Chapter 1 in this Volume.

with the German and French codes, when there was an urgent need to introduce modern codes to Japan in order to catch up with the West.

The Meiji Restoration of 1868 began the modernisation of Japanese political and social systems. The restoration marked the end of Japan's feudal government (the shogunate government of the Samurai) and the beginning of the imperial rule by Emperor Meiji. The leaders of the Meiji Restoration tried to strengthen Japan against the threat of Western colonial powers. Until then, Japan maintained an isolationist policy. However, after 300 years of national isolation, Japan's leaders tried to introduce Western culture to Japan. Above all, they tried to terminate the shogunate feudal government by placing the vast lands owned by the feudal lords under government control and abolishing the caste system that favoured the Samurai.

The model of the new political system began as a constitutional monarchy, but there was an urgent need to introduce modern civil and penal codes to dismantle the unequal treaties introduced by Western countries, which, demanding the modernisation of legal systems, deprived Japan of certain benefits, such as tariff autonomy. The ruling elites were therefore very eager to study foreign ideas on legislation, which led to the translation of some of Bentham's works.[36]

The first two of Bentham's works that were translated into Japanese were 'Principles of the Civil Code' and 'Principles of the Penal Code', translated by Reishi Ka and Saburo Shimada, respectively, in 1876 and 1877. The original texts of these translations were chapters from Richard Hildreth's edition of *Theory of Legislation: Translated from the French of Etienne Dumont* (1840), published in Boston. Shimada also translated and published *Principles of Legislation* from Hildreth's edition of *Theory of Legislation*. In so doing, Ka and Shimada, even though the latter was the secretary of a provisional legislature, tried to respond to the need for legislation at the time.[37] It is possible that Bentham's theory of law as orders of the sovereign was particularly appealing to them.

In the 1880s, the movements for drafting a constitutional code and setting up a diet became serious, and many private drafts for the National Constitution, some of which were liberal and democratic, as well as influenced by foreign ideas, were written and submitted. The objectives in translating Bentham's works changed accordingly, and in 1882, Shiro Fujita translated

[36] T. Uchida, *The Birth of Legal Study: What Was 'Law' for Modern Japan* (Chikuma Shobo, 2018) 138–9.

[37] Y. Fukagai and M. Kaino (eds.), *The Challenges of Jeremy Bentham* (Nakanishiya Publishing. 2015) 170–1.

and published Bentham's *Fragment on Government*, in which Bentham criticized Blackstone's conservative constitutional theory, with a Japanese publisher called the 'Free Publishing Company'. In the same year, although it had only thirty-six pages and its original text was unknown, *Jeremy Bentham's Principles of Constitution* was published by Shimada. Remarkably, the second edition of *An Introduction to the Principles of Morals and Legislation*, one of the magnum opus of Bentham, was also translated and published in two volumes by Munemitsu Mutu, a famous politician and diplomat, in 1883 and 1884. Bentham's writings on parliament and freedom of speech also received attention after the imperial edict for the opening of the National Diet was issued. Thus, in 1883, Tanehichiro Noda translated and published Bentham's 'On the Liberty of the Press, and Public Discussion' from Volume 2 of the Bowring edition of Bentham's works (which were originally published in 1843).[38]

However, the Meiji Constitution, promulgated in 1889, followed the examples of the Constitution of the German Empire and its Imperial Constitution. Although there was the so-called Freedom and People's Rights Movement in the 1880s, known as Ziyuu Minken Undou, of which the series of translations of Bentham's works was certainly a part, the movement soon lost momentum and disbanded. The new Constitutional Code was anti-liberal. Article 23 of the Meiji Constitution, for example, provided for the due process of law and was influenced by Article 29 of Magna Carta ('The body of a free man is not to be arrested, or imprisoned [...] except by judgment of his peers or by the law of the land'). However, this provision and the other provisions protecting human rights could be suspended easily. Hirobumi Ito, who led the way in the introduction of the Meiji Constitution, noted that Magna Carta was a document imposed on King John by the barons. He argued that Magna Carta and the ideas derived from it were unsuitable for the new Meiji and oligarchic government as they would incite conflicts between the Emperor and his subjects.

German influence was evident in not only the Constitutional Code but also the Criminal Code (1907) and the Criminal Procedure Code (1890), even though these were initially based on the French codes. The Civil Code (1896, 1898) was also written in light of the drafts of the Bürgerliches Gesetzbuch (BGB). This was in part because Japanese law had been based on a statutory law system even before the Meiji Restoration.[39] As mentioned above, Bentham was critical of the case law system and proposed his Pannomion – a complete code

38 Ibid., 173–4.

39 Y. Nagai, *Jeremy Bentham: Critical Biography of British Intellectuals* (Kenkyusha, 2013) 137.

of laws – to several countries. However, it seemed that Japanese lawyers in the Meiji period considered Bentham's codes too incomplete to meet their urgent need to enact the codes. The other reason why Bentham's legal theory made little impact on the Japanese codification process is related to Japan's nationalism. Nobushige Hozumi, a leading jurist and statesman of the Meiji period who was a professor of comparative law at Tokyo Imperial University (the most prestigious university in Japan), and was awarded the first doctorate of law in Japan, acknowledged that while Bentham and his codification system were developing a strong reputation among his colleagues, Bentham's plan disregarded the sentiments of nationalism.[40] According to Hozumi, Bentham's plan of universal codification was impractical because Bentham did not understand the importance of borders and took the existence of national sentiments too lightly.[41]

Harding suggested that some laws are analogous to mobile phones, while others are more like K-pop songs, meaning that some laws which have complex relations to culture are not easy to transplant.[42] Family laws are certainly among those that have a deeper relation to culture. Hozumi was once involved in an argument on the codification of family law in the 1890s. He was against the direct transplantation of the European Civil Code written by the French legal scholar, Gustave Émile Boissonade (1825–1910). The introduction of the codes modelled after Western codes had not been easy. The Meiji Government at first invited Boissonade and commissioned him to draw up the Civil Code along with the Criminal Code and Criminal Procedure Code. Boissonade began his work in 1879; after about ten years of work, he completed the draft Civil Code, which was scheduled to be promulgated in January of 1893. However, some legal scholars argued for the postponement and abolition of Boissonade's Civil Code, focusing especially on the part about family law. The argument was summarized by a phrase coined by Yatuka Hozumi, the younger brother of Nobushige Hozumi and himself also a legal scholar at Tokyo Imperial University: '(Boissonade's) Civil Code would destroy Japanese Confucian morality'.[43] Although the family law part of the Civil Code was actually drawn up by Japanese officials, the influence of Boissonade's Western or liberal view of family relations was evident. Boissonade's Civil Code draft, for example, gave women legal rights such as the right of inheritance. It also

40 N. Hozumi, *Hoso Yawa* (Iwanami Shoten, 1980) 266.

41 Uchida (n. 36) 159.

42 Harding, 'The Legal Transplants Debate: Getting beyond the Impasse?', Chapter 1 in this Volume.

43 Uchida (n. 36) 154.

allowed wives to file for a divorce by themselves, which had not been allowed in Japan at that time.

Nobushige Hozumi successfully led the way to the postponement and abolition of Boissonade's Civil Code. Criticism of Boissonade's Civil Code argued that it wholly failed to take Japanese customary law into consideration. Critics also asserted that the draft should first be discussed among the Japanese people and then adjusted according to the customs of the Japanese people. Meanwhile, Hozumi pointed out that the debate on Boissonade's Civil Code was parallel to the debate between Anton Thibaut and Savigny. As is well known, Savigny in the 1810s criticized Thibaut, who tried to introduce the Civil Code, modelled after the French Civil Code (Code Napoléon), into Germany. Influenced by the German historical school led by Savigny, Hozumi seemed to have identified himself with Savigny, who argued that law, like language, has a folk character and should accord with the Volksgeist (national spirit). Hozumi once argued in Parliament that to impose a major code with hundreds of provisions without regard to the country's history or tradition is a reckless attempt that is unprecedented in human history.[44] Hozumi's prestige is said to have helped those who were against Boissonade's Civil Code, leading to the formal postponement of its introduction in 1892. Instead, a more conservative Civil Code was introduced in 1896 and 1898. The composition of the Code was based on a Pandekten style modelled after the BGB. The content of family law was made to reflect Japanese Confucian morality, which, for example, deprived women of any legal power.

It is fair to say that Bentham's plan for the Pannomion did not have any influence on the Civil Code or other codes in Japan. However, Bentham's 'Place and Time' was not fully discussed in the Meiji era. As discussed above, Bentham's Pannomion was supposed to be based on abstract utility, or 'the true interests' of the people of the donee countries. Bentham's means of introducing the Pannomion were also incremental, beginning with freedom of the press and public discussion. Bentham was fully aware of the stubbornness of the irrational or prejudiced custom. Thus, although Bentham often argued that consensual homosexual acts are harmless, he also proposed that consensual homosexual acts should be punished by banishment instead of by hanging, in the face of strong prejudice against homosexual acts and the anticipated unpopularity of decriminalized homosexual behaviour in nineteenth-century England. Concerning women's franchise, although Bentham's position was that the exclusion of women was based on prejudice, he 'was

44 Ibid., 157.

prepared to surrender to that prejudice, and wait the arrival of more enlightened attitudes'.[45] Thus, Bentham's legal transplant theory was not as unrealistic as it seemed. Harding noted that the objective of legal transplant is not to reflect society but to change or reform it.[46] Bentham can be said to be providing clear-cut criteria (the abstract utility of the Pannomion) and a reasonable methodology (freedom of the press and public discussion) for legal transplant and social reform.

In what follows, I discuss Bentham's plan for transplanting his Constitutional Charter into despotic countries. Bentham attempted to introduce freedom of the press and public discussion into despotic countries through the Charter in order to increase security. Bentham's argument seemingly provided a solid foundation for his entire Pannomion scheme.

IV BENTHAM'S 'SECURITIES AGAINST MISRULE'

Bentham fully developed his attitude toward despots in one of the volumes in the *Collected Works of Jeremy Bentham: Securities against Misrule and Other Constitutional Writings for Tripoli and Greece*.[47] This work includes 'Account of Tripoli', 'Securities against Misrule' and 'Letters to John Quincy Adams', which were mainly written in 1822. 'Securities against Misrule' was divided into 'Constitutional Securities of Tripolitan Nation' and 'Preliminary Examinations'.

I begin by examining the rationale of the Constitutional Charter developed in 'Preliminary Examinations'. In this work, Bentham examined the remedy for social instability arising from the Pasha's arbitrary power. First, he divided the shapes of misrule as follows:

1. Shape 1. Sufferers all determinate: the individuals all determinate and assignable. Examples: Homicide, Confinement, Banishment [. . .].
2. Shape 2. Sufferers, altogether undeterminate. Examples: Waste of public money: Act of engaging in unnecessary war. In this case the evil may be called purely public.
3. Shape 3. Immediate sufferers determinate, but the greater part of the evil composed of the sufferings of individuals altogether undeterminate. Examples: 1. Political gagging [. . .]. 2. National debilitation [. . .].

[45] Quinn (n. 33) 79.

[46] Harding, 'The Legal Transplants Debate: Getting beyond the Impasse?', Chapter 1 in this Volume.

[47] J. Bentham, *Securities against Misrule and Other Constitutional Writings for Tripoli and Greece*, ed. P. Schofield (Oxford University Press, 1990).

> In this case the evil may be said to be mixt; or public through the medium of private.[48]

According to Bentham, the remedy for these misrules arising from the arbitrary power of the Pasha is publicity:

> So much for the disease. Now as to the remedy. A single word, *publicity*, has been employed for the designation of it. For this purpose, another expression—*Public Opinion*—might have been employed.[49]

According to Bentham, the main subjects of publicity in Tripoli were ordinances and the transgression of ordinances. The ordinances mean the Constitutional Charter, which Bentham devized. The contents of the Constitutional Charter developed in 'Constitutional Securities of Tripolitan Nation' were divided into securities in favour of the nation and those in favour of individuals. The former comprized mainly security against vexation on account of religion and the security of appeal. The latter comprised mainly securities against secret confinement, injurious banishment, secret and unlawful homicide, misuse of private writings and official oppression, among others.

Bentham argued that publicity is important for stopping misrule because:

> the greater the number of the members of the whole community to whom the existence of an act of oppression has been made known, the greater is the number of those by whom, on the occasion of an endeavour to exercise other acts of a similar nature, supposing the past act notified to them, not only may obedience withholden, but resistance opposed.[50]

To make this function of publicity work, Bentham developed the concept of a public opinion tribunal, which will be discussed in the next section.

However, it is not clear why the Pasha should adopt the Constitutional Charter and give publicity to acts of misrule, which would certainly reduce his power. According to Bentham, the main problem in Tripoli was that:

> Neither for life nor for liberty, for neither of those possessions, against resentment, fear, concupiscence or erroneous conception in the breast of Sovereign, can any permanent security be possessed by any one individual in the community in the present state of the government. In respect of property all labour under insecurity, not merely in that shape in which it involves danger and alarm in respect of what they have already, but in that shape

48 Ibid., 26.

49 Ibid., 27.

50 Ibid., 30.

likewise in which by the sense of it they are prevented from making all those additions to it to which a feeling of security such as is enjoyed even in the worst-governed European nation is sufficient to give birth.[51]

Bentham thought that the Pasha would profit from a Constitutional Charter because it would increase security and make the country wealthier. Thus, while in 'Place and Time', freedom of the press and public discussion was a means of bringing net utility into line with abstract utility, in 'Securities against Misrule', publicity, which is enhanced by freedom of the press and public discussion, brought about security.

We saw in the preceding section that, although widely discussed and well known in academic circles, Bentham's plan for the Pannomion did not have any influence on the Civil Code or the other codes in Japan. On the other hand, Bentham's 'Securities against Misrule' was not introduced nor discussed in or after the Meiji era of Japan. However, even if it had been introduced, Japanese politics would have been too immature for the scheme. In 1925, the Universal Manhood Suffrage Act was introduced in Japan. However, the Maintenance of Public Order Law was also introduced in the same year. This law, prohibiting speeches and activities advocating changes of national polity, virtually prohibited any criticisms of the government. This law contributed to the birth of a militaristic government in the late 1930s and early 1940s, which suppressed freedom of the press and public discussion and led Japanese society to the catastrophic World War II.

V BENTHAM'S PUBLIC OPINION TRIBUNAL

In this section, I will examine Bentham's concept of the public opinion tribunal. As outlined above, Bentham argued that misrule could be prevented only through publicity, and the public opinion tribunal played a central part in this. In Bentham's own words, public opinion is 'the only source which is not included in the force of government: the only force therefore from which the force of government when operating in a sinister direction can experience any the least impediment to its course'.[52]

This public opinion tribunal is one of the key concepts of Bentham's theory. Concerning the function of the public opinion tribunal, Bentham said that the tribunal primarily carries out a statistic or evidence-furnishing

[51] Ibid., 108–9.
[52] Ibid., 121.

function (delivering information and evidence of misrule), a censorial function (rendering judgments) and an executive function (punishing and rewarding).[53] The newspaper has a leading role in each of these functions. To be more specific, newspapers deliver information concerning misrule among the people and examine and criticize the misrule. People then put their judgment into effect through social sanctions such as 'all obstructions to the exaction of taxes the produce of which is at the disposal of the sovereign' and 'all obstructions capable of being opposed to the execution of the judgment of the several regularly constituted judicatories'.[54] Ultimately, Bentham included in the social sanction the withdrawal of all obedience to the power of the sovereign.

Bentham tried to introduce the public opinion tribunal in Tripoli; he argued that even despots including the Pasha of Tripoli should admit freedom of the press and public discussion. Further, the main subjects of publicity in Tripoli were ordinances, which comprised Bentham's Constitutional Charter, and the transgression of these ordinances. The ordinances of the Constitutional Charter and their transgression were to be delivered among the people of Tripoli, which would punish the conductors of misrule through social sanctions.

In 'On the Liberty of Press, and Public Discussion', Bentham defended the liberty of the press and public discussion as universally desirable, arguing that both were 'indispensable, at all times and every where'.[55] The public opinion tribunal was also thought to be universally desirable, as it would provide security all around the world.

Postema recently argued that Bentham's concept of the public opinion tribunal was relevant to his theory of rule of law. According to Postema, Bentham tried to constrain arbitrary exercises of the powers, or 'the rule of man', by subjecting governmental action of every sort to public opinion tribunal and its sanctions. Postema convincingly argues that Bentham had a strategy for 'securing ordinary law-subjects against the arbitrary exercise of power at the hands of ruling officials'.[56] After World War II, the new

53 J. Bentham, *Constitutional Code*, ed. F. Rosen and J. H. Burns (Oxford University Press, 1983) 37–9.

54 Bentham (n. 47) 124.

55 J. Bentham, 'On the Liberty of Press, and Public Discussion', in C. Pease-Watkin and P. Schofield (eds.), *On the Liberty of Press, and Public Discussion and Other Legal and Political Writings for Spain and Portugal* (Oxford University Press, 2012) 4.

56 G. Postema, 'The Soul of Justice: Bentham on Publicity, Law, and the Rule of Law' in X. Zhai and M. Quinn (eds.), *Bentham's Theory of Law and Public Opinion* (Cambridge University Press, 2014) 42.

Constitutional Code was introduced in Japan, which guarantees a right to freedom of the press and public discussion. Although Bentham had nothing to do with the introduction of this Constitutional Code, a kind of public opinion tribunal was established in Japan. This public opinion tribunal helped maintain the rule of law in Japan and it is now more difficult for officials to exercise power arbitrarily than it was in the late 1930s and early 1940s.

VI CONCLUSION

In this paper, I have discussed Bentham as 'the legislator of the world'. I examined Bentham's work, 'Place and Time', and discussed his theory of legal transplants. In the preceding sections, the main subjects were articles from *Securities against Misrule and Other Constitutional Writings for Tripoli and Greece*. There, I examined Bentham's attitude towards tyrannies and his concept of the public opinion tribunal.

Here I firstly want to briefly examine Bentham's theory of legal transplants in a global context by comparing it with the theories of John Locke (1632–1704) and John Stuart Mill (1806–73). The most remarkable point in the comparison of Locke and Bentham is that the coercion of natural law is absent from Bentham's theory. What Bentham tried to do was to guide individuals to find the abstract utility, or their true interests, and adopt his Pannomion through freedom of the press and public discussion. On the other hand, Mill's paternalism towards the East is also absent in Bentham. Bentham thought that people themselves would choose the Pannomion if they were fully enlightened. Although Bentham's Pannomion was based on abstract utility, it was the people of each country who decided whether it could lead to their happiness. Bentham's plan of bringing net utility in line with abstract utility through the introduction of his Pannomion seems radical at first. If, however, as Harding showed, the objective of legal transplant is to change society,[57] Bentham seems to show a quite reasonable and realistic way of doing so.

In addition, Bentham's Pannomion and public opinion tribunal were based on his analysis that security is universally pursued regardless of place and time. In Bentham's theory, security is 'maximized by limiting the possibilities of oppression either by one citizen over another or by the

[57] Harding, 'The Legal Transplants Debate: Getting beyond the Impasse?', Chapter 1 in this Volume.

government over the citizen'.[58] The former securities are established by the Pannomion and the latter by the public opinion tribunal. I think it is quite difficult to refute Bentham's postulation on security. As John Stuart Mill argued, security is:

> to every one's feelings the most vital of all interests. Nearly all other earthly benefits are needed by one person, not needed by another; and many of them can, if necessary, be cheerfully foregone, or replaced by something else; but security no human being can possibly do without.[59]

Bentham's concept of security and his principle of utility were dependent not on values but on people's interests or pleasures.[60] What mattered was an empirical or factual question as to whether freedom of the press, free public discussion and above all the Pannomion would lead to increased security. Bentham certainly thought that they would.

We may also emphasize the explanation behind Bentham's theory of legal transplants. Bentham's Pannomion was based on the notion of abstract utility or the 'true interests' of human beings. Bentham tried to lead people to find their 'true interests' through freedom of the press and public discussion, and abandon laws that were at odds with his Pannomion. For example, Bentham argued that from the principle of utility, women should have the same legal rights as men and expected that through freedom of the press and public discussion, people in due course would be enlightened enough to accept this argument. In Japan, after World War II, the family law, which had deprived women of any legal power, was removed; as a result, women now enjoy the same legal rights as men. This change was introduced in occupied Japan after World War II by the United States, which tried to modify Japanese feudal society. At the time of this change, some reactionary critics argued that the change was against traditional Japanese Confucian morality, but today, very few people in Japan would argue that women should not have the same legal powers as men. The enlightened public opinion brought about by the freedom of the press and public discussion played a role in these changes. So, as far as legal transplants in Japan is

58 F. Rosen, *Jeremy Bentham and the Representative Democracy* (Oxford University Press, 1983) 75.

59 J. S. Mill, '*Utilitarianism*', in G. Williams (ed.), *Utilitarianism, On Liberty, Considerations on Representative Government* (Everyman's Library, 1993) 56.

60 P. Schofield, 'Jeremy Bentham, the Principle of Utility, and Legal Positivism', *Current Legal Problems* 56 (1) (2003), 1, 27.

concerned, Bentham's theory of legal transplants seems to explain the situation very well. Bentham's theory of legal transplants did not have any concrete effects on Japanese law, but his point about how legal transplants should be accomplished incrementally with the help of freedom of the press and public discussion explains the success of transplants of Western laws in Japan.

VII BIBLIOGRAPHY

Bentham, J., 'A General View of a Complete Code of Laws', in Bowring J.(ed.), *The Works of Jeremy Bentham*, vol. 3 (Russell and Russell, 1962).

An Introduction to the Principles of Morals and Legislation, ed. Burns, J. H. and Hart, H. L. A. (The Athlone Press, 1970).

A Comment on the Commentaries and a Fragment on Government, ed. Burns, J. H. and Hart, H. L. A. (The Athlone Press, 1977).

Constitutional Code, ed. Rosen, F. and Burns, J. H. (Oxford University Press, 1983).

Securities against Misrule and Other Constitutional Writings for Tripoli and Greece, ed. Schofield, P. (Oxford University Press, 1990).

Legislator of the World: Writings on Codification, Law and Education, ed. Schofield, P. and Harris, J. (Oxford University Press, 1998).

ed. Schofield, P. and Engelmann, S. 'Place and Time' in Engelmann, S. (ed.), *Selected Writings: Jeremy Bentham* (Yale University Press, 2011).

'On the Liberty of Press, and Public Discussion', in Pease-Watkin, C. and Schofield, P. (eds.), *On the Liberty of Press, and Public Discussion and Other Legal and Political Writings for Spain and Portugal* (Oxford University Press, 2012).

Burns, J. H., 'Utilitarianism and Reform: Social Theory and Social Change, 1750–1800', *Utilitas* 1 (2) (1989), 211.

Fukagai, Y. and Kaino, M. (eds.), *The Challenges of Jeremy Bentham* (Nakanishiya Publishing, 2015).

Hozumi, N., *Hoso Yawa* (Iwanami Shoten, 1980).

Mill, J. S., *'Utilitarianism'*, in Williams, G. (ed.), *Utilitarianism, On Liberty, Considerations on Representative Government* (Everyman's Library, 1993).

Nagai, Y., *Jeremy Bentham: Critical Biography of British Intellectuals* (Kenkyusha, 2013).

Postema, G., 'Interests, Universal and Particular: Bentham's Utilitarian Theory of Value', *Utilitas* 18 (2) (2006), 109.

'The Soul of Justice: Bentham on Publicity, Law, and the Rule of Law' in Zhai X. and Quinn, M. (eds.), *Bentham's Theory of Law and Public Opinion* (Cambridge University Press, 2014).

Quinn, M., 'Popular Prejudices, Real Pains: What Is the Legislator to Do When the People Err in Assigning Mischief' in Zhai, X. and Quinn, M. (eds.), *Bentham's Theory of Law and Public Opinion* (Cambridge University Press, 2014).

Rosen, F., *Jeremy Bentham and the Representative Democracy* (Oxford University Press, 1983).

Schofield, P. and Bentham, J. 'The Principle of Utility, and Legal Positivism', *Current Legal Problems* 56 (1) (2003), 1.
Uchida, T., *The Birth of Legal Study: What Was 'Law' for Modern Japan* (Chikuma Shobo, 2018).
Warke, T., 'Classical Utilitarianism and the Methodology of Determinate Choice in Economics and in Ethics', *Journal of Economic Methodology* 7 (3) (2000), 373.

4

On the Hardingian Renovation of Legal Transplants

Benjamen Gussen

I INTRODUCTION

In his chapter, Andrew Harding entertains the proposition of moving beyond the unhelpful dichotomy of effectiveness/ineffectiveness of transplantation. This paper provides a grounded (theory) approach as to how this can be achieved in relation to constitutional designs. If we apply the mechanism of inheritance to constitutions (as a transport phenomenon), and limit our analysis to federalism (as a modality of hypotaxis), and more specifically to the construct of vertical division of powers within federalism, would we be able to ascertain how such powers were adapted to local conditions in the constitutional designs of these different jurisdictions? The objective is to see if there has been such evolution, and the change in the inherited traits in the pre-constitutional phase (the design phase). The hypothesis is that the evolution of the constitutional systems in Canada and Australia can be illustrated as an intercourse between the principles of hypotaxis (the distribution of vertical powers), Walter Bagehot's dichotomy of the dignified (theoretical) and efficient (practical) constitutions,[1] and Lamarck's theory of (soft) inheritance.[2]

The paper is inspired by Harding's proposition of moving beyond the legal transplants debate. Harding provides a trichotomy of 'legal transplantation' (limited to imperial transplantation to colonies), 'legal mimesis' (limited to twenty-first century law reform) and 'legal reception' (limited to the Great

[1] W. Bagehot, *The English Constitution* 5th edn (Kegan Paul, Trench & Co, 1888). Another useful dichotomy is that of Thorstein Veblen where he distinguishes between the 'ceremonial' constitution (looking at the past) and the 'instrumental' (or 'technological') constitution (looking at the future). See T. Veblen, *The Theory of the Leisure Class: An Economic Study of Institutions* (Penguin, 1994). See also D. A. Reisman, *The Social Economics of Thorstein Veblen* (Edward Elgar, 2012).

[2] A. Watson, *Legal Transplants: An Approach to Comparative Law* (University of Georgia Press, 1993).

Reception of Roman law). In this paper, the idea of a 'legal transplant' (the first category) is replaced with a process from biology. The proposition is to analogize institutional innovation (in the context of constitutional designs) to evolutionary biology. More specifically, the analysis is modelled after Lamarckian evolution (inheritance of acquired characteristics).[3] The theory (below) is therefore structured around two themes, which in terms of constitutions can be stated as follows: (1) evolved constitutions tend to exhibit increasing complexity; and (2) adaptation of constitutions to local conditions.[4] Constitutional designs exhibit characteristics that are inherited from 'parent' constitutions but adapted to achieve higher efficiency (signified by increased complexity).[5] The efficiency criteria are analogous to those employed in law-and-economics. Hence, mechanisms such as diffusion are conceived using an evolutionary discourse. More precisely, we can theorize the evolution of constitutional designs, as seen in the vertical division of

[3] See, e.g., R. Burkhardt, *The Spirit of System: Lamarck and Evolutionary Biology* (Harvard University Press, 1977).

[4] This is in line with the *general theory of morphogenesis* where complexity is defined in terms of the change of scale (μ) with respect to degrees of freedom (τ):

$$\pi \triangleq \frac{d\mu}{d\tau} = k\frac{d^2\sigma_k}{d\tau^2} + \left(\frac{d\sigma_x}{d\tau} - \frac{d\sigma_{dx}}{d\tau}\right)\frac{dx}{d\tau} \tag{4a}$$

$$\mu \triangleq k\frac{d\sigma_k}{d\tau} + dk\frac{d\sigma_{dk}}{d\tau} \tag{4b}$$

Where κ refers to the quantum of matter in the system (e.g. the number of agents). Quantum (κ) can be thought of as a form of generalized mass. There are two symmetries in the definition. The first σ_κ is in relation to the symmetry of the existing quantum. The second symmetry is $\sigma_{d\kappa}$ and refers to the symmetry in the change of the existing quantum, which allows for growth in the population of existing matter in the system. Under this formulation, entropy is taken to be analogous to symmetry. More precisely, it is a condition that maximizes symmetry:

$$S : \frac{d\sigma}{d\tau} \to 0 \tag{4c}$$

It follows that negentropy (J) is a condition on symmetry such that:

$$J : \frac{d^2\sigma}{d\tau^2} \to 0 \tag{4d}$$

Under the general theory of morphogenesis, evolution is a process of change where:

$$\frac{d\pi}{d\tau} = \frac{d^2\mu}{d\tau^2} > 0 \tag{4e}$$

Evolution therefore understood as a process that leads to increased (morphological) complexity. See B. F. Gussen, 'On the Problem of Scale: A General Theory of Morphogenesis and Normative Policy Signals for Economic Evolution', *Evolutionary and Institutional Economic Review* 12 (2015), 81.

[5] For the causal nexus between efficiency and complexity, see F. Ruzzenenti and R. Basosi, 'On the Relationship between Energy Efficiency and Complexity: Insights on the Causality Chain', *International Journal of Design & Nature and Ecodynamics* 3 (2) (2008), 95.

legislative powers, in the three great Anglo-American federations. The model in Figure 4.1 (below) gives a two-period explanation of the evolution of hypotaxis (the division of vertical powers) within the jurisdictions of the United States, Canada, and Australia.[6]

II A (GROUNDED) THEORY OF CONSTITUTIONAL EVOLUTION

Figure 4.1 represents a two-period model. The first period signified by the 1867 Canadian Constitution.[7] The second period, by the adoption of the (current) 1900 Australian Constitution.[8] The arrow in Figure 4.1 indicates the evolution direction of the acquired characteristics, namely hypotaxis and efficiency.

The objective is to maximize efficiency (e) (as defined below) through changes to constitutional designs ($D_i, \forall i \in \{Canada, Australia\}$) with respect to the two characteristics (τ_1, τ_2), namely, the US division of powers and the English overlap of powers, respectively:[9]

$$\max_{e} \frac{\partial^2 D_i}{\partial \tau_1 \partial \tau_2} \tag{1}$$

where ∂ represents a partial derivative, i.e. the change of the constitutional design with respect to the (inherited) characteristics. The change in relation to the overlap of powers, $\frac{\partial}{\partial_2}$, is seen in an extension of the overlap from horizontal (executive and legislative powers) to vertical (legislative) powers. The change in relation to the division of powers, $\frac{\partial}{\partial_1}$, is seen in the introduction of concurrent powers between the federal and sub-national governments.

Efficiency is defined following Bagehot, that is, increasing with overlap of powers.[10] The rationale for this understanding flows directly from the

6 See also B. F. Gussen, 'Reflections on La Fata Morgana: Watsonian "prestige" and Bagehotian "efficiency"', *The Journal of Comparative Law* 12 (1) (2017), 80 (ISSN 1477–0814). For evolutionary law-and-economics, see G. von Wangenheim, 'Evolutionary Theories in Law and Economics and Their Use for Comparative Legal Theory', *Review of Law & Economics* 7(3) (2011), 737. M. J. Roe, 'Chaos and Evolution in Law and Economics', *Harvard Law Review* 109 (3) (1996), 641; G. Atkinson and S. P. Paschall, *Law and Economics from an Evolutionary Perspective* (Edward Elgar, 2016); P. Zumbansen and G.-P. Calliess (eds.), *Law, Economics and Evolutionary Theory* (Edward Elgar, 2011).

7 British North American Act 1867 (Imp), hereafter referred to as the Canadian Constitution.

8 Clause 9 of the Commonwealth of Australia Constitution Act 1900 (Imp). Hereafter referred to as the Australian Constitution.

9 This is why the evolutionary model adopted in this paper can be seen as Lamarckian rather than Darwinian; in other words, change is driven by an objective function.

10 Bagehot (n. 1) 2, 13, 15.

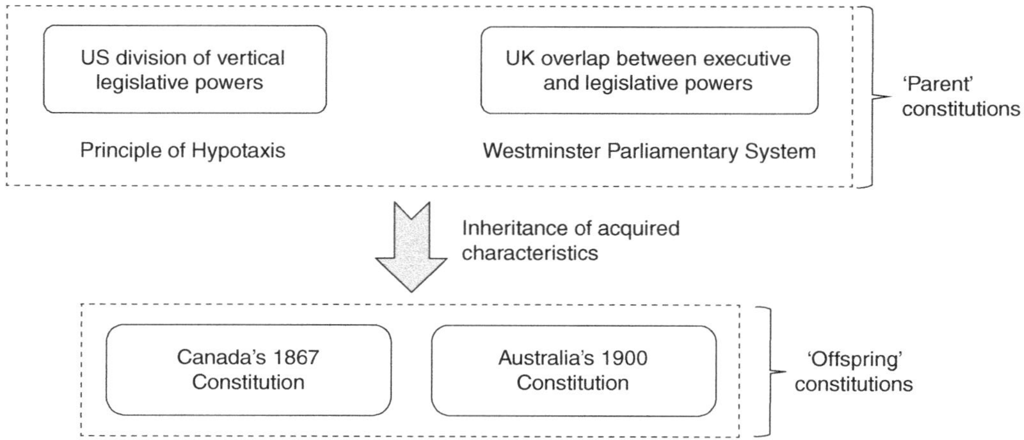

FIGURE 4.1: Two-period model for the evolution of residuum of power designs in the USA, Canada, and Australia

efficiency principle of the Coase Theorem, namely where governments (or branches of government in the case of horizontal overlap) are able to bargain together effectively (e.g. through institutions such as legislatures or informal institutions such as the cabinet) and can effectively implement their decisions, then the outcomes will tend to be efficient. Horizontal and vertical overlap allows for this bargaining process more than where there is strict division of powers.[11] This conception of efficiency extends the information problem, where there are two polar solutions: transmission to a centralized planner or to autonomous decentralized decision-makers. The former incurs communication and computation costs, while the latter incurs costs of consistency and coordination. In the case of constitutional designs, the solution is to create a 'political market' à la Buchanan and Tullock.[12] The overlap allows for internal 'transfer prices' between different (horizontal) branches or (vertical) levels of government.

Note that the constitution (C) of a given jurisdiction i is then formulated as follows:

$$C_i = f\left(D_i, I_i(t)\right) \tag{2}$$

In other words, the constitution is also a function of $I_i(t)$, the constitutional interpretation adopted by the court of constitutional original jurisdiction, which itself is a function of time.

The assertion is that:

$$D_{Canada} = f(D_{US}, D_{UK}) \tag{3}$$

That is, the hypotactic design (i.e. the division of vertical powers) in the Canadian Constitution is a function of the earlier US design of 1788 (through the Tenth Amendment of 1791[13]) and UK design that can be traced back to constitutional conventions.[14] In other words, the Canadian design evolved

[11] R. H. Coase, 'The Nature of the Firm', *Economica* 4 (16) (1937), 386; M. Klaes, 'Historical Economics and Evolutionary Economic Policy – Coasean Perspectives' in K. Dopfer (ed.), *Economics, Evolution and the State: The Governance of Complexity* (Edward Elgar, 2005) 78, 83.

[12] J. Buchanan and G. Tullock, *The Calculus of Consent: Logical Foundations of Constitutional Democracy* (University of Michigan Press, 1962) 16–19.

[13] US Constitution Amendment X.

[14] The convention that ministers must be Members of either the House of Commons or the House of Lords. Bagehot (n. 1) 15. See also A. V. Dicey, *Introduction to the Study of the Law of the Constitution* (Liberty Classics, 1982) ch. 14.

posteriori from the US design. It was adapted to local conditions to maximize the *a priori* efficiency of the constitutional design.[15] Similarly,

$$D_{Australia} = f(D_{US}, D_{UK}) \tag{4}$$

The hypotactic design found in the 1900 Australian Constitution is a function of the US and UK designs. Note that the Australian design is also influenced, if only indirectly, by the acquired characteristics in the Canadian design. However, in our model, this application does not add to the inheritance from the USA and UK, and hence, is not reflected in Equation (4) above. The Australian design was, however, informed *posteriori* by *praxis* flowing from the earlier Canadian design and adapted the same for higher efficiency. The influence is one of process (in relation to maximizing efficiency) rather than substance (in relation to the heritable traits).

The objective of maximizing efficiency takes place over two phases: a pre-constitutional phase where D (the constitutional design) is adopted and adapted from interior (or past) designs through the inheritance of constitutional characteristics. This adoption and adaptation signals a bifurcation that is followed, in the post-constitutional phase, by a period where the design settles into a coherent (initial) *praxis* ($\equiv I_i(0)$)—for example, in terms of interpretation methodology by a constitutional court. Later, the *praxis* enters into a (longer) steady-state phase, which represents an efficient equilibrium. As shown in Figure 4.2, the changing local circumstances ensure the dynamic nature of this equilibrium. Further evolution results from further intercourse between legal designs and the ensuing transient and steady-state (evolutionary) phases.

Note that these interpretive changes to the constitutional design represent a second order maximization beyond the original inherited traits:

$$\max_{e} \frac{\partial C_i}{\partial t} \tag{5}$$

Unlike first-order optimization, intra-jurisdictional optimization is a function of time. An example of these phases is the shift from originalism to textualism in interpreting the residuum powers found in the Australian (Commonwealth) constitutional design.[16]

[15] This assertion that Canadian federalism was influenced by the US model does not preclude the influence of multinationalism, in particular, the argument that French Canadians were the driving force behind federalism. The assertion is that Canada adopted federalism and was influenced by the US model.

[16] See in particular *Amalgamated Society of Engineers* v. *Adelaide Steamship Co Ltd (Engineers case)* [1920] HCA 54, (1920) 28 CLR 129. For phase shift in Canada, see, e.g., *Canadian*

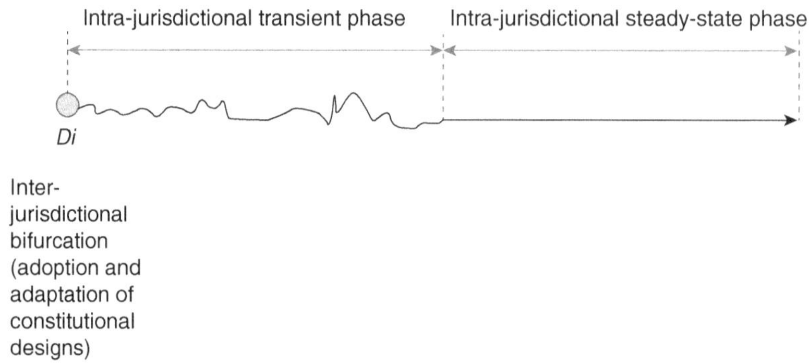

FIGURE 4.2: Intra-jurisdictional (post-constitutional) transient and steady-state phases

The rest of the paper elaborates these constructs in the context of the Constitutions of the United States, Canada, and Australia.

III THE HERITABLE TRAITS

While Alan Watson's 'legal transplants' model attempts to analyze the diffusion of legal constructs from one jurisdiction to another (inter-jurisdictional diffusion),[17] the theory proposed earlier (and detailed below) uses Lamarckian evolution to explain the inheritance of (acquired) traits in the designs of offspring constitutions: Canada and Australia. Under this theory, 'transplanting' occurs by the official promulgation of heritable traits (from 'parent' constitutions). The three great Anglo-American federations (and the United Kingdom) represent case studies where one country (Canada and later Australia) inherited some of its constitutional traits from 'parent' countries (the United Kingdom and the United States); see Figure 4.1 above. Hence, while the Watsonian model was a scholarship about the sociology of law (where Watson argues that legal transplants occur at a rate higher than that of the evolution of the receiving society, which hence would vitiate any potential fit between legal systems and their social milieu), the paper adapts the model to inheritance in hypotactic constitutional designs as embedded in

Western Bank v. *Alberta* [2007] 2 SCR 3 in relation to the disapproval of the inter-jurisdictional immunity doctrine in Canada. In the US context see *Planned Parenthood of Southeastern Pennsylvania* v. *Casey* 505 US 833 (1992) for the role normative signals play in constitutional interpretation.

17 Watson (n. 2). For a general discussion of legal transplants, see D. Nelken and J. Feest, *Adapting Legal Cultures* (Bloomsbury Publishing, 2001).

a canonical constitutional text. This logic allows for a (pragmatic) plasticity in the 'efficient' constitution, closer to the spirit of the law-as-literature and law-as-communication movements.[18]

The model in this paper uses two (constitutional) traits. The first is based on a "corner" solution of the principle of hypotaxis, namely federalism, where there is complete division of vertical powers.[19] Hypotaxis refers to the rules of grammar that govern the modalities of coordination among clauses. By extension, the principle of hypotaxis refers to the constitutional principle that decides the sharing of legislative powers between vertical levels of governments (at the national and sub-national scales). Federalism represents only one modality of hypotaxis, where there is a division of powers rather than a sharing of the same, and only between two levels of government, namely, the federal government, and a sub-national government, such as the provinces in Canada, and the states in Australia. Generally, federalism does not afford other governments, such as local governments, any constitutional recognition. In Catholic social doctrine, the principle is known as 'subsidiarity,' while in Protestant doctrine it is referred to as 'spheres of sovereignty.' The doctrine has its origin in Judaism (through the Judges period)[20] and can also be seen in Islam (through the Constitution of Madinah).[21] I use 'hypotaxis', instead of other terms, to maintain a religion-neutral analysis.[22]

In the context of the United States, federalism can be seen in James Madison's concept of 'residuum powers' and its 'enumerated powers' conjugate.[23] The concept provides an option for constitutional designs where there is need to divide sovereignty between different levels of government (namely the federal or central versus the state or provincial levels). This

18 See, e.g., R. Posner, *Law and Literature: A Misunderstood Relation* (Harvard University Press, 1988); A. Scalia, *A Matter of Interpretation* (Princeton University Press, 1997); B. Cardozo, 'Law and Literature', *Yale Review* 14 (1925), 699; M. Van Hoecke, *Law as Communication* (Hart Publishing, 2002); M. Adams and D. Heirbaut (eds.), *The Method and Culture of Comparative Law: Essays in Honour of Mark Van Hoecke* (Hart Publishing, 2014).

19 See B. F. Gussen, 'Australian Constitutionalism between Subsidiarity and Federalism', *Monash University Law Review* 42 (2) (2016), 383, 388.

20 J.-B. D'Onorio, *La Subsidiarité* (Téqui, 1995) 13.

21 S. Nu Nu Htay and S. A. Salman, 'Transaction Cost Theory, Political Theory and Resource Dependency Theory in Light of Unconventional Aspect', *IOSP Journal of Humanities and Social Science* 12 (5) (2013), 89, 92.

22 P. M. Brennan, 'Subsidiarity in the Tradition of Catholic Social Doctrine' in M. Evans and A. Zimmermann (eds.), *Global Perspectives on Subsidiarity* (Springer, 2014) 29, 34.

23 P. B. Kurland and R. Lerner, *The Founders Constitution*, vol. 5 (Liberty Fund, 2001) 20. See also T. O. Hueglin, *Comparative Federalism: a Systematic Inquiry* (University of Toronto Press Incorporated, 2006), especially ch. 6.

theory allows for the vertical division of legislative powers by assigning to one level of government restricted legislative powers, while assigning to the other non-restricted legislative powers. The restriction of such powers is (usually) achieved by specifying the powers given to one level of government, the *subordinated* level of government. The non-restricted government, the *sub-ordinator* government, would then be presumed to have the capacity to legislate on all other matters not specified in the restricted powers 'menu'. Because the restricted powers are enumerated (written into the canonical constitution), these are relatively narrower than the powers held by the principal level of government, although still capable of giving rise to implied powers. This hypotactic design represents a continuum between two polar ideals (in the Weberian sense).[24] The first is the confederal ideal where central government powers are sharply limited. The second polar type is the unitary ideal where the only powers of regional or local governments are those delegated by the central government. Under this ideal type, the central government controls local government functions through funding instruments such as (general and specific) transfers. There are of course difficulties with these polar types. The exaggerated power separation found in the confederal ideal is difficult to implement given incidental, implied, or emergency powers that (from time to time) might need to be claimed by central governments. On the other hand, ethical and economic considerations require vesting elected local and regional governments with powers which they already have the competencies to assume. In practice, constitutional designs are restricted to the spectrum between these two ideals. Arguably, the (historical) American, Swiss and German confederations illustrate the limitations of the acephalous confederal ideal.[25]

Decentralization models help explain how constitutional designs gravitate toward a polar ideal (either confederal or unitary). Administrative decentralization (such as deconcentration, delegation and devolution) allows sub-national governments a role in implementing national policies, but not a legislative power. While fiscal decentralisation, for example in the form of fiscal transfers from the central government to sub-national levels, does not require a re-division of powers. It could hence be implemented under the same 'residuum powers' design, but with considerably different outcomes. Under fiscal decentralization, which usually goes hand-in-hand with

[24] M. Weber, *The Methodology of the Social Sciences*, ed. and trans. E. Shils and H. Finch (Free Press, 1949) 90.

[25] See, e.g., O. Ola, 'Confederal Systems: A Comparative Analysis', *Civilisations* 18 (2) (1968), 270; C. Church and P. Dardanelli, 'The Dynamics of Confederalism and Federalism: Comparing Switzerland and the EU', *Regional & Federal Studies* 15 (2) (2005), 163.

administrative decentralization, the central government maintains a monopoly on powers, and incentivizes sub-national governments to participate under a principal-agent framework where local and regional governments are restricted to the 'four corners' of national policies set by the central government.[26]

The second trait comes from the Westminster horizontal overlap between the executive and legislative branches of government as seen in the Cabinet of the Government of the United Kingdom. Note that the heritable trait is not the horizontal overlap per se, but rather the 'meme' that there can be an overlap of powers in a given constitutional design. This overlap trait was later extrapolated to the vertical overlap of powers in a federal constitutional design. This Westminster overlap also provides the starting point for the efficiency criterion that will be used to explain how inheritance works.

According to Bagehot, in his scholarship on the English Constitution, there is a distinction between the canonical parts of constitutions, which are based on institutional authority (in the economic sense), and the efficient parts of constitutions, based on the actual division of powers.[27] Bagehot therefore declares the fusion of the executive and legislative powers in the Cabinet to be the English 'efficient constitution'.[28] His dichotomy is used in this paper to distinguish between the canonical provisions based on the hypotactic 'residuum of powers', and the efficient (conjugate) provisions introducing (enumeration and) concurrency.

Hence, the paper extends this Bagehotian efficiency from a *horizontal* overlap of powers between the executive and the legislative branches of government, to a *vertical* overlap between federal and state (or in the case of Canada, provincial) governments. This overlap can be seen in the concurrent powers (or lack thereof) in the constitutional design of the US, Canada and Australia as shown in Figure 4.3 below.

The intuition behind this Bagehotian efficiency is the flexibility brought about where there is overlap, or concurrency, in the powers assigned to the federal and sub-national governments.

26 A third type of decentralization: political decentralization, expands formal democratic channels to entrust individuals with a larger role in formulating and implementing policies, but does not inform the constitutional division of powers between different vertical levels of government.

27 Ibid.

28 Ibid. See also G. W. Cox, *The Efficient Secret: The Cabinet and the Development of Political Parties in Victorian England* (Cambridge University Press, 2005) 5.

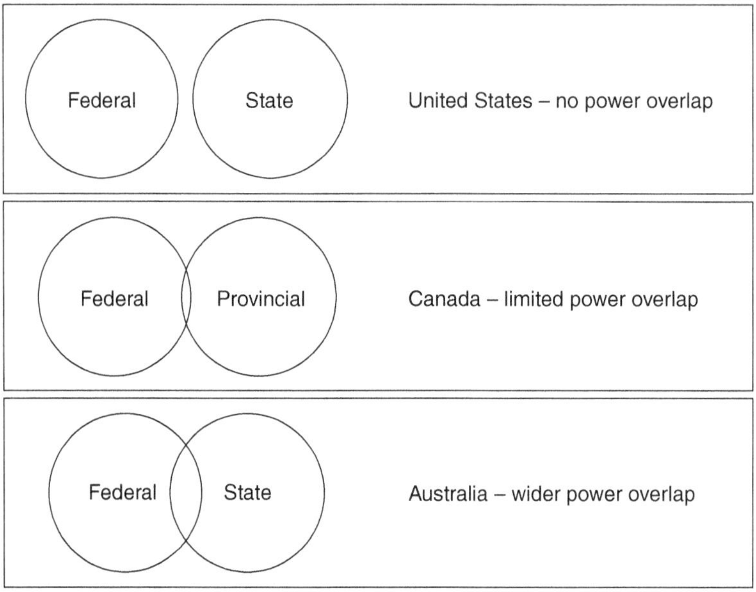

FIGURE 4.3: A vignette depicting the Bagehotian (vertical) efficiency in the federal Constitutions of the United States, Canada, and Australia

In summary, the heritable traits are represented by: (1) the horizontal overlap between the executive and legislative branches of government as seen in England; and (2) the vertical division between the federal government and state governments as seen in the United States of America. In the first period, these traits were diffused from the USA and UK to Canada. As a result, a more efficient version of the design (in the Bagehotian sense) was implemented in the 1867 Canadian Constitution, where the efficiency is represented by an (vertical) overlap in the powers federal and provincial governments. In the second period, a more efficient version of the design appeared in the 1900 Australian Constitution. This increase in efficiency provides a Hardingian (evolutionary) qualitative assessment of the constitutional design.

The rest of the chapter will flesh out the above hypothesis.

IV CODING THE HERITABLE TRAITS

This part traces the design implementing the US and UK traits in the Constitutions of the three great Anglo-American federations: United States, Canada and Australia.

In the United States,[29] the Constitution assigned the 'subordinator' government to the states.[30] The Federal Government was assigned a narrow (enumerated) set of powers.[31]The same division of powers can still be seen in the 1775 and 1781 Articles of Confederation.[32] The express vertical division of powers, however, was not part of the US Constitution that came into force in 1789. The division was introduced through the Tenth Amendment in 1791 (see below). This was the original hypotactic provision, which was later passed on to Canada (and Australia):[33]

> **Tenth Amendment:**
> The powers not delegated to the United States by the Constitution, nor prohibited by it to the States, are reserved to the States respectively, or to the people.

Before proceeding with the analysis, we need to ascertain the heritable trait from this design. The trait differs from the actual provision in a way similar to the difference between a *ratio decidendi* and a *res adjudicata*. In order for the trait to be inherited, we need to introduce a level of abstraction in capturing the key idea or meme represented by the Tenth Amendment. Hence, we can write:

$$\tau_1 \equiv vertical\ separation\ of\ power \tag{6}$$

Note how the trait captures only two ideas. The first is the ability to separate powers, and how this separation assigns these powers to two levels of government. Based on this understanding, the inheritance has taken place notwithstanding that the approach for allocating powers in Canada is diametrically opposed to the one in the United States.[34] In the Canadian Constitution the residuum powers were assigned to the Federal Government (the subordinator) rather than to the Provinces (the subordinated). Moreover, enumeration was applied to both, the subordinator and subordinated levels of government,

29 For a general discussion of the US federal system, refer to M. Tushnet, *The Constitution of the United States of America: A Contextual Analysis* 2nd edn (Hart, 2015).

30 US Constitution Amendment X (Federal Reserved Powers – Residual State legislative powers).

31 J. Madison, 'The Federalist No. 45: "The Alleged Danger from the Powers of the Union to the State Governments Considered"' in A. Hamilton, J. Madison and J. Jay (eds.), *The Federalist* (Barnes & Noble Classics, 2006) 204.

32 Articles of Confederation 1775, Articles of Confederation 1781.

33 US Constitution Amendment X.

34 See J. Webber, *The Constitution of Canada: A Contextual Analysis* (Hart, 2015) 31–32; W. P. M. Kennedy, 'The Judicial Process and Canadian Legislative Powers', *Washington University Law Review* 25 (2) (1940), 215. A. H. F. Lefroy, *Canada's Federal System* (The Lawbook Exchange, 2006).

TABLE 4.1 *The Canadian and Australian renditions of the first heritable trait*

Provision	Text
Tenth Amendment of the US Constitution (1791)	The powers not delegated to the United States by the Constitution, nor prohibited by it to the States, are reserved to the States respectively, or to the people.
Section 91 of the Canadian Constitution (1867)	It shall be lawful for the Queen, by and with the Advice and Consent of the Senate and House of Commons, to make Laws for the Peace, Order, and good Government of Canada, in relation to all Matters not coming within the Classes of Subjects by this Act assigned exclusively to the Legislatures of the Provinces . . .
Section 107 of the Australian Constitution (1900)	Every power of the Parliament of a Colony which has become or becomes a State, shall, unless it is by this Constitution exclusively vested in the Parliament of the Commonwealth or withdrawn from the Parliament of the State, continue as at the establishment of the Commonwealth, or as at the admission or establishment of the State, as the case may be.

rather than the US approach of enumerating only power assigned to the subordinated government. In other words, expressly the Canadian approach indicated the assignment of residuum powers but went on to also enumerate some of these.

Table 1 below shows how the trait appears in the constitutions of Canada and Australia.

The trait as seen in the US Constitution under the Tenth Amendment, and in the 1867 Canadian Constitution under section 91, was later diffused into Australia. Table 1 (above) shows that the trait did not undergo considerable change from the original Tenth Amendment design.[35] The first 1791 rendition explained residuum powers as those not delegated to the Federal Government or prohibited to the states by the Constitution. The second rendition, 76 years later, does not use the word 'reserved' but the word 'exclusively' instead. This rendition explains residuum powers as those not assigned exclusively to the Provinces. The effect is nonetheless the same in terms of dividing legislative powers between the national and sub-national governments. However, Section 91 went further than the Tenth Amendment in enumerating some thirty powers of the national government 'for greater certainty', but without

[35] See J. Quick and R. R. Garran, *The Annotated Constitution of the Australian Commonwealth* (LexisNexis Butterworths, 2015).

restricting the residuum powers assigned to the Federal Government. The most exclusive federal powers came under subsections (7), (11), and (25) in relation to national security and international affairs.

The Australian rendition[36] came 109 years after the US Tenth Amendment,[37] but only 33 years after Canada's section 91.[38] The provision adopts a text closer to the Canadian one and uses the same 'exclusivity' approach. Residuum powers are explained as those not exclusively vested in the Federal Government. This does not negate the proposition that the trait was inherited in Canada and Australia. The language of exclusivity was used because of the explicit (and implied) power concurrency that was built into the Constitutions of Canada and Australia (see below).

In all three renditions the residuum powers existed before the act of federation. Simply, the constitutional instrument was intended not to extinguish them. Note however, that in the US and Australian versions, these powers were assigned to the states, while in the Canadian case they were assigned to the federal government. However, the language of exclusivity seen in the Canadian and Australian renditions – a succinct way of stating the non-delegation and non-prohibition language in the US rendition – had quite different effects on the efficient constitutions in these jurisdiction (as discussed below). This can be seen in the different enumeration approaches in these constitutions.

However, before we continue our efficiency analysis we need to make explicit our formulation of the second heritable trait. This trait comes from the United Kingdom constitutional convention where there is overlap between the powers of the legislative and executive branches of government.[39] The overlap that we are interested in is that between the executive and legislative branches of government.[40] The abstracted trait from this design can be stated as follows:

$$\tau_2 \equiv \textit{horizontal overlap of powers} \qquad (7)$$

This trait can be seen in Canada through the constitutional convention, with few exceptions, that only Members of Parliament (MPs) can serve as ministers.[41] In the Australian case, this overlap is required by section 64 of the Constitution:[42]

36 Commonwealth of Australia Constitution Act (1900), s. 107.
37 US Constitution, Amendment X.
38 British North America Act 1867 (Imp), s. 91.
39 Bagehot (n. 1) 13.
40 See, e.g., P. Leyland, *The Constitution of the United Kingdom: A Contextual Analysis* (Bloomsbury, 2016).
41 Webber, above (n. 36), 96.
42 Commonwealth of Australia Constitution Act (1900), s. 64.

> **Ministers of State**
> The Governor-General may appoint officers to administer such departments of State of the Commonwealth as the Governor-General in Council may establish.
> Such officers shall hold office during the pleasure of the Governor-General. They shall be members of the Federal Executive Council, and shall be the Queen's Ministers of State for the Commonwealth.
>
> **Ministers to sit in Parliament**
> After the first general election no Minister of State shall hold office for a longer period than three months unless he is or becomes a senator or a member of the House of Representatives.

Hence, while a minister does not have to be an MP, s. 64 requires the minister to become a member of either the House of Representatives (lower house) or the Senate (upper house) within three months.

We now have the two heritable traits that will be analysed to ascertain their evolution in the offspring constitutions (of Canada and Australia). In other words, we will look at how the two traits (τ_1 and τ_2) will combine to produce new traits in the offspring constitutions. The prediction is that:

$$\tau_{Offspring} = \tau_1 \oplus \tau_2 \tag{8a}$$

$$\tau_{Offspring} \equiv \mathit{vertical\ overlap\ of\ powers} \tag{8b}$$

The evolution in the offspring constitutions is driven by an objective function, namely, maximizing efficiency (see Equation (1)). This efficiency is interpreted in the Bagehotian sense, as an overlap of powers, as seen in the Westminster system horizontal overlap between the legislative and executive branches. The offspring constitutions inherit the symmetric difference between the two heritable traits (τ_1 and τ_2). This means that the constitutions of Canada and Australia will exhibit an overlap in the distribution of vertical powers, as shown below. This symmetric difference is intended to maximize the efficiency in the design of the offspring constitutions. Hence, the proposition is that the residuum powers in the Australian design is more efficient than that in Canada due to the competition between the American and Canadian versions when drafting of the Australian version. The proposition is that:

$$e_{Australia} > e_{Canada} \tag{9}$$

This proposition is motivated by the fact that the drafters of the Australian Constitution had the advantage of studying the Canadian Constitution before deciding on an Australian version, especially in relation to concurrent powers. This advantage results from later designs being a function of earlier ones.

There is hence evidence from the records of the Australasian Federal Conventions of the 1890s that the delegates were influenced by the US (and Canadian Constitutions):

> We have had a great many analogies drawn between the United States and the Dominion of Canada. No doubt there is a partial analogy in many respects between ourselves and those countries, but, on the other hand, there are essential differences. For example, we are an island continent. No matter how volt subdivide the different parts of Australia into different sections, you must give to each of them a large sea – coast, with its harbours and valuable commerce, together with all the other possibilities of national life. But the position of the United States or of Canada is that of a congery of littoral states depending for their commerce upon the interior states, which in their turn naturally depend upon the others for the means of getting their products to the markets of the world.[43]

It therefore follows that the Canadian Constitution is less efficient as the drafters did not have the benefit of studying the practical effects of enumeration and concurrency. Hence, while Canada introduced implicit concurrency in the powers assigned to the federal and state (provincial) governments, Australia created explicit concurrency. This explains (at least in part) the higher intensity of change in Canada to reach efficiency (through the cultural competition between Quebec and English-speaking Canada).[44] Note, however, that this improvement is one of degree rather than a bifurcation as seen in Figure 2. It is, therefore, treated as part of the traits in the US and UK designs. The rest of this part elaborates on these points.[45]

The hypotactic 'residuum powers' has a conjugate, namely the 'enumerated powers'. In the US Constitution, enumeration is stated as follows:[46]

> **Article I, section 8.** The Congress shall have Power To lay and collect Taxes, Duties, Imposts and Excises, to pay the Debts and provide for the common Defence and general Welfare of the United States; but all Duties, Imposts and Excises shall be uniform throughout the United States;
>
> To borrow Money on the credit of the United States;

[43] Official Record of the Debates of the Australasian Federal Convention, Melbourne, 12 February 1890, 53 (W. McMillan).

[44] See U. Mattei, 'Efficiency in Legal Transplants: an Essay in Comparative Law and Economics', *International Review of Law and Economics* 14 (1994), 3, 10–11 for the point on efficiency and competition.

[45] See also Gussen (n. 6).

[46] US Constitution, Art. I, s. 8.

> To regulate Commerce with foreign Nations, and among the several States, and with the Indian Tribes;
>
> . . .
>
> To make all Laws which shall be necessary and proper for carrying into Execution the foregoing Powers, and all other Powers vested by this Constitution in the Government of the United States, or in any Department or Officer thereof.

While there was no concurrency in the US design, enumeration later resulted in concurrent powers in the vertical distribution as seen in Canada and Australia. In terms of our model, we have:

$$\tau_3 = \frac{\partial D_i}{\partial_1 \partial_2} \equiv concurrent\, powers \tag{10}$$

Table 2 below gives a summary of concurrent powers as seen in the US, Canadian and Australian Constitutions. Note that under the US Article I, section 8 enumeration, none of these powers was concurrent powers. This was the initial implementation of the theory of residuum of powers. Under section 92 of the Canadian Constitution, enumerates the exclusive powers assigned to the Provinces.[47] There are sixteen such (heads of) powers.[48] These powers are limited and read narrowly where subsets of those powers are expressly conferred on the Federal Government.

Unlike the US Constitution, the Canadian Constitution has three concurrent powers, namely old age pension, agriculture, and immigration. These powers are stated in sections 94A and 95 of the Constitution. Note, however, that the word 'concurrent' appears only in the margin of section 95.[49]

The fact that the Canadian concurrent powers are limited resulted in the allocation of powers through what came to be known as the 'principle of exhaustiveness'. The principle ensures that there are no gaps in the distribution of power – at least one level of government is able to legislate on any given issue.[50] Hence, while there was an efficiency improvement in the Canadian design, it was still embryonic, and relied more on the evolution that came later on through doctrines of constitutional interpretation. In the case of Canada, we find that both Federal and Provincial governments have enumerated powers in the constitution. In total the Canadian Constitution has 48

47 British North America Act 1867 (Imp), s. 92.

48 The power under s. 92(1) was repealed in 1982 by the Constitution Act 1982 and substituted by s. 45 of that Act. The section authorizes provincial legislatures to make laws amending their respective constitutions.

49 Section 94A was an amendment to the original Constitution, added in 1964.

50 See Reference Re Same-Sex Marriage (2004) 3 SCR 698., para. 34; cited in Webber (n. 36) 145.

enumerated heads of power. Of these 30 are assigned to the central government, 16 are assigned to the provinces, and three (in two provisions) are concurrent. In practice however, the courts used the doctrine of 'double aspect' to enlarge the concurrent or overlapping powers between the central and provincial governments.[51] In essence, the 'exclusive' lists in section 91 and 92 were found to be in fact overlapping.

In the Australia version we now find explicit concurrency. However, unlike the Canadian Constitution, there is no parallel list of state powers to counterbalance the construction of federal powers. Instead, the Commonwealth Government can only exercise specific exclusive powers, while most of the enumerated powers are held concurrently. As a result, the federal powers have been given a broad interpretation.[52]

Unlike the Canadian Constitution, the Australian Constitution does not have a chapter dedicated for the division of powers. Enumeration comes under the 'concurrent' powers in section 51, Chapter I: The [Commonwealth] Parliament, in Part V (Powers of the Parliament). This is essentially the same 'peace, order, and good government' (POGG) power that we see in section 91 of the Canadian Constitution. Although there is no equivalent for section 109 in the Canadian Constitution (see Table 2 above). Another key difference between the Canadian and Australian constitutions is that there is no counterpart to section 51(xxxvii) (Table 2). In fact, in Canada, the Supreme Court prohibited the delegation of powers from one level of government to the other,[53] because 'inter-delegation of powers between legislatures undermines public accountability and electoral responsibility for decisions and might make it difficult to unscramble the jurisdiction'.[54]

In the Australian Constitution,[55] the federal exclusive powers come under section 52 (Chapter I), sections 90 and 105 (Chapter IV: Finance and Trade),

[51] For the origin of this doctrine see *Hodge* v. *The Queen* (1883) 9 App Cas 117.

[52] Webber (n. 36) 145. Another key difference between Canada and Australia is accentuated by the regional diversity that Quebec provides. Australia and the US are in this sense territorial federations, while Canada is a cultural one. See T. O Hueglin, *Comparative Federalism: A Systematic Inquiry* (University of Toronto Press, 2006).

[53] *Attorney-General of Nova Scotia* v. *Attorney-General of Canada* (1951) SCR 31 (The Nova Scotia Interdelegation Case).

[54] Webber (n. 36) 169–70. Notwithstanding there is 'administrative inter-delegation' where both levels delegate their powers to an administrative agency, and there is 'incorporation by reference' where one level incorporates the rules applied by the other level. Similar arrangements are used to coordinate action where there is jurisdictional overlap.

[55] Commonwealth of Australia Constitution Act 1900 (Imp).

TABLE 4.2 *Enumeration and concurrency in the Constitutions of the US, Canada, and Australia*

Provision	Text
Canadian Constitution (1867)	**Section 94A.** The Parliament of Canada may make laws in relation to old age pensions and supplementary benefits, including survivors' and disability benefits irrespective of age, but no such law shall affect the operation of any law present or future of a provincial legislature in relation to any such matter.
	Section 95. In each Province the Legislature may make Laws in relation to Agriculture in the Province, and to Immigration into the Province; and it is hereby declared that the Parliament of Canada may from Time to Time make Laws in relation to Agriculture in all or any of the Provinces, and to Immigration into all or any of the Provinces; and any Law of the Legislature of a Province relative to Agriculture or to Immigration shall have effect in and for the Province as long and as far only as it is not repugnant to any Act of the Parliament of Canada.
Australian Constitution (1900)	**Section 51.** The Parliament shall, subject to this Constitution, have power to make laws for the peace, order, and good government of the Commonwealth with respect to . . .
	Section 109. Inconsistency of laws: When a law of a State is inconsistent with a law of the Commonwealth, the latter shall prevail, and the former shall, to the extent of the inconsistency, be invalid.
	section 51(xxxvii). Matters referred to the Parliament of the Commonwealth by the Parliament or Parliaments of any State or States, but so that the law shall extend only to States by whose Parliaments the matter is referred, or which afterwards adopt the law.

section 114 and 115 (Chapter V: The States), and section 122 (Chapter VI New States). The residual powers (to the States) are preserved in section 107 (Chapter V: The States), but no enumeration is given of these powers.

In summary, the hypotactic residuum of powers was inherited from the United States. Similarly, the (Westminster) horizontal overlap between executive and legislative governments was inherited from the United Kingdom. In the US and Australia, the residuum was given to the States, while in Canada, the Federal Government was assigned these powers. The conjugate to these powers was enumerated. There are 18 enumerated heads of powers under Article I, section 8, in the United States Constitution, compared to 30 heads of power under section 91, and 15 heads under section 92 in Canada; and

40 heads under section 51 in Australia.[56] The enumeration and concurrency provisions resulted in a *sui generis* evolution of the trait (the residuum of powers) in these jurisdictions. This change in enumeration can be represented as follows:

$$\left(\frac{\partial D_{Canada}}{\partial_1 \partial_2}\right) < \left(\frac{\partial D_{Australia}}{\partial_1 \partial_2}\right) \tag{11}$$

As discussed above, the increase in enumeration was partly to account for a concurrency menu (of the legislative powers) between the federal government and the sub-national governments. This concurrency is an extrapolation of the Bagehotian horizontal (*trias politica*) overlap between the executive and legislative governments. The hypotactic concurrency used the same 'meme' to design vertical concurrency of legislative powers into the Constitutions of Canada and Australia.

This change in enumeration is understood as maximizing the efficiency of the constitutional design (D).[57] The motivation for this understanding can be gleaned from Bagehot's analysis of the English Cabinet. Bagehot explains how the division of the legislative and executive branches weakens both. Citing the US Constitution, Bagehot explains how the US legislative branch does not have the same power to change the executive, as it does in the UK.[58] In a presidential system, challenging the executive will generally have to wait for the electoral cycle. He adds: 'In England a strong cabinet can obtain the concurrence of the legislature in all acts which facilitates its administration; it is itself, so to say, the legislature'.[59] This (horizontal) overlap efficiency was extrapolated to a (vertical) overlap efficiency between national and sub-national governments, in the form of concurrency of legislative powers as seen in the Canadian and Australian Constitutions. The rationale for the efficiency of this overlap is analogous to that given by Bagehot in relation to the overlap in the Westminster system. The concurrency does not only allow for migrating powers to the federal government, but also envisages a reversal of such investiture where circumstances so require. It also envisages a cooperative form of federalism that is less likely to obtain where concurrency is not a feature of the design.[60]

56 There are more enumerated powers in other parts of these Constitutions. This provided list focuses on the concurrency aspects in Canada and Australia.

57 For an empirical analysis of this efficiency, refer to Gussen (n. 6).

58 Bagehot (n. 1) 21.

59 Ibid., 23.

60 It should be noted that Bagehot was opposed to the principle of hypotaxis, at least in its federal rendition. Hence, he opines that 'a new country need not fall back into the fatal division of powers incidental to a presidential government; it may if, other conditions serve, obtain the

V CONCLUSION

The paper expounds the Hardingian rationale for replacing the 'legal transplants' model. The proposed alternative here is a version of 'Lamarckian evolution' –a subset of the wider paradigm of the evolution of legal systems. This can be thought of as a bifurcation point in the evolution of the offspring jurisdiction. Efficiency evolves these constitutions to a *sui generis* form. This efficiency is evidenced in the constitutional design phase (through concurrency of heads of powers enumerated in the constitution) as well as in the post-constitutional phase (through constitutional interpretation that enlarges the concurrency or modifies it to optimize net benefits from assigning a given head of power to one level of government). The first heritable trait can be seen in the hypotactic vertical division of legislative powers inherited from the United States (first used in Canada, and later on in Australia). What was inherited at the bifurcation point (in Figure 2) was the constitutional design where powers are divided between two levels of government, irrespective of which level receives the plenary (residuum) powers and which receives the enumerated powers. While Canada and Australia assign the plenary powers to different levels of government, the trait is still the same, namely the constitutional design where one level of government is given plenary powers, while the other is restricted to a limited (enumerated) menu of powers.

The second rationale is evident in the overlap of these powers, using enumeration and concurrency. This adaptation occurred intra-jurisdictionally in the constitutional design phase (and before the transient and steady-state phases after promulgation). The residuum trait was embedded into a canonical constitution that enumerated the powers associated with this residuum design. As we move from the eighteenth century to the twentieth century, these constitutional designs show a clear preference for more enumeration (and hence complexity). This delineation of powers achieves efficiency gains by enabling a bargaining process between the federal and sub-national levels of government. In addition, later designs emphasized concurrency of powers, first (generally) impliedly as in the Canadian Constitution, and later on, explicitly as in the Australian Constitution. In the case of the United States and Australia, we see a shift of the residuum from the sub-national level to the central government due to enumeration and (in the case of Australia) concurrency, while in the Canadian case we see the exact opposite (given that the residuum was assigned to the federal government). In each case, the efficient constitution restricts the

ready, well-placed, identical sort of sovereignty which belongs to the English Constitution, under the unroyal form of Parliamentary Government': Bagehot (n. 1) 253.

plenary design found in the canonical constitution. This suggests, at least in relation to these three jurisdictions, that there is an evolution beyond the original traits. There was an adaptation of the 'parent' traits to *sui generis* (colonial) local conditions.

To gauge the successfulness (or otherwise) of the inheritance mechanism, it was necessary to look at how the Canadian and Australian designs allowed for efficiency gains through a *posteriori* adaptation of the US and UK designs (in terms of the vertical division of legislative powers and the horizontal overlap between executive and legislative powers respectively). The timespans separating the Canadian and Australian designs, namely from 1867 to 1900, allowed for a form of 'feedback' (loop) on the effectiveness of the Canadian designs. These insights provided for a different approach to conjugate powers – the greater use of concurrent powers in later constitutional designs. In essence, gauging the success of the inter-jurisdictional inheritance of residuum powers is a function of its adaptation to local requirements (i.e. its evolution) in the constitutional design phase. Later, in the post-constitutional phase, the construction of these provisions by constitutional courts allows for intra-jurisdictional evolution in the transient phase (acquired characteristics). That then is followed by a steady-state (equilibrium) phase that is (usually) 'punctured' again through new inter-jurisdictional 'intercourse'.

It should be reiterated that this paper presents a *grounded* theory of how efficiency can be used to go beyond the dichotomy of successful/unsuccessful transplantation. The discussion is embedded in the constitutional designs of the UK, USA, Canada, and Australia. The assertion made in terms of residuum powers and the efficiency of their (Lamarckian) use should not be extrapolated beyond this context. Arguably, the very complexity of the mechanism of inheritance of legal designs militates against any general evolutionary theory. At best, it is hoped that there could be a streamlined approach to the analysis of legal systems evolution. Namely, the application of efficiency criteria from the discourse of evolutionary biology to explain the adoption and adaptation of legal designs.

It is hoped that the above discourse on Lamarckian evolution will be enriched by the application of systems theory and complexity theory. The adoption of (economic) efficiency criteria to gauge the success of inheritance (in terms of use and disuse), and the application of analytical models from evolutionary (law-and-economics), can potentially provide a useful platform for a more scientific approach.

While this paper limited its inquiry into Hardingian transplantation, there could well be applications of Lamarckian evolution to 'legal mimesis' and 'legal reception'. Again, the proposition is not for a general theory, but rather for a methodology that can allow for intercourse between (heterodox) explanations of the change in legal systems over time. Future research in this area is also likely to enhance the application of model-building in legal analysis, and the drive for an imperial application of efficiency analysis as seen in law-and-economics.

VI BIBLIOGRAPHY

Adams, M. and Heirbaut, D. (eds.), *The Method and Culture of Comparative Law: Essays in Honour of Mark Van Hoecke* (Hart Publishing, 2014).

Atkinson, G. and Paschall, S. P., *Law and Economics from an Evolutionary Perspective* (Edward Elgar, 2016).

Bagehot, W., *The English Constitution* 5th edn (Kegan Paul, Trench & Co, 1888).

Brennan, P. M., 'Subsidiarity in the Tradition of Catholic Social Doctrine' in Evans, M. and Zimmermann, A. (eds.), *Global Perspectives on Subsidiarity* (Springer, 2014) 29.

Buchanan, J. and Tullock, G., *The Calculus of Consent: Logical Foundations of Constitutional Democracy* (University of Michigan Press, 1962).

Burkhardt, R., *The Spirit of System: Lamarck and Evolutionary Biology* (Harvard University Press, 1977).

Cardozo, B., 'Law and Literature', *Yale Review* 14 (1925), 699.

Church, C., and Dardanelli, P., 'The Dynamics of Confederalism and Federalism: Comparing Swizerland and the EU', *Regional & Federal Studies* 15 (2) (2005), 163.

Coase, R. H., 'The Nature of the Firm', *Economica* 4 (16) (1937), 386;

Cox, G. W., *The Efficient Secret: The Cabinet and the Development of Political Parties in Victorian England* (Cambridge University Press, 2005).

D'Onorio, J.-B., *La Subsidiarité* (Téqui, 1995).

Dicey, A. V., *Introduction to the Study of the Law of the Constitution* (Liberty Classics, 1982).

Gussen, B. F., 'On the Problem of Scale: A General Theory of Morphogenesis and Normative Policy Signals for Economic Evolution', *Evolutionary and Institutional Economic Review* 12 (2015), 81.

'Australian Constitutionalism between Subsidiarity and Federalism', *Monash University Law Review* 42 (2) (2016), 383.

'Reflections on La Fata Morgana: Watsonian "prestige" and Bagehotian "efficiency"', *The Journal of Comparative Law* 12 (1) (2017), 80 (ISSN 1477–0814).

Htay, S. N. N. and Salman, S. A., 'Transaction Cost Theory, Political Theory and Resource Dependency Theory in Light of Unconventional Aspect', *IOSP Journal of Humanities and Social Science* 12 (5) (2013), 89.

Hueglin, T. O., *Comparative Federalism : A Ssystematic Inquiry* (University of Toronto Press, 2006).

Kennedy, W. P. M., 'The Judicial Process and Canadian Legislative Powers', *Washington University Law Review* 25 (2) (1940), 215.

Klaes, M., 'Historical Economics and Evolutionary Economic Policy: Coasean Perspectives' in Dopfer, K. (ed.), *Economics, Evolution and the State: The Governance of Complexity* (Edward Elgar, 2005), 78.

Kurland, P. B. and Lerner, R., *The Founders Constitution*, vol. 5 (Liberty Fund, 2001), 20.

Lefroy, A. H. F., *Canada's Federal System* (The Lawbook Exchange, 2006).

Leyland, P., *The Constitution of the United Kingdom: A Contextual Analysis* (Bloomsbury, 2016).

Madison, J., "The Federalist No. 45: "The Alleged Danger from the Powers of the Union to the State Governments Considered"' in Hamilton, A., Madison, J. and Jay, J. (eds.), *The Federalist* (Barnes & Noble Classics, 2006).

Mattei, U., 'Efficiency in Legal Transplants: an Essay in Comparative Law and Economics', *International Review of Law and Economics* 14 (1994), 3.

Nelken, D. and Feest, J., *Adapting Legal Cultures* (Bloomsbury Publishing, 2001).

Ola, O., 'Confederal Systems: A Comparative Analysis', *Civilisations* 18 (2) (1968), 270.

Posner, R., *Law and Literature: A Misunderstood Relation* (Harvard University Press, 1988).

Quick, J. and Garran, R. R., *The Annotated Constitution of the Australian Commonwealth* (LexisNexis Butterworths, 2015).

Reisman, D. A., *The Social Economics of Thorstein Veblen* (Edward Elgar, 2012).

Roe, M. J., 'Chaos and Evolution in Law and Economics', *Harvard Law Review* 109 (3) (1996), 641.

Ruzzenenti, F. and Basosi, R., 'On the Relationship between Energy Efficiency and Complexity: Insights on the Causality Chain', *International Journal of Design & Nature and Ecodynamics* 3 (2) (2008), 95.

Scalia, A., *A Matter of Interpretation* (Princeton University Press, 1997).

Tushnet, M., *The Constitution of the United States of America: A Contextual Analysis* 2nd edn (Hart, 2015).

Van Hoecke, M., *Law as Communication* (Hart Publishing, 2002);

Veblen, T., *The Theory of the Leisure Class: An Economic Study of Institutions* (Penguin, 1994).

von Wangenheim, G., 'Evolutionary Theories in Law and Economics and Their Use for Comparative Legal Theory', *Review of Law & Economics* 7 (3) (2011), 737.

Watson, A., *Legal Transplants: An Approach to Comparative Law* (University of Georgia Press, 1993).

Webber, J., *The Constitution of Canada: A Contextual Analysis* (Hart, 2015).

Weber, M., *The Methodology of the Social Sciences*, eds. and trans. Shils, E. and Finch, H. (Free Press, 1949).

Zumbansen, P. and Calliess, G.-P. (eds.), *Law, Economics and Evolutionary Theory* (Edward Elgar, 2011).

PART II

5

The Incomplete Legal Transplant – Good Faith and the Common Law

Anthony Gray

The aim of any mature system of contract law must be to promote the observance of good faith and fair dealing in the conclusion and performance of contracts.[1]

I INTRODUCTION

This chapter will consider a legal transplant that is potentially still occurring – the broad recognition of notions of 'good faith' in relation to contracts. Whilst notions of good faith surround early conceptions of contractual relations, as will be seen, the common law, whilst initially apparently accepting good faith as part of the law of contract, set its face against such a doctrine, except in relation to insurance contracts. That resistance had been stoic for many years, until finally in recent years, the United Kingdom Supreme Court accepted the doctrine as a principle applicable to contracts,[2] at least to some extent. In so doing, it followed in the footsteps of the Canadian Supreme Court, which finally recognized a general doctrine of good faith earlier in the same year.[3] The doctrine is broadly recognized in the United States.[4] However, the transplant remains incomplete, with the High Court of Australia maintaining its stubborn refusal to finally decide on the fate of the doctrine, although it made somewhat encouraging 'noises' suggesting it might accept the doctrine in a recent decision.[5] There is evident lack of

1 Lord Steyn 'Role of Good Faith and Fair Dealing in Contract Law: A Hair-Shirt Philosophy', *Denning Law Journal* 6 (1991), 131, 131.

2 *Telefonica O2 UK Ltd* v. *British Telecommunications Plc* [2014] UKSC 42, [37] (Lord Sumption, for the Court).

3 *Bhasin* v. *Hrynew* [2014] 3 SCR 494.

4 Section 205 Restatement of the Law, Second (Contracts) (1979) s. 1-203 United States Uniform Commercial Code.

5 *Commonwealth Bank of Australia* v. *Barker* (2014) 253 CLR 169, 195 (French CJ Bell and Keane JJ), 213–14 (Kiefel J).

clarity in the United Kingdom approach, uncertainty which also affects Asian legal systems which, at least traditionally, paid great respect to United Kingdom law, particularly in the commercial sphere, namely Singapore and Hong Kong. The article is premised on the basis, as Harding points out, that legal transplants must fit. It is believed that good faith is a good fit within the common law 'family'.

II RATIONALE FOR ACCEPTANCE OR NON-ACCEPTANCE OF GOOD FAITH

The precise meaning of good faith is contested, as will be elaborated upon below. Having said that, various rationales have been offered for either the acceptance or rejection of the good faith principle. Those who reject such a principle might conceive of a contract as an agreement between two rational actors, interested in maximizing their utility in relation to the transaction. The transaction is usually conceived of as a one-off, by parties who are strangers to each other. Trust is relatively low between the parties. There is relatively equal bargaining power, and each is able to 'look after themselves' in terms of the negotiation process.[6] Access to information is relatively equal. Because bargaining power is relatively equal, each party is able to price in risks associated with the contract, including risks that the other contracting party will not perform their obligations as expected, or act in a capricious, arbitrary, dishonest or unreasonable way.[7] The relationship between the parties is seen as somewhat adversarial in nature,[8] in that each party has remedies for breach of contract. Reflecting a Hobbesian view of human nature, rules of contracting are necessary. They exist to ensure that parties do the right thing, or pay for the consequences of doing the wrong thing. The primary remedy for breach of

[6] G. Kuehne, 'Implied Obligations of Good Faith and Reasonableness in the Performance of Contracts: Old Wine in New Bottles?', *University of Western Australia Law Review* 33 (2006), 63, 98: 'commercial contracts are likely to be the product of extensive negotiation and advice; representing an allocation of risks and interests too nuanced to be reconciled with a general, mandatory obligation of good faith or reasonableness'.

[7] 'If there is one thing which more than another public policy requires it is that men of full and competent understanding shall have the utmost liberty of contracting, and that their contracts when entered into freely and voluntarily shall be held sacred and shall be enforced by courts of justice. Therefore you have this paramount public policy to consider – that you are not lightly to interfere with this freedom of contract': *Printing and Numerical Registering Co* v. *Sampson* (1875) LR 19 Eq. 462, 465 (George Jessell MR).

[8] P. Girard 'Good Faith in Contract Performance: Principle or Placebo?', *Supreme Court Law Review* 5 (1983) 309, 326: 'the common law doctrines relating to contract performance all assume that the parties are in an adversarial relationship'.

contract is payment of damages, rather than restoration of the contractual relationship.[9]

However, others view contracts in a different light. This is the relational view of contracts, most often associated with scholars such as Macneil and Macaulay.[10] A relational view of contracts sees contracts as typically involving a high level of trust. The parties will often have dealt with each other in the past. The relationship between the parties is important.[11] Parties are not necessarily just motivated to maximize the utility of this one contract, but are concerned with the ongoing harmonious relationship between the parties, involving give and take. Where disputes arise, parties prefer to, and usually do, resolve them themselves, without recourse to formal legal proceedings. And if formal legal proceedings are taken, as a last resort, the emphasis would be on bringing the parties back together, getting them to meet their contractual obligations, as opposed to merely accepting the parties' relationship has ended, and assessing what has been lost as a result with a view to paying damages. Empirical studies are used to show this is the more realistic view of how contracts actually work.[12] As is obvious, a doctrine of good faith, depending on how it is defined, fits much better within the relational view of contracts. It eschews the black letter, in favour of the 'spirit' of the agreement between the parties.[13] In a relational view of contracts, parties are entitled to expect honesty and perhaps reasonableness from the other side.

9 It should be conceded that doctrines of equity would sometimes be utilized to take some of the 'hard edges' out of the common law of contract.

10 I. Macneil 'Contracts: Adjustment of Long-Term Economic Relations under Classical Neoclassical and Relational Contract Law', *Northwestern University Law Review* 72 (1978), 854; I. Macneil 'Relational Contract: What We Do and Do Not Know', *Wisconsin Law Review* (1985), 483; S. Macaulay 'Non-Contractual Relations in Business: A Preliminary Study', *American Sociological Review* 28 (1963), 55; S. Macaulay 'The Real and the Paper Deal: Empirical Pictures of Relationships, Complexity and the Urge for Transparent Simple Rules', *Modern Law Review* 66 (2003), 44; R. Summers 'The General Duty of Good Faith – Its Recognition and Conceptualization', *Cornell Law Review* 67 (1982), 810.

11 P. Finn 'Commerce, the Common Law and Morality', *Melbourne University Law Review* 17 (1989), 87, 98.

12 H. Beale and T. Dugdale 'Contracts between Businessmen: Planning and the Use of Contractual Remedies', *British Journal of Law and Society* 2 (1975), 45, 47: 'even if plans had been made to cover possible disruptions, there was usually thought to be no need to fall back on legal rights if the disruption materialized. It was made very clear to us that, besides there being a common acceptance of certain norms, within the trade, there was a considerable degree of trust among firms'; A. Arrighetti, R. Bachmann and S. Deakin 'Contract Law, Social Norms and Inter-Firm Co-Operation', *Cambridge Journal of Economics* 21 (1997), 171.

13 A. Duke 'A Universal Duty of Good Faith: An Economic Perspective', *Monash University Law Review* 33 (2007), 182, 196; M. Van Alstine 'Of Textualism, Party Autonomy and Good Faith', *William and Mary Law Review* 40 (1999), 1223, 1274.

Another idea is that the law should conform to, and not be antagonistic towards, the nature of contracts which it purports to regulate. If a contract is truly relational in nature, the law that regulates it should recognize the concept of good faith.

III GOOD FAITH IN CIVIL LAW SYSTEMS

The doctrine of good faith has an ancient vintage in systems we would now recognize as 'civil law' systems.[14] Some claim it existed in the second century BC.[15] Cicero (106 BC–43 BC) refers to it as the foundation of justice, comprising consistency and truth regarding promises and compacts. He stated that:

> [t]hese words, good faith, have a very broad meaning. They express all the honest sentiments of a good conscience, without requiring a scrupulousness which could turn selflessness into sacrifice; the law banishes from contracts ruses and clever manoeuvres, dishonest dealings, fraudulent calculations, dissimulations and perfidious simulations, and malice, which under the guise of prudence and skill, takes advantage of credulity, simplicity and ignorance.[16]

It appears in two treatises of Roman law, the second century AD's *Institutes of Gaius*, and the sixth century's *Corpus Iuris Civilis*.[17] Anyone wishing to bring a claim under this system of law was required to fit within particular categories (forms of action) case recognized by that legal system. One such form of action was the *bona fide judicia*.[18] In time, the list of situations which could attract such a claim expanded.[19] Of all types of contract, good faith was most

[14] M. Van Alstine 'Of Textualism, Party Autonomy and Good Faith', *William and Mary Law Review* 40 (1999), 1223, 1230: 'in one form or another, an obligation of good faith performance has existed from the earliest formulations of the law governing private obligational relationships'.

[15] B. Nicholas *An Introduction to Roman Law* (Oxford University Press, 1962) 163.

[16] Cicero, *De Officiis*, cited in *European Contract Law: Materials for a Common Frame of Reference: Terminology, General Principles, Model Rules* (2008) 152.

[17] 'It cannot be provided by agreement that a person shall not be responsible for bad faith': Justinian's Digest, II.XIV27.3 (Scott, *The Civil Law: Translations of Roman Text*, 1932).

[18] L. Trakman 'The Binding Force of Agreements to Negotiate in Good Faith', *Cambridge Law Journal* 73 (2014), 598: 'at the outset, Roman law established an obligation ex bona fide, or obligation to act in good faith, by which parties were required to act in good conscience in fulfilling their obligations. Canon law perpetuated this obligatio ex bono fide'; R. Zimmermann *The Law of Obligations: Roman Foundations of the Civilian Tradition* (Clarendon Press, 1990); R. Pound *Jurisprudence*, vol. 1 (Harvard University Press, 1959) 409.

[19] Lawson, *A Common Lawyer Looks at the Civil Law* (University of Michigan, 1955).

prevalent in the context of commercial contracts.[20] Good faith closely approximated a requirement of reasonableness, as conceived in this time.[21] It was inherent in those contracts to which it applied.[22]

These doctrines found their way into civil law in various European nations.[23] Pollock and Maitland relate the practice in jurisdictions now known as part of modern France and modern Italy in 'early times' of a binding ceremony pertaining to contracts, the *fides facta*.[24] They refer also to contracting parties making faith upon a wand or holly stick. A handshake represented the 'faith' pertaining to the agreement. Parties were answerable to a higher body if they breached this faith. This exchange of promises often took place in the presence of a third party *fideiussor*. This person often held a religious position, and had coercive powers over those making promises. The *fideiussor* 'holds the promisor's faith in his hands and can constrain him to redeem it by ecclesiastical censure of temporal distress'. Good faith is referred to during the eleventh and twelfth centuries.[25]

Good faith appears in Article 7(1) of the United Nations Convention on Contracts for the International Sale of Goods, Article 1.7 of the UNIDROIT Principles of International Commercial Contracts (2004) and Article 1.106(2) and 201 of the Principles of European Contract Law. It appears in Articles 1134 and 1135 of the French Civil Code, s. 242 of the German Civil Code and Article 1175 and 1337 of the Italian Civil Code. Article 6.2 of the Dutch Civil Code refers to an obligation of 'reasonableness and fairness'. It was referred to as a 'principle of civil law' by the European Court of Justice in *Messner v. Kruuger*.[26]

20 S. Corcoran 'Good Faith as a Principle of Interpretation: What Is the Positive Content of Good Faith?', *Australian Bar Review* 36 (2012), 1, 4.

21 A. Farnsworth 'Good Faith Performance and Commercial Reasonableness under the Uniform Commercial Code', *University of Chicago Law Review* 30 (1963), 666, 668–70; R. Pound (n. 18) 413: 'the parties were bound to perform what could be required fairly and reasonably under the circumstances of the case'.

22 Corcoran (n. 20), 1, 44.

23 Corcoran (n. 20), 1, 5 notes that 'the duty of good faith in contract formation entered continental European law with the reception of Roman law in the renaissance and has been a fundamental doctrine of European jurisdictions since then'.

24 F. Pollock and F. Maitland *The History of English Law Vol.* 2 (Cambridge University Press, 1895) 185–9; *fides* from the Latin meaning faith, trust, belief, confidence, loyalty and honesty; *facta* from factum, meaning to make, do, cause or practise.

25 W. Tetley 'Good Faith in Contract, Particularly in the Contracts of Arbitration and Chartering', *Journal of Maritime Law and Commerce* 36 (2004), 561, 567.

26 [2009] C489/07.

Outside Europe, good faith is also recognized in Article 6 of the Contract Law of the People's Republic of China (1999). It mirrors Confucian concern with the spirit (*li*) as well as the letter (*fa*) of law.[27]

IV GOOD FAITH IN COMMON-LAW SYSTEMS

Notions of good faith have had a somewhat turbulent path in the common law. In the late eighteenth century commercial law master Lord Mansfield declared it was the 'governing principle ... to all contracts and dealings'.[28] Others took a similar view during this time.[29] However, as the years progressed, the doctrine became applicable only in the narrow circumstances of insurance contracts. Perhaps, in the period of the industrial revolution where commerce and industry was to be accommodated and encouraged at all costs, it was thought that notions of good faith were an impediment.[30] Good faith notions appear much more readily in equitable principles, though equity typically uses other words to describe the kind of behaviour to which good faith might otherwise be applied. It was (in)famously dismissed as being 'unworkable' by the House of Lords in *Walford* v. *Miles*.[31] The traditional difference in this respect between the common law and other systems was acknowledged by Lord Bingham:

> In many civil law systems, and perhaps in most legal systems outside the common law world, the law of obligations recognises and enforces an overriding principle that in making and carrying out contracts parties should act in good faith ... English law has characteristically committed itself to no

27 See Liming Wang and Chuanxi Xu 'Fundamental Principles of China's Contract Law', *Columbia Journal of Asian Law* 13 (1999), 1; G. Wang 'The New Contract Law of China', *Journal of Contract Law* 3 (2000), 242; C. Leonard 'A Legal Chameleon: An Examination of the Doctrine of Good Faith in Chinese and American Contract Law', *Connecticut Journal of International Law* 25 (2010), 305.

28 *Carter* v. *Boehm* (1766) 3 Burr. 1905, 1909; 97 ER 1162, 1164.

29 'In contracts of all kinds, it is of the highest importance that courts of law should compel the observance of honesty and good faith': *Mellish* v. *Motteux* (1792) 170 ER 113, 114; *Pawson* v. *Watson* (1778) 2 Cowp 786, 788: 'by the law of merchants, all dealings must be fair and honest'.

30 A. Farnsworth 'Good Faith Performance and Commercial Reasonableness under the Uniform Commercial Code', *University of Chicago Law Review* 30 (1963), 666, 670; R. Hui 'The Doctrine of Good Faith in Contract: Greater Acknowledgement in Hong Kong? A Comparative Study', *City University of Hong Kong Law Review* 5 (2015), 85, 94: 'the paucity in positive acknowledgement of good faith can be attributed to notions of freedom of contract and the dictates of laissez-faire economics prevalent since the industrial revolution'.

31 [1992] 2 AC 128, 138: 'the concept of a duty to carry on negotiations in good faith is inherently repugnant to the adversarial position of the parties when involved in negotiations ... a duty to negotiate in good faith is as unworkable in practice as it is inherently inconsistent'.

such overriding principle, but has developed piecemeal solutions in response to demonstrated problems of unfairness.[32]

Despite this, after the *Walford* decision, members of the English High Court and Court of Appeal appeared to assert the existence of a doctrine of good faith.[33] In 2003 in the House of Lords, Lord Bingham (with whom Lord Steyn agreed) declared that parties to a contract 'will assume the honesty and good faith or the other; absent such an assumption they would not deal'.[34] An influential single judge decision in 2013 again asserted its existence.[35] It noted that United Kingdom law was 'swimming against the tide' in its attitude towards good faith.[36] Finally, in 2014 the United Kingdom Supreme Court in *British Telecommunications Plc* unanimously agreed that it should be assumed, absent clear evidence of intent to the contrary, that a contractual discretion was to be exercised in good faith.[37] The court dealt with the matter extremely briefly, surprising given they were changing the law as it had previously been stated. The court's consideration is contained in one paragraph of the judgment. The court used the concept of good faith in contradistinction to conduct that was arbitrary, capricious or inconsistent with the purpose of the contract.

Notwithstanding the Court's decision in *British Telecommunications*, doubt remains as to the current position in the United Kingdom. Some cases apparently continue to deny that a general obligation to exercise good faith exists,[38] seeking to limit the finding in *British Telecommunications* to categories of case, as opposed to a statement about a general contracting

[32] *Interfoto Picture Library Ltd* v. *Stilletto Visual Programmes Ltd* [1989] 1 QB 433, 439 (Lord Bingham).

[33] *Abu Dhabi National Tanker Co* v. *Product Star Shipping (The Product Star)*(No. 2) [1993] 1 Lloyd's Rep 397 (CA); *Paragon Finance Plc* v. *Nash* [2001] EWCA Civ 1466 (CA); *Socimer International Bank Ltd (In Liquidation)* v. *Standard Bank London Ltd* (No. 2) [2008] EWCA Civ 116 (CA); *JML Direct Ltd* v. *Freesat UK Ltd* [2010] EWCA Civ 34 (CA); *Compass Group UK and Ireland Ltd* v. *Mid Essex Hospital Services NHS Trust* [2013] EWCA Civ 200 (CA); *Horkulak* v. *Cantor Fitzgerald International* [2004] EWCA Civ 1287 (CA).

[34] *HIH Casualty and General Insurance Ltd* v. *Chase Manhattan Bank* [2003] UKHL 6, [15]. Lord Hoffmann agreed that contracting parties expected honest dealing.

[35] *Yam Seng Pte Ltd* v. *International Trade Corp Ltd* [2013] EWHC 111 (Leggatt J), [154]: 'I respectfully suggest that the traditional English hostility towards a doctrine of good faith in the performance of contracts, to the extent it still persists, is misplaced'.

[36] Ibid., [125].

[37] *Telefonica O2 UK Ltd* v. *British Telecommunications Plc* [2014] UKSC 43, [37] (Lord Sumption, for the Court).

[38] *Compass Group UK and Ireland Ltd (t/a Medirest)* v. *Mid Essex Hospital Services NHS Trust* [2013] EWCA Civ 200; *MSC Mediterranean Shipping Co SA* v. *Cottonex Anstalt* [2016] EWCA Civ 789, [45]; *Carewatch Care Services Ltd* v. *Focus Caring Services* [2014] EWHC 2313 (Ch).

principle.[39] Others have apparently embraced good faith as a concept implicit in contracts to which United Kingdom law applies.[40]

Others have now re-asserted a very narrow interpretation to be given to the concept of 'reasonableness' in the good faith context, seeking to argue that it relates to how the concept of 'reasonableness' is used in the very different context of judicial review, namely so-called '*Wednesbury* unreasonableness'. This is the sense that only exercises of discretion to which no rational person would have agreed are vulnerable to challenge. Members of the United Kingdom Supreme Court recently suggested this should be used in assessing the exercise of a contractual discretion.[41] However, somewhat confusingly, members of the Court also appeared to refer to contractual discretion being conditioned by broader concepts of 'honesty, good faith and genuineness … (to avoid) arbitrariness, capriciousness, perversity and irrationality'.[42] Now, obviously, whether good faith is defined to include all of these things and the compendium term 'good faith' is used, or whether the term is defined narrowly but all of these other concepts are also used, the result in almost all cases will be the same. However, it is believed that a definition of good faith which includes reasonableness, expected to include concepts such as lack of arbitrariness and capriciousness, would be a more efficient way for the law to develop, rather than expect the court to grapple with the meaning behind a range of words that broadly apply in the same area of law.

With respect, it is highly dubious that a doctrine developed in the very different context of judicial review of an administrative decision can or should be utilized in relation to review of what occurred within a contracting environment. For example, contracts are typically relational in nature, very much unlike a decision that a government organisation makes with respect to an individual. It is doubtful that a *Wednesbury* unreasonableness approach accords with the relational nature of contracts; it does not reflect the general ongoing, trust-based relationship between contracting parties. The relationship between government decision-maker, for example

[39] For example, it has been suggested that the good faith requirement would not apply to the exercise of a discretion where the decision was in reality a binary choice as to whether or not to exercise an absolute contractual right: *Myers* v. *Kestrel Acquisitions Ltd* [2015] EWHC 916 (Ch); *Monde Petroleum SA* v. *WesternZagros Ltd* [2016] EWHC 1472 (Comm).

[40] *Bristol Groundschool Ltd* v. *Intelligent Data Capture Ltd* [2014] EWHC 2145 (Ch); *D and G Cars Ltd* v. *Essex Police Authority* [2015] EWHC 226 (QB); *Globe Motors Inc* v. *TRW Lucas Varity Electric Steering Ltd* [2016] EWCA Civ 396, [105].

[41] *Braganza* v. *BP Shipping Limited and Another* [2015] 1 WLR 1661, [28]–[32] (Lady Hale, with whom Lord Kerr agreed); [53] (Lord Hodge, with whom Lord Kerr agreed); [102]-[104] (Lord Neuberger, with whom Lord Wilson agreed).

[42] [104] (Lord Neuberger, with whom Lord Wilson agreed).

a government minister, and one who is affected by a government decision, is very different.

Until recently, the common law of Canada was relatively uncertain in relation to good faith principle. Lower court decisions had reached conflicting views on the doctrine, with some apparently accepting its existence, and others denying it. The uncertainty was resolved in the landmark Supreme Court of Canada decision in *Bhasin* v. *Hrynew*.[43] There the Supreme Court accepted that good faith was an 'organising principle' of Canadian contract law. It rejected the common law's past reluctance to embrace notions of good faith, and noted the apparent anomaly where notions apparently very similar to good faith had been accepted and applied elsewhere in the common law of contract, with little difficulty. Another reason the Court gave for embracing notions of good faith was that it had been accepted and applied in civil law jurisdictions, with little evident difficulty, as well as in the United States.[44] It appeared in Canadian statutes, and had proven to be workable.

Unfortunately, the resolution of the position in Canadian contract law by the highest court has not been replicated (yet?) in the case of Australia. Lower courts have taken inconsistent positions, with some accepting that good faith applies to contracts,[45] and others not. The High Court of Australia has to date avoided the issue,[46] and most recently maintained this position, despite some dicta that might appear to be vaguely supportive.[47] It is to be regretted that (a) a suitable case has not appeared for the court to determine the issue one way or the other, and/or (b) the Court has not suggested to parties that they may wish to make submissions about good faith, in a case where the doctrine might

43 [2014] 3 SCR 494.

44 [32] (Cromwell J, for the Court). Good faith appears in section 1–203 of the United States Uniform Commercial Code and s. 205 of the Restatement of Contracts (Second).

45 *Renard Constructions (ME) Pty Ltd* v. *Canada (Minister of Public Works)* (1992) 26 NSWLR 234; *Burger King Corp* v. *Hungry Jack's Pty Ltd* [2001] NSWCA 187; *Alcatel Australia Ltd* v. *Scarcella and Ors* [1998] NSWSC 483; *Vodafone Pacific Ltd* v. *Mobile Innovations Ltd* [2004] NSWCA 15; *United Group Rail Services Ltd* v. *Rail Corporation* (NSW) [2009] NSWCA 177; *Cordon Investments Pty Ltd* v. *Lesdor Properties Pty Ltd* [2012] NSWCA 184; *Esso Australia Resources Pty Ltd* v. *Southern Pacific Petroleum* [2005] VSCA 228; *Androvitsaneas* v. *Members First Broker Network Pty Ltd* [2013] VSCA 212.

46 *Royal Botanic Gardens and Domain Trust* v. *South Sydney City Council* (2002) 240 CLR 45.

47 *Commonwealth Bank of Australia* v. *Barker* (2014) 253 CLR 169, 195–6 (French CJ Bell and Keane JJ, clarifying that their rejection of an implied duty of trust and confidence in employment contracts was not intended to reflect on the existence or otherwise of a duty of good faith, when the parties had not even made submissions about good faith), 213–14 (Kiefel J) (five justices heard the case).

potentially apply. In that most recent decision Kiefel J noted the doctrine had been accepted in civil law countries, and in the United States.[48]

The position of Edelman J should be noted. He expressed his views in a single judge decision of the Federal Court in *Mineralogy Pty Ltd* v. *Sino Iron (No. 6)*.[49] Obviously, his views are particularly important given his recent elevation to the High Court of Australia. In that case, Edelman J rejected the suggestion that good faith was a universal implication to be made with respect to contracts generally.[50] The inquiry should be a case specific one, focused on the particular contract at issue. He opined that suggestions that, where good faith did apply, it was confined to notions of honesty would mean the doctrine would have very little content, given that parties already had legitimate expectations of the honesty of another.[51] He found it could embrace in some cases notions of reasonableness, and where it did so, that word would not necessarily be confined to notions of *Wednesbury* unreasonableness, as some members of the United Kingdom had suggested in *Braganza*.[52]

There is evidence in some Asian legal systems of acceptance and application of the prior English approach disfavouring the use of good faith.[53] For example, in the Hong Kong High Court decision of *GDH Ltd* v. *Creditor Co Ltd*, To J found no general obligation of good faith in the law of Hong Kong. In so doing, he cited English authorities, including Atiyah and the 1989 English decision in *Interfoto*. To J concluded that there was no general good faith obligation to be applied in contracts to which Hong Kong law applied, unless the parties were in a fiduciary relationship. He gave examples of such contracts as including insurance contracts, partnership agreements, and employment agreements.[54] Obviously, given that Chinese contract law embraces notions of good faith, it is possible that in future Hong Kong law will move to accept it.[55]

The Singaporean Court of Appeal specifically left open in its recent decision the question of whether a general duty of good faith should be implied

[48] *Commonwealth Bank of Australia* v. *Barker* (2014) 253 CLR 169, 213. Kiefel J specifically declined to determine whether the doctrine was part of the law of Australia (214).

[49] [2015] FCA 825.

[50] [1007].

[51] [1008].

[52] [1015].

[53] *Hyundai Engineering and Construction Co Ltd* v. *Vigour Ltd* [2005] 3 HKLRD 723 (CA).

[54] *GDH Ltd* v. *Creditor Co Ltd* [2008] HCA 1462/2006, [57]. An appeal against this decision failed, but the Court of Appeal did not elaborate upon the good faith issue.

[55] For an argument in favour of recognition of good faith in Hong Kong contract law see Hui (n. 30), 85.

into contracts.[56] It also found that usually, where a contract required one of the parties to obtain the permission of a third party in order that a contractual pre-condition could be satisfied, it would be implied that the party would use reasonable endeavours in order to achieve that pre-condition.[57] Some would view this as being included within the broader notion of good faith. In some cases the Singaporean courts appear to support notions of good faith. In the Court of Appeal decision in *Straits Advisors Pte Ltd v. Behringer Holdings (Pte) Ltd*, it concluded that one of the parties must exercise one of their contractual discretions 'in good faith and for proper purposes'.[58] Elsewhere there appear suggestions denying or at least doubting the existence of a general contractual obligation of good faith,[59] but it must be conceded that in some of these cases, there is reference to English law apparently denying a general good faith obligation.[60] As noted above, the precise English position is somewhat uncertain at present.

V THE HISTORY OF COMMERCIAL LAW IN THE COMMON LAW

It is considered that there are some salutary lessons for the current discussion of good faith in the field of contract law from the history of commercial law. Legal historians often trace English commercial law back to 1280's *The Little*

56 *The One Suites Pty Ltd* v. *Pacific Motor Credit (Pte) Ltd* [2015] SGCA 21, [44] (Menon CJ Tin and Leong JJ).

57 [43]. The Singaporean courts have also left open whether an implied duty of trust and confidence applies in the employment context: *Wee Kim San Lawrence Bernard* v. *Robinson and Co (Singapore) Pty Ltd* [2014] 4 SLR 357.

58 [2010] 1 SLR 760 (CA), [18] (Phang JA for the Court); see also *Indulge Food Pte Ltd* v. *Torabi Marashi Bahram* [2010] 2 SLR 540 (High Court, per Ang J) (contractual discretion to be exercised in good faith for legitimate purposes and reasonably ([14]–[15]); *Edwards Jason Glenn* v. *Australia and New Zealand Banking Group Ltd* [2012] SGHC 61 (Tay J) (contractual discretion must not be exercised arbitrarily, capriciously, perversely, parties must act honestly and in good faith in relation to their contracting powers)([101]-[102]). For discussion of these cases, and an argument in favour of recognition of good faith in Singaporean contract law, see C. Liew 'A Leap of Good Faith in Singapore Contract Law', *Singapore Journal of Legal Studies* [2012], 416.

59 *Chua Choon Cheng* v. *Allgreen Properties Ltd* [2009] 3 SLR (R) 724 (CA), [83]: 'the common law does not recognize a principle of good faith, in the sense of fair dealing, to be of general application'.

60 *ARIEF (Singapore I) Pte Ltd* v. *NTUC Fairprice Co-Operative Ltd and Another Matter* [2015] SGHC 28 (Coomaraswamy J) [63]–[64], citing *Walford* v. *Miles*, as did the Court of Appeal in *Ng Giap Hon* v. *Westcomb Securities Pty Ltd* [2009] 3 SLR(R) 518, [55]. The decision and authority of *Walford* must itself be in some doubt after the United Kingdom Supreme Court decision in *British Telecommunications Plc*. An express clause requiring parties to act in good faith will be enforced: *HSBC International Trust Services* [2012] 4 SLR 738.

Red Book of Bristol. Inherent in the content of the book is the idea that merchants themselves should hear and resolve commercial disputes. A specialized commercial court, the Court of Pie Powder, was developed. The court was generally regarded as a success; it used streamlined procedures, and was presided over by expert merchant decision-makers. Decisions were based on standard commercial practice. A consequence of this was that the commercial law as applied in the common-law courts ossified to some extent, due to the small volume of cases in comparison with the specialized court. By the eighteenth century England's commercial activity had grown exponentially, but was hampered by its relatively underdeveloped set of commercial law principles. Lord Mansfield earned his place in British legal history for his resolve, and achievement, in reshaping English commercial law to make it more coherent with actual commercial practice. Indeed, there is evidence that he looked to civilian law systems in doing so. Writing of Lord Mansfield's contribution to English commercial law, legal historian Holdsworth notes:

> Few lawyers indeed recognized that the legal principles underlying these commercial customs could be learned only from the writings of the foreign *civilians* [emphasis added] ... but these works were not easy for a common lawyer to read, and so they remained unread. It was not until the common law obtained in Lord Mansfield a judge who was a master of this learning that the rules deducible from the many varied commercial customs which had come before the courts were formed into a coherent system, and completely incorporated with the common law.[61]

The problem of mismatch between commercial practice, and commercial law, had been identified, and steps taken to remedy it.

It may be trite to observe that those who ignore the lessons of history are condemned to repeat it, but the lesson from the above experience is considered particularly important in the current context. Specifically, if it is in fact true that contracts typically reflect established relations between parties, rather than one-off, discrete transactions, it does seem anomalous to treat parties as rational utility maximizers who have low levels of trust between one another, and whose behaviour must be strictly curtailed and regulated by written terms. When the parties in the vast majority of cases resolve disputes themselves, it seems incongruous to assume an adversarial, I-win-you-lose situation.[62] And if

61 Vol. 5 *A History of English Law* (1924) 147.

62 D. Pliener 'Are English Courts Still Hostile to a Doctrine of Good Faith?', *Journal of International Banking and Financial Law* 1 (2017), 19: 'the Darwinian struggle of litigation does not reflect commercial reality, where businesses often recognise that co-operation and reciprocity are the underlying, if often unexpressed, drivers of the contract'.

contracts are frequently entered into between parties of different bargaining power, it seems inconsistent to apply contract law rules to them that assume they have relatively equal bargaining power. Lord Steyn reflected on this more broadly:

> A theme that runs through our law of contract is that the reasonable expectations of honest men must be protected. It is not a rule or principle of law. It is the objective which has been and still is the principal moulding force of our law of contract . . . if the prima facie solution to a problem runs counter to the reasonable expectations of honest men, this criterion sometimes requires a rigorous examination of the problem to ascertain whether the law does indeed compel demonstrable unfairness.[63]

Now, the limitations of coming up with a set of contracting principles that are to apply to a vast array of contract types are readily conceded. It is conceded that not all contracts are relational in nature; some are easier to discern as 'relational', for example an employment contract, or an agency contract. And not all parties will act in a trustworthy manner; some will act in an adversarial manner. However, the law must make a choice as to the set of assumptions it uses to formulate its rules. We know that the assumptions will sometimes be incorrect in a given case; however, we understand the imperative for the development of a set of legal rules and principles governing contracts in general. We also know that rules can be self-perpetuating, in the sense that by their assumptions, they can encourage behaviour that mirrors such assumptions. Given the empirical evidence suggesting that on most occasions parties adopt a relational stance to others, and given the low number of contractual disputes that in fact end in litigation, it seems preferable to make the relational contract assumption. As indicated above, notions of good faith are entirely consistent with the relational contract approach, and quite at odds with the adversarial, traditional common-law approach. And good faith reduces the transaction costs associated with contracting,[64] something to which any society should aspire.

63 *First Energy (UK) Ltd* v. *Hungarian International Bank Ltd* [1993] 2 Lloyd's Rep 194 (CA); Lord Steyn 'Contract Law: Fulfilling the Reasonable Expectations of Honest Men', *Law Quarterly Review* 113 (1997), 433; similarly Lord Devlin observed that 'an economic system which did not include as part of itself . . . machinery for settling commercial differences in accordance with the idea of commercial men would be bad for trade'; J. Allsop 'Good Faith and Australian Contract Law: A Practical Issue and a Question of Theory and Principle', *Australian Law Journal* 85 (2011), 341, 342: 'commercial law is, or to a significant degree should be, the reflection of society's facilitation, not hindrance, of commercial endeavour'.

64 'A world saturated with bad faith is very costly': L. T. Garvin 'Adequate Assurance of Forbearance of Risk, Duress and Cognition', *University of Colorado Law Review* 69 (1998), 71, 120; 'promoting trust and cooperation is an extremely effective way of fostering efficiency':

VI THE PRECISE MEANING OF GOOD FAITH

One of the vexed issues that any jurisdiction recognizing the doctrine of good faith would need to deal with is its precise meaning. And indeed criticism of the doctrine of good faith often revolves around the fact its meaning is said to be imprecise, leading to uncertainty.[65] Of course, business people should legitimately expect that the commercial law will provide as much certainty as possible. At the risk of simplification, the key bone of contention in this debate is between those who would confine good faith to notions of honesty, however defined, and those who would include within in some kind of concept of 'reasonableness' or similar. This confusion may be traced to the very origins of the doctrine. Some say that, at its origin, the doctrine essentially referred to notions of reasonableness, but that as its reach expanded to questions of formation of contract, rather than just performance, some sought to limit its meaning to something like honesty.

This historical difference may explain the otherwise anomalous disparity that appears in the Uniform Commercial Code. Article 1–201 of the Code appears to define good faith in terms of honesty, whilst Article 2–103(1)(b) of the same Code appears to include within it concepts of reasonableness. This confusion also appears, with respect, in the landmark decision of the Supreme Court of Canada in *Bhasin* v. *Hrynew*.[66] Cromwell J in that case delivered the decision of the court. Confusion arises because one passage seems to confine good faith to honesty:

> The key question is ... whether we ought to create a new common law duty under the broad umbrella of the organising principle of good faith performance of contracts. In my view, we should ... there is a general duty of honesty in contractual performance. This means simply that parties must not lie or otherwise knowingly mislead each other.[67]

Duke (n. 13), 182, 194: 'promoting trust and cooperation is an extremely effective way of fostering efficiency'; A. Johnson 'Correctly Interpreting Long Term Leases Pursuant to Modern Contract Law: Towards a Theory of Relational Leases', *Virginia Law Review* 74 (1988), 751, 754.

65 Lord Justice Staughton 'Good Faith and Fairness in Commercial Contract Law', *Journal of Contract Law* 7 (1994), 193, 194; M. Bridge 'Does Anglo-Canadian Contract Law Need a Doctrine of Good Faith?', *Canadian Business Law Journal* 9 (1984), 385, 412, dismissing good faith as 'an imperfect translation of an ethical standard into legal (rules) ... its appropriate home is the University where it can (stimulate debate and scholarship) without wreaking practical mischief', both cited in R. Hui 'The Doctrine of Good Faith in Contract: Greater Acknowledgement in Hong Kong? A Comparative Study', *City University of Hong Kong Law Review* 5 (2015), 85, 90.

66 [2014] 3 SCR 494.

67 [72]–[73].

However, in the same judgment the following statement appears in relation to the 'organising principle' of good faith:

> [T]hat organising principle is simply that parties generally must perform their contractual duties honestly and reasonably and not capriciously or arbitrarily.[68]

So, with respect, any judgment, legislation, code or restatement which relates to good faith must, as a priority, be clear on what is meant by the concept.

Having said that, there exists a range of literature on this issue, in terms of academic statement and case law. Most of it tends to suggest that good faith should be defined in way that includes concepts of reasonableness. For instance, the work of Summers:

> What about honesty? Is not acting in good faith equivalent to acting honestly? Numerous judges appear to have thought so, but this is wrong unless, of course, the definition of honesty is stretched beyond recognition. Honesty only rules out dishonesty in its various forms. But good faith, as used by many judges, excludes numerous forms of contractual bad faith besides dishonesty. For one thing, dishonesty is necessarily immoral, but in the eyes of many judges contractual bad faith is not necessarily immoral at all. A party may, for example, abuse his bargaining power, undercut the other party's efforts to perform, or act capriciously without having the guilty mind that would make his actions immoral – indeed, a party might even think this conduct is in the other party's own best interests. And despite this purity of mind, many judges could be counted on to say that such conduct conflicts with requirements of contractual good faith. As one judge stated, good faith in law is not to be measured always by a man's own standard of right, but by that which it has adopted and prescribed as a standard for the observation of all men in their dealings with each other.[69]

Notions of good faith as including reasonableness also appear in numerous other academic works,[70] including a scholarly article by a former

68 [63]; at [69] there is a reference to 'honesty and reasonableness'.

69 R. Summers 'Good Faith in General Contract Law and the Sales Provisions of the Uniform Commercial Code', *Virginia Law Review* 54 (1968), 195, 204.

70 Corcoran '(n. 20), 3: 'it is the idea of the good that focuses any analysis of good faith not only on questions of honesty in fact, but on motivation, integrity and fairness. Modern articulations using honesty in fact as a synonym for good faith miss part of the richness of the concept'; Pound(n. 18) 414: 'the parties were bound to perform what could be required fairly and reasonably under the circumstances of the case'.

Australian Chief Justice[71] and a former judicial member of the House of Lords.[72] Notions of good faith as including reasonableness appear in the judgment of Kiefel J (as she then was) in *Barker*,[73] and in Australian lower court decisions.[74] Notions of reasonableness appear in the United States case law, and in some of the British decisions that have accepted good faith.[75] They also appear in a recent decision of the Singaporean Court of Appeal.[76]

Reasonableness does not usually suggest that a fiduciary duty is owed. In other words, a requirement that a contracting party act reasonably to the other contracting party does not require them to act in the best interests of the other party or to subjugate their own interests to those of the other party. In that light, existing precedents to the effect that fiduciary obligations generally do not attach to parties in a commercial relationship[77] are not implicated by any acceptance of the doctrine of good faith as embracing reasonableness.

[71] Sir Anthony Mason 'Contract, Good Faith and Equitable Standards in Fair Dealing', *Law Quarterly Review* 116 (2000), 66, 69; see also Chief Justice of the Federal Court J. Allsop 'Good Faith and Australian Contract Law: A Practical Issue and a Question of Theory and Principle', *Australian Law Journal* 85 (2011), 341, 346: 'good faith is an expression that includes honesty, but goes beyond it'.

[72] Lord Steyn (n. 63), 433, 438 where he defined good faith to include: 'the observance of reasonable commercial standards of fair dealing in the conclusion and performance of the transaction concerned'.

[73] (2014) 253 CLR 169, 213: 'fairness in dealings as between contracting parties may be understood as an aspect of a duty of good faith, which has been accepted in other legal systems, and is wider than that of honesty'.

[74] *Cordon Investments Pty Ltd* v. *Lesdor Properties Pty Ltd* [2012] NSWCA 184, [145] and [167] (Bathurst CJ, Macfarlan JA and Meagher JA agreeing); *Silverbrook Research Pty Ltd* v. *Lindley* [2010] NSWCA 357; *Burger King Corp* v. *Hungry Jack's Pty Ltd* [2001] NSWCA 187; *Renard Constructions (ME) Pty Ltd* v. *Canada (Minister of Public Works)* (1992) 26 NSWLR 234, 258 (Priestley JA, with whom Handley JA agreed); *Esso Australia Resources Pty Ltd* v. *Southern Pacific Petroleum* [2005] VSCA 228; *Androvitsaneas* v. *Members First Broker Network Pty Ltd* [2013] VSCA 212.

[75] *Yam Seng Pty Ltd* v. *International Trade Corp Ltd* [2013] EWHC 111 (QB), [138] (Leggatt LJ), and [144]: 'the test of good faith is objective in the sense that it depends not on either party's perception of whether particular conduct is improper but on whether in the particular context the conduct would be regarded as commercially unacceptable'.

[76] *HSBC Institutional Trust Services (Singapore) Ltd (Trustee of Starhill Global Real Estate Investment Trust)* v. *Toshin Development Singapore Pty Ltd* [2012] SGCA 48, [45]: 'at its core, the concept of good faith encompasses the threshold subjective requirement of acting honestly, as well as the objective requirement of observing accepted commercial standards of fair dealing in the performance of the identified obligations. This encompasses a duty to act fairly, having regard to the legitimate interests of the other party.' (Rajah JA for the Court).

[77] *Hospital Products Ltd* v. *United States Surgical Corporation* (1984) 156 CLR 41.

It must be conceded that a limited number of commentators,[78] and judges,[79] have confined the meaning of good faith to notions of honesty, though in some cases their definition itself refers to unreasonableness. As Edelman J noted recently, confining good faith to mere honesty would largely deprive it of any substantive effect.[80]

I should briefly address the issue of whether good faith should be seen as an implied term, a question of construction, or an assumption or expectation underlying contracts. Given this issue is not central to the theme of transplants, it will be dealt with relatively briefly here. In essence, there are significant difficulties in asserting that good faith should be considered to be an implied term, whether in fact or in law. The tests for whether a term should be implied in fact are notoriously extremely restrictive and difficult to satisfy,[81] and some argue they are themselves uncertain. Even the test for a term to be implied by law is one based on 'necessity', also very difficult to satisfy.[82] Even if it is satisfied, it applies only to certain classes of contract.

The suggestion is sometimes made that good faith might be seen as being part of a contract through a process of construction of the contract. Sometimes, it is suggested that the implication of terms is really just an

78 J. Carter and E. Peden 'Good Faith in Australian Contract Law', *Journal of Contract Law* 19 (2003) 155, 157 (though their definition of honesty is said to exclude actions that no reasonable person would think unreasonable); E. Peden 'When Common Law Trumps Equity: The Rise of Good Faith and Reasonableness and the Demise of Unconscionability', *Journal of Contract Law* 21 (2005), 226, 236: 'to equate an obligation of reasonableness and one of good faith is misconceived'; J. Carter and A. Stewart 'Interpretation, Good Faith and the True Meaning of Contracts: The *Royal Botanic* Decision', *Journal of Contract Law* 18 (2002), 182, 192; J. Carter and W. Courtney 'Good Faith in Contracts: Is There an Implied Promise to Act Honestly?', *Cambridge Law Journal* 75 (2016), 608; R. Hooley 'Controlling Contractual Discretion', *Cambridge Law Journal* 72 (1) (2013), 65, 74: 'good faith refers to a subjective state of mind generally characterised by honesty'.

79 *United Group Rail Services Ltd* v. *Rail Corporation* (NSW) [2009] NSWCA 177; *Strzelecki Holdings Pty Ltd* v. *Cable Sands Pty Ltd* [2010] WASCA 222; *Dura (Australia) Constructions Pty Ltd* v. *Hue Boutique Living Pty Ltd* (No. 3) [2012] VSC 99, [422].

80 *Mineralogy Pty Ltd* v. *Sino Iron* (No. 6) [2015] FCA 825, [1008].

81 *BP Refinery (Westernport) Pty Ltd* v. *Shire of Hastings* (1977) 180 CLR 266, 282–3 (Lord Simons) (Privy Council); *Codelfa Constructions Pty Ltd* v. *State Rail Authority of NSW* (1982) 149 CLR 337, 347 (Mason J) and 405–6 (Brennan J) where the Court stated five requirements for the implication of a term by fact: (a) must be reasonable and equitable; (b) must be necessary to give business efficacy to the contract, so no term will be implied if the contract is effective without it; (c) must be so obvious it goes without saying; (d) must be capable of clear expression; and (e) must not contradict any express term of the contract. In *Yam Seng Pte Ltd* v. *International Trade Corp Ltd* [2013] EWHC 111, Leggatt J spoke of good faith as a doctrine implied by fact: [131].

82 *Byrne* v. *Australian Airlines Ltd* (1995) 185 CLR 410, 450 (McHugh and Gummow JJ).

exercise in construction.[83] However, in some of the cases, it is quite clear that the parties did not expressly include a good faith doctrine. With respect, it really does not matter how many times the contract is read, it still will not easily yield an interpretation that accords with good faith. But at a deeper level, to so search may be to misinterpret what good faith is, in any event. Former Chief Justice of the Australian High Court Murray Gleeson stated that:

> For a number of reasons, some to do with the work of legislatures, some to do with judicial lawmaking, and some to do with the temper and spirit of the times, we can no longer say that, in all but exceptional cases, the rights and liabilities of parties to a written contract can be discovered by reading the contract.[84]

Perhaps a better way of viewing good faith is that it is a general presumption or expectation that underlies the contract. It reflects the parties' general expectations of how the other will behave during the life of the contract. I interpret the doctrine as usually being inherent in the notion of a contract. Thus conceived, it is not necessary to 'imply' it; nor is it necessary to try to discern it from the actual terms used. It is inherently there, reflective of general norms of behaviour that command societal acceptance, as Leggatt J put it in *Yam Seng*.[85] Chief Justice of the Australian Federal Court Allsop CJ refers to it as an 'informing principle, expectation or maxim' of the common law,[86] that parties are assumed to act in accord with good faith. It is close to how the Supreme Court of Canada conceived of the doctrine in *Bhasin*.[87] In short, the doctrine should not be tied into a discussion of implied terms; rather, it should be seen as inherent in contracts, reflecting parties' reasonable expectations. Now, on this approach, the parties would be free to contract out of a general obligation of good faith. Clearly, parties could not have a reasonable expectation that the other will act in good faith, if the contract clearly specified that such should not be assumed. It is expected that such cases would be very rare. Parties to such a contract would be on notice of the possible behaviour of the other, and price their contract risk accordingly.

83 *Attorney-General of Belize* v. *Belize Telecom Ltd* [2009] UKPC 10, [19] (Lord Hoffmann, for the Court); this approach has been praised (Richard Hooley 'Implied Terms after Belize Telecom', *Cambridge Law Journal* 73 (2) (2014), 313) and criticized (W. Courtney and J. Carter 'Implied Terms: What is the Role of Construction?', *Journal of Contract Law* 31 (2014), 151).

84 'Individualised Justice – The Holy Grail', *Australian Law Journal* 69 (1995), 421, 428.

85 *Yam Seng Pty Ltd* v. *International Finance Trade Corp* [2013] EWHC 111, [134].

86 'Good Faith and Australian Contract Law: A Practical Issue and a Question of Theory and Principle', *Australian Law Journal* 85 (2011), 341, 357.

87 The Supreme Court did not refer or rely on notions of implied terms in its discussion of good faith, preferring to cast it in terms of an 'organising principle' of contract law, reflecting what commercial parties could reasonably expect of the other: [60] (Cromwell J, for the Court).

VII CONCLUSION – THE INCOMPLETE TRANSPLANT

From its genesis in Roman law, good faith has been fully embraced in civil law legal systems around the world, in international contracting conventions and standards, and in the American commercial law. However, its transplantation into other common-law countries and jurisdictions has been piecemeal and tentative. The doyen of commercial law Lord Mansfield hailed its arrival and acceptance in British commercial law, but the common law seemed to 'reject' the transplant during the period of nineteenth century individualism and freedom of contract. It has been very reluctant to try again. However, some brave individual justices have consistently advocated for it. It seemed to have been accepted by the United Kingdom Supreme Court in *Telefonica*, but the terse way in which the judgment seemed to accept good faith, at least as applied to contractual discretion, did not bode well for its acceptance as a general principle in United Kingdom commercial law. The result has been ongoing uncertainty in United Kingdom law, with some of the courts seemingly intent on the 'rejection' path, and others apparently sympathetic to the doctrine. This confusion has subsequently itself been transplanted to Asian common-law systems which traditionally looked to the United Kingdom for guidance, in particular Singapore and Hong Kong. In Australia too the position is one of uncertainty – in the medical vernacular, it depends which doctor you speak to, as to whether good faith has been transplanted into Australian law. And the most senior court continues to look for ways to get out of deciding whether to operate or not, but sometimes whispers it may be prepared to do so. Commendably, the Canadian Supreme Court has boldly stepped into the operating theatre, and though, with respect, some mistakes may have been made during surgery, the transplant was completed successfully.

It has been argued that the common law should embrace good faith. Such a doctrine is 'compatible' with the common law. It fits well with the relational nature of most contracts, and with the idea that contracts should reflect ordinary commercial practice, and the reasonable expectations of commercial parties. Common-law systems already embrace and apply principles similar in nature to good faith, though they may call them something else. Regarding its meaning, it has been argued to mean something like reasonableness. It is something more than honesty. It should be seen as a reasonable assumption that parties make when contracting, rather than an implied term. The law of insurance readily applies a doctrine of good faith. In such circumstances, it is difficult to see why the transplant should continue to be rejected, resisted or doubted by common-law legal systems. Good faith is 'compatible' with the general corpus of the law of common-law jurisdictions. It should not be rejected any more.

VIII BIBLIOGRAPHY

Allsop J., 'Good Faith and Australian Contract Law: A Practical Issue and a Question of Theory and Principle', *Australian Law Journal* 85 (2011),341.

American Law Institute *Restatement of the Law, Second (Contracts)* 1979.

Arrighetti, A, Bachmann, R. and Deakin, S., 'Contract Law, Social Norms and Inter-Firm Co-Operation', *Cambridge Journal of Economics* 21 (1997),171.

Beale H. and Dugdale, T., 'Contracts between Businessmen: Planning and the Use of Contractual Remedies', *British Journal of Law and Society* 2 (1975), 45.

Bridge M., 'Does Anglo-Canadian Contract Law Need a Doctrine of Good Faith?', *Canadian Business Law Journal* 9 (1984), 385.

Carter J. and Peden, E., 'Good Faith in Australian Contract Law', *Journal of Contract Law* 19 (2003), 155.

Carter J. and Stewart, A., 'Interpretation, Good Faith and the True Meaning of Contracts: The *Royal Botanic* Decision', *Journal of Contract Law* 18 (2002), 182.

Corcoran S., 'Good Faith as a Principle of Interpretation: What Is the Positive Content of Good Faith?', *Australian Bar Review* 26 (2012), 3.

Courtney W. and Carter, J., 'Implied Terms: What Is the Role of Construction?', *Journal of Contract Law* 31 (2014), 151.

Duke A., 'A Universal Duty of Good Faith: An Economic Perspective', *Monash University Law Review* 33 (2007), 182.

Farnsworth A., 'Good Faith Performance and Commercial Reasonableness under the Uniform Commercial Code', *University of Chicago Law Review* 30 (1963), 666.

Finn P., 'Commerce, the Common Law and Morality', *Melbourne University Law Review* 17 (1989), 87.

Garvin L., 'Adequate Assurance of Forbearance of Risk, Duress and Cognition', *University of Colorado Law Review* 69 (1998), 71.

Girard P., 'Good Faith in Contract Performance: Principle or Placebo?', *Supreme Court Law Review* 5 (1983), 309.

Gleeson M., 'Individualised Justice: The Holy Grail', *Australian Law Journal* 69 (1995), 421.

Holdsworth W., *A History of English Law* (Methuen, 1922).

Hooley R., 'Controlling Contractual Discretion', *Cambridge Law Journal* 72 (1) (2013), 65.

Hui R., 'The Doctrine of Good Faith in Contract: Greater Acknowledgement in Hong Kong? A Comparative Study', *City University of Hong Kong Law Review* 5 (2015), 85.

Johnson A., 'Correctly Interpreting Long-Term Leases Pursuant to Modern Contract Law: Toward a Theory of Relational Leases', *Virginia Law Review* 74 (1988), 731.

Kuehne G., 'Implied Obligations of Good Faith and Reasonableness in the Performance of Contracts: Old Wine in New Bottles?', *University of Western Australia Law Review* 33 (2006), 63.

Lawson F. H., *A Common Lawyer Looks at the Civil Law* (University of Michigan, 1955).

Leonard C., 'A Legal Chameleon: An Examination of the Doctrine of Good Faith in Chines and American Contract Law, *Connecticut Journal of International Law* 25 (2010), 305.

Liew C., 'A Leap of Good Faith in Singapore Contract Law', *Singapore Journal of Legal Studies* [2012], 416.
Macneil I., 'Contracts: Adjustments of Long-Term Economic Relations under a Classical, Neoclassical and Relational Contract Law', *Northwestern University Law Review* 72 (1978), 854.
Macneil I., 'Relational Contract: What We Do and Do Not Know', *Wisconsin Law Review* (1985), 483.
Mason A., 'Contract, Good Faith and Equitable Standards in Fair Dealing', *Law Quarterly Review* 116 (2000), 66.
Nicholas B., *An Introduction to Roman Law* (Clarendon Press, 1975).
Peden E., 'The Meaning of Contractual Good Faith', *Australian Bar Review* 22 (2002), 235.
Peden E., 'When Common Law Trumps Equity: The Rise of Good Faith and Reasonableness and the Demise of Unconscionability', *Journal of Contract Law* 21 (2005), 226.
Pliener D., 'Are English Courts Still Hostile to a Doctrine of Good Faith?', *Journal of International Banking and Financial Law* 1 (2017), 19.
Pollock F. and Maitland, F., *The History of English Law* (Cambridge University Press, 1895).
Pound R., *Jurisprudence* (Harvard University Press, 1943).
Powers P., 'Defining the Undefinable: Good Faith and the United Nations Convention on Contracts for the International Sale of Goods', *Journal of Law and Commerce* 18 (1999), 349.
Scott S. P., *The Civil Law: Translations of Roman Text* (AMS Press, 1973).
Staughton C., 'Good Faith and Fairness in Commercial Contract Law', *Journal of Contract Law* 7 (1994), 193.
Steyn J., 'Role of Good Faith and Fair Dealing in Contract Law: A Hair-Shirt Philosophy', *Denning Law Journal* 6 (1991), 131.
Steyn J., 'Contract Law: Fulfilling the Reasonable Expectations of Honest Men', *Law Quarterly Review* 113 (1997), 433.
Summers R., 'Good Faith in General Contract Law and the Sales Provisions of the Uniform Commercial Code', *Virginia Law Review* 54 (1968), 195.
Summers R., 'The General Duty of Good Faith – Its Recognition and Conceptualisation', *Cornell Law Review* 67 (1982),810.
Tetley W., 'Good Faith in Contract, Particularly in the Contracts of Arbitration and Chartering', *Journal of Maritime Law and Commerce* 36 (2004), 561.
Trakman L., 'The Binding Force of Agreements to Negotiate in Good Faith', *Cambridge Law Journal* 73 (2014), 598.
Van Alstine M., 'Of Textualism, Party Autonomy and Good Faith', *William and Mary Law Review* 40 (1999), 1223.
Wang G., 'The New Contract Law of China', *Journal of Contract Law* 3 (2000), 242.
Wang L. and Xu, C., 'Fundamental Principles of China's Contract Law', *Columbian Journal of Asian Law* 13 (1999), 1.
Zimmermann R., *The Law of Obligations: Roman Foundations of the Civilian Tradition* (Clarendon Press, 1990).

6

How Long Is Too Long to Determine the Success of a Legal Transplant? International Doctrines and Contract Law in Oceania

Jessica Viven-Wilksch[1]

I INTRODUCTION

Legal transplants have captivated comparative scholars for more than four decades. Their definition,[2] their relevance,[3] their possible occurrence,[4] and their danger[5] have been analyzed. Legal transplants do exist and have been occurring for centuries.[6] What the debate has highlighted over time is the fact that transplanting a legal doctrine, an institution, or a structure is a 'dynamic process'.[7] Contrary to Watson's assertion that transplanting is socially easy,[8]

[1] The author would like to thank Ms Ailie Shaw for her work as a research assistant during the early stages of this chapter.

[2] A. Watson, *Legal Transplants: An Approach to Comparative Law* (University of Georgia Press, 1974).

[3] P. Legrand, 'The Impossibility of Legal Transplants', *Maastricht Journal of European and Comparative Law* 4 (1997), 111.

[4] For instance, P. M. Nichols, 'The Viability of Transplanted Law: Kazakhstani Reception of a Transplanted Foreign Investment Code', *University of Pennsylvania Journal of International Economic Law* 18 (4) (1997), 1235; H. Kanda and C. J. Milhaupt, 'Re-Examining Legal Transplants: The Director's Fiduciary Duty in Japanese Corporate Law', *American Journal of Comparative Law* 51 (4) (2003), 887; M. Chen-Wishart, 'Legal Transplant and Undue Influence: Lost in Translation or a Working Misunderstanding?', *International and Comparative Law Quarterly* 62 (1) (2013), 1; A. Alshorbagy, 'On the Failure of a Legal Transplant: The Case of Egyptian Takeover Law', *Indiana International and Comparative Law Review* 22 (2) (2012), 237.

[5] G. Teubner, 'Legal Irritants: Good Faith in British Law or How Unifying Law Ends Up in New Divergences', *Modern Law Review* 61 (1998), 11; H. Cooke Gutteridge, *Comparative Law: An Introduction to the Comparative Method of Legal Study and Research* (Cambridge University Press, 1949) 25.

[6] As Watson famously stated, referring to the Code of Hammurabi. Watson (n. 2) 23.

[7] J. Fedkte, 'Legal Transplants' in J. S. Smits (ed.), *Elgar Encyclopedia of Comparative Law* (Elgar, 2006) 434, 435.

[8] Watson (n. 2) 695.

the dynamic nature of the transplant process shows how complex the process can really be.[9] Indeed it can take years for a legal system to identify a gap, for legal reform to be discussed, and for a legal system with a relevant 'gap filler' to be identified. This is only the start of a process that will lead to legal reform as a notion is merged with a legal system's existing laws. And then the waiting game begins. The focus of this chapter is on this waiting period: how long is long enough to determine the success of a legal transplant.

Examples will be drawn from international commercial law and its impact on Australian contract law based on current debates as well as developments in this legal field. A caveat must be given. This chapter will focus on the case law provided by the courts. The author recognizes the importance of arbitral decisions in practice and for businesses, but the aim of the chapter is to see what domestic law looks like when a doctrine from an international body of law is used by two branches of the state: the judiciary and the legislature. Beyond this, issues of interpretation and enforcement of the law will be considered, using the Convention on Contracts for the International Sale of Goods[10] (hereafter the Convention) as the main case study due to its implementation in national law.

The chapter will start with a snapshot of the theories on legal transplants to ground its discussion of time. Indeed, the next part will present the reasons why timing is relevant. The chapter will then present a quick chronological history of the UNIDROIT Principles of International Commercial Contracts and the Convention on Contracts for the International Sale of Goods to provide context to the examples given in the last part of the chapter, which will highlight the challenges the Australian legal system has had in transplanting doctrines into contract law. While this chapter cannot be the forum for a macro-comparative approach,[11] examples will also be drawn from neighbouring jurisdictions to provide points of difference. The aim of the chapter is to explain why time is a relevant criterion, too often overlooked in the legal transplant debate, why it matters and how the lack of use of the Principles and the Convention does not mean the surgery has failed and these transplants have been rejected. However, some action must be taken to avoid such a failure and rejection.

9 Fedtke (n.7) 435.

10 Convention on Contracts for the International Sale of Goods (adopted 11 April 1980, entered into force 1 January 1988) 1489 UNTS 3 (CISG).

11 'Be modest and practical' stated Harding. Andrew Harding, 'The Legal Transplants Debate: Getting beyond the Impasse', Chapter 1 in this Volume, 1, 3.

II THEORIES AND PUSHING THE METAPHOR; THE ORGANIC NATURE OF THE TRANSPLANT

Since Alan Watson coined the expression in the 1970s,[12] the notion of legal transplant has been used to define the process according to which countries use notions from another legal system to fill a gap in and improve their own legal system. Metaphors are part of the scholarly discussion on legal transplants. Harding's introductory chapter to this collection makes a reference to gardening.[13] This is echoed by Teubner and the 'organismic' nature of the transplant.[14] He continues by saying that transplants 'need cultivation and implantation'.[15] But the origins of the expression are not found in gardening but in medicine.[16] The use of the word transplant can be traced back to the fact that at the time of Watson's writing progress in medical organ transplants was occurring, and this pushed some scholars to use the metaphor.[17] Of course a legal transplant is not truly the same as a surgical transplant since there is no displacement of the doctrine in the donor country. Still, the legal surgery imagery has merit for the following reasons.

Firstly, organ transplants require an organ, and donor and recipient bodies. Similarly, legal transplants require a legal doctrine, structure, or institution to be transplanted, a legal system that already uses it and a receiving legal system. Secondly, the two bodies are matched according to particular criteria to maximize the chances of success of the transplant. The donor and receiving legal systems must be matched according to the similarities of their branches of law, structure and values. Thirdly, the surgery is complex and the role of the surgeon is important. In the case of a legal transplant, the institution(s) in charge of the surgery is important. Fourthly, the organ transplant will fill a need in the receiving body. The legal transplant will also be used to fill a gap in and/or improve a legal system. Fifthly, following the surgery, medicine is used to prevent rejection and help the receiving body to recover. Following the legal surgery, a need for post-surgery care will be demonstrated through education to ensure the transplant does not remain law only in the books. One must note that post-surgery care can also create problems and the possibility of further difficulties for the recovering body. The legal transplant

12 Watson (n. 2).

13 Harding (n. 11) 11.

14 Teubner (n. 5) 12.

15 Ibid.

16 Ibid., 13.

17 Indeed Alan Watson was not the first or only one. See J. W. Cairns, 'Watson, Walton and the History of Legal Transplants', *Georgia Journal of International and Comparative Law* 41 (3) (2013), 637, 643.

can be transplanted with success, become a legal irritant[18] that disrupts the balance of the legal body of rules in the receiving country, or be rejected by that body. This chapter will provide examples that focus on the assessment of post-surgery care in Australian contract law for both domestic and international commercial transactions.

Some Commonalities: A Focus on Time

In legal transplants, like organ transplants, timing is crucial. The time of the legal surgery and the help given to the legal transplant to support its integration and to ensure the receiving body of laws survives the legal surgery do matter. The receiving body has to integrate the newly acquired legal organ and this is what will truly determine whether the surgery is ultimately successful. This chapter will illustrate this metaphor further through the example of international commercial law and its impact on the Australian legal system. However, the notion of time as a determinant of the success of legal transplants is not subject or jurisdiction specific. In fact, the question of how long we should wait to determine if a legal system has successfully accommodated concepts of foreign legal systems is universal.

As the comparison between organ transplants and legal transplants shows, time is a very relevant factor in the planning of the surgery, its occurrence and post-surgical care. Indeed, it takes time to identify the problem in a domestic legal system and the possible compatible donor legal system whose legal institution could be transplanted. The medical surgery is complex, and it can take years to see if the new organ is truly accepted and integrated by the body. The same applies to the legal surgery. Furthermore, the actual timing of the surgery is extremely important to ensure not only the readiness of the receiving body, the speed of the recovery, and ultimately the success of the surgery. The actual process of the transplant, the merger with other laws in the body of the receiving system, and the post-surgery monitoring will highlight, once again, that time is an important factor. But what it is that is being monitored? Is it legal change? Under which form? As Harding states:

> Do we judge by the objectives of those promoting the legal change? If so, over what period of time? What if, as is typical, a legal change is largely accepted, but fails in the short-to-medium term to deliver to a substantial extent what was desired, and leads to other problems which are being addressed by further proposals for legal change? Or what if it appears to work in the sense of being

[18] Teubner (n. 5).

> complied with, but at much greater economic, social or political cost than was anticipated?[19]

Through the example of international commercial law and its transplant into Australia, this chapter will demonstrate the complexity of the operation, and the practical challenges that are encountered when seeking legal change. One element however seems relatively easy to identify: the surgery itself. The timing of the surgery of a legal transplant depends on the notion, legal idea or doctrine that is transplanted. For the Convention on Contracts for the International Sale of Goods, that will be its ratification and entry into force as well as its statutory recognition in Australian domestic law. For the UNIDROIT Principles of International Commercial Contracts, it will be their use by businesses, courts and legislatures. But first, let us look at these chosen instruments.

III INTERNATIONAL LAW AS A DONOR 'SYSTEM': EXAMPLES IN CONTRACT LAW IN SOUTH EAST ASIA AND OCEANIA WITH A FOCUS ON AUSTRALIA

International Law as a Donor System

Harding has highlighted the importance of international law as a source of legal reform, and of the transplantation of legal ideas into domestic law.[20] This is because one of the purposes of legal transplants is to reform and develop a legal system.[21] In the context of this chapter, the donor system is international commercial law represented not as a legal system but as a 'body of texts'.[22] The focus will be on two instruments, which are also the transplants: the Convention and the Principles. The receiving country is Australia. The reason for the surgery is to answer the call to reform Australian contract law and harmonize domestic and international transactions. Developing and promoting international trade at the domestic level provides a safe legal environment in which such trade can increase and ultimately thrive. Global governance and the development of a transnational legal culture promote certain values

19 Harding (n. 11) 12.
20 Ibid., 7.
21 Ibid., 1.
22 There are examples of transplants from international law beyond commercial law. For instance, China has used the Hague Conference conventions in private international law to improve its domestic rules and transplant legal ideas such as the concept of habitual residence. For a review see, e.g., W. Chen and G. Goldstein, 'The Asian Principles of Private International Law: objectives, contents, structure and selected topics on choice of law', *Journal of Private International Law* 13 (2) (2017), 411.

and norms. From Adam Smith[23] to Ricardo,[24] the concepts of international exchange and globalization have transformed economies and their regulation.[25] Indeed, following the specialization of countries in the production of particular goods and services, companies across the world have exported goods to respond to the demand from external markets. This plethora of exchanges has led to the questioning of the laws applicable to them, and the proposed development of a harmonized law that would only apply to international trade.[26] Yet as we will see, legal pluralism prevails.[27] While this preserves individualized fit and promotes regulatory competition, it has come at the expense of 'predictability, clear guidance, and the efficient settlement of a conflict' in international commercial law.[28]

Relevant to this situation is the type of transplant. Here we are dealing with global instruments instead of a donor legal *system* or jurisdiction. This does not mean that a transplant is impossible. In fact, it highlights the change in the legal environment and the adaptability of the notion of legal transplants. We must keep in mind that, to have any chance of success, a legal transplant must be voluntary, and not externally dictated.[29] The author argues that the need to reform contract law and the use of the Convention and the Principles demonstrate a certain willingness to draw new legal doctrines into the Australian contract law sphere. As we will see later, there is no clear time limit after which such a transplant can be deemed to be useless, but patience among some scholars is running thin.

IV THE CONVENTION ON CONTRACTS FOR THE INTERNATIONAL SALE OF GOODS

Today the Convention is considered the pinnacle of international sales law,[30] a discipline which has developed over time.[31] Through this international

23 A. Smith, *Wealth of Nations* (Strahan and Cadell, 1776).

24 D. Ricardo, *On the Principles of Political Economy and Taxation* (John Murray, 1817).

25 See, e.g., A.-M. Slaughter, *A New World Order* (Princeton University Press, 2005).

26 I. Schwenzer, 'Global Unification of Contract Law', *Uniform Law Review* 21 (2016), 60, 60.

27 E. O'Hara O'Connor, 'The Role of the CISG in Promoting Healthy Jurisdictional Competition for Contract Law', *Uniform Law Review* 21 (2016), 41, 44.

28 Ibid., 44.

29 J. M. Miller, 'A Typology of Legal Transplants: Using Sociology, Legal History and Argentine Examples to Explain the Transplant Process', *American Journal of Comparative Law* 51 (2003), 839.

30 L. DiMatteo, 'Global Challenges of International Sales Law' in L. DiMatteo (ed.), *International Sales Law: A Global Challenge* (Cambridge University Press, 2014) 725.

31 K. Sono, 'The Vienna Sales Convention: History and Perspective' in P. Sarcevic and P. Volken (eds.), *International Sale of Goods: Dubrovnik Lectures* (Oceana Publications, 1985) 1, 12.

convention, international commercial law is showing itself to be a very sophisticated *body* of law. The Convention was itself a long time in the making. Bringing uniformity to international contracts is not a new idea. Back in the 1920s, it was suggested that the law of the international sale of goods be unified.[32] Following an archaeological trail,[33] the spirit of the Convention can be found, in its infancy, in 1964 when a discussion on international instruments regulating the formation of contracts, and sales contracts in particular, occurred within the United Nations Commission on International Trade Law.[34] However, only nine states ratified the Convention Relating to a Uniform Law on the International Sale of Goods, which led to a rethinking of the instruments used for such harmonization. Later in the twentieth century, two instruments provided steps towards the uniformity of international commercial contract law: the Convention is one of them, the other is the Principles.

The structure of the Convention makes it truly a law for merchants. The Convention is the most important body of law governing international sales.[35] The characteristics of the Convention include simplicity, practicality and clarity.[36] The Convention came into force in 1988 and eighty-nine states have acceded to it.[37] In spite of notable absences among contracting parties,[38] 'still on the whole there can be no doubt that the CISG provides a most valuable and fairly innovative normative regime for international sales contracts'.[39] The purpose of the Convention is to provide a modern, uniform, and fair regime for contracts for the international sale of goods, and it has introduced certainty in commercial exchanges.[40] Today the Convention governs more than eighty per cent of international trade.[41] Consequently, it

32 I. Schwenzer (ed.), *Schlechtriem & Schwenzer: Commentary on the UN Convention on the International Sale of Goods (CISG)* 3rd edn (Oxford University Press, 2010) 1.

33 J. Honnold, *Uniform Law for International Sales under the 1980 United Nations Convention* (Wolters Kluwer, 1982) 37; O. Lando, 'CISG and its Followers: A Proposal to Adopt Some International Principles of Contract Law', *American Journal of Comparative Law* 53 (2005) 379, 379.

34 Honnold (n. 33) 37; Convention Relating to a Uniform Law on the International Sale of Goods (adopted 1 July 1964, entered into force 23 August 1972) 834 UNTS 169.

35 D. J. Smythe, 'Reasonable Standards for Contract Interpretation under the CISG', *Cardozo Journal of International and Comparative Law* 25 (2016), 1, 2.

36 Sono (n. 31) 7.

37 CISG status table www.uncitral.org/uncitral/en/uncitral_texts/sale_goods/1980CISG_status.html accessed 20 June 2018.

38 Such as the UK and India.

39 M. J. Bonell, 'The CISG, European Contract Law and the Development of a World Contract Law', *American Journal of Comparative Law* 56 (2008), 1, 4.

40 CISG preamble.

41 Schwenzer (n. 32) 1.

is considered *'the most successful and noteworthy result of unification of international contract law'*.[42] The Convention contains substantive rules that can apply to international contracts. It is a law-making treaty, a *traité-loi*.[43] For instance, according to the Convention, offer and acceptance are core requirements of a contract for the sale of goods.[44] The Convention therefore provides an alternative set of norms applicable to the international sale of goods in a commercial setting.[45]

The Convention was opened for signature in 1980. Australia ratified the Convention on 17 March 1988 and each Australian state and territory enacted uniform legislation.[46] Article 99 of the Convention required that, to enter into force, the Convention needed a minimum of ten instruments of ratification, acceptance, approval or accession. This happened on 1 January 1988. The Convention may consequently apply to commercial contracts for the international sale of goods. The Convention entered into force in Australia on 1 April 1989.

The Convention does not regulate the validity of a contract,[47] or the liability of the seller for personal injury.[48] Certain categories of contract are excluded from its scope, including the sale of goods bought for personal, family or household use, sales by auction or on execution or otherwise by authority of law; and sale of stocks, shares, investment securities, negotiable instruments or money.[49] It applies automatically in contracts regulating the international sale of goods, whether or not it is expressly adopted by the parties, and regardless of rules of private international law nominating the law of a contracting state as the law applicable to the contract.[50] However, parties can expressly exclude its

42 N. Hofmann, 'Interpretation Rules and Good Faith as Obstacles to the UK's Ratification of the CISG and to the Harmonization of Contract Law in Europe', *Pace International Law Review* 22 (2010), 145, 146.

43 P. Volken, 'The Vienna Sales Convention: Scope, Interpretation and Gap-Filling' in P. Sarcevic and P. Volken (eds.), *International Sale of Goods: Dubrovnik Lectures* (Oceana Publications, 1985) 19, 20.

44 CISG Art. 14, Art. 23.

45 O'Connor (n. 27) 53.

46 Sale of Goods (Vienna Convention) Act 1987 (ACT); Sale of Goods (Vienna Convention) Act 1986 (NSW); Sale of Goods (Vienna Convention) Act 1987 (NT); Sale of Goods (Vienna Convention) Act 1986 (Qld); Sale of Goods (Vienna Convention) Act 1986 (SA); Sale of Goods (Vienna Convention) Act 1987 (Tas); Sale of Goods (Vienna Convention) Act 1987 (Vic); Sale of Goods (Vienna Convention) Act 1986 (WA); Vienna Convention on the Law of Treaties (adopted 23 May 1969, entered into force 27 January 1980) 1155 UNTS 331.

47 CISG Art. 4.

48 CISG Art. 5.

49 CISG Art. 2 also includes sale of ships, vessels, hovercraft or aircraft; and of electricity. Bonell (n. 39).

50 CISG Art. 1.

application and have often done so,[51] limiting the case law available in the jurisdictions that have acceded to the Convention.[52]

V HISTORY OF THE PRINCIPLES

The International Institute for the Unification of Private Law, also called UNIDROIT, was created in 1926 as an auxiliary organ of the League of Nations. Since the collapse of the latter, it is now an independent organism. Australia, Brazil, Egypt, India, and France are some of the sixty-three member states of the organization, 'representing a variety of different legal, economic and political systems as well as different cultural backgrounds'.[53] Interestingly, in South East Asia, only Australia and Indonesia are members of this institution.

The Principles are part of the *lex mercatoria* and are not part of the 'hard' international sales law that includes the Convention. Yet, it is important to highlight certain aspects of the Principles since some argue that the Principles have become 'background law'.[54] Like the Convention, the Principles took time to be drafted. Indeed,

> It was as long ago as 1971 that the Governing Council decided to include this subject in the Work Programme of the Institute. A small Steering Committee, composed of Professors René David, Clive M. Schmitthoff and Tudor Popescu, representing the civil law, the common law and the socialist systems, was set up with the task of conducting preliminary inquiries into the feasibility of such a project.[55]

A working group was established in 1980, the year the Convention was opened for signature, to work on the Principles. As a consequence, the Principles were influenced by the Convention.[56] It is also an interesting example of the actors involved with the development of fairness in contractual dealings, be they national, supranational, or in this instance international.

51 CISG Art. 6.

52 L. Nottage, 'Who's Afraid of the Vienna Sales Convention (CISG)? A New Zealander's View from Australia and Japan', *Victoria University of Wellington Law Review* 36 (2005), 815, 817; see also J. F. Coyle, 'The Role of the CISG in US Contract Practice: An Empirical Study', *University of Pennsylvania Journal of International Law* 38 (2016), 195.

53 Details of the membership of UNIDROIT are available at: www.unidroit.org/about-unidroit/membership accessed 20 June 2018.

54 R. Michaels, 'The UNIDROIT Principles as Global Background Law', *Uniform Law Review* 19(4) (2014), 643.

55 UNIDROIT Principles of International Commercial Contracts 1994 (PICC) Introduction, viii.

56 Lando (n. 33) 381.

The 2016 Principles are the latest version of a document first published in 1994. Parties can specify that their contract is governed by the Principles, or the *lex mercatoria* more generally.[57] The Principles can also apply through the application of private international law rules if the parties have not chosen any law to regulate their agreement.[58] For the Principles to be applicable to the situation *ratione materiae*, the contract must be international, meaning involving different states or relating to international trade. The contract must also be between commercial parties as the Principles do not apply to consumer contracts.[59] The Principles present a definition of a legal agreement. They recognize its binding nature if it is validly entered into by two consenting parties.[60] Their mere agreement is sufficient.[61]

One advantage the Principles hold over the Convention is that they are not a treaty. This means that they can be more easily amended, as they were in 2004, 2010 and 2016. The concern to provide better guidance to parties in long-term international commercial contracts is not new. Indeed, it was brought to the attention of the working group in charge of amending the Principles in 2010. However, for lack of time, the relevant provisions were not analyzed and integrated into the revised Principles. This highlights the challenges for international law to meaningfully address quotidian situations faced by parties in international long-term ventures. The question is therefore whether these concerns could be better addressed. Prior to their fourth edition in 2016, the Principles only referred incidentally to long-term contracts. This was highlighted in a 2013 memorandum from the Secretariat in 2013 to the Governing Council.[62] The following year, acting upon a request from the Governing Council, the Secretariat prepared a new memorandum relating to more specific issues faced by parties in long-term contracts. This memorandum highlighted the need for the Principles to provide more fairness to parties in long-term contracts to ensure the establishment and success of new international commercial ventures. A working group was created to address these concerns and provide amendments

57 PICC 2016 preamble.

58 Ibid; see also *Rules of Arbitration of the International Chamber of Commerce* (1998) Art. 17(1); *Rules of the Arbitration Institute of the Stockholm Chamber of Commerce* Art. 24(1).

59 PICC 2016 preamble.

60 PICC 2016 Art. 2.1.1.

61 PICC 2016 Art. 3.1.2.

62 Memorandum prepared by the Secretariat, Item No. 4 on the agenda: International Commercial Contracts –

(b) Possible future work on long-term contracts' UNIDROIT 2013 – C.D. (92) 4(b)) www.unidroit.org/english/governments/councildocuments/2013session/cd92-04b-e.pdf accessed 24 July 2018.

to the Principles.[63] Proposed amendments addressed particular situations that parties in long-term international contracts can face. These included: the express agreement to negotiate in good faith; cooperation between the parties in long-term contracts; and termination due to irreparable breakdown of mutual trust. Amendments were submitted for adoption and adopted in May 2016.[64] The latest iteration of the Principles now reflects the specificities of long-term contracts.[65] This further echoes scholarly work, especially on the importance of so-called relational contracts and the need to ensure fairness throughout these dealings.[66] So, unlike the Convention, the Principles are still being refined as time goes by. In contrast to the Convention, the Principles have also acted as a restatement.[67] The success of the Principles is not determined by ratification by states but by use of the Principles by businesses.[68] However, as not many contracts are made publicly available, it can be difficult to determine the use and reliance on the Principles by Australian businesses and parties.

VI THE CONVENTION AND THE PRINCIPLES AS MODEL LAW

Model Laws: Explicit Statements in the Texts

Besides being used by parties as the law applicable to a contract,[69] the Convention can be used as a model law.[70] In fact,

63 Michael Joachim Bonell, 'The UNIDROIT Principles of International Commercial Contracts and Long-Term Contracts' (position paper prepared for the Working Group on Long-Term Contracts, Principles of International Commercial Contracts, First session, Rome, 19–23 January 2015) www.unidroit.org/english/documents/2014/study50/s-50-126-e.pdf accessed 16 July 2018.

64 UNIDROIT Secretariat, 'Report to Working Group on Long-Term Contracts Second Session' (Hamburg, 26–29 October 2015) see [43], [69], [19] respectively www.unidroit.org/english/documents/2016/study50/s-50-misc32-e.pdf accessed 16 July 2018.

65 Governing Council UNIDROIT 2016, '95th session CD (95) Misc 2 Summary of the Conclusions' (Rome, 18–20 May 2016) www.unidroit.org/meetings/governing-council/1986-95th-session-rome-18-20-may-2016 accessed 30 October 2016.

66 I. MacNeil, 'Relational Contract Theory: Challenges and Queries', *Northwestern University Law Review* 94 (3) (2000) 877; D. Robertson, 'Long-Term Relational Contracts and the UNIDROIT Principles of International Commercial Contracts', *Australian International Law Journal* 17 (2010), 185.

67 D. Oser, *The Unidroit Principles of International Commercial Contracts: A Governing Law?* (Brill, 2008) 11.

68 Ibid., 13.

69 For a discussion of the jurisdictions of Germany, France and the USA, see P. S. Berman, 'The Inevitable Legal Pluralism within Universal Harmonization Regimes: The Case of the CISG', *Uniform Law Review* 21 (2016), 23, 23.

70 For instance, in the EU see Directive of 25 May 1999 on certain aspects of the sale of consumer goods and associated guarantees – consumer sales 1999/441EC, 1999 OJ L 171 12 (EC): Art. 2 is almost identical to CISG Art. 35 and Art. 3 to CISG Arts. 36, 46, 49 and 50. However, this

> domestic law based on the Convention would be enriched by this body of thought and experience, and students and practitioners would gain wider horizons and opportunities by this contact with the world of international commerce.[71]

To allow this, international case law and scholarship are freely available on the Pace and UNILEX databases.[72] In fact, to ensure uniform interpretation of the Convention among the ratifying states, domestic institutions need to be able to access decisions of other countries.[73] Today, there are more than 3,152 Convention references in decisions from both the judiciary and arbitration.[74]

An explicit purpose of the Principles is to be used as a model by both national and international legislators.[75] The commentary in the preamble expressly recommends the use of the Principles as a means of interpreting and supplementing international uniform law instruments.[76] In 2000, the Court of Appeal of New Zealand did exactly that by stating that the Principles were a restatement of international commercial contract law which 'refines and expands the principles' contained in the Convention.[77] The Principles could be used to interpret and supplement domestic law. Australian cases have used them to discuss the duty of good faith in contract, albeit in *obiter*.[78] Finally, the preamble states that 'the Principles may be particularly useful to those countries which lack a developed body of legal rules relating to contracts and which intend to update their law, at least with respect to foreign economic relationships, to current international standards'.[79] This has been the case in China[80] and also the USA.[81]

directive goes further than the CISG by imposing responsibility on the seller for the quality and performance of the goods.

71 Honnold (n. 33) 15.

72 For instance, UNILEX is available at: www.unilex.info/; and CISG Pace at http://iicl.law.pace.edu/cisg/cisg.

73 Volken (n. 43) 41.

74 See PACE CISG database www.cisg.law.pace.edu/cisg/text/casecit.html accessed 21 June 2018.

75 PICC 2016 preamble.

76 PICC 2016 preamble, commentary [5].

77 *Yoshimoto* v. *Canterbury Golf International Ltd* [2000] NZCA 350 [89].

78 *Alcatel Australia Ltd* v. *Scarcella* (1998) 44 NSWLR 349, 365; *Hughes Aircraft Systems International* v. *Airservices Australia* [1997] FCA 558.

79 PICC 2016 preamble, commentary [7].

80 H. Dahan, 'The UNIDROIT Principles and their Influence in the Modernisation of Contract Law in the People's Republic of China', *Uniform Law Review* 8 (2003), 107.

81 B. Zeller, 'The Unidroit Principles of Contract Law; Is There Room for Their Inclusion into Domestic Contracts?', *Journal of Law and Commerce* 26 (2006–2007), 115, 121.

Not a Wide Practice by the Courts

The Convention[82] was highly influential in the drafting of the Principles of European Contract Law (PECL).[83] The PECL bore some resemblance to the Principles and the Convention, and formed part of a *lex mercatoria*.[84] This is not the place to discuss this instrument in detail. However, it is worth noting the multitude of sources used by the Lando Commission.[85]

In Australia, this has been echoed by some members of the judiciary. In *Alcatel*,[86] Sheller JA recognized the need for good faith to be used, even though he acknowledged that it would be a significant adjustment for Australian contract law. The judge referred to using the Convention and Principles to reach this point.[87] This was also the case in *Hughes Aircraft v. Airservices Australia* in which Justice Finn referred to the Principles when discussing the duty of good faith, ultimately applied to a tender process in that instance.[88] It is worth noting that Professor Finn is also an active scholar in this area and a contributor to the revision of the Principles; therefore he is well informed on their content.[89]

Over time, the impact of the Convention on some domestic legislation is undeniable.[90] In a recent article, Chianale shows how

[82] It is extensively referred to in O. Lando and H. Beale (eds.), *Principles of European Contract Law, Parts I and II (Combined and Revised)* prepared by the Commission of European Contract Law (Kluwer Law International, 2000).

[83] Even though the latter takes good faith from the confines of interpretation (CISG Art. 7; PECL Art. 1:106) into formation, performance and enforcement (PECL Art. 1:201); see Lando and Beale (n. 82) xxv–xxvi. The CISG has furthermore influenced the Common European Sales Law regime, regulating transactions between businesses: G. Wagner, 'Termination and Cure under the Common European Sales Law', *Common Market Law Review* 50 (2013), 147, 162.

[84] For a comparison of these instruments, see also L. A. DiMatteo, 'Contract Talk: Reviewing the Historical and Practical Significance of the Principles of European Contract Law', *Harvard International Law Journal* 43 (2002), 569; J. Felemegas, 'Comparative Editorial Remarks on the Concept of Good Faith in the CISG and the PECL', *Pace International Law Review* 13 (2001), 399.

[85] See Lando and Beale (n. 82); Lando (n. 33).

[86] *Alcatel Australia Ltd* (n. 78) 349.

[87] Ibid., 365.

[88] *Hughes Aircraft Systems International* (n. 78).

[89] PICC 2016 x; P. Finn, 'The UNIDROIT Principles: An Australian Perspective', *Australian International Law Journal* 17 (2010), 193; P. Finn, 'Fiduciary and Good Faith Obligations under Long Term Contracts' in K. Dharmananda and L. Firios (eds.), *Long Term Contracts* (Federation Press, 2013) 136.

[90] Berman (n. 69) 35; P. Finn, 'Internationalization or Isolation: The Australian Cul de Sac? The Case of Contract Law' in E. Bant and M. Harding (eds.), *Exploring Private Law* (Cambridge University Press, 2010) 41, 53.

> [n]eutrality with respect to the various national solutions, and above all neutrality with respect to politically or ideologically sensitive legislative choices, constitutes a profound characteristic of the CISG that makes it perfectly suitable as a base for the various attempts at regional harmonisation.[91]

He provides many examples of jurisdictions and regional organizations that have transplanted the CISG into their domestic legislation, from Nordic countries[92] to China.[93] Closer to home, Australia, New Zealand, and ASEAN countries are negotiating a free trade agreement. As one of the top three trading partners of Australia, ASEAN represented $93.2 billion of Australia's total trade in 2016, most of it being in goods. ASEAN countries have already agreed on the ASEAN Trade in Goods Agreement,[94] whose preamble calls for 'a legal framework to realise free flow of goods in the region'. The Convention may well be a good model for ASEAN to explore due to its prestige and intrinsic equilibrium – because it was drafted with influences from both the common law and the civil law.[95] Yet, it is worth noting that, out of the ASEAN members, only Vietnam and Singapore have ratified the Convention.

VII TRANSPLANT AND MODEL LAW: PRACTICAL CHALLENGES

Today over eighty-nine jurisdictions are party to the Convention. As the reader is likely to be aware, signatory countries to international conventions can make objections to certain parts of the Convention. Which objections are possible within each international instrument is text-dependent. Article 95 of this Convention allows a state to declare that it is not bound by Article 1(1)(b). This means that the Convention would only apply if the legal dispute concerns a contract for the sale of goods between parties whose places of business

[91] A. Chianale, 'The CISG as a Model Law: A Comparative Law Approach', *Singapore Journal of Legal Studies* [2016] 29, 45.

[92] Ibid., 33; L. Sevon, 'The New Scandinavian Codification on the Sale of Goods and the 1980 United Nations Convention on Contracts for the International Sale of Goods' in P. Schlechtriem (ed.), *Einheitliches Kaufrecht and nationales Obligationenrecht: Referate and Diskussionen der Fachtagung Einheitliches Kaufrecht am 16-17 2 1987* (Nomos Verlagsgesellschaft, 1987) 343; L. Spagnolo, 'Law Wars: Australian Contract Law Reform v. CISG v. CESL', *Villanova Law Review* 58 (4) (2013), 623, 636.

[93] Chianale (n. 91) 34, citing Bruno Zeller, 'CISG and China' in M. R. Will (ed.), *The CISG and China: Dialog Deutschland-Schweiz VII* (Faculté de droit, Universite de Genève, 1999) 7.

[94] Adopted 26 February 2009, entered into force 17 May 2010.

[95] Chianale (n. 91) 38–44.

are in different states and these states are Contracting States. Singapore, an ASEAN member, has made such a declaration.[96] Vietnam, the other ASEAN member that is also party to this Convention, has not made such a declaration following its accession on 18 December 2015. New Zealand, another close trading partner of Australia,[97] is also a party to the Convention. Australia and New Zealand have made similar declarations on the basis of Article 93 of the Convention. These declarations limit the geographical application of the convention by excluding the Cook Islands, Niue and Tokelau in New Zealand, and Christmas Island, the Cocos (Keeling) Islands and the Ashmore and Cartier Islands in Australia. Therefore, prior to applying the Convention, it is important to pay particular attention to the declarations of contracting states to ensure the Convention does indeed apply to the situation at stake.

The situation is different for the Principles as they do not require signature, accession or ratification. This is because they are soft law and not an international treaty. They are redacted by a community of legal practitioners, judges and scholars in the relevant area of law, here international commercial contracts.[98] It is left to the parties of a contract to decide to make the Principles, as a whole or partly, the proper law of the contract. However, it is worth noting that, while Australia is a member of UNIDROIT, the only ASEAN member that is a party is Indonesia. New Zealand is not party to it.[99]

Lack of Use and Understanding

According to the UNILEX database, out of 239 cases worldwide that have referenced the Principles, only fourteen have been Australian.[100] The main discussion in these cases refers to the good faith section of the Principles. The discussion in these references has usually led to the rejection of the Principles, making the instrument an anti-model instead of a model for domestic legislation,[101] in spite of its preamble. Unfortunately, the statistics

96 Sale of Goods (United Nations Convention) Act (Singapore, Chapter 283a, 1995) Art. 3.

97 Australia and New Zealand are also party to the bilateral Australia-New Zealand Closer Economic Relations Trade Agreement (1984) 1329 UNTS 175.

98 UNIDROIT, 'Working Group for the Preparation of the Unidroit Principles 2016' in PICC 2016 x–xi.

99 UNIDROIT's membership is available at: www.unidroit.org/about-unidroit/membership accessed 16 July 2018.

100 In comparison, there are five cases in France, one in Germany, twenty-eight in the Russian Federation. See UNILEX www.unilex.info/dynasite.cfm?dssid=2377&dsmid=13619&x=1 accessed 18 June 2018.

101 Michaels (n. 54) 651.

on the Convention reflect a similar fate. Indeed, despite the Convention being part of Australian law, it has been rarely used. In comparison, French courts have referred to the Convention six times more often than Australian courts.[102] Furthermore, only a handful of Australian cases actually apply some provisions of the Convention while the other cases refer to the Convention in *obiter*. Australian cases mostly refer to the Convention and the Principles but do not often apply the provisions of these international instruments.[103] Out of 946 cases on the Convention, only twelve are Australian.[104]

Perhaps a more worrying development is that Australian courts are also giving in to domestic bias, meaning contracts to which the Convention applies are interpreted using domestic principles instead of the Convention,[105] or the Convention is not enforced even when it applies. In *Perry Engineering Pty Ltd* v. *Bernold* AG, the Supreme Court of South Australia stated that, even though the Convention applied, as the buyer had not argued under it, the Court could not award damages based on it.[106] In *Playcorp Pty Ltd* v. *Taiyo Kogyo Ltd*, the Supreme Court of Victoria noted the applicability of the Convention, as part of Australian law. However, as the Court had not been persuaded that a different outcome would result from the application of the Convention, it held it unnecessary to apply it.[107] In *Attorney-General of Botswana* v. *Aussie Diamond Products Pty Ltd*, the Supreme Court of Western Australia was aware that the Convention forms part of the law of Australia and was applicable in this case. However, the Court noted that

> [n]either party in this case has suggested that there are provisions of the Convention which require consideration, or that the provisions of the Convention would operate inconsistently with the application of the Act in the circumstances of this case, and the general law of Western Australia. Having regard to the way the case was run it is unnecessary to refer to the Convention further.[108]

This showed the ignorance not only of the judge but also of the counsel in their pleadings. This trend can partly be explained by the fact that 'in common

[102] UNILEX Database on CISG www.unilex.info/dynasite.cfm?dssid=2376&dsmid=13354&x=1 accessed 16 July 2018.

[103] Oser (n. 67) 153.

[104] In comparison, there are in eighty-four cases in France and 210 in Germany. See UNILEX www.unilex.info/dynasite.cfm?dssid=2376&dsmid=13354&x=1 accessed 18 June 2018.

[105] This is a common phenomenon in the USA, as per Smythe (n. 35), 26–7, but as we will see this trend is also found in Australia.

[106] *Perry Engineering Pty Ltd* v. *Bernold AG* [2001] SASC 15.

[107] *Playcorp Pty Ltd* v. *Taiyo Kogyo Ltd* [2003] VSC 108 [235].

[108] *Attorney-General of Botswana* v. *Aussie Diamond Products Pty Ltd* [2010] WASC 141 [210].

law systems such as Australia parties and the courts are generally limited by the pleadings, it remains open even to an Australian court to apply the CISG indirectly by rejecting an argument based on an inapplicable domestic law'.[109] There have been instances where a court has considered the applicability of the Convention to the legal dispute and applied it, albeit rarely.[110]

Interpretation

While the Convention is a cornerstone of international commercial law, its text is ambiguous.[111] This has left courts using their domestic legal principles to interpret provisions of the Convention instead of the Convention itself,[112] although the Convention mandates an interpretation in line with the international character of the text.[113] One of the most controversial aspects of the Convention relates to its use of good faith. To understand the controversy, one must go back to the proposal of the working group for the draft Convention on the formation of contracts. Article 6 of this draft stated: 'in the course of the formation of the contract the parties must observe the principle of fair dealing and act in good faith'. This provision was debated during the writing of the Convention and a compromise was reached to restrict the application of the principle to the interpretation of the Convention.[114] The UK did not want good faith recognized as a duty applicable to parties whose contract is governed by the Convention.[115] Yet, while the principle is only mentioned in one article, it is present throughout the Convention, at least in spirit.[116]

Article 7(1) stipulates that the Convention must be interpreted in such a way that it observes good faith in international trade. Article 7(1) imposes good faith only in regard to the interpretation of the Convention. The text does not impose a duty of good faith upon the parties in an international sale of goods.[117] The explanatory notes detail the need to understand 'good faith in

109 B. Hayward, 'The CISG in Australia – The Jigsaw Puzzle Missing a Piece', *Vindobona Journal of International Commercial Law and Arbitration* 14 (2) (2010), 193, 196.

110 See, e.g., *Castel Electronics Pty Ltd* v. *Toshiba Singapore Pte Ltd* [2011] FCAFC 55.

111 Berman (n. 69) 27.

112 *Downs Investments Pty Ltd (in liq)* v. *Perwaja Steel SDN BHD* [2002] 2 Qd R 462.

113 CISG Art. 7.

114 Honnold (n. 33) 94.

115 Yet, in spite of this, the UK is yet to ratify the Convention. See S. Moss, 'Why the United Kingdom Has Not Ratified the CISG', *Journal of Law and Commerce* 25 (2005–2006), 483.

116 F. G. Mazzotta, 'Good Faith Principle: Vexatio Questio' in DiMatteo (n. 30) 120, 128; see for instance CISG Art. 16(2)(b), Art. 21(2), Art. 29(2), Art. 40.

117 Felemegas (n. 84) 401: 'The wording was agreed upon only after lengthy deliberations and it was meant as a final rejection of more far-reaching proposals to apply the principle of "good faith and fair dealing" to the obligations and the behavior of the parties themselves';

international trade' across legal systems, without reference to the domestic understanding of the notion, in order to promote a uniform approach to the interpretation.[118] There is yet to be a 'universal' interpretation of the doctrine of good faith in international contract law.

Therefore, according to the text of the Convention and its commentary, good faith can be used as an aid to interpretation. This however poses the question of its use and content. It has been said of this doctrine that it is an 'elusive and easily stretchable concept'.[119] While the Convention aims to promote uniformity in international sales law, the lack of a 'common core of meaning'[120] has meant the notion of good faith is not easily understood, interpreted or applied. This has led to a homeward trend bias, an 'ethnocentric trap'[121] whereby judges revert to their own understanding to interpret the Convention. This can partly be explained by a lack of clear interpretative methodology in the Convention.[122] Due to the lack of guidelines within the Convention as to what good faith in international trade means, a US court has used private international law mechanisms to ultimately guide the American interpretation.[123] France has also used Article 7 to impose a duty of good faith upon the parties. For instance, the Court of Appeal of Grenoble decided that,

> by not telling the seller the ultimate destination of the goods and by sending them to another location than the one stated in the contract, the buyer breaches article 7 CISG as such conduct is contrary to the principle of good faith in international trade laid down in article 7 CISG.[124]

Schwenzer (n. 32) 121–2; see also M. Wesiack, 'Is the CISG Too Much Influenced by Civil Law Principles of Contract Law Rather Than Common Law Principles of Contract Law? Should the CISG Contain a Rule on the Passing of Property?' (2004) CISG Database www.cisg.law.pace.edu/cisg/biblio/wesiack.html accessed 21 June 2018; T. Keily, 'Good Faith and the Vienna Convention on Contracts for the International Sale of Goods (CISG)', *Vindobona Journal of International Commercial Law and Arbitration* 3 (1) (1999), 15.

118 B. Zeller, 'Four-Corners – The Methodology for Interpretation and Application of the UN Convention on Contracts for the International Sale of Goods' (2003) CISC Database, article 7 www.cisg.law.pace.edu/cisg/biblio/4corners.html accessed 21 June 2018.

119 Mazzotta (n. 116) 134.

120 Honnold (n. 33) 95.

121 Zeller (n. 79) 119.

122 L. Di Matteo, L. Dhooge, S. Greene, V. Maurer and M. Pagnattaro, 'The Interpretive Turn in International Sales Law: An Analysis of Fifteen Years of CISG Jurisprudence', *Northwestern Journal of International Law & Business* 34 (2004), 299, 437; *Beijing Metals & Minerals* v. *M Bus Ctr In* 993 F2d 1178 (5th cir, 1993).

123 *Schmitz-Werke GmbH & Co* v. *Rockland Industrie Inc; Rockland International FSC Inc* (2002) 37 Fed Appx 687; *Forestal Guarani SA* v. *Daros International* United States Court of Appeals for the Third Circuit No. 08-4488 (2010).

124 *BRI Production 'Bonaventure'* v. *Pan African Export* CA Grenoble France, 22 February 1995 No. 93-3275.

Article 7 has also been used to decide 'to allow a buyer to declare the contract void at the time of trial [which] would violate the principle of good faith'.[125] The rationale for these approaches is that 'Parties derive their rights and duties from the contract in accordance with the CISG; the CISG is to be interpreted in accordance with good faith; therefore the parties' rights and duties are subject to good faith'.[126] Generally, good faith has been mentioned in cases in Australia[127] and across the world[128] but has only been applied in a limited number of them.[129] This shows that, while Article 7(1) is the only reference to good faith in the text, judicial activism in some jurisdictions has created an obligation to act in good faith in contracts submitted to the application of the Convention. While it is fair to recognize that the doctrines of reasonableness, loyalty and cooperation are present within the text and throughout the Convention,[130] it is quite another thing to consider that the text mandates a duty to act in good faith, when negotiations during the drafting process show the difficulties of reaching a consensus on the question.[131] Zeller argues that, by incorporating the Convention into its domestic law, Australia has integrated the notion of good faith in domestic law.[132] However, this approach adopts the broader interpretation of Article 7 and departs from the literal interpretation of the Convention.[133] It is reasonable to suggest that Legrand was right,[134] and that this shows the pervasive nature of domestic interpretation and the inability to detach cultural and societal values from the interpretation of any transplanted legal idea.[135] The added difficulty here may well be that, unlike EU law and the guidance on its interpretation by the European Court of Justice, domestic courts are left to their own devices. Maybe at the core of the issue of transplanting the Convention and the Principles successfully is Harding's idea that global doctrine can become local

125 Keily (n. 117) 17.

126 M. G. Bridge, *The International Sale of Goods* 3rd edn (Oxford University Press, 2014) [10.41], cited in M. Bridge, 'Good Faith, the Common Law, and the CISG', *Uniform Law Review* 22 (1) (2017), 98, 114.

127 *Renard Constructions (ME) Pty Ltd* v. *Minister for Public Works* (1992) 26 NSWLR 234.

128 See Bridge (n. 126) 101.

129 B. Sheehy, 'Good Faith in the CISG: The Interpretation Problems of Art 7' (2007) *Review of the Convention on Contracts for the International Sale of Goods* 153.

130 Schwenzer (n. 32) 5.

131 For a history of the Convention see Schwenzer (n. 32), Introduction.

132 B. Zeller, 'Good Faith – Is It a Contractual Obligation?', *Bond Law Review* 15 (2) (2003), 215, 217.

133 A position echoed by Bridge (n. 126) 109.

134 The position of Legrand is developed in Harding (n. 11), Chapter 1 in this Volume; see also Legrand (n.3).

135 Legrand (n. 3); Harding (n. 11) 4.

knowledge.[136] While I agree that a law needs context to be properly understood, how one addresses the understanding of international law requires finding the right balance between internationalisation and domestication of legal ideas. This will always take time and mistakes are likely to be made. But how long can we keep monitoring the situation?

Using the Convention and the Principles for Law Reform: Has It Been too Long for Australia?

As argued in the previous paragraphs, interpretation and separation from domestic law are the 'missing pieces' of Australia's relationship with the Convention.[137] However, both the Convention and the Principles were drafted in the context of international commercial contracts. Indeed, their wording and commentaries emphasize the importance of not confusing the international trade context with the domestic circumstances of a legal system. Both instruments also state that, in spite of the differences, the Convention and the Principles can be used to direct reform of domestic contract law. This is because of the need to promote a harmonized approach to facilitate business both domestic and international.[138] The reverse should not however be occurring, that is, domestic law should not be used to interpret the Convention or the Principles. Unfortunately, practice seems to have followed the later path.

In Australia, the impact of these international instruments is linked to the state of Australian contract law. For some time now, scholars have highlighted the lack of coherence[139] and the need for reform of contract law in Australia.[140] In 2010, Paul Finn highlighted the need to look at the Principles to rejuvenate contract law in Australia, which he described as 'a little tired, a little inadequate to the world in which it now finds itself'.[141] For instance, good faith is yet to be formally recognized in Australian contract law despite the concept being accepted throughout the world, although there is debate as to whether Australian contract law needs such a duty or legal concept. Yet, scholarly papers, debates and courts decisions may refer to international instruments to help interpret doctrines, especially the doctrine of good faith.

136 Harding (n. 11) 10.

137 Hayward (n. 9) 217–21.

138 Smythe (n. 35).

139 J. Carter, 'Good Faith in Contract: Why Australian Law Is Incoherent' (Legal Studies Research Paper No. 14/38, Sydney Law School, 2014) https://ssrn.com/abstract=2421117 accessed 21 June 2018; A. Stewart, 'What's Wrong with the Australian Law of Contract?', *Journal of Contract Law* 29 (2012), 74.

140 Finn (n. 89).

141 Ibid., 193.

In 2012, the Attorney General's department released a discussion paper on the possible reform of Australian contract law, inviting submissions.[142] Part of the paper discussed the Convention and the UNIDROIT Principles, and the possible internationalization of Australian contract law.[143] Unfortunately, while the debate surrounding the possible internationalisation of Australian contract law surfaced, it did not take off, and the reform lost momentum after submissions closed in July 2012. One issue that transpired from the submissions was the fact that, as Spagnolo rightly pointed out, 'Australia suffers from many legislative and common law overlaps. The existence of legislation often will not prevent application of the common law, resulting in a range of remedies pursuant to statute and common law.'[144]

Where does this leave the legal transplant of the Convention and the Principles in Australia? Is it a failure? First, it is worth remembering that any legal change, and perhaps especially change to domestic contract law, cannot happen overnight. Such a change is incremental and takes time.[145] Unlike the 24/7 cycle of our current society, where changes can happen rapidly, this movement is slower. This is not a run, but a marathon. If there is movement there is hope, and topical references to the two international instruments in this chapter show there is such movement, albeit sometimes almost anecdotal. As long as there is still a link between the recipient country and the international instrument there is still time. In 1996, a report of the Australian Law Reform Commission referred to the fact that the Principles could not only be applied by legislatures but also domestic courts.[146] There is still the possibility of doing more with the Principles in relation to domestic contract law reform[147] and this is because more and more, in the context of contract law, judges and legislators have to justify their decision against a 'global consensus'.[148]

To some extent, the two instruments discussed here represent the best of both worlds, hard law and constantly reformed soft law that could help interpret the Convention. The author argues that there is now an opportunity to correct Australia's trajectory and start using the Convention and the

142 Australian Government, Attorney General's Department, Improving Australia's Law and Justice Framework a Discussion Paper to Explore the Scope for Reforming Australian Contract Law (2012).

143 For a review of the discussion paper and the submissions see Spagnolo (n. 92) 630–3.

144 Ibid., 626.

145 A characteristic of common-law countries like Australia: see *Perre* v. *Apand* [1999] HCA 36.

146 Australian Law Reform Commission, 'Legal Risk in International Transactions' (Report 80, 1996) [3.37].

147 Michaels (n. 54), 656–7.

148 Ibid., 658.

Principles better.[149] The transplant of the Convention has already taken place. While there might not be a drive to reform Australian contract law to align with these instruments, more can be done to ensure legal change and avoid the mistakes mentioned here.

Reflecting back on the surgery metaphor, any transplant is monitored, and medicine is given to ensure the transplant is not rejected by the recipient body. It would be naïve to think the same does not apply to a legal transplant. The dilemma is deciding which institution should monitor the success of the legal transplant. Courts now need to play by the rule book and not give in to the domestic bias trend. Instead they should promote the Convention in all questions regarding contract interpretation when the Convention applies.[150] This is the first step and is also applicable to the Principles. A recent example from the High Court shows that a court can draw attention to the bad pleadings of the parties.[151] While this shows that the reasoning of counsels may be mistaken, to correct it requires more education. This call for better teaching is not new. In 2005, Nottage stated that 'Australia and New Zealand need to take measures to ensure that their accession continues to generate maximum benefits'.[152] This could be done by informing law students and practitioners of the existence of various freely available databases that could help counsel in building their argument: the Pace University CISG Database, the Global Sales Law Project, UNILEX and UNCITRAL's Case Law on UNCITRAL Texts project (CLOUT). If, as Nottage argues, 'a problem for lawyers is that they prefer the familiar',[153] let us make the Convention and the Principles part of their familiar. In 2017, the Law Society of New South Wales' Commission of Enquiry on the Future of Law and Innovation in the Profession noted that globalization is one of the challenges of the legal profession.[154] One recommendation was to teach private international law, a core discipline to the proper application of the Convention and the Principles.[155] This call to arms for educators applies not only within Australian borders but beyond, in ASEAN countries and Oceania.[156]

149 J. A. E. Faria, 'Future Directions of Legal Harmonisation and Law Reform: Stormy Seas or Prosperous Voyage?', *Uniform Law Review* 14 (2009), 5, 18.

150 Smythe (n. 35), 25–6.

151 *Commonwealth Bank of Australia* v. *Barker* [2014] HCA 32 [107] (Kiefel J).

152 Nottage (n. 52) 827.

153 Ibid., 830.

154 Law Society of New South Wales, 'The Future of Law and Innovation in the Profession' (2017) 94 www.lawsociety.com.au/sites/default/files/2018-03/1272952.pdf accessed 21 June 2018.

155 Ibid., 97.

156 See, e.g., the recognition of the need for better understanding of the UNIDROIT Principles in Vietnam in Le Net, 'Rules of Interpretation of Contracts under the UNIDROIT Principles and their Possible Adoption in Vietnamese Law', *Uniform Law Review* 4 (2002) 1017, 1028–9.

VIII CONCLUSION: THEORIES AND MOVING FORWARD

Legal transplants, or the process of promoting legal change by integrating a model law into the domestic law of a receiving jurisdiction, are complex. Like surgeries, there needs to be preparation, careful operation and constant monitoring. The literature on legal transplants often discusses the process or the preparation, yet seldom considers an efficient monitoring system. By looking at the Convention and the Principles through the lenses of transplantation in Australian contract law, this contribution shows the complexity beyond the surgery. How to define success is complex. By examining the time taken and the need to further promote these instruments without a deadline, it has moved beyond the binary of success or failure. Instead, this chapter calls for a stronger involvement not only of legal reformers and courts but also educators to redirect Australian contract law to make it relevant in a globalized world. We can then enter a new cycle where legal change is motivated by the benefits of having the Convention and the Principles reshape Australian law and Australian legal professionals. The relevance goes beyond Australian borders. Indeed, ASEAN countries and Oceania should take on the lessons of the past, ensure these are not repeated in this part of the world and promote a better understanding and application of these legal instruments.[157] This is particularly relevant as we negotiate the contents of a free trade agreement in this region. We should follow the example of the European Union, where both the Convention and the Principles are much more widely known, applied and enforced.

IX BIBLIOGRAPHY

Alshorbagy, A., 'On the Failure of a Legal Transplant: The Case of Egyptian Takeover Law', *Indiana International and Comparative Law Review* 22 (2) (2012), 237.

Australian Government, Attorney General's Department, Improving Australia's Law and Justice Framework a Discussion Paper to Explore the Scope for Reforming Australian Contract Law (2012).

Bant, E. and Harding M. (eds.), *Exploring Private Law* (Cambridge University Press, 2010) 41.

Berman, P. S., 'The Inevitable Legal Pluralism within Universal Harmonization Regimes: The Case of the CISG', *Uniform Law Review* 21 (2016), 23.

Bonell, M. J., 'The UNIDROIT Principles of International Commercial Contracts and Long-Term Contracts' (position paper prepared for the Working Group on Long-Term Contracts, Principles of International Commercial Contracts, First session,

[157] Department of Foreign Affairs and Trade, 'New Colombo Plan' http://dfat.gov.au/people-to-people/new-colombo-plan/Pages/new-colombo-plan.aspx accessed 21 June 2018.

Rome, 19–23 January 2015) www.unidroit.org/english/documents/2014/study50/s-50–126-e.pdf accessed 16 July 2018.

Bonell, M. J. 'The CISG, European Contract Law and the Development of a World Contract Law', *American Journal of Comparative Law* 56 (2008),1.

Bridge, Michael G, 'Good Faith, the Common Law, and the CISG', *Uniform Law Review* 22 (1) (2017), 98.

Cairns J. W., 'Watson, Walton and the History of Legal Transplants', *Georgia Journal of International and Comparative Law* 41 (3) (2013), 637.

Carter, John, 'Good Faith in Contract: Why Australian Law Is Incoherent' (Legal Studies Research Paper No 14/38, Sydney Law School, 2014) https://ssrn.com/abstract=2421117 accessed 21 June 2018.

Chen-Wishart, M., 'Legal Transplant and Undue Influence: Lost in Translation or a Working Misunderstanding?', *International and Comparative Law Quarterly* 62 (1) (2013), 1.

Chianale, A., 'The CISG as a Model Law: A Comparative Law Approach', *Singapore Journal of Law Studies* [2016], 29.

Coyle, J. F., 'The Role of the CISG in US Contract Practice: An Empirical Study', *University of Pennsylvania Journal of International Law* 38 (2016), 195.

Department of Foreign Affairs and Trade, 'New Colombo Plan' http://dfat.gov.au/people-to-people/new-colombo-plan/pages/new-colombo-plan.aspx accessed 21 June 2018.

Dharmananda K. and Firios L. (eds.), *Long Term Contracts* (Federation Press, 2013), 136.

DiMatteo, L. (ed.), *International Sales Law: A Global Challenge* (Cambridge University Press, 2014)

Dhooge L., Greene S., Maurer, V. and Pagnattaro M. 'The Interpretive Turn in International Sales Law: An Analysis of Fifteen Years of CISG Jurisprudence', *Northwestern Journal of International Law & Business* 34 (2004), 299.

'Contract Talk: Reviewing the Historical and Practical Significance of the Principles of European Contract Law', *Harvard International Law Journal* 43 (2002), 569.

Estrella Faria, J. A., 'Future Directions of Legal Harmonisation and Law Reform: Stormy Seas or Prosperous Voyage?', *Uniform Law Review* 14 (2009), 5.

Felemegas, J., 'Comparative Editorial Remarks on the Concept of Good Faith in the CISG and the PECL', *Pace International Law Review* 13 (2001), 399.

Finn, P., 'The UNIDROIT Principles: An Australian Perspective', *Australian International Law Journal* 17 (2010), 193.

Gutteridge, H. C., *Comparative Law: An Introduction to the Comparative Method of Legal Study and Research* (Cambridge University Press, 1949), 25.

Hayward, B., 'The CISG in Australia – The Jigsaw Puzzle Missing a Piece', *Vindobona Journal of International Commercial Law and Arbitration* 14 (2) (2010), 193

Hofmann, N., 'Interpretation Rules and Good Faith as Obstacles to the UK's Ratification of the CISG and to the Harmonization of Contract Law in Europe', *Pace International Law Review* 22 (2010), 145.

Honnold, J., *Uniform Law for International Sales under the 1980 United Nations Convention* (Wolters Kluwer, 1982).

Dahan, H., 'The UNIDROIT Principles and their Influence in the Modernisation of Contract Law in the People's Republic of China', *Uniform Law Review* 8 (2003), 107.

Kanda, H. and Milhaupt C. J., 'Re-Examining Legal Transplants: The Director's Fiduciary Duty in Japanese Corporate Law', *American Journal of Comparative Law* 51 (4) (2003), 887.

Keily, T., 'Good Faith and the Vienna Convention on Contracts for the International Sale of Goods (CISG)', *Vindobona Journal of International Commercial Law and Arbitration* 3 (1) (1999), 15.

Lando, O., 'CISG and its Followers: A Proposal to Adopt Some International Principles of Contract Law', *American Journal of Comparative Law* 53 (2005), 379.

Le N., 'Rules of Interpretation of Contracts under the UNIDROIT Principles and Their Possible Adoption in Vietnamese Law', *Uniform Law Review* 4 (2002), 1017, 1028–9.

Legrand, P., 'The Impossibility of Legal Transplants', *Maastricht Journal of European and Comparative Law* 4 (1997), 111.

MacNeil, I., 'Relational Contract Theory: Challenges and Queries', *Northwestern University Law Review* 94 (3) (2000), 877.

Michaels, R., 'The UNIDROIT Principles as Global Background Law', *Uniform Law Review* 19 (4) (2014), 643.

Miller, J. M., 'A Typology of Legal Transplants: Using Sociology, Legal History and Argentine Examples to Explain the Transplant Process', *American Journal of Comparative Law* 51 (2003), 839.

Moss S., 'Why the United Kingdom Has Not Ratified the CISG', *Journal of Law and Commerce* 25 (2005–2006), 483.

Nichols, P. M., 'The Viability of Transplanted Law: Kazakhstani Reception of a Transplanted Foreign Investment Code', *University of Pennsylvania Journal of International Economic Law* 18 (4) (1997), 1235.

Nottage, L., 'Who's Afraid of the Vienna Sales Convention (CISG)? A New Zealander's View from Australia and Japan', *Victoria University of Wellington Law Review* 36 (2005), 815.

O'Hara O'Connor, E., 'The Role of the CISG in Promoting Healthy Jurisdictional Competition for Contract Law', *Uniform Law Review* 21 (2016), 41.

Oser, D., *The Unidroit Principles of International Commercial Contracts: A Governing Law?* (Brill, 2008).

Ricardo, D., *On the Principles of Political Economy and Taxation* (John Murray, 1817).

Robertson, D., 'Long-Term Relational Contracts and the UNIDROIT Principles of International Commercial Contracts', *Australian International Law Journal* 17 (2010), 185.

Schlechtriem, P.(ed.), *Einheitliches Kaufrecht and Nationales Obligationenrecht: Referate and Diskussionen der Fachtagung Einheitliches Kaufrecht am 16–17 2 1987* (Nomos Verlagsgesellschaft, 1987).

Schwenzer, I., 'Global Unification of Contract Law', *Uniform Law Review* 21 (2016), 60.

Schlechtriem & Schwenzer: Commentary on the UN Convention on the International Sale of Goods (CISG) 3rd edn (Oxford University Press, 2010)

Sheehy B., 'Good Faith in the CISG: The Interpretation Problems of Art 7', *Review of the Convention on Contracts for the International Sale of Goods* (2007) 153.

Slaughter, A. M., A *New World Order* (Princeton University Press, 2005).

Smith, A., *Wealth of Nations* (Strahan and Cadell, 1776).

Smits, J. S. (ed.), *Elgar Encyclopedia of Comparative Law* (Elgar, 2006) 434, 435.

Smythe, D. J., 'Reasonable Standards for Contract Interpretation under the CISG', *Cardozo Journal of International and Comparative Law* 25 (2016), 1.

Sarcevic P. and Volken P. (eds.), *International Sale of Goods: Dubrovnik Lectures* (Oceana Publications, 1985), 1.

Spagnolo L., 'Law Wars: Australian Contract Law Reform v. CISG v. CESL', *Villanova Law Review* 58 (4) (2013), 623.

Stewart, A., 'What's Wrong with the Australian Law of Contract?', *Journal of Contract Law* 29 (2012), 74.

Teubner, G., 'Legal Irritants: Good Faith in British Law or How Unifying Law Ends Up in New Divergences', *Modern Law Review* 61 (1998), 11.

UNIDROIT Secretariat, 'Report to Working Group on Long-Term Contracts Second Session' (Hamburg, 26–29 October 2015) see [43], [69], [19] respectively www.unidroit.org/english/documents/2016/study50/s-50-misc32-e.pdf accessed 16 July 2018.

Item No. 4 on the agenda: International Commercial Contracts – (b) Possible future work on long-term contracts' UNIDROIT 2013 – C.D. (92) 4(b)) www.unidroit.org/english/governments/councildocuments/2013session/cd92-04b-e.pdf accessed 24 July 2018.

Wagner G., 'Termination and Cure under the Common European Sales Law', *Common Market Law Review* 50 (2013), 147.

Watson A., *Legal Transplants: An Approach to Comparative Law* (University of Georgia Press, 1974).

Wesiack, M., 'Is the CISG Too Much Influenced by Civil Law Principles of Contract Law Rather Than Common Law Principles of Contract Law? Should the CISG Contain a Rule on the Passing of Property?' (2004) CISG Database www.cisg.law.pace.edu/cisg/biblio/wesiack.html accessed 21 June 2018.

Zeller, B., The Unidroit Principles of Contract Law; Is There Room for Their Inclusion into Domestic Contracts?', *Journal of Law and Commerce* 26 (2006–2007), 115.

"Four-Corners – The Methodology for Interpretation and Application of the UN Convention on Contracts for the International Sale of Goods' (2003) CISC Database, Article 7 www.cisg.law.pace.edu/cisg/biblio/4corners.html accessed 21 June 2018.

'Good Faith – Is It a Contractual Obligation?', *Bond Law Review* 15 (2) (2003), 215.

7

Proportionality in Australian Public Law

Colin Campbell and H. P. Lee

I INTRODUCTION

Andrew Harding, in his excursus on 'legal transplantation', observed: '[W]e do live in a world of legal connectivity in which we share common problems which can only be addressed by a limited range of solutions which are unlikely not to have been tried before'.[1] This prescient remark is apt in the context of the growing importance of the proportionality concept in the Australian public law arena. The proportionality concept attained particular prominence when the High Court of Australia found a freedom of political communication impliedly embedded in the Constitution.[2] It was inevitable that with the establishment of such an implied fundamental constitutional guarantee, the High Court had to craft a principle to enable the saving or invalidation of legislation claimed to be in violation of the implied freedom.

Ever since then, the 'proportionality' concept has taken off on a rising trajectory as an area of burgeoning interest among public law jurists[3] and

1 A. Harding, 'The Legal Transplants Debate: Getting beyond the Impasse?', Chapter 1 in this Volume.

2 *Nationwide News Pty Ltd* v. *Wills* [1992] HCA 46; (1992) 177 CLR 1 and *Australian Capital Television Pty Ltd* v. *Commonwealth* [1992] HCA 45; (1992) 177 CLR 106.

3 B. F. Fitzgerald, 'Proportionality and Australian Constitutionalism', *University of Tasmania Law Review* 12 (1993), 49; J. Kirk, 'Constitutional Guarantees, Characterisation and the Concept of Proportionality', *Melbourne University Law Review* 21 (1997), 1; P. Quirk, 'Australian Looks at German Proportionality', *University of Notre Dame Australia Law Review* 1 (1999), 39; P. Loftus. 'Proportionality, Australian Constitutionalism and Governmental Theory – Changing the Grundnorm', *Southern Cross University Law Review* 3 (1999), 30; H. P. Lee, 'The "Reasonably Appropriate and Adapted" Test and the Implied Freedom of Political Communication' in M. Groves (ed.), *Law and Government in Australia* (Federation Press, 2005) 59; G. J. Appleby, 'Proportionality and Federalism: Can Australia Learn from the European Community, the US and Canada?', *University of Tasmania Law Review* 26 (2007), 1; S. McDonald, 'Involuntary Detention and the Separation of Judicial Power', *Federal Law Review* 35 (2007), 25, 39–52; D. Meagher, 'The Brennan Conception of

emerged as an issue of practical importance in a number of areas of Australian public law. In 2015, in *McCloy* v. *NSW*,[4] the Justices of the High Court of Australia engaged in an exegesis on this concept and a plurality sought to craft a highly structured proportionality analytical framework incorporating a three-stage test. In this chapter we seek to provide a contemporary perspective on the scope and application of the proportionality concept in the broad areas of constitutional law and administrative law in Australia.[5]

II THE MIGRATION OF PROPORTIONALITY INTO AUSTRALIA

In 2012, Aharon Barak, a former President of the Supreme Court of Israel (1995–2006), published an influential book on the concept of proportionality.[6] In it he traced the 'historical roots' of proportionality to 'eighteenth-century German administrative law'.[7] Over the course of time proportionality was developed and accorded a central place in German constitutional law by the German Constitutional Court.[8] Barak said:

> The German approach to proportionality expanded beyond Germany. This is one of the prime examples of migration – or transplantation – of constitutional models in the modern era. Indeed it is possible to argue ... that proportionality is the post-war paradigm of human rights protection. Today, proportionality serves as a major component of the constitutional model shared by many democracies.[9]

The German doctrine migrated into the human rights jurisprudence of the European Court of Justice and the European Court of Human Rights. In 1993, Gummow J observed that in Australia the concept of 'reasonable

the Implied Freedom: Theory, Proportionality and Deference', *University of Queensland Law Journal* 30 (1) (2011), 119; The Hon Justice Hon Justice Susan Kiefel, 'Proportionality: A Rule of Reason', *Public Law Review* 23 (2012), 85; M. Wesson, 'Crafting a Concept of Deference for the Implied Freedom of Political Communication', *Public Law Review* 27 (2016), 87; B. Challenor, 'The Balancing Act: A Case for Structured Proportionality under the Second Limb of the *Lange* Test', *The University of Western Australia Law Review* 40 (2015), 304; A. Carter, 'Proportionality in Australian Constitutional Law: Towards Transnationalism?', *Heidelberg Journal of International Law* 76 (2016), 951.

4 [2015] HCA 34.

5 This concept was covered in a lucid manner by the Hon Sir Anthony Mason, 'The Use of Proportionality in Australian Constitutional Law', *Public Law Review* 27 (2016), 109.

6 A. Barak, *Proportionality: Constitutional Rights and Their Limitations* (Cambridge University Press, 2012).

7 Ibid., 177.

8 Ibid., 179–81.

9 Ibid., 180–1.

proportionality' as a criterion for assessment of validity in constitutional and administrative law 'appears to have entered from the jurisprudence of the Court of Justice of the European Communities and the European Court of Human Rights'.[10] He added that the doctrine has 'taken root and, indeed, extended its reach into the heartland of federal constitutional law in Australia'.[11]

Today, it is clear that the doctrine has become an entrenched feature of Australian constitutional law. Broadly speaking, the proportionality concept is deployed in two main areas of Australian constitutional law. First, it is an important tool which enables the invalidation of federal legislation in the 'characterisation' of federal legislation in relation to its connection to 'purposive' powers, such as the defence power and the incidental power. Secondly, the concept becomes operative whenever an express constitutional guarantee, such as section 92, is involved.[12] The proportionality concept is becoming increasingly prominent following the High Court's recognition of an implied freedom of political communication in 1992. Given that the implied freedom, just like the express guarantees, is not an absolute freedom, it is necessary to apply the proportionality concept to determine the validity of legislative and executive acts which impinge on the implied freedom. The extent to which the doctrine has reached into the heartlands of Australian administrative law is rather uncertain.

III THE IMPLIED FREEDOM OF POLITICAL COMMUNICATION

The High Court asserted the existence of an implied freedom of political communication in two cases decided at about the same time: *Nationwide News Pty Ltd* v. *Wills*[13] and *Australian Capital Television Pty Ltd* v. *Commonwealth*.[14] Eventually, after a period of controversy, the High

[10] *Minister for Resources* v. *Dover Fisheries Pty Ltd* (1993) 116 ALR 54, 64.

[11] Ibid., 65.

[12] The Hon Justice Susan Kiefel, 'Section 92: Markets, Protectionism and proportionality – Australian and European Perspectives', *Monash University Law Review* 36 (2) (2009), 1; G. V. Puig, 'Abridged Proportionality in Australian Constitutional Review: A Doctrinal Critique of the Cole *v.* Whitfield Saving Test for Section 92 of the Australian Constitution' (Conference Paper, 7th World Congress of the International Association of Constitutional Law, Athens, 14 June 2007, Workshop 15); G. V. Puig, 'A European Saving Test for Section 92 of the Australian Constitution', *Deakin Law Review* 13 (1) (2008), 99; G. V. Puig, *The High Court and Section 92 of the Australian Constitution* (Lawbook, 2008) 145–54.

[13] [1992] HCA 46; (1992) 177 CLR 1.

[14] [1992] HCA 45; (1992) 177 CLR 106.

Court consolidated its position in a unanimous decision in *Lange v. Australian Broadcasting Corporation*.[15]

In *Lange*, the following formula was established to determine whether the implied freedom was infringed:

> When a law of a State or Federal Parliament or a Territory legislature is alleged to infringe the requirement of freedom of communication imposed by ss.7, 24, 64 or 128 of the Constitution, two questions must be answered before the validity of the law can be determined.
>
> Firstly, does the law effectively burden freedom of communication about government or political matters either in its terms, operation or effect?
>
> Secondly, if the law effectively burdens that freedom, is the law reasonably appropriate and adapted to serve a legitimate end the fulfilment of which is compatible with the maintenance of the constitutionally prescribed system of representative and responsible government and the procedure prescribed by s.128 for submitting a proposed amendment of the Constitution to the informed decision of the people … If the first question is answered 'yes' and the second 'no', the law is invalid.[16]

The second limb of the *Lange* test was subsequently reformulated in *Coleman v. Power*[17] to ask whether the law is 'reasonably appropriate and adapted to serve a legitimate end [in a manner] which is compatible with the maintenance of the constitutionally prescribed system of representative and responsible government?'

We will not traverse the rather stale debates about the constitutional basis for such an implication. Conscious of the deficiency in relying on a 'free-standing principle' of representative democracy, the Court shifted gear and moved to a more traditional technique of focusing on the provisions of the Constitution. In *Lange*, the Court explained that the Australian Constitution gives effect to the institution of representative government 'only to the extent that the text and structure of the Constitution establish it'. Thus 'the relevant question is not, "What is required by representative and responsible government?" It is, "What do the terms and structure of the Constitution prohibit, authorise or require?"'[18]

15 (1997) 189 CLR 520.

16 (1997) 189 CLR 520, 567–8.

17 (2004) 220 CLR 1.

18 (1997) 189 CLR 520, 566–7. See A. Stone, 'The Limits of Constitutional Text and Structure: Standards of Review and the Freedom of Political Communication', *Melbourne University Law Review* 23 (1992), 668, 673; A. Stone, 'The Limits of Constitutional Text and Structure Revisited', *University of New South Wales Law Journal* 11 (2005), 8.

Much water has flowed under the bridge since 1992 and the Court has laid down many settled propositions in relation to the implied freedom. We will simply highlight a few of these settled propositions relevant for purpose of our exposition:

(1) Sections 7 and 24 and related sections of the Constitutions effect a protection of freedom of communication between the people concerning 'political or government matters' which enables a 'free and informed choice' to be made by the people as electors;
(2) The provisions stated in (1) do not confer 'personal rights' on individuals; rather, they prevent legislative or executive power being exercised to curtail the freedom;
(3) The implied freedom of political communication is 'not absolute'.

In respect of proposition (2), the Court endorsed the statement of Brennan J in *Cunliffe* v. *Commonwealth*:[19] 'The implication is negative: it invalidates laws and consequently creates an area of immunity from legal control, particularly from legislative control.'[20]

The third settled proposition that the implied freedom is not an absolute freedom requires the Court to formulate a test to determine what would constitute a legitimate legislative or executive incursion into the implied freedom. Basically what is required is to identify the *end* sought to be achieved by the law and the *means* selected to achieve that end. Gageler J in *Tajjour* v. NSW[21] said:

> The degree of fit between means and end sufficient to justify a law as reasonably appropriate and adapted to serve that end can be alternatively described as one of "proportionality" or of "reasonable necessity". Whatever description is used, the examination is in every case directed to the sufficiency of the justification for the burden on communication on governmental or political matter which the law has been identified to have at the first step in the analysis.[22]

Thus, according to him, where an effective burden is 'undue' it is 'unjustified' and thus not afforded the constitutional protection.[23]

19 (1994) 182 CLR 272.
20 Ibid., 326.
21 [2014] HCA 35.
22 Ibid., [149].
23 Gageler J added: 'Means which come at too great a cost to the system of representative and responsible government established by the Constitution must be abandoned or refined. Means which are overbroad may need to be narrowed' – ibid., [163].

In *Lange*,[24] the Court had remarked that '[d]ifferent formulae have been used by members of this Court in other cases to express the test whether the freedom provided by the Constitution has been infringed'.[25] Some judges invoked a 'reasonably appropriate and adapted' test, while others described it as one of 'proportionality'.[26]

In *Lange*, the Court opted for the 'reasonably appropriate and adapted' formulation for 'ease of expression'.[27] However, Kirby J, in *Mulholland* v. *Australian Electoral Commission*,[28] described the 'appropriate and adapted' formulation as an 'ungainly and edifying phrase'.[29] In *Coleman*, he criticized the use of the 'appropriate and adapted' formula as 'an unhelpful formula for distinguishing permissible from impermissible or inadequate constitutional connection',[30] and expressed a preference for the 'proportionality' formula.[31] Gleeson CJ in *Mulholland* said that either formula would be acceptable to him.[32]

Despite the clash of views over the correct label, the authoritativeness of the *Lange* formula has never been questioned. Gageler J in *Tajjour* v. *NSW*[33] neatly explains how the *Lange* analytical framework works in practice. The first step requires the establishment of a restriction which would 'effectively burden' the implied freedom. The second step which Gageler J labels as 'Justification?' considers just 'whether there is sufficient justification for the burden which the [impugned law] imposes on communication on governmental or political matter in pursuit of that legitimate end'.[34]

French CJ, Hayne, Crennan, Kiefel and Bell JJ in *Unions NSW* v. *NSW*[35] explained that, in relation to whether an impugned law effectively burdens the freedom of political communication either in its terms, operation or effect, 'the identification of the extent of the burden imposed on the freedom

24 (1997) 189 CLR 520.
25 (1997) 189 CLR 520, 562.
26 Ibid.
27 Ibid.
28 (2004) 220 CLR 181.
29 Ibid., [247]. H. P. Lee, 'The "Reasonably Appropriate and Adapted" Test and the Implied Freedom of Political Communication' in M. Groves (ed.), *Law and Government in Australia* (Federation Press, 2005) 59, 71–3.
30 Ibid., [235].
31 Ibid., [236]. However, he acknowledged that: 'Any phrase used will only convey imperfectly the idea of valid constitutional connection to the source of the law-making power.'
32 (2004) 220 CLR 181, [39].
33 [2014] HCA 35.
34 Ibid., at [161].
35 [2013] HCA 58.

is not relevant' to this inquiry.[36] This was reinforced by Hayne J in *Tajjour* v. NSW.[37]

IV CONSTITUTIONAL ADJUDICATION POST-*LANGE*

A number of cases were decided through the operation of the *Lange* formula. In *Coleman* v. *Power*,[38] the impugned legislation, section 7(1)(d) of the Vagrants, Gaming and Other Offences Act 1931 (Qld), rendered the use of insulting words an offence. Coleman who was convicted under this law had his conviction quashed by the High Court on appeal. Three judges (Gleeson CJ, Callinan and Heydon JJ) found the object of the impugned legislation was 'the preservation of order in public places in the interests of the amenity and security of citizens' and that this was compatible with the implied freedom. Three judges (Gummow, Kirby and Hayne JJ) read the law down to require an intention to provoke an unlawful physical violence, and thus was not applicable to the facts of the case. McHugh J held the law to be invalid.

In *Monis* v. *The Queen*,[39] the impugned law, section 471.12 of the Criminal Code (Cth), made it an offence to use the postal service in an 'offensive' way or in a 'harassing' manner. Three judges (Crennan, Kiefel and Bell JJ) found that as the purpose of the impugned law was to protect citizens against the misuse of the postal services to effect intrusions of 'seriously offensive' material into a person's home or workplace, there was no impermissible burdening of the implied freedom. Three judges (French CJ, Hayne and Heydon JJ) found to the contrary, resulting in the appealed decision being affirmed via the operation of section 23 of the Judiciary Act 1903 (Cth). The lack of unanimity in arriving at a conclusion while applying the same test illustrates starkly that at the end of the day, the process is value-laden. The judges are highly conscious of the separation of powers doctrine when they are called upon to determine whether a law is 'appropriate and adapted' or 'proportionate'. In *McCloy* v. NSW,[40] an attempt was made to amplify the *Lange* formula to make the process more transparent.

36 Ibid., [40].

37 [2014] HCA 35, [61].

38 (2004) 220 CLR 1. See A. Stone and S. Evans, 'Australia: Freedom of speech and Insult in the High Court of Australia', *International Journal of Constitutional Law* 4 (4) (2006), 677–88.

39 (2013) 249 CLR 92.

40 [2015] HCA 34. See A. Carter, 'Political Donations, Political Communication and the Place of Proportionality Analysis: Case Note on McCloy v New South Wales', *Public Law Review* 26 (2015), 245; S. Chordia, 'The Trajectory of Structured Proportionality in Implied Freedom of Political Communication cases: *Brown* v. *Tasmania*' (2017) *AusPubLaw* https://auspublaw.org/2017/11/the-trajectory-of-structured-proportionality/ accessed 21 January 2019.

V THE QUEST FOR A NEW STRUCTURED PROPORTIONALITY

In *McCloy* v. *NSW*, the High Court was called on to determine whether certain provisions of the Election Funding Expenditure and Disclosure Act 1981 (NSW) infringed the implied freedom of political communication. The impugned provisions place caps on political donations and also make it unlawful for 'property developers' to make political donations. McCloy was subjected by the Independent Commission against Corruption (ICAC) to a compulsory examination regarding donations he had made in a NSW state elections and whether they violated these provisions. He challenged the validity of these provisions.

A majority of the High Court (French CJ, Bell and Keane JJ; Gageler J and Gordon J) upheld all the impugned provisions. Nettle J held invalid the impugned provision as it applied to property developers.

A full convergence with the European doctrine is reflected in the joint judgment of four of the High Court judges. French CJ, Kiefel, Bell and Keane JJ elaborated on the *Lange* test:

> The question whether a law exceeds the implied limitation depends upon the answers to the following questions, reflecting those propounded in *Lange* as modified in *Coleman* v. *Power*:
>
> 1. Does the law effectively burden the freedom in its terms, operation or effect?
>
>   If 'no', then the law does not exceed the implied limitation and the enquiry as to validity ends.
> 2. If 'yes' to question 1, are the purpose of the law and the means adopted to achieve that purpose legitimate, in the sense that they are compatible with the maintenance of the constitutionally prescribed system of representative government? This question reflects what is referred to in these reasons as 'compatibility testing'.
>
>   The answer to that question will be in the affirmative if the purpose of the law and the means adopted are identified and are compatible with the constitutionally prescribed system in the sense that they do not adversely impinge upon the functioning of the system of representative government.
>
>   If the answer to question 2 is 'no', then the law exceeds the implied limitation and the enquiry as to validity ends.
> 3. If 'yes' to question 2, is the law reasonably appropriate and adapted to advance that legitimate object? This question involves what is referred to in these reasons as 'proportionality testing' to determine whether the restriction which the provision imposes on the freedom is justified.

> The proportionality test involves consideration of the extent of the burden effected by the impugned provision on the freedom. There are three stages to the test – these are the enquiries as to whether the law is justified as suitable, necessary and adequate in its balance in the following senses:
>
> ***suitable*** – as having a rational connection to the purpose of the provision;
> ***necessary*** – in the sense that there is no obvious and compelling alternative, reasonably practicable means of achieving the same purpose which has a less restrictive effect on the freedom;
> ***adequate in its balance*** – a criterion requiring a value judgment, consistently with the limits of the judicial function, describing the balance between the importance of the purpose served by the restrictive measure and the extent of the restriction it imposes on the freedom.
>
> If the measure does not meet these criteria of proportionality testing, then the answer to question 3 will be 'no' and the measure will exceed the implied limitation on legislative power.[41]

The quest for High Court unanimity in support of the *McCloy* formula may be a futile exercise. Two of the judges in *McCloy* showed either strong opposition to it or a lack of enthusiasm for it. Gageler J remarked that the 'content and consequences' of a majority of the Court 'must await consideration in future cases'.[42] He expressed two reservations. He is not convinced that 'one size fits all', adding: 'I am not convinced that standardized criteria, expressed in unqualified terms of "suitability" and "necessity", are appropriate to be applied to every law which imposes a legal or practical restriction on political communication irrespective of the subject-matter of the law and no matter how large or small, focussed or incidental, that restriction on political communication might be.' He is also 'not convinced that to require a law which burdens political communication to be "adequate in its balance" is to adopt a criterion of validity which is sufficiently focussed adequately to reflect the reasons for the implication of the constitutional freedom and adequately to capture considerations relevant to the making of a judicial determination as to whether or not the implied freedom has been infringed.'[43]

Gordon J was of the view that the structure proposed by the plurality 'does not yield in this case an answer any different from that reached by the accepted

41 Ibid., at [2].
42 Ibid., at [141].
43 Ibid., at [145].

modes of reasoning'.[44] Quite clearly, the two questions posed by *Lange* formula 'have been applied without apparent difficulty since the decision in *Lange*'.[45] At the end of the day, the two questions 'call for judgment' and that 'opinions may differ about the answers that should be given to them in a particular case'.[46] Given that Gordon and Gageler JJ both have strong reservations, the convergence of the *Lange* formula into an equivalent of the European proportionality doctrine does not at this stage command overwhelming support in the High Court.

In *Murphy* v. *Electoral Commissioner*,[47] Gageler J reiterated his reservations 'about the appropriateness of importing such a structured and prescriptive, and ultimately open-ended, form of proportionality testing into our constitutional setting'.[48] He added: 'What is at best an ill-fitted analytical tool has become the master, and has taken on a life of its own.'[49] French CJ responded: 'The adoption of that approach in *McCloy* did not reflect the birth of some exotic jurisprudential pest destructive of the delicate ecology of Australian public law. It is a mode of analysis applicable to some cases involving the general proportionality criterion, but not necessarily all.'[50]

In *Brown* v. *Tasmania*,[51] Kiefel CJ, Bell and Keane JJ, accepting a suggestion from the Commonwealth, reframed Questions 2 and 3 in *McCloy* in the following terms:

> 2. If 'yes' to question 1, is the purpose of the law legitimate, in the sense that it is compatible with the maintenance of the constitutionally prescribed system of representative government?
> 3. If 'yes' to question 2, is the law reasonably appropriate and adapted to advance that legitimate object in a manner that is compatible with the maintenance of the constitutionally prescribed system of representative government?[52]

44 Ibid., at [311].
45 Ibid., at [310].
46 Ibid., at [310].
47 [2016] HCA 36.
48 Ibid., at [101].
49 Ibid.
50 Ibid., at [37]. French CJ referred to the following observation of Kiefel J in *Rowe* : 'A test of reasonable necessity, by reference to alternative measures, may not always be available or appropriate having regard to the nature and effect of the legislative measures in question.'
51 [2017] HCA 43. See: A. Carter, 'Brown v. Tasmania: Proportionality and the Reformulation of the Lange Test', *Public Law Review* 29 (3) (2018), 14; Chordia(n. 40).
52 Ibid., at [104]. Nettle J, at [277], expressed his agreement with this restatement.

Gageler J kept up his criticism of the framework of proportionality analysis advanced by the plurality in *McCloy*. He agreed that the Court should put paid to the notion that the last of the three questions must always or sometimes be answered through application of three-staged 'proportionality testing'.[53] He added: 'Three-staged proportionality testing was not sought to be characterized in *McCloy* as anything more than a tool of analysis, not to be confused with the constitutional principle it served . . . *McCloy* does not elevate three-staged proportionality testing to the level of principle; and *McCloy* does not endow it with precedential status. The point is one of emphasising that the tool is, at best, a tool. For my own part, I have never considered it to be a useful tool.'[54]

Gageler J said that the structure imposed by the three-staged proportionality testing was 'not tailored to the constitutional freedom of political communication, which is not concerned with rights, and which exists solely as the result of a structural implication concerned not with attempting to improve on outcomes of the political process but with maintaining the integrity of the system which produces those outcomes.'

He criticized the 'suitability' stage as one that 'can be quite perfunctory'; the 'necessity' stage as 'too prescriptive and can be quite mechanical if confined to an inquiry into 'less restrictive means'; and the third 'adequacy of balance' stage as 'too open-ended, providing no guidance as to how the incommensurables to be balanced are to be weighted or as to how the adequacy of their balance is to be gauged'.

VI PROPORTIONALITY, CHARACTERIZATION, AND PURPOSIVE POWERS

In *Murphy*, Gordon J observed: 'The concept of proportionality is applied in a variety of areas of Australian jurisprudence. It should not be assumed that, because a particular test for proportionality has been adopted in one particular constitutional context, it can be uncritically transferred into another context, constitutional or otherwise, even within the same jurisdiction.'[55]

The other constitutional context in which proportionality comes into play is in respect of the characterisation of federal legislation enacted pursuant to a *purposive* head of power. It is now an established proposition that where a law is made under a purposive head of power there must be a proportionality

53 Ibid., at [157].
54 Ibid., at [158]–[159].
55 [2016] HCA 36 at [296].

between the end and the means chosen to achieve the end. The defence power in section 51(vi) of the Constitution, empowering the Commonwealth Parliament to make laws with respect to '[t]he naval and military defence of the Commonwealth and of the several States, and the control of the forces to execute and maintain the law of the Commonwealth', is often highlighted to exemplify this.[56]

In *Marcus Clark & Co Ltd* v. *Commonwealth*[57], McTiernan J described the defence power as authorising 'the Parliament to take such measures as are proportionate to the end for which the Constitution created the defence power' and that the end is 'for the protection of Australia against invasion and the dangers of war'.[58] The 'appropriate and adapted ' formula drew on the words of Marshall CJ in *McCulloch* v. *Maryland*:[59] 'Let the end be legitimate, let it be within the scope of the constitution, and all means which are appropriate, which are plainly adapted to that end, which are not prohibited, but consist with the letter and end of the constitution, are constitutional.'[60]

The incidental power, express and implied, is another head of power in which the proportionality doctrine has been invoked. In *Davis* v. *Commonwealth* (the *Bicentennial Case*),[61] the High Court invalidated impugned provisions of the Australian Bicentennial Authority Act 1980 (Cth) which mandated the need to obtain the consent in writing of the Authority before a business, trade, profession, or occupation could use certain prescribed expressions: 'Bicentenary', 'Bicentennial', '200 years', 'Australia', 'Sydney' and 'Melbourne' in conjunction with '1788', '1988' or '88'. Mason CJ, Deane and Gaudron JJ said that in arming the authority with 'this extraordinary power' the impugned legislation provided for a regime of protection which was 'grossly disproportionate to the need to protect the commemoration and the Authority'.[62] They added: 'Although the statutory regime may be related to a constitutionally legitimate end, the provisions in question reach too far. This extraordinary intrusion into freedom of expression is not reasonably and appropriately adapted to achieve the ends that lie within the limits of constitutional power.'[63]

The external affairs power in section 51(xxix) of the Constitution is not in itself regarded as a purposive power. However, the proportionality doctrine is

56 See *Stenhouse* v. *Coleman* (1944) 69 CLR 457.
57 (1952) 87 CLR 177.
58 Ibid., 226.
59 7 US 316 (1819).
60 Ibid., 321.
61 (1988) 166 CLR 79.
62 Ibid., 100.
63 Ibid.

brought into play when the purpose of the challenged Commonwealth legislation is to achieve the implementation of a treaty obligation (of obtaining an international benefit). Deane J provided this 'extravagant example' to illustrate the point: '[A] law requiring that all sheep in Australia be slaughtered would not be sustainable as a law with respect to external affairs merely because Australia was a party to some international convention which required the taking of steps to safeguard against the spread of some obscure sheep disease which had been detected in sheep in a foreign country and which had not reached these shores. The absence of any reasonable proportionality between the law and the purpose of discharging the obligation under the convention would preclude characterisation as a law with respect to external affairs notwithstanding that Tweedledee might, "contrariwise", perceive logic in the proposition that the most effective way of preventing the spread of any disease among sheep would be the elimination of all sheep.'[64]

VII PROPORTIONALITY IN AUSTRALIAN ADMINISTRATIVE LAW: THE VIEW OF AUSTRALIAN COURTS

Until recently, Australian judges tended to be, at best, 'tentative'[65] about the possibility of proportionality serving as a basis upon which administrative decisions might be impugned pursuant to applications for judicial review. Hence, although that possibility enjoyed support among some judges, others held grave reservations. For instance, in *Cunliffe* v. *Commonwealth*, Dawson J, after noting that 'the principle of proportionality appears to have its origin in European Countries ... ' observed that as 'far as administrative law is concerned [proportionality] exists as part of a larger framework which finds no counterpart in the common law'[66] – it was thus 'an unlikely European transplant'.[67] And in *Bruce* v. *Cole*, Spiegelman CJ stated that the notion existed only 'at the boundaries of accepted administrative law'.[68]

That position appears now to have changed, with suggestions from a majority of the High Court that proportionality, if not a ground of review on its own account, may form part of the *Wednesbury* unreasonableness

64 *Commonwealth* v. *Tasmania* (1983) 158 CLR 1, 260.

65 M. Aronson and M. Groves, *Judicial Review of Administrative Action* 5th edn (Lawbook Co, 2013) 376.

66 (1994) 182 CLR 272, 356.

67 Aronson and Groves (n. 65) 376.

68 (1998) 45 NSWLR 163 at 185. See Aronson and Groves (n. 65) 376–7 and J. Boughey, 'The Reasonableness of Proportionality in the Australian Administrative Law Context', *Federal Law Review* 43 (2015), 59, 61–3 for a more detailed consideration of the Australian position.

ground. In *Minister for Immigration and Citizenship* v. *Li*,[69] Ms Li's application for a skilled independent overseas student residence visa was denied by the Minister's delegate on the basis that the 'skills assessment', obtained from Trades Recognition Australian (TRA), and which accompanied the application, was (although through no fault on Ms Li's part) based on false information and so fraudulent. Ms Li then sought review of the delegate's decision in the Migration Review Tribunal (the MRT) and applied to TRA for a new skills assessment. This second skills assessment was obtained by Ms Li prior to the hearing before the MRT, but was unfavourable to Ms Li. However, the new skills assessment contained two fundamental errors, and so Ms Li asked TRA to review it. Ms Li also sought an adjournment of the hearing of her matter before the MRT until after TRA had reviewed this second skills assessment. However, this request was denied on the basis that Ms Li had 'been provided with enough opportunities to present her case'.[70] Instead, the MRT made its decision in reliance on the first skills assessment. Unsurprisingly, (because this skills assessment was attended by fraud) the MRT upheld the original decision of the Minister's delegate, denying Ms Li the visa.

Although the matter was decided on other bases,[71] a majority of the Court's five judges[72] considered whether the MRT's exercise of its discretion, in not granting the adjournment, might have been unreasonable on the basis that the MRT had accorded disproportionate weight to the fact that Ms Li had already had the opportunity to be heard. Hayne, Kiefel and Bell JJ noted, that as 'a presumption of law ... [t]he legislature is taken to intend that a discretionary power, statutorily conferred, will be exercised reasonably'.[73] Then, in reliance on the judgment of Mason J in *Minister for Aboriginal Affairs* v. *Peko-Wallsend*,[74] and on Allars' analysis of the basis on which decisions may be found to be *Wednesbury* unreasonable,[75] (as endorsed by Gummow J in a Federal Court judgment)[76], the judges observed that if a decision-maker, in making the decision under statute has 'given disproportionate weight to some factor ... the final conclusion will ... be that the decision-maker has

69 (2013) 249 CLR 332.
70 Ibid., 339 [3], 368 [80].
71 See ibid., 352 [31], 369 [85].
72 Hayne, Kiefel and Bell JJ.
73 *Minister for Immigration and Citizenship* v. *Li* (2013) 249 CLR 332, 362 [63].
74 (1986) 162 CLR 24 at 41, Gibbs CJ and Dawson J agreeing at 30, 71, referred to at *Minister for Immigration and Citizenship* v. *Li* 362 (2013) 249 CLR 332, 365–6 [72].
75 Allars, *Introduction to Australian Administrative Law* (Butterworths, 1990) 188–91 [5.54]–[5.57].
76 *In Re Fares Rural Meat and Livestock Corporation Pty Ltd* v. *Australian Meat and Live-Stock Corporation* (1990) 96 ALR 153 [49].

been unreasonable in a legal sense.'[77] The judges concluded their consideration of proportionality by contemplating whether, on the facts of the case at hand, 'consideration could be given to whether the Tribunal gave excessive weight – more than was reasonably necessary – to the fact that Ms Li had had an opportunity to present her case'.[78] Although the judges did not decide the matter – the submissions in the case did 'not draw upon such an analysis"[79] – they observed that "an obviously disproportionate response is one path by which a conclusion of unreasonableness may be reached.'[80]

French CJ also seems to have been receptive towards the idea that an administrative decision may be able to be impugned on the basis a lack of proportionality. Hence he observed that:

> a disproportionate exercise of an administrative discretion, taking a sledgehammer to crack a nut, may be characterised as irrational and also as unreasonable simply on the basis that it exceeds what, on any view, is necessary for the purpose it serves.[81]

Further support from the High Court for the notion that proportionality (or, rather, lack of proportionality) may be relied on to impugn an administrative decision has been provided even more recently in *McCloy* v. *New South Wales*.[82] Although *McCloy* principally concerned the legality of legislation, the majority of the High Court, in discussing the notion of proportionality, made it clear that it could be relied upon to seek to impugn an administrative decision, at least where the power, pursuant to which the decision was purported to be made, has purposive limits.[83] The court did not say much more about the notion of proportionality in this context, although its observation that proportionality is 'analytical tool rather than . . . a doctrine',[84] lends at least some support to the idea that proportionality, as means of impugning administrative decisions, is not a freestanding ground of review but, rather, is part of the broader *Wednesbury* ground.

To the extent that the notion of proportionality does now form part of the *Wednesbury* ground of review, it is not entirely clear what form its 'doctrinal structure'[85] would take. However, it is reasonable to assume that it would be

77 *Minister for Immigration and Citizenship* v. *Li* 362 (2013) 249 CLR 332, 366 [72].
78 Ibid., 366 [74].
79 Ibid.
80 Ibid.
81 Ibid., 352 [30].
82 (2015) 257 CLR 178.
83 *McCloy* v. *New South Wales* (2015) 257 CLR 178, 195 [3].
84 Ibid., 215 [72].
85 Aronson and Groves (n. 65) 374.

very similar to that articulated, in a constitutional law context, in *McCloy*, but suitably modified to accommodate review of administrative decisions in a non-constitutional law context.[86]

VIII PROPORTIONALITY'S PRINCIPAL VIRTUE

The principal virtue of proportionality, as a means of impugning administrative decisions, is claimed to be that the determination, by the court, of whether a decision lacks the relevant proportionality, is highly structured, and transparent,[87] with the result that the basis on which the decision is struck down (if that occurs) will be 'identifiable and ascertainable'.[88] Hence (assuming an approach similar to that articulated in *McCloy* is adopted) the court will have to determine, amongst other things, whether the decision is: 'suitable', in the sense that there is a 'rational connection' between the purpose of the empowering provision and the decision in question;[89] 'necessary' in the sense that 'there is no obvious and compelling alternative, reasonably practicable means of achieving the same purpose which has a less restrictive effect on the freedom', right or interest in question;[90] and 'adequate in its balance' in the sense that the decision properly strikes the balance between, on the one hand 'the importance of the purpose served by the decision in question' and, on the other, 'the extent of the restriction it imposes'.[91] In determining those matters, so the argument would go, the court's reasoning will be laid bare, including, especially, the value judgment that it makes with regard to whether the decision is 'adequate in its balance.'

This claimed virtue of proportionality is usually articulated alongside an examination of the way in which *Wednesbury* unreasonableness, traditionally understood, operates, with the contrast thought to reflect positively on proportionality. As Jowell and Lester famously observed,[92] Lord Greene MR's

86 See M. Aronson, M. Groves and G. Weeks, *Judicial Review of Administrative Action and Government Liability* 6th edn (Lawbook Co, 2017), 379–80.

87 See, e.g., P. Craig, 'Unreasonableness and Proportionality in UK Law', in E. Ellis (ed.), *The Principle of Proportionality in the Laws of Europe* (Hart Publishing, 1999), 99–100. For an outlining of the 'normative foundations' of proportionality as a basis for review of administrative decisions generally, see P. Craig, "Proportionality, Rationality and Review", *New Zealand Law Review* [2010] 265, 271–3.

88 Ibid., 100.

89 *McCloy* v. *New South Wales* (2015) 257 CLR 178, 195[2].

90 Ibid.

91 Ibid.

92 A. Lester and J. Jowell, 'Beyond Wednesbury: substantive principles of administrative law', *Public Law* [1987], 368, 372.

formulation of *Wednesbury* unreasonableness – that a decision will be unreasonable in the relevant sense if it is 'so unreasonable that no reasonable [decision-maker] could ever have come to it'[93] – is tautologous. It does not follow from this that the application of the *Wednesbury* unreasonableness ground by the courts is necessarily a merely intuitive exercise. Rather, when a decision has been found to be *Wednesbury* unreasonable, this has often been on the basis that, in the view of the reviewing judge, the decision contravenes one or more substantive principles, which exist independently of the empowering statute.[94] However, when such principles are relied upon by the reviewing court, these are usually not articulated in court's reasons for its decision but, rather, remain 'hidden'.[95] The consequence is that the basis on which decisions are held to be *Wednesbury* unreasonable is often obscure, with one commentator going so far as to say that the law surrounding the availability of the *Wednesbury* unreasonableness ground is '(almost) resolutely opaque'.[96]

If lack of proportionality, in an Australian context, is simply one basis on which *Wednesbury* unreasonableness can be made out (as seems to be the suggestion of the court in *Li*), rather than a separate ground of review, there is less of a need, than might otherwise be the case, to evaluate the virtues of one vis-à-vis the other; proportionality can be understood as complementing *Wednesbury* unreasonableness as traditionally understood, rather than as being an alternative to it.

However, even if proportionality does become an accepted part of the *Wednesbury* unreasonableness ground, it should not be thought that all of the problems with *Wednesbury* unreasonableness will be resolved. Hence, one difficulty with *Wednesbury* unreasonableness as traditionally conceived is that, because of the lack of clarity about what factors will result in a decision being *Wednesbury* unreasonable, it will be difficult for the parties to a review

93 *Associated Provincial Picture Houses Ltd* v. *Wednesbury* [1948] 1 KB 223, 229.

94 Anthony Lester and Jeffrey Jowell, 'Beyond Wednesbury: substantive principles of administrative law', *Public Law* [1987] 368, 369, 370. See also M. Allars, *Introduction to Australian Administrative Law* (Butterworths, 1990) 188–191 [5.54]–[5.57]; P. Daly, 'Wednesbury's reason and structure', *Public Law* [2011] 238.

95 A. Lester and J. Jowell, 'Beyond Wednesbury: substantive principles of administrative law', *Public Law* [1987] 368, 377. It is worth noting, however, that there are some cases, decided on the basis of *Wednesbury* unreasonableness, where the courts are quite explicit about the substantive principle that is contravened by the decision in question (and, therefore, the basis on which the decision is held to be *Wednesbury* unreasonable): see, for instance, the decision of the UK Supreme Court in *R (Rotherham Borough Metropolitan Borough Council)* v. *Secretary of State for Business, Innovation and Skills* [2015] UKSC 6, referred to in M. Elliott and J. Varuhas, *Administrative Law, Texts and Materials* 5th edn (Oxford University Press, 2017) 272.

96 P. Daly, 'Wednesbury's reason and structure', *Public Law* [2011] 238, 242.

application to form a view as to the likelihood of a decision being found to be *Wednesbury* unreasonable. But the same difficulty may arise with regard to proportionality. Even if proportionality is confined in its operation to 'rights',[97] it is still the case that there is a variety of matters that will make it difficult to ascertain whether a decision will be impugned because of lack of proportionality. These include 'the relative importance of the right [...], the range of justificatory responses open to the government ... and the fact that the same right ... can be deployed in very different circumstances ... '.[98]

IX CONCERNS WITH REGARD TO THE ADOPTION OF PROPORTIONALITY

Commentators have raised a number of concerns about the notion of proportionality being used to impugn administrative decisions as part of the judicial review process. Several of these, centring on the idea of rights, will be considered below.

Customarily, proportionality is used as a mechanism in situations where rights have been conferred, either by a Constitution, or by legislation, to determine whether interference with the stipulated rights is legally permissible.[99] However, in Australia, at a Commonwealth level, there is no Bill of Rights. Accordingly, if proportionality is going to be used in judicial review in Australia the courts must either i) ascertain a way of determining what counts as rights for the purposes of proportionality review; or ii) give effect to proportionality review in respect of a broader range of 'interests'. There are problems with both approaches.

Determining What Are Rights

There are real difficulties for the courts in arriving at an approach for determining when an interest will count as a 'right' in the relevant sense, that can be relied upon, in turn, by administrative decision-makers (who, after all, in making their decisions, must not fall foul of a lack of proportionality, lest their decisions be impugned upon review). Hence, as Boughey points out,

97 See below, the text under the heading 'Concerns with Regard to the Adoption of Proportionality'.

98 P. Craig, 'Proportionality, Rationality and Review', *New Zealand Law Review* [2010], 265, 297. For a discussion of the indeterminacy of the very balancing process itself, see C. Henckels, 'Proportionality and the Separation of Powers in Constitutional Review: Examining the Role of Judicial Deference', *Federal Law Review* 45 (2017) 181, 187–8.

99 With regard to rights conferred by legislation, see Human Rights Act 1998 (UK), Schedule 1.

relying on international law as a source of such rights would require decision-makers to undertake the impossible task of 'being aware of, and giving genuine consideration to, the large number of frequently conflicting international human rights treaties'.[100] Although Boughey realizes that there would also be difficulties with relying on common-law rights – 'due to the absence of any fixed points of reference'[101] – she is slightly more comfortable with the common law as a source of 'rights' for proportionality review. This is because judges 'are certainly accustomed to defining and applying common law rights in other circumstances, such as in the context of . . . the principle of legality'.[102] However, it may be that we are entitled to be concerned about the common law as a source of rights for proportionality review, too. As Groves and Weeks point out, the Australian courts do not seem to have arrived at any coherent methodology – or, really at any articulated methodology at all – for determining what will be a 'right' for the purposes of the principle of legality.[103] There is no particular reason for thinking that the courts would be any more successful in arriving at such a methodology for the purposes of determining what constitutes a 'right' for the purposes of proportionality than they have been in the context of the principle of legality. And in the absence of an articulated methodology, or even a test, it would be difficult for decision-makers to know whether a particular interest constituted a right, at least in the absence of prior judicial consideration of the matter.

Problems with Interests

If the courts cannot arrive at an appropriate approach for determining what are rights for the purposes of proportionality review, the question remains whether the court may simply consider the plaintiff's interests (rather than any rights they may possess), in determining whether the decision-maker has acted disproportionately. Certainly, for instance, Craig, writing in a UK context, thinks that such an approach is unproblematic.[104]

However, it is not clear that a plaintiff's interests – rather than rights – *should* be protected by way of proportionality review. One argument that has

[100] J. Boughey, 'The Reasonableness of Proportionality in the Australian Administrative Law Context', *Federal Law Review* 43 (2015), 59, 88.

[101] Ibid.

[102] Ibid.

[103] M. Groves and G. Weeks, 'Substantive (Procedural) Review in Australia', in H. Wilberg and M. Elliott, *The Scope and Intensity of Substantive Review, Traversing Taggart's Rainbow* (Hart Publishing, 2015), 154.

[104] P. Craig, 'Proportionality, Rationality and Review', *New Zealand Law Review* [2010] 265, 297.

been made to such an effect concerns the nature of judicial review. Judicial review, so the argument would go, is principally concerned with the decision-maker's abuses of power, rather than the infringement of the plaintiff's rights (or interests).[105] The proportionality ground, by contrast, is explicitly concerned with the protection of the plaintiff's rights (or interests). Whatever the range of the rights possessed by an applicant for judicial review (and the breadth of those rights), the range of interests possessed by the plaintiff (and the breadth of those interests) would be much greater. Accordingly, if proportionality operated in respect of the plaintiff's interests, the nature of judicial review would become distorted, with its focus shifting from the decision-makers' abuse of power to plaintiffs' interests.[106]

It is suggested, however, that this argument is unpersuasive, for a number of reasons. Firstly, it is not immediately clear why such a change of focus would be undesirable[107], especially given that most applications for judicial review are brought by people whose interests have been adversely affected by the decision sought to be impugned. As long as provision was made for applications for review to be brought by public interest groups – such provision not being inconsistent with a conception of judicial review that focused principally, but not wholly, on the interests of the applicant – then it is difficult to see what the adverse consequences would be of such a change in focus.[108]

Secondly, the argument outlined above seems overstated. Even if proportionality were accepted as part of judicial review, and, in determining whether a decision were disproportionate, the court would focus on the plaintiff's interests, (lack of) proportionality would not be the only basis on which a decision could be impugned. All of the other established grounds – improper purpose, irrelevant considerations etc. – that are concerned with abuses of power, would remain. It seems to be going too far to suggest that proportionality would be sought to be relied on in every case, and, when it was relied on, that it would be the only ground relied upon.

Thirdly, as Boughey points out, judicial review is concerned, to at least an extent, with the protection of the plaintiff's interests. As she says, certain aspects of judicial review, 'particularly natural justice and standing requirements … have always been directed towards individual interests as

105 J. Boughey, 'The Reasonableness of Proportionality in the Australian Administrative Law Context', *Federal Law Review* 43 (2015), 59, 71.

106 Ibid.

107 See, for instance, T. R. S. Allan, *Constitutional Justice* (Oxford University Press, 2001), 172.

108 For Allan's view on representative standing, see T. R. S. Allan, *Law, Liberty and Justice* (Oxford University Press, 1993), 234, note 98.

opposed to the public interest in legality'.[109] To these aspects of judicial review can be added at least certain of the discretionary factors that the courts take into account in determining whether to decline a remedy pursuant to what would otherwise be a successful review application. For instance, the court's disinclination to grant relief to an applicant, even though the decision-maker has acted illegally in making the decision (and so abused her power), where the granting of relief would not benefit the applicant, seems to reflect a concern with the applicant's interests, rather than with abuse of power per se.[110]

Another, perhaps more serious argument, concerns the relative importance of, or weight accorded to, interests, by contrast to the importance of, or weight accorded to, rights. Assuming that it is the plaintiff's interests (rather than rights) that are considered in proportionality review then, as Hickman states, 'applying a proportionality test requires the interests affected by the [decision] to be given a priority and importance over those served by the [decision].'[111] This priority manifests in at least two ways in the approach to proportionality articulated in *McCloy* and referred to, in an administrative law context, above. First, if there is, in fact, an 'obvious and compelling alternative, reasonably practicable means of achieving the same purpose which has a less restrictive effect on the' interest in question, then the decision will be disproportionate and be impugned upon review. Secondly, even if there is no such alternative means, the decision will still be impugned if the impact on the interest is adjudged to be too severe. But, as Hickman suggests, it is difficult to see why an individual's interests – which have not been categorized as rights – should be so prioritized over public interests to begin with.[112]

One possible solution would be for the courts to differentiate between different sorts of interests. Those, that are regarded as more serious or important could be accorded much more weight in the proportionality analysis, with those that are regarded as less serious or important being accorded less weight. However, if the court cannot arrive at a workable test for determining whether certain interests qualify as 'rights', it is not at all clear that they would be able to arrive at a workable approach for distinguishing between, on the one hand 'more important' interests, and, on the other, those that are less important.

109 Boughey (n. 105), 59, 88.

110 See, for instance, *R* v. *Secretary of State for Foreign and Commonwealth Affairs, ex p Everett* [1989] 1 QB 811 at 819 per O'Connor LJ.

111 T. Hickman, 'Problems for Proportionality', *New Zealand Law Review* [2010] 303, 322.

112 Ibid. See also Boughey (n. 105), 59, 71.

X CONCLUSION

Barak, after noting that the concept has become part of the shared constitutional discourse among jurists, said:

> In some cases, after migrating to a new legal system, the concept of proportionality retained all of the components of the German approach. In other cases, the receiving legal system adopted only some components while rejecting others.[113]

It can be seen that the proportionality doctrine has permeated into many aspects of public law in Australia. The proportionality doctrine from the European legal arena continues to shape the constitutional discourse in Australia. However, there is a lack of unanimity about accepting all the components of the transplant. While a plurality in *McCloy* seek to effect a full transplant of the European model, there is a strong resistance, especially from Gageler J and Gordon J. It is uncertain at this stage whether the plurality's *McCloy* formula will eventually prevail as the sole analytical framework in determining proportionality.

XI BIBLIOGRAPHY

Allan, T. R. S., *Constitutional Justice: A Liberal Theory of the Rule of Law* 1st edn (Oxford University Press, 2001).

Law, Liberty, and Justice: The Legal Foundations of British Constitutionalism (Clarendon Press; Oxford University Press, 2003).

Allars, M., *Introduction to Australian Administrative Law* (Butterworths, 1990).

Appleby, G., 'Proportionality and Federalism: Can Australia Learn from the European Community, the US and Canada?' *University of Tasmania Law Review* 26, no. 1 (2007), 1–33.

Aronson, M., Groves, M. and Weeks, G., *Judicial Review of Administrative Action and Government Liability* 6th edn (Thomson Reuters (Professional) Australia Limited, 2017).

Aharon, B., *Proportionality Constitutional Rights and Their Limitations* (Cambridge University Press, 2012).

Boughey, J., 'The Reasonableness of Proportionality in the Australian Administrative Law Context' *Federal Law Review* 43, no. 1 (2015), 59.

Carter, A., 'McCloy v. New South Wales: Political Donations, Political Communication and the Place of Proportionality Analysis' *Public Law Review* 26, no. 4 (2015), 245–54.

'Proportionality in Australian Constitutional Law: Towards Transnationalism?', *Heidelberg Journal of International Law* 76 (2016), 951.

[113] A, Barak (n. 6), 181.

'Brown v Tasmania: Proportionality and the Reformulation of the Lange Test', *Public Law Review* 29 (3) (2018), 14.

Chordia S., 'The Trajectory of Structured Proportionality in Implied Freedom of Political Communication cases: *Brown v Tasmania*' (2017) *AusPubLaw* https://auspublaw.org/2017/11/the-trajectory-of-structured-proportionality/ accessed 21 January 2019.

Craig, P., 'Proportionality, Rationality and Review' *New Zealand Law Review* no. 2 (2010), 265–301.

'Unreasonableness and Proportionality in UK Law' in *The Principle of Proportionality in the Laws of Europe*, edited by E. Ellis (Hart Publishing, 1999), 85–102.

Daly, P., 'Wednesbury's Reason and Structure', *Public Law* April issue (n.d.) 2011, 238–59.

Elliott, M. and Varuhas, J. N. E., *Administrative Law: Text and Materials* 5th edn (Oxford University Press, 2016).

Ellis, Evelyn, ed. *The Principle of Proportionality in the Laws of Europe* (Hart Publishing, 1999).

Fitzgerald, B., 'Proportionality and Australian Constitutionalism' *University of Tasmania Law Review* 16, no. 3 (n.d.), 263.

Groves, M., ed. *Law and Government in Australia*(Federation Press, 2005).

Groves, M., and Weeks, G., 'Substantive (Procedural) Review in Australia' in *The Scope and Intensity of Substantive Review: Traversing Taggart's Rainbow*, edited by Wilberg, H. and Elliott, M. Hart Studies in Comparative Public Law, volume 8 (Hart Publishing, 2015), 154–70.

Henckels, C., 'Proportionality and the Separation of Powers in Constitutional Review: Examining the Role of Judicial Deference' *Federal Law Review* 45, no. 2 (2017), 181–97.

Hickman, T., 'Problems for Proportionality', *New Zealand Law Review*, no. 2 (2010), 303.

Jowell, J., and Lester, A., 'Beyond Wednesbury: Substantive Principles of Administrative Law', *Commonwealth Law Bulletin* 14, no. 2 (1988), 858–70 https://doi.org/10.1080/03050718.1988.9985971.

Kiefel, S., 'Proportionality: A Rule of Reason (Australia)' *Public Law Review* 23, no. 2 (2012), 85–93.

'Section 92: Markets, Protectionism and Proportionality – Australian and European Perspectives', *Monash University Law Review* 36, no. 2 (2010), 1–15.

Kirk, J., 'Constitutional Guarantees, Characterisation and the Concept of Proportionality', *Melbourne University Law Review* 21, no. 1 (June 1997), 1.

Lee, H. P., 'Proportionality in Australian Constitutional Adjudication' in *Future Directions in Australian Constitutional Law* edited by Lindell, G. (Federation Press, 1994) 126.

'The "Reasonably Appropriate and Adapted' in *Law and Government in Australia*, edited by Groves, M. (Sydney: Federation Press, 2005).

Loftus, P., 'Proportionality, Australian Constitutionalism and Governmental Theory: Changing the Grundnorm' *Southern Cross University Law Review*, no. 3 (1999), 30–84.

Mason, A., 'The Use of Proportionality in Australian Constitutional Law' *Public Law Review* 27, no. 2 (2016), 109–23.
Mcdonald, S., 'Involuntary Detention and the Separation of Judicial Power (Australia)' *Federal Law Review* 35, no. 1 (2007), 25–79. https://doi.org/10.22145/flr.35.1.2.
Mason A., 'The Use of Proportionality in Australian Constitutional Law', *Public Law Review* 27 (2016), 109.
Meagher, D., 'The Brennan Conception of the Implied Freedom: Theory, Proportionality and Deference' *University of Queensland Law Journal* 30, no. 1 (2011), 119–33.
Quirk, P., 'An Australian Looks at German "Proportionality"' *University of Notre Dame Australia Law Review* 1 (1999), 39.
Stone, A., 'The Limits of Constitutional Text and Structure Revisited (Freedom of Speech: Contemporary Issues)', *University of New South Wales Law Journal* 28, no. 3 (2005), 842–51.
'The Limits of Constitutional Text and Structure: Standards of Review and the Freedom of Political Communication (Australia)', *Melbourne University Law Review* 23, no. 3 (1999), 668–708.
and Evans, S. 'Australia: Freedom of Speech and Insult in the High Court of Australia', *International Journal of Constitutional Law* 4, no. 4 (2006,), 677–88. https://doi.org/10.1093/icon/mol030.
Villalta Puig, G., *The High Court of Australia and Section 92 of the Australian Constitution: A Critique of the Cole v Whitfield Test* (Thomson/Lawbook Co, 2008) https://trove.nla.gov.au/version/44567726.
Wilberg, H., and Elliott, M. (eds.). *The Scope and Intensity of Substantive Review: Traversing Taggart's Rainbow*. Hart Studies in Comparative Public Law, volume 8 (Hart Publishing, 2015).

CASE LAW

Australian Capital Television Pty Ltd v. *Commonwealth* [1992] HCA 45; (1992) 177 CLR 1.

Brown v. *Tasmania* [2017] HCA 43.

Commonwealth v. *Tasmania* (1983) 158 CLR 1,

Davis v. *Commonwealth* (1988) 166 CLR 79.

Marcus Clark & Co Ltd v. *Commonwealth* (1952) 87 CLR 177.

McCulloch v. *Maryland* 7 US 316 (1819).

McCloy v. NSW [2015] HCA 34.

Metropolitan Borough Council v. *Secretary of State for Business, Innovation and Skills* [2015] UKSC 6.

Minister for Aboriginal Affairs v. *Peko-Wallsend* (1986) 162 CLR 24.

Minister for Immigration and Citizenship v. *Li* 362 (2013) 249 CLR 332, 362 [63].

Minister for Resources v. *Dover Fisheries Pty Ltd* (1993) 116 ALR 54,

Monis v. *The Queen* [2013] 249 CLR 92.

Mulholland v. *Australian electoral Commission* (2004) 220 CLR 181.

Nationwide News Pty Ltd v. *Wills* [1992] HCA 46; (1992) 177 CLR 1
Re Fares Rural Meat and Livestock Corporation Pty Ltd v. *Australian Meat and Live-Stock Corporation* (1990) 96 ALR 153.
R v. *Secretary of State for Foreign and Commonwealth Affairs, ex p Everett* [1989] 1 QB
Tajjour v. NSW [2014] HCA 35.

8

Legal Transfer and 'Hybrid' International Commercial Dispute Resolution Procedures: Lessons from the Singapore International Commercial Court

Drossos Stamboulakis

I INTRODUCTION

The recent genesis of international commercial courts has given rise to a new conception of 'hybridized' dispute resolution procedures, crafted by a liberal drawing from perceived global best practice across both international commercial arbitration and litigation. As these courts depend upon an exclusive choice of forum to support their jurisdiction, the hybridity reflected in these procedures is intended to represent an attractive balance between the flexibility inherent in arbitration, and the greater degree of judicial compulsion and guidance seen in traditional national courts. This form of hybridity is perhaps best represented by the genesis of the Singapore International Commercial Court ('SICC'), driven by the perceived dominance of arbitration in transnational dispute resolution, as well as the sheer growth of transnational trade both globally and regionally in East Asia (and the resulting need for greater transnational dispute resolution services).[1] Given the focus of this collection, this procedural hybridity can be analyzed as a form of legal transfer, as it directly involves the idea of engaging legal borrowings and adaptation, with the ultimate aim of attracting and serving the needs of foreign disputants. This phenomenon however, is not confined to Singapore, as the SICC represents only the tip of the iceberg:[2] lurking beneath the surface are

[1] Chief Justice Sundaresh Menon, 'International Commercial Courts: Towards a Transnational System of Dispute Resolution' (Opening Lecture for the DIFC Courts Lecture Series 2015, Dubai, 2015) [22]–[23].

[2] The idea of an international commercial court no doubt takes significant inspiration from perhaps the most successful example enduring over centuries – the Commercial Court of England and Wales. The SICC, like several courts centred in or around the United Arab Emirates, such as the Abu Dhabi Global Market, the DIFC Courts and the Qatar Commercial Courts, all draw heavily on this experience, and rely upon close reference to English common

a range of international commercial courts in several key jurisdictions, including in China and in a range of jurisdictions in the European Union.[3] Although the precise features of these institutions are far from settled, based on what detail has emerged, it is likely they will adopt, at least in part, some aspects of hybridized procedure. The focus on crafting hybrid procedures for these new 'breed' of courts thus immediately begs the question – to what extent can this process of legal creation be readily analyzed as one that either is a transplant, or involves aspects of, transplantation?

This chapter focuses on the extent to which a broader idea of legal transfer can explain the creation of the SICC's hybrid procedures, allowing it to be compared across national law boundaries, and across the epistemological divide traditionally seen in arbitration vis-à-vis litigation. To do so, Section I of this chapter commences by exploring the comparative law ideas of 'legal borrowings' – as represented by terms such as transplant and transfer – and their conceptual limitations. I make the case for a broader conception of the traditional comparative law idea of 'legal transplant', towards a richer idea of 'legal transfer'. Doing so is particularly useful for understanding borrowings involving transnational elements – including the procedures of international commercial courts like the SICC – and more readily supports the call for detailed consideration of transfers as 'flows' of legal information; rather than a singular 'transplanted' organism. Additionally, a richer conception of

law and the perception of the attractiveness of English (or at least common) law and procedure: see Z. Sharar and M. Al Khulaifi, 'The Courts in Qatar Financial Centre and Dubai International Financial Centre: A Comparative Analysis', *Hong Kong Law Journal* 46 (2016), 529. At the same time, the SICC (and other mooted international commercial courts that follow in its footsteps) can be distinguished from 'traditional' commercial courts based upon their explicit genesis, mandate and focus on attracting foreign disputants.

[3] Although at early stages of development, other international commercial courts, drawing explicitly on the SICC experience, have been proposed in a diverse range of jurisdictions including the Netherlands, Belgium, the region of Frankfurt and China: de Rechtspraak [Judiciary of the Netherlands], 'Plan tot oprichting van de Netherlands commercial court [Plan to establish the Netherlands commercial court]' (2015); Council of Ministers, 'Instauration de la Brussels International Business Court [Establishment of the Brussels International Business Court]' (2017) Press Release www.presscenter.org/fr/pressrelease/20171027/instauration-de-la-brussels-international-business-court accessed 7 December 2017; Frankfurt Regional Court [Landgericht Frankfurt am Main], 'Gerichtsstandort Frankfurt wird gestärkt: Englischsprachige Kammer für Handelssachen ab Januar 2018 [Strengthening Frankfurt as a Venue: English-Speaking Chamber for Commercial Matters Starting January 2018]' (2017) Press Release; Supreme People's Court Monitor, 'SPC Reveals New Belt & Road-Related Initiatives' (*Supreme People's Court Monitor*, 7 October 2017) https://supremepeoplescourtmonitor.com/2017/10/07/spc-reveals-new-belt-road-related-initiatives/ accessed 18 December 2017. At the time of writing, the most advanced of these proposed transnational courts is that of the Netherlands Commercial Court, which has published a draft set of procedures, and one is slated to commence operation in the second half of 2018.

transfer, considering a broader variety of socio-legal factors and impacts, is also likely to have greater explanatory force than a bare legal analysis in considering attempts to transfer law or laws. Section II applies this broader conception of transfer, by analysing an exemplar of the SICC's hybrid procedures, and the cultural factors impacting on and surrounding the initial creation of the SICC. To do so, I set out the nature of the SICC and what it is aiming to achieve, including a brief sketch of some of its 'transferred' procedures that represent a hybrid from aspects of international arbitration and international litigation dispute resolution procedures. My aim in so doing is not to exhaustively map the hybridity of the SICC's transferred procedures – or their sources – but to illustrate how reference to broader cultural factors can inform even a bare functionalist analysis of legal borrowings. In other words, the SICC's hybridized transnational dispute resolution procedures serve to highlight the inevitable pressures for a legal transfer to adapt to a local culture. This idea of transfer (with adaptation) can be enhanced by considering each of the SICC's hybridized procedures as a series of individual standalone transfers, or, as a possible whole, where transfer represents the process and method of re-combining these procedures to form one institution. Doing so will provide insight into understanding both the genesis and operation of the SICC and its hybridized procedures, and possibly also extend to assisting in mooted efforts in other jurisdictions to develop international commercial courts, notably, including jurisdictions in East Asia (and Oceania).[4]

II INSTITUTIONAL 'BORROWINGS': FROM TRANSPLANT TO TRANSFER?

Conceiving of Legal Borrowings

The idea of whether 'legal borrowings' can and do occur has permeated much comparative law literature – including many chapters in this collection – for decades. Yet, as Professor Andrew Harding argues in Chapter 1 of this collection, this debate has often proved 'trapped', and fixated on a range of binary outcomes.[5] Framed, perhaps at its broadest, references to this act of

[4] See, e.g., the call by Justice Croft and Chief Justice Warren (Supreme Court of Victoria, Australia) for an 'integrated commercial court' in Australia, which, similar to the SICC is aimed at attracting both regional and 'global disputants': Justice Croft and Chief Justice Warren, 'An International Commercial Court for Australia – Looking beyond the New York Convention' (2016) Commercial CPD Seminar Series 34–5.

[5] Andrew Harding, 'The Legal Transplants Debate: Getting beyond the Impasse?', Chapter 1 in this Volume.

'borrowing' must encapsulate the entire range of events that arise over the 'process, activity and problem' of attempting to 'borrow' one or more rules of law, that come to be used in some shape or form outside of their original context. In part reflecting the debate as to the role of 'borrowings' as solely a legal task, as distinct from a socio-legal concern accounting for 'culture', comparative law literature is replete with competing terminology that variously focuses on categorizing aspects of the process of borrowing; highlighting the inevitable problems with adaptation of legal rules, or acting as a descriptive metaphor for the act of borrowing. This chapter is not intended to set out the full gamut of terms that are used – nor to evaluate their relative merits – but a brief review of these terms highlights that conceptions of 'legal borrowing' stretch from the prosaic and process-driven to the floridly metaphoric. The early metaphor of 'transplant' suggests the seamless excision of one organ from one body, to be placed into another. Yet, it is at the same time recognized by critical scholars that this attempted transplant is likely to be a difficult process; 'more delicate than heart transplants'.[6] The metaphors that follow reflect their own cultural and legal influences. In no particular order, and without aiming to be exhaustive, these terms include legal 'adaptation', 'borrowing', 'circulation', 'diffusion', 'evolution', 'expansion', 'exports', 'formants', 'imports', 'imposition', 'influence', 'irritants', 'migration', 'mutation', 'reception', 'spread', 'transfrontier mobility', 'translation', 'transmigration', or 'transposition'.[7] Comparative law has also succumbed to the temptation to 'modernize' in the face of technology, extending – often in a critical fashion – the terminology used to describe the borrowing process as an incidence of 'copy and paste',[8] as well as 'uploads and downloads'.[9] Yet, this divergence of terminology is not merely cosmetic; instead, it masks an array of methodological complexity. The danger is that when some of these metaphors are taken,

[6] G. Frankenberg, *Comparative Law as Critique* (Edward Elgar, 2016) 231.

[7] This very brief survey of terms stems primarily from the following works, the authors of which respectively prefer the term "legal transfer" and "legal diffusion": G. Frankenberg, 'Constitutions as Commodities: Notes on a Theory of Transfer' in G. Frankenberg (ed.), *Order from Transfer: Comparative Constitutional Design and Legal Culture* (Edward Elgar, 2013) 4; W. Twining, 'Diffusion of Law: A Global Perspective', *The Journal of Legal Pluralism and Unofficial Law* 36 (2004), 1, 5.

[8] Michaels critically analyzes this critical terminology, noting that this metaphor can be expanded to reflect the various formatting options available in modern word processors ('text only', 'keep source formatting', 'match destination formatting'), modelling the complexities faced by the comparative task: R. Michaels, '"One Size Can Fit All" – On the Mass Production of Legal Transplants' in G. Frankenberg (ed.), *Order from Transfer: Comparative Constitutional Design and Legal Culture* (Edward Elgar, 2013) 57.

[9] H. Koh, 'Why Transnational Law Matters', *Penn State International Law Review* 24 (2006), 745.

at least to some extent, literally, this will over-simplify the complexity – and potential problems – with adapting legal borrowings.

It assists to unpack one commonly used phrase – that of legal transplant – to highlight some of the complexities the terminology masks. The term legal transplant serves as a useful example, as despite criticism of its 'misleading' nature, it still has widespread use (including in the title of this collection).[10] The term came to prominence in the 1960-70s, and was popularized in a book by Alan Watson on comparative law and transplant.[11] Watson, drawing upon selected historical case studies, argues that transplants are the major source of legal change and occur regularly (and with relative ease).[12] The reception of the concept of 'transplant' was at the time – and remains – mixed, based primarily on perceived failings in abstracting away 'culture' ('societal values') from the act or process of borrowing.[13] Watson, in a subsequent revision, concedes that borrowing occurs with some degree of 'adaptation',[14] but maintains that 'transplants' still take place relatively insulated from surrounding reference to social and cultural factors. Taking issue with this conception of 'transplant', the traditional retort, represented perhaps most stridently in Legrand's work,[15] emphasizes the 'impossibility' of transplant due to the concept's failure to account for the ever-present 'culture'. That is, even if there can be technical integration of a legal borrowing, the rule's meaning 'does not survive the journey':[16] when a transplant encounters the surrounding "deep structures" of law – including legal culture, mentality, myth and the legal unconsciousness – it takes on a new dimension that is not captured within the idea of transplant.[17] This view is shared by other contributors to this collection, who describe it as

[10] See, e.g., the groundbreaking work of Teubner in the context of good faith: G. Teubner, 'Legal Irritants: Good Faith in British Law or How Unifying Law Ends up in New Divergences', *The Modern Law Review* 61 (1998), 11. Teubner expressly notes the misleading nature of attempting to categorize legal borrowings as a form of 'transplant' – preferring instead the concept of 'legal irritants' which highlights the "transformations of meaning" any borrowing must undergo: ibid., 11–12.

[11] A. Watson, *Legal Transplants: An Approach to Comparative Law* 2nd edn (University of Georgia Press, 1993). The first edition was published in 1974.

[12] Ibid., 95.

[13] See, for an overview of the early critiques of Watson's focus on transplant, with emphasis on issues arising from abstracting away from 'culture' or 'societal values': J. Cairns, 'Watson, Walton, and the History of Legal Transplants', *Georgia Journal of International & Comparative Law* 41 (2014), 637.

[14] One of the most cited comparative law terminologies is Watson's updated definition of a transplant as a form of 'borrowing (with adaptation)': Watson (n. 11) 7.

[15] With the aptly titled article: P. Legrand, 'The Impossibility of "Legal Transplants"', *Maastricht Journal of European and Comparative Law* 4 (1997), 111, 116–20.

[16] Ibid., 117.

[17] Teubner (n. 10) 21.

a 'mistake' to say that the law can always be detached from societal conditions in the recipient jurisdiction.[18] Consequently, utilizing the language of 'transplant' may be misleading as it suggests a narrower array of uses (an involuntary transplant?) than other terms, and cloaks the inherent problems of any movement of laws – which face inevitable difficulties due to an array of socio-legal concerns, such as culture, existing institutional structures and hegemonic influences.[19] This brief example serves simply to highlight the conceptual and methodological masks that inevitably arise in trying to summarize a complex task of borrowings under a single metaphorical heading.

For the purposes of this chapter, it is not necessary to delve further into this metaphorical and methodological debate regarding the terminology used to describe this process of 'transplant'.[20] Put simply, concerns arise with all terminology. For example, as Twining suggests, some terms direct us to the *source* of the legal transfer (such as 'export'), as distinct from others that direct attention to the *recipient* of the borrowing (e.g., 'transposition').[21] Yet, even this critique of terminology pre-supposes a conception of legal borrowings based on a unilateral transfer of one rule from one legal system to another. The use of many of the terms briefly surveyed above can also be criticized by reference to the uncertainty they engender by being 'ill-adapted' to capturing either gradual diffusion or continuous change through appropriation of foreign ideas.[22] Further and additionally, many terms – and underlying methodologies – do not fully capture the 'multifold, simultaneous, and iterative' borrowing processes inherent to any transnational dealings, which implicate 'disparate actors, applications, and flows in multiple directions'.[23] Instead, to begin to model these complexities, the comparative task – and the methodology and terminology utilized – should increasingly focus on 'pathways', rather than 'one way streets' – including the way in which law can be commoditized and 'tapped' on a transnational level.[24] For this reason, I adopt for the purposes of

[18] A. Harding in 'The Legal Transplants Debate: Getting beyond the Impasse?', Chapter 1 of this Volume.

[19] Frankenberg, 'Constitutions as Commodities: Notes on a Theory of Transfer' (n. 7) 8.

[20] This continues to be done extensively elsewhere – including in this collection: see, e.g., A. Harding, 'The Legal Transplants Debate: Getting beyond the Impasse?', Chapter 1 in this Volume.

[21] Twining (n. 7) 5 (note 6).

[22] M. Graziadei, 'Comparative Law as the Study of Transplants and Receptions' in M. Reimann and R. Zimmermann (eds.), *The Oxford Handbook of Comparative Law* (Oxford University Press, 2006) 443.

[23] G. Shaffer, 'Transnational Legal Ordering and State Change' in G. Shaffer (ed.), *Transnational Legal Ordering and State Change* (Cambridge University Press, 2012) 9.

[24] Frankenberg, 'Constitutions as Commodities: Notes on a Theory of Transfer' (n. 7) 8.

this chapter – still with hesitation – the terminology of 'legal *transfer*'. That is, rather than viewing hybridized procedures – and new legal developments in general – as static 'copies' or 'transplants', greater insight can be gleaned from considering this legal evolution or creation as a dynamic act of transfer, rather than a simple transplant analysis of where practices have been sourced.

As Section II sets out, the SICC's novel recombination of transnational dispute resolution procedures supports the idea of legal transfer; suggesting that there is more to this process than simply considering legal rules as a raft of independent organs 'transplanted' into a new body. Of course, the organs are essential, but so to the product: the creation, composition and adaptation to living of Frankenstein (or, in this case, an international commercial court) is of more consequence. In this sense, the genesis of the SICC stands as a particularly stark example, as its entire composition must be traced back across a series of pathways, themselves each involving a significant degree of borrowing, sharing and interrelationship in and across transnational dispute resolution and commercial court practice. Transfer also brings to the fore the inescapable issues of adaptation, and can, conceivably, extend to capturing iterative transnational processes from a wider socio-legal lens, including, for example, the commodification of so-called 'global' or 'transnational' 'best practices'.[25] The idea of transfer is thus of assistance in considering the design and operation of the SICC – a body that consciously seeks to transfer (to itself) 'best practice' dispute resolution processes, and then to adapt these processes in a hybrid way, to advance the goals of the SICC overall in its cultural context.

Towards a Richer Conception of Legal Transfer?

To begin to unpack the creation of the SICC as an incidence of transfer, it assists to recall that any legal rule or collection of legal rules – including those precipitated by legal transfer – represent only a 'generalization denoting a collage of legal artefacts'.[26] In Frankenberg's words, because law is both 'omnipresent' and 'ambiguous':

> to locate [law] only here or there would like trying to nail a pudding to the wall. We have to trace it everywhere: in texts, institutions, actions, ideas and fantasies – a rather disquieting but also fascinating prospect[27]

[25] As Frankenberg notes, the use of 'transfer' qualifies legal borrowings as problematic – rather than 'socially easy' and 'organic' (as in the case of transplant). It also assists in incorporating a broader array of socio-legal concerns: ibid.

[26] Graziadei (n. 22) 471.

[27] G. Frankenberg, 'Critical Comparisons: Re-Thinking Comparative Law', *Harvard International Law Journal* 26 (1985), 411, 452.

Considering the popularity of the term legal transplant, the dominant mode of analysis with respect to legal 'borrowings' has traditionally been one of formalism: attempts abound which aim to answer how legal rules are transplanted in a legal fashion based primarily on formal legal sources (cases, treaties, statute). In other words, attempting to nail the pudding to the wall. This has been criticized from a range of perspectives, including from the perspective of functionalism.[28] In this way, focus on a 'thicker' socio-legal *transfer* in this chapter sidesteps the debate of 'gaps and hopes' surrounding the possibility of legal transplant, and, instead, actively brings to the fore the methodological maelstrom arising from divergent functionalist, formalist or contextual analysis in considering legal borrowings.[29] This, at the least, suggests that a transfer is not a simple or natural processes.

In the context of the SICC, this means there may be utility when considering legal transfer to go further than a bare legal analysis of transferred procedures, and focus more closely on some aspects of 'thick comparison' in the constitution of the SICC overall. Doing so aids in moving beyond *a priori* debates around mere textualism or formalism versus contextualism ('law' versus 'culture').[30] That is, instead of considering whether transplants exist – or can exist – the more 'interesting question' is *how* transfer happens, and 'what happens when [transfer] happens': namely, exploring the processes or conditions which facilitate or hinder this transfer.[31] This requires moving beyond conceptions of legal legitimacy – a mere consideration of the legal validity of the transfer process – into broader concerns of acceptance ('cultural legitimacy' or 'authoritativeness' in the language of transnational legal ordering), assessing the extent to which the transfer is aided by or congruent with the social context, cultural values and political preferences of the adopting

28 See, e.g., early comparative law methodological criticisms in Frankenberg, 'Critical Comparisons' (n. 27). Brand takes this argument further, and considers that there are 'real problems' with the use of functional method in comparative law, querying its continued prominence given the significant methodological flaws: O. Brand, 'Conceptual Comparisons: Towards a Coherent Methodology of Comparative Legal Studies', *Brooklyn Journal of International Law* 32 (2007), 415 (and following): http://brooklynworks.brooklaw.edu/bjil/vol32/iss2/3 accessed 10 January 2019.

29 M. Seckelmann, 'Clotted History and Chemical Reactions – On the Possibility of Constitutional Transfer' in G. Frankenberg (ed.), *Order from Transfer: Comparative Constitutional Design and Legal Culture* (Edward Elgar, 2013) 40.

30 Frankenberg, *Comparative Law as Critique* (n. 6) 227.

31 Frankenberg, 'Constitutions as Commodities: Notes on a Theory of Transfer' (n. 7) 25. Frankenberg's comments are made in the context of considering constitutional transfer, but much of this approach can be applied more broadly, e.g. to 'institutional transfer'.

entity.[32] Focusing on the cultural factors facilitating reception of the transfer then implicates a range of actors – a particularly broad array in any field that touches on transnational elements – for example, extending potentially to various state authorities, public or private transnational authorities, domestic and international interest groups, and academic or professional elites. These actors can all play a role in 'transforming' the transferred rules – that is, attempting to adapt rules to culture.[33] Consequently, the use of legal transfers reminds us to consider the role of both legal and extra-legal impacts and actors across the spectrum of legal borrowings, their use as a source of legal development, and the likely impact on the 'success' of any transfer.

To further investigate the socio-legal aspects of transfer, it assists to explore how policy ideas and institutions transfer from one legal context to another, a process that takes inspirations from a diverse range of sources, including 'legal transplantation in comparative law, lesson drawing, policy transfer and policy convergence in political science'.[34] Applying a 'blend of legal, political and cultural academic insights' serves to make explicit the dichotomy between formal and informal institutions.[35] The former can broadly be aligned with formalism: a consideration of rules, regulations and procedures; the latter introduces a socio-legal aspect to any process of transfer, necessitating a consideration of social practice (stemming from norms and culture). Setting out this dichotomy makes clear the process of adaptation, and brings to light the difficult causative question – usually abstracted way from in a formalist approach – of how informal institutional preconditions may impact on the legitimacy of any transfer of formal institutions.[36] Utilizing the language of Gillespie, this process of transfer requires exploration of the 'regulatory conversations' between interpretative communities that share similar epistemological world views: it is this thinking which ultimately shapes the way in which legal transfers are adapted to a particular culture.[37] In this way,

[32] M. de Jong and S. Stoter, 'Institutional Transplantation and the Rule of Law: How This Interdisciplinary Method Can Enhance the Legitimacy of International Organisations', *Erasmus Law Review* 2 (2009), 311, 316. See, also, for efforts to categorize other domestic-to-domestic transfers as an incidence of transfer – and attempts to draw wider lessons from a range of empirical studies – the edited collection in: M. de Jong, K. Lalenis and V. Mamadouh (eds.), *The Theory and Practice of Institutional Transplantation: Experiences with the Transfer of Policy Institutions* (Springer, 2002).

[33] Graziadei (n. 22) 470.

[34] de Jong and Stoter (n. 32) 318.

[35] Ibid.

[36] Ibid., 319.

[37] J. Gillespie, 'Towards a Discursive Analysis of Legal Transfers into Developing East Asia', *New York University Journal of International Law and Politics* 40 (2007–2008), 657, 713.

rather than solely isolating the formal sources of legal rules that are transferred, a consideration of a broader idea of transfer built on legal culture offers greater explanatory force. Consequently, moving towards a thicker form of analysis opens the comparative task of transfer to 'local knowledge' in a 'context-sensitive' way, can assist in overcoming reductionism in surface-level formalist or functionalist approaches.[38]

Yet, to move from a reductionist comparison of transfer – and to instead engage with the performative act of comparison and its attendant political and ethical ramifications – is a much more difficult task than the traditional idea of legal borrowings captured by transplant: 'more like grasping a proverb, catching an allusion, seeing a joke – or . . . reading a poem'.[39] Given that the precise bounds of cultural influences are perhaps limitless, involving a multitude of actors and reaching far back to historical path dependencies, no one text – this chapter included – aims to do so, or perhaps even can do so, in an authoritative way. Indeed, due to difficulties in proving causation in any complex transfer, it is unlikely that even a 'thicker' analytical process can deterministically map any legal transfer, including the creation of the SICC.[40] Nonetheless, introducing aspects of thicker analysis via a richer idea of transfer acts to reposition the evaluative lens of borrowings to encompass not only the transferred rules from a legalistic perspective, but also a broader range of socio-legal (or 'cultural') factors that impact on the operation of these rules or the overall efficacy of the transfer process. Doing so offers greater explanatory force in considering the creation of the SICC as a process of transfer, and has the potential to inform subsequent efforts to develop other international commercial courts that may take inspiration from the SICC's approach.

III TRANSFER AND THE SICC

Transfer and Hybrid Adaptation: Dispute Resolution Procedures of the SICC

Despite influences from a range of transnational dispute resolution mechanisms and procedures, the SICC is unique in its genesis, in that it uses dispute resolution practices and procedures drawn from mixing and adapting elements of both international arbitration and litigation practice. It adapts these

[38] Frankenberg, *Comparative Law as Critique* (n. 6) 227.

[39] Ibid., 232, citing C. Geertz, 'From the Native's Point of View: On the Nature of Anthropological Understanding' in C. Geertz (ed.), *Further Essays in Interpretive Anthropology* (Basic Books, 1983).

[40] Gillespie (n. 37) 713.

practices in a 'hybrid' fashion,[41] attempting to balance the greater flexibility of many procedures of parties to arbitration, with the greater degree of control of judicial proceedings: the former is premised upon dispute users' autonomy, but the latter likely involves a greater consideration of public interests or public governance in transnational dispute resolution.[42] Because of this, the SICC likely represents a 'new model' for transnational litigation and commercial court practice.[43] Of course, traditional domestic courts or divisions of courts with a cross-border commercial focus – and often different procedures from other judicial organs – are not an entirely new creation: much of this focus can be traced back to the approach of some English courts, who have for centuries viewed their role as one that spans multiple jurisdictions, particularly with respect to trading matters.[44] However, the express design of the SICC to attract international disputants via its hybridity means that the SICC fundamentally differs from the traditional 'default' role of most national courts. At the same time, it is true that the SICC remains at its core – both in composition and approach – closer to extant commercial courts than it is to any arbitral institution or tribunal.[45] It is in this context of novel hybridity that the idea of legal transfer as an explanatory tool arises. Each of the procedures that constitute the SICC, or their overall 'repackaging' in the context of the

[41] M. Yip, 'Singapore International Commercial Court: A New Model for Transnational Commercial Litigation' in Y.-J. Ma (ed.), *Chinese (Taiwan) Yearbook of International Law and Affairs*, vol. 32 (Brill, 2016) 163. See also M. Hwang, 'Commercial Courts and International Arbitration–Competitors or Partners?', *Arbitration International* 31 (2015), 193, 201.

[42] See, e.g., a broad overview of the 'push' and 'pull' factors – including governance issues – away from arbitration to international litigation in S. Menon, 'International Commercial Courts: Towards a Transnational System of Dispute Resolution' (2015) Opening Lecture for the DIFC Courts Lecture Series 2015 8 (and following).

[43] It is clearly distinct from most commercial courts that are not designed in this way. Even its closest competitor – the DIFC Courts – were not expressly tailored to this purpose, serving instead to cater for a new economic zone within the Emirates: Yip (n. 41) 6.

[44] An early example of English courts that were tasked with attempting to resolve complex transnational disputes includes the Admiralty Courts, operating in various forms from as early as the fourteenth century: see, further, J. H. Baker, *The Oxford History of the Laws of England: 1483–1558* (Oxford University Press, 2003) ch. 11 (Admiralty Courts and Court Martial).

[45] See, e.g., ss. 18C and 18I of the Supreme Court of Judicature Act (Cap 322) 1969, which clarify that subject to the specific hybrid procedures adapted to the SICC, the SICC remains bound by all other rules of court in the same way as the High Court (including the subsidiary 'Rules of Court' as set out in Rule 5). Additionally, for example, despite deriving (and adapting) many procedures from arbitration, the procedures of the SICC have been styled closely, and explicitly, on the Commercial Court of England and Wales (a specialist court within the Queen's Bench Division of the High Court of Justice in the United Kingdom): Singapore International Commercial Court Committee, 'Report of the Singapore International Court Committee' (2013) [29].

operation of the SICC, can be analyzed as a series of transfers that offer insights on at least two levels: first, as to the operation and genesis of the SICC, and its potential appeal to disputants (and their legal counsel); and, second, the extent to which the transfer (or series of transfers) leading to the creation or operation of the SICC is likely itself to be transferrable beyond Singapore and the SICC.

Nature and Processes of the SICC

The SICC is established under Singaporean law to hear a diverse range of international commercial cases. To do so, it employs a range of procedures which are not available in other traditional domestic courts (including in Singapore). This means that despite its 'international' moniker and focus on providing for commercial disputants transnationally, the SICC remains a product of, and firmly rooted in, municipal (domestic) law, including its rules of private international law.[46] It thus remains an 'open question' whether the SICC can be correctly described as an 'international court' under accepted legal taxonomy.[47] Yet, for the purpose of this chapter the SICC's undoubted 'internationality' arises in one key respect – its attempt to attract and provide for foreign disputants – is what has allowed the transfer (with adaptation) of novel approaches to dispute resolution for a commercial court. This transfer process includes the incorporation of a 'strong influence' of the flexibility of arbitral practice throughout many of its procedures,[48] many of which differ significantly from domestic court procedures. For example, the SICC offers relatively flexible and accommodating approaches – compared with other courts – with respect to confidentiality, proof of foreign law and rules of evidence.[49] Ultimately, because the SICC's procedures derive in large part from elsewhere, their genesis can be initially explored as an incidence of legal transfer.

46 For example, all formative aspects of the SICC – including its constitution, jurisdiction and procedure – are set out in Singapore's Supreme Court of Judicature Act (Cap 322) ss. 18A-18M. All subsequent references to statutory provisions are to this Act, unless otherwise specified. These statutory powers are expanded upon in the SICC's Practice Directions: Singapore International Commercial Court, 'Singapore International Commercial Court Practice Directions' (2017).

47 D. H. Wong, 'The Rise of the International Commercial Court: What Is It and Will It Work?', *Civil Justice Quarterly* 33 (2014), 215, utilizing academic taxonomy on the definition of an international court notes that the SICC satisfies only four of the seven requirements.

48 M. Yip, 'The Resolution of Disputes before the Singapore International Commercial Court', *International and Comparative Law Quarterly* [2016] 439, 6.

49 Yip (n. 41) 156.

Many of the SICC's procedures aim to navigate the murky waters of procedural hybridity by balancing judicial direction (or compulsion) with deference to the wishes of the parties (party autonomy). Framed alternatively, the process of transfer embedded in each of the SICC's procedures represents an attempt to adapt transferred procedures in a way that is consistent with the judiciary's significant 'public governance' role, but also in a way that also supports 'private rights'.[50] This is, of course, not easy to balance. Arbitration procedures have been criticized for giving greater support to the latter as compared with courts;[51] but the criticism can be reversed in that courts do not give sufficient heed to private rights.[52] The idea of giving greater deference to private rights is, in no small part, based on a conscious policy decision to accord greater procedural flexibility to private disputants who have chosen their dispute resolution mechanism and forum. This idea permeates international arbitration, as its procedures are for the most part justified upon disputants' autonomy to choose a forum to hear their disputes.[53] The same cannot be said for litigants that end up in a domestic court due to the operational of default jurisdictional or private international law rules. It is here, however, that the SICC's attempt to 'hybridize' these procedures arise: the SICC recognizes that procedural flexibility is valuable for international commercial disputants, and hence aims to bridge the traditional divide between the 'flexibility' of arbitration and the default rules-driven approach of most national courts, adopting aspects of procedures that may make the SICC attractive to disputants who actively select a dispute resolution forum.[54]

[50] See, for an overview of the private-public governance mechanisms in both arbitration and litigation: C. Whytock, 'Litigation, Arbitration, and the Transnational Shadow of Law', *Duke Journal of Comparative & International Law* 18 (2008), 449.

[51] See, e.g., Wong (n. 47),) 205, 206.

[52] See, e.g., S. Menon, 'The Transnational Protection of Private Rights: Issues, Challenges, and Possible Solutions', *Asian Journal of International Law* 5 (2015), 219. Menon notes a range of 'improvements' aimed at promoting the transnational protections of private rights, including via reformed court-based mechanisms: 239 (and following).

[53] M. Yip, 'The Resolution of Disputes before the Singapore International Commercial Court', *International and Comparative Law Quarterly* [2016] 439, 6.

[54] Although it is difficult to source data for a new institution (and dispute resolution model that is emerging), the arbitration experience may prove instructive. In the context of international arbitration, over 38 per cent of respondents to a major empirical survey on user perceptions of arbitration suggest that such flexibility is one of arbitration's 'most valuable characteristics': White & Case and Queen Mary University of London, *International Arbitration Survey 2015: Improvements and Innovations in International Arbitration* (October 2015) www.arbitration.qmul.ac.uk/research/2015/ accessed 21 January 2019 ('2015 Arbitration Survey').

Exploring Hybridity: the Composition of the SICC

Rather than set out the hybridity of the SICC's procedures in an exhaustive fashion – which has been done comprehensively elsewhere[55] – it assists to consider an example that highlights the complexity of hybridization and its interaction with legal transfer. Doing so sheds light on the extent to which a richer conception of legal transfer – involving iterative flows of information, rules and norms across a range of jurisdictions, as well as mapping the idea of adaptation of any transfer to reflect the surrounding legal culture – may offer explanatory force. To do so, I select as a key exemplar of the SICC's hybridity, the way in which the court is constituted (i.e. the ways in which a decision maker or makers are selected or appointed). This is because in this respect the SICC draws heavily from arbitration, but this inspiration is tempered by the introduction of a significant degree of judicial control.

Reflecting influence from arbitration, the SICC is able to be constituted by both or either 'local' and international jurists, rather than solely jurists trained in a domestic legal tradition. These international jurists, termed 'International Judges' in the SICC, do not serve merely as figureheads or in an honorary role: they can hear and determine disputes in the first instance, sit on appeals from the SICC, and even be appointed to serve as President of the SICC Supreme Court of Judicature Act (Cap 322) 1969 sections 5A, 18B. Presently designated International Judges come from a diverse range of jurisdictions – including, for example, Australia, England, the United States, France, Japan, and Austria.[56] A brief consideration of three randomly selected International Judges highlights the wealth of transnational dispute resolution and commercial experience that doing so can bring: the Hon Justice Berger has decades of experience serving as a judge in Delaware (one of the most active corporate law jurisdictions in the United States); the Hon Justice Hascher presently serves as a judge of the Supreme Judicial Court of France, and has previously been heavily involved in international arbitration; and, the Hon Justice Bergin served for almost twenty years as a Commercial List judge in the Supreme Court of New South Wales, which likely has the heaviest commercial case-load of any court in Australia. In this sense, the International Judges able to resolve SICC disputes are specifically chosen for their expertise in different legal traditions and areas of commercial law.

[55] See, e.g.: Wong (n. 51); Hwang (n. 41); J. Landbrecht, 'The Singapore International Commercial Court (SICC) – An Alternative to International Arbitration?', ASA *Bulletin* 34 (2016), 112; Yip (n. 41); Man Yip (n. 48).

[56] See 'SICC – Judges' www.sicc.gov.sg/Judges.aspx?id=30 accessed 3 October 2016.

At the risk of stating the obvious, the use of specialized and expert International Judges diverges significantly from national court practice in Singapore (and most of the world), where judges are drawn almost exclusively from a local judiciary. Perhaps the most analogous scenario of international jurists serving in a foreign jurisdiction is what is termed the 'expatriate model': commonly seen where judges trained in a common-law legal tradition work within jurisdictions linked by Commonwealth ties (such as in a range of Pacific islands). Yet, this practice is far from the ordinary course, is usually conducted at the appellate level, and is predominantly utilized as a mechanism to bolster local judicial resources predominantly in developing countries (by drawing upon the expertise of foreign-trained legal professionals). As Stephen Eliot Smith, 'The Way We Do Things Back Home: Do Expatriate Judges Preferentially Cite the Jurisprudence of Their Home Countries?', *Oxford University Commonwealth Law Journal* 13 (2013), 331. finds, however, these expatriate judges often have a tendency to 'favour the jurisprudence of their home jurisdiction'". The SICC similarly predominantly employs Commonwealth-trained judges, who may yet be subject to the same criticism. Yet their purpose and rationale can be contrasted: International Judges in the context of the SICC are not intended to bridge a lack of resources, but instead are selected to add to Singapore's already strong reputation for resolving business disputes. In this sense, the SICC leverages upon the reputation of International Judges to further entrench its own reputation as a premier forum for commercial dispute resolution. Consequently, despite limited uses of 'foreign' judges in some (predominantly developing) jurisdictions, it is likely that SICC's approach remains without parallel in court-based transnational commercial dispute resolution.

At the same time, for those familiar with arbitral practice, the idea that disputants may prefer, and be able to select, their decision-maker(s) – usually with expertise in the subject matter of the commercial relationship, or in international dispute resolution generally – goes without saying. The common wisdom in transnational commercial dispute resolution models and reflects this refrain, namely that Yves Dezalay and Bryant G. Garth, *Dealing in Virtue: International Commercial Arbitration and the Construction of a Transnational Legal Order* (University of Chicago Press, 1996) 8. Unlike official court systems, where public judges are assigned more or less randomly to individual cases and are supposed to operate according to clearly established procedures and substantive laws, arbitration allows the parties to select their judges.

It is here that the nuanced contours of the SICC's novel attempt to introduce greater deference via a process of hybridity can be seen. While the use of International Jurists is a novel procedural innovation, drawing upon the flexibility inherent in international arbitration, the SICC retains judicial discretion to determine which judge will hear a dispute. That is, rather than considering the selection of the decision-maker from the central position of party autonomy (as in international arbitration), or relatively 'randomly' (as most traditional domestic courts do, even where they may employ a 'foreign' jurist), the selection of International Judges occurs via the grant of a broad discretion to the Chief Justice to select the judges to hear a particular dispute or a class of disputes.[57] This discretion can encompass – and indeed will likely be predominantly be exercised based upon – a deference to disputant wishes.

The carefully crafted balancing act the SICC undertakes to navigate hybridity can be seen perhaps most clearly in procedures applicable to determining the number of judges that will hear a dispute. In international arbitration, this remains strictly a matter for party autonomy.[58] By contrast, in traditional courts, this is usually subject to mandatory procedural rules that disputants have little say in or control over. Like arbitral practice, the SICC allows disputants to assist in determining whether the court will be constituted by a single judge or three judges.[59] However – and again diverging from the significant deference to party autonomy in international arbitration – this autonomy is qualified: the Chief Justice of the SICC can, on a discretionary basis, direct that the matter be heard by either one or three judges, even if this is contrary to the express wishes of the parties. The language of Practice Direction 23(2) neatly demonstrates the nature of this balancing act: it provides that proceedings in the SICC 'must' be heard by three judges if the Chief Justice determines that 'that three Judges should hear the cause of the matter', or where all parties agree so agree, '*unless the Chief Justice directs otherwise*'. In this way, the SICC signals it will be guided broadly by the wishes of disputants, but retains a residual control over the composition of judges on the Court via the Chief Justice's discretion. Yet, the mere existence of a discretion is where an attempt to model a transfer in a bare legal formalist fashion ends: unfortunately, this says little about how this discretion is likely to be exercised.

57 Section 9(4)(b) confers discretion on the Chief Justice to appoint an 'International Judge' to sit in the SICC to hear and determine 'any case . . . or such classes of cases' in the SICC as the Chief Justice determines (and is paralleled by s. 29(4) for appeals).

58 This is true even for institutional arbitration that provides greater guidance to the parties. See, e.g., Art. 7 of the United Nations Commission on International Trade Law, 'UNCITRAL Arbitration Rules' (2013), which leaves the number of arbitrators largely to party agreement (with a self-executing default of three arbitrators if the parties cannot agree in a timely fashion).

59 See Order 110, Rule 53(1) of the Rules of the Court; see also Singapore International Commercial Court (n. 46) Practice Direction 23 (and Practice Direction 24 for the constitution of the Court of Appeal in SICC matters).

As has been argued in the context of recognising and enforcing arbitral awards, broad 'discretions' are rarely, if ever, unfettered or completely 'open-ended' in practice.[60] This seems to be consistent with the view of the Singaporean Court of Appeal, which, in an oft-cited extracted – albeit in a case testing executive discretion in detention matters – noted that the very 'notion of a subjective or unfettered discretion is contrary to the rule of law'.[61] Indeed, sometimes a 'formal' legal discretion masks an established body of rules or norms that govern what otherwise appears to be an unbounded discretionary decision.[62] As Hall suggests in the context of enforcing arbitral awards pursuant to the New York Convention,[63] despite the appearance of an unfettered discretion apparent in a literal reading of the Convention, years of practice have given rise to a 'general rule' that if a defence is established 'enforcement will be (and should be) refused'.[64] In this way norms embedded in the 'spirit and intent' of this Convention can potentially transcend national law boundaries, and shape the contours of what otherwise appears to be an unfettered and entirely domestic discretionary concern. Applied to the SICC in the context of legal transfer, this suggests that, a mere legal formalist analysis does not divulge the practice of how legal rules containing a discretion are likely to be applied or adapted, particularly when they draw directly upon perceived best practice across a range of transnational dispute resolution mechanisms.

From only this brief exemplar of the SICC's compositional procedures, it is immediately apparent that an understanding of legal transfer that considers the SICC's hybrid procedures as simply representing a 'transplant' as a 'copy' of legal borrowings is deficient. For example, a formalist overview of transfer can say little about the contours of the SICC's reliance upon judicial discretion to carve a 'hybrid' path to a range of its dispute resolution procedures.[65] Yet, given the SICC's strong drive to attract foreign litigants, it is unlikely that such discretion will be exercised capriciously (or unreasonably). In this way, as Section 2.2 elaborates further, the SICC's procedures are shaped by the

[60] J. Hill, 'The Exercise of Judicial Discretion in Relation to Applications to Enforce Arbitral Awards under the New York Convention 1958', *Oxford Journal of Legal Studies* 36 (2016), 304, 306.

[61] *Chng Suan Tze* v. *Minister for Home Affairs* [1988] 2 SLR(R) 525 at [86].

[62] Hill (n. 60) 306.

[63] United Nations Convention on the Recognition and Enforcement of Foreign Arbitral Awards 38.

[64] Hill (n. 60) 333.

[65] For example, the SICC also has a broad discretion to apply 'other rules of evidence' (s. 18K), and to order that a 'question of foreign law be determined on the basis of submissions instead of proof' (s. 18L): Supreme Court of Judicature Act (Cap 322) (n. 45).

surrounding socio-legal cultural landscape: without consideration of these factors, a bare legal transfer lacks explanatory depth. This is because such a conception of legal formalism cannot begin to comprehend the contours of some adaptations to transfer. It is precisely these 'adaptations', however, that have significant practical import for disputants. These remain ultimately a product of the surrounding local, institutional, and transnational culture, as applied and understood by the SICC. Thus, as the exemplar of the SICC's hybridity in composition suggests, the SICC and its dispute resolution procedures cannot be fulsomely explained simply by reference to legality or legal formalism in transfer.

Culture and Transfer: the Creation of the SICC

As Section 2.1.1 establishes, a level of formal legal analysis is needed to isolate the operative procedures of the SICC, and the extent to which these procedures may represent a form of legal transfer. However, these innovations only become truly comprehensible in the context of the wider socio-legal context of the creation of the SICC overall. In particular, the genesis of the SICC represents a willingness to break with the structure of traditional dispute resolution mechanisms and develop an institution that adopts elements of hybridity; essentially re-conceptualizing the role of transnational dispute resolution mechanisms. In large part, this approach depends on embedded cultural features that have been utilized and built upon to support the ambitious creation of the SICC. These include, for example, Singapore's stable institutional and legal structures, including its strong support for the rule of law, deference to commercial disputants where this is not contrary to the rule of law, and the ongoing relationships and close interaction between different arms of the Singaporean government.[66] These factors combined allowed the SICC to develop as an idea – and subsequently an institution – at a pace that is perhaps without parallel in institutional development (let alone in the development of commercial courts). At the same time, however, it must be recalled that it is difficult – if not 'impossible' – to attempt to deterministically model legal transfers.[67] In other words, it is hard to prove causality in the transfer process by identifying essential pre-conditions for a transfer's success. Even

[66] Although far outside of this chapter – and perhaps of less import from an international commercial law perspective – see for a critical analysis of the concept of the rule of law in general, including the common critique of Singapore's purported rule *by* law – rather than rule *of* law: L.-A. Thio, 'Between Apology and Apogee, Autochthony: The "Rule of Law" beyond the Rules of Law in Singapore', *Singapore Journal of Legal Studies* [2012] 269.

[67] Gillespie (n. 37) 713. See also Section 1.2, above.

without attempting this task, however, exploring the process of transfer (and adaptation) can still go some way to explaining how and why a particular procedure operates.

The first outcome that offers some insight into the culture surrounding the creation of the SICC and its hybrid procedures is the speed at which the SICC developed. Each timeframe in the SICC's establishment – from the public airing of the *idea* of the SICC (early 2013), to its development, support and implementation as a legal framework (late 2014), on to a fully constituted and operational organ embedded in the Singaporean judiciary (early 2015) – is perhaps without precedent in the development of a complex commercial court. As to the first, the idea of the SICC was first publicly mooted in a speech by the Chief Justice of Singapore at the opening of the Singaporean Legal year on 4 January 2013,[68] and developed from idea to institution at a rapid pace. From its constitution, it took a specially appointed SICC Committee – the body tasked with establishing the SICC – only approximately seven months to submit its final report to the Singaporean Government.[69] Less than a week later, the Ministry of Law formally welcomed the SICC Committee's report,[70] and established a period of public consultation: itself relatively expeditious given the time of year – from 3 December to 31 January 2014.[71] By early October 2014, the legal framework to establish the SICC – which included significant amendments to the Singaporean Constitution,[72] the Supreme Court Act,[73] and some SICC-related amendments in the Legal Profession Act[74] – had been introduced into Parliament. This framework was finalized in the final quarter of 2014, and on 5 January 2015, the SICC was launched. It bears repeating at this point that the precise constitution and approach of the SICC, including the way of navigating hybrid dispute resolution procedures, was at the time, and yet remains, a novel development for judiciaries

68 S. Menon, 'Response by Chief Justice Sundaresh Menon' (2013) Speech delivered at the Singapore Opening of Legal Year 2013 www.sal.org.sg/Lists/Speeches/DispForm.aspx?ID=112 accessed 1 January 2017.

69 Singapore International Commercial Court Committee (n. 45).

70 Ministry of Law (Singapore), 'Government Welcomes Recommendations to Establish Singapore International Commercial Court' (2013) Press Release www.mlaw.gov.sg/news/press-releases/government-welcomes-recommendation-to-establish-SICC.html accessed 1 January 2017.

71 Ministry of Law (Singapore), 'Public Consultation on the Report of the Singapore International Commercial Court Committee' (2013) Public Consultation www.mlaw.gov.sg/news/press-releases/government-welcomes-recommendation-to-establish-SICC.html accessed 1 January 2017.

72 Constitution of the Republic of Singapore (Amendment) Act 2014 (Act 39 of 2014).

73 Supreme Court of Judicature (Amendment) Act 2014 (Act 42 of 2014).

74 Legal Profession (Amendment) Act 2014 (Act 40 of 2014).

anywhere in the world.[75] Not surprisingly, given the sheer speed at which the SICC developed, this did not escape practitioners or commentators: early views, dating back more than a year before the SICC came into existence in January 2015, suggested that the SICC – and the expeditious way it had been conceived – constituted a 'bold, visionary and entrepreneurial approach' representing a 'masterstroke' of deft concerted action within Singapore, that was likely to resound on a transnational level.[76]

Ultimately, the speed at which the SICC could develop as an institution can be related back to the strong relationships and close interlinkages between arms of the Singaporean government: for the most part, an assemblage of (unwritten) cultural factors and legal norms. In this way, the SICC reflects perhaps the highpoint of 'voluntary adoption' of a legal transfer, driven by arms of government working together in an expeditious and seamlessly integrated fashion. This is seen clearly even in the relationships of actors constituting (and leading) key legal roles within Singapore. For example, the SICC Committee was co-chaired by the then Minister for Law and the then Judge of Appeal Justice V K Rajah. Justice Rajah then assumed office as Attorney-General in 2014, further highlighting the close links between executive and judicial branches of government. Yet this linkage is not unique: Justice Rajah's predecessor, The Hon Steven Chong was appointed as Attorney-General from his role as a Judge on the Supreme Court, and after serving two years in that role, returned to the bench. Additionally, the predecessor of Steven Chong, the Hon Sundaresh Menon, went on to serve as Chief Justice of Singapore, and continues to play an active role in promoting the SICC.[77] The most recent appointment of Lucien Wong as Attorney-General of Singapore (19 December 2016) serves as an exception that proves the rule of strong linkages between the executive government and the judiciary: Wong is the first Attorney-General of Singapore who has not spent time as a judge or within

[75] It is argued, in this vein, that the SICC in particular offers a "new model of litigation for international disputes" as it was expressly designed entirely for this purpose: Yip (n. 41) 6.

[76] Clifford Chance and Cavenagh Law LLP, 'The Singapore International Commercial Court – A Masterstroke' (2013) Briefing Note www.cliffordchance.com/briefings/2013/12/the_singapore_internationalcommercialcourt.html accessed 29 March 2017.

[77] See, e.g., a range of speeches and academic works centreed upon justice and governance in an era of transnationalization and arbitration – many of which are cited in this chapter – including: S. Menon, 'Transnational Commercial Law: Realities, Challenges and a Call for Meaningful Convergence', *Singapore Journal of Legal Studies* 2013 (2013), 231; S. Menon, 'The Somewhat Uncommon Law of Commerce', *Singapore Academy of Law Journal* 26 (2014), 23; Menon, 'The Transnational Protection of Private Rights' (n. 52); Menon, 'International Commercial Courts: Towards a Transnational System of Dispute Resolution' (n. 42).

the Attorney-General's chambers. On balance, it is likely that this fluidity between executive and judicial positions enables greater cooperation between arms of government than is seen in other legal systems that employ a stricter separation of powers – and is likely to be a unique product of the tight-knit Singaporean legal culture.[78]

Close interlinkages and trust between different arms of government, rather than a strict separation of powers, are also seen directly from the outset of the creation of the SICC, including in the initial formation of the idea of the SICC, and the composition of the SICC Committee. Demonstrating these close relationships, the original Secretariat to this Committee was a combined product of a mix of representatives drawn from all three key governmental legal institutions – the Attorney-General's Chambers, the Supreme Court and the Ministry of Law. Additionally, and from the outset, the Secretariat, combining these three key legal arms of government, was comfortable in diverging in approach from the traditional parochial domestic concerns of most domestic law reformers. In particular, the Secretariat was concerned with capturing 'global best practice' in its procedures, and to facilitate this goal appointed a significant number of Committee members with no necessary link to Singapore. The Committee membership thus represents a broad swathe of the who's who in transnational dispute resolution (albeit predominantly those with a common-law perspective): extending to a diverse range of individuals from around the globe, including experienced legal practitioners, legal academics and judges. Importantly, these individuals are able to offer centuries of combined experience in transnational dispute resolution practice, including in both arbitration and litigation, across a range of key commercial jurisdictions. To grasp the extent of the international and transnational expertise employed in the SICC Committee – ranging from all aspects of private practice and government – it helps to set out the list in its entirety:[79]

> [2] On 13 May 2013, the Minister for Law appointed the following members to the SICC Committee:
> (a) Mr Ang Cheng Hock SC, Partner (Allen & Gledhill LLP);
> (b) Dr Beh Swan Gin, Permanent Secretary (Ministry of Law);

[78] Consider, e.g., the 'de-linking' of the separation of powers from the rule of law in the context of Singapore. G. Silverstein, 'Singapore: The Exception That Proves Rules Matter' in T. Ginsburg and T. Moustafa (eds.), *Rule by Law: the Politics of Courts in Authoritarian Regimes* (Cambridge University Press, 2008) 83–4. The Singaporean government is intimately concerned with the latter (including international perceptions of Singapore's rule of law) particularly in business matters, indicating a decoupling of the two concepts.

[79] Singapore International Commercial Court Committee (n. 45) [2].

(c) Mr Cavinder Bull SC, Deputy Chairman of Singapore International Arbitration Centre SIAC Court of Arbitration, Director (Drew & Napier LLC);
(d) Mr Chan Leng Sun SC, Principal (Dispute Resolution, Baker & McKenzie. Wong & Leow);
(e) Mr Chong Yee Leong, Partner (Allen & Gledhill LLP);
(f) Lord Peter Goldsmith QC PC, former Attorney General of England and Wales, Partner (Debevoise & Plimpton LLP)
(g) Professor Jan Paulsson, President (International Council for Commercial Arbitration)
(h) The Honourable Justice Judith Prakash, Judge (Supreme Court of Singapore);
(i) Ms Juthika Ramanathan, Chief Executive (Supreme Court of Singapore);
(j) Mr Harish Salve, former Solicitor General of India, Senior Advocate (Supreme Court of India);
(k) Mr Joe Smouha QC, Barrister (Essex Court Chambers);
(l) The Honourable James Jacob Spigelman, AC QC, former Chief Justice of the Supreme Court of New South Wales;
(m) Professor Tan Lee Meng, former Judge of the Supreme Court of Singapore, Professor (National University of Singapore);
(n) Mr Thio Shen Yi SC, Joint Managing Director (TSMP Law Corporation);
(o) Mr Robert Weber, Senior Vice President, Legal and Regulatory Affairs, and General Counsel (IBM);
(p) Ms Ariel Ye, Head of Cross-Border Dispute Resolution (King & Wood Mallesons (PRC)); and
(q) Mr Andre Yeap SC, Senior Partner (Rajah & Tann LLP).

In this way, the SICC Committee's origin – which, somewhat uniquely for the creation of a domestic legal institution much more closely represents the composition of an expert working group of a transnational legal body, constituted by a as broad range of specialized international experts – drove directly and explicitly the strong transnational focus of the SICC's procedures. The speed by which the SICC came into being is thus perhaps even more surprising, given that the Committee's composition closely models a transnational expert grouping – the 'law-making' of which usually progress at the slower pace of 'incrementalisms'.[80] It is perhaps no surprise, then, that one of the SICC Committee's 'key recommendations' was that,

[80] See, e.g., S. Block-Lieb and T. Halliday, 'Incrementalisms in Global Lawmaking', *Brooklyn Journal of International Law* 32 (2007).

as a starting rule, 'international best practice for commercial dispute resolution' be followed.[81] This broad transnational creation story of the SICC is no doubt a critical component that allows it to successfully craft and navigate its own novel approach to complex transnational issues.[82] Where matters are ambiguous – or subject to judicial discretion – they can thus be interpreted with this transnational business-friendly focus in mind. In no small part, then, the method and precise composition of the SICC reflects a product of Singaporean reformist legal culture in international business matters. This legal culture was initially – and remains – a key contributing factor to the SICC's success in 'hybridizing' complex dispute resolution procedures in a novel fashion for transnational dispute resolution.

IV CONCLUDING REMARKS

This chapter has demonstrated the difficulties of conceiving of legal borrowings as a process of one-way legal 'transplantation' in the context of the SICC. Given the process of hybridity embedded in the SICC's practices, there is no doubt some truth to the idea that the act of adapting a legal borrowing to another jurisdiction recreates the legal borrowing in an entirely distinct way. It is thus somewhat artificial to separate out each process by subject area – or even the SICC as a whole – and comment on the degree of transfer as it is a process of 'copying'; instead, the act of transfer creates new rules, approaches, and as we see with the SICC, has the potential to create new and novel procedures and even institutions on a transnational scale. Instead of transplants, reference instead to the idea of 'legal transfer' can prove useful, as it suggests that multiple pathways, models and frameworks are 'tapped' or 'mined' and then evaluated for their explanatory utility. Doing so in the context of procedures that take inspiration from a raft of transnational dispute resolution procedures – and 'hybridizing' them in a novel way – begins to offer a richer view of ongoing legal developments or evolutions. Conceiving of legal borrowings as a broader form of transfer thus offers first steps towards garnering analytical insight into complex adaptations such as attempts to hybridize disparate resolution procedures, and provides space for consideration of

81 Singapore International Commercial Court Committee (n. 45) [29].

82 See, e.g., G. Shaffer, 'The Dimensions and Determinants of State Change' in G. Shaffer (ed.), *Transnational Legal Ordering and State Change* (Cambridge University Press, 2012) 23–31.

the role and impact of socio-legal factors such as the amorphous idea of culture.

At the same time, despite artfully navigating the creation of novel hybrid procedures in a manner consistent with its transnational focus, the extent to which the SICC is likely to serve as a 'best practice' model for other international commercial courts is yet unclear. Although far from an empirical finding, no other mooted international commercial court goes as far in adopting hybridity and re-imagining court procedures as the SICC.[83] On the other hand, the initial reception of the SICC's judgments – at present, only representing judgments in matters transferred from the High Court to the SICC – has been overwhelmingly positive.[84] For example, a number of international law firms have expressly noted the SICC's potential advantages over other forms of dispute resolution, including arbitration, based in part on the SICC's track record of resolving disputes in both a 'reliable', 'speedy' and 'expeditious' fashion.[85] This may suggest that while the transfer process leading to the SICC – and the operation of the SICC itself – is difficult to replicate in other jurisdictions, it still shows signs of transnational legitimacy amongst dispute users. However, the true 'success' of the SICC will take many years to determine: as it is aimed at attracting foreign disputants, the ultimate measure will be when contracting parties (or their legal representatives) actively choose to submit their disputes – real or potential – to the SICC, and this active selection filters down to an eventual dispute heard in the SICC. Pending any further empirical study, then, the success of any transferred procedure is likely to remain an open question. Nonetheless, as Professor Andrew Harding argues in opening this Volume, the difficulty of assessing such success should not act as an inhibitor to undertaking true legal change built upon transfer.[86]

83 See the constitutive documents for a range of mooted international commercial courts, set out at n. 3, above.

84 See 'SICC – Hearings & Judgments' www.sicc.gov.sg/HearingsJudgments.aspx?id=72 accessed 12 June 2017.

85 'Full Steam Ahead: Singapore International Commercial Court ('SICC') Issues Judgment Clarifying the Position on What Constitutes an Offshore Case' (*Herbert Smith Freehills – Asia disputes notes*, July 2016) http://hsfnotes.com/asiadisputes/2016/07/22/full-steam-ahead-singapore-international-commercial-court-sicc-issues-judgment-clarifying-the-position-on-what-constitutes-an-offshore-case/ accessed 12 June 2017; 'KWM | The Singapore International Commercial Court – Two Years On' www.kwm.com/en/au/knowledge/insights/singapore-international-commercial-court-two-years-on-20170529 accessed 12 June 2017.

86 A. Harding, 'The Legal Transplants Debate: Getting beyond the Impasse?', Chapter 1 of this Volume.

V BIBLIOGRAPHY

Baker, J. H., *The Oxford History of the Laws of England: 1483–1558* (Oxford University Press, 2003).

Block-Lieb, S. and Halliday T., 'Incrementalisms in Global Lawmaking', *Brooklyn Journal of International Law* 32 (2007).

Brand, O., 'Conceptual Comparisons: Towards a Coherent Methodology of Comparative Legal Studies', *Brooklyn Journal of International Law* 32 (2007) http://brooklynworks.brooklaw.edu/bjil/vol32/iss2/3.

Cairns J., 'Watson, Walton, and the History of Legal Transplants', *Georgia Journal of International & Comparative Law* 41 (2014), 637.

Clifford Chance and Cavenagh Law LLP, 'The Singapore International Commercial Court – A Masterstroke' (2013) Briefing Note www.cliffordchance.com/briefings/2013/12/the_singapore_internationalcommercialcourt.html accessed 29 March 2017.

Council of Ministers, 'Instauration de la Brussels International Business Court [Establishment of the Brussels International Business Court]' (2017) Press Release www.presscenter.org/fr/pressrelease/20171027/instauration-de-la-brussels-international-business-court accessed 7 December 2017.

de Jong, M., Lalenis K. and Mamadouh V. (eds.), *The Theory and Practice of Institutional Transplantation: Experiences with the Transfer of Policy Institutions* (Springer, 2002).

de Jong M. and Stoter S., 'Institutional Transplantation and the Rule of Law: How This Interdisciplinary Method Can Enhance the Legitimacy of International Organisations', *Erasmus Law Review* 2 (2009),311.

de Rechtspraak [Judiciary of the Netherlands], 'Plan tot oprichting van de Netherlands commercial court [Plan to establish the Netherlands commercial court]' (2015).

Dezalay Y. and Garth B. G., *Dealing in Virtue: International Commercial Arbitration and the Construction of a Transnational Legal Order* (University of Chicago Press, 1996).

Frankenberg G., 'Critical Comparisons: Re-Thinking Comparative Law', *Harvard International Law Journal* 26 (1985), 411.

Frankenberg, G., 'Constitutions as Commodities: Notes on a Theory of Transfer' in Frankenberg, G. (ed.), *Order from Transfer: Comparative Constitutional Design and Legal Culture* (Edward Elgar, 2013).

Frankenberg, G., *Comparative Law as Critique* (Edward Elgar, 2016).

Frankfurt Regional Court [Landgericht Frankfurt am Main], 'Gerichtsstandort Frankfurt wird gestärkt: Englischsprachige Kammer für Handelssachen ab Januar 2018 [Strengthening Frankfurt as a Venue: English-Speaking Chamber for Commercial Matters Starting January 2018]' (2017) Press Release.

'Full Steam Ahead: Singapore International Commercial Court ("SICC") Issues Judgment Clarifying the Position on What Constitutes an Offshore Case' (*Herbert Smith Freehills – Asia disputes notes*, July 2016) http://hsfnotes.com/asiadisputes/2016/07/22/full-steam-ahead-singapore-international-commercial-court-sicc-issues-judgment-clarifying-the-position-on-what-constitutes-an-offshore-case/ accessed 12 June 2017.

Geertz, C., 'From the Native's Point of View: On the Nature of Anthropological Understanding' in Clifford Geertz (ed.), *Further Essays in Interpretive Anthropology* (Basic Books, 1983).

Gillespie, J., 'Towards a Discursive Analysis of Legal Transfers into Developing East Asia', *New York University Journal of International Law and Politics* 40 (2007–2008), 657.

Graziadei, M., 'Comparative Law as the Study of Transplants and Receptions' in Mathias Reimann and Reinhard Zimmermann (eds.), *The Oxford Handbook of Comparative Law* (Oxford University Press, 2006).

Hill, J., 'The Exercise of Judicial Discretion in Relation to Applications to Enforce Arbitral Awards under the New York Convention 1958', *Oxford Journal of Legal Studies* 36 (2016),304.

Hwang M., 'Commercial Courts and International Arbitration–Competitors or Partners?', *Arbitration International* 31 (2015), 193.

Justice Croft and Chief Justice Warren, 'An International Commercial Court for Australia – Looking beyond the New York Convention' (2016) Commercial CPD Seminar Series.

Koh, H., 'Why Transnational Law Matters', *Penn State International Law Review* 24 (2006), 745.

'KWM : The Singapore International Commercial Court – Two Years On' www.kwm.com/en/au/knowledge/insights/singapore-international-commercial-court-two-years-on-20170529 accessed 12 June 2017.

Landbrecht, J., 'The Singapore International Commercial Court (SICC) – An Alternative to International Arbitration?', *ASA Bulletin* 34 (2016), 112.

Legrand, P., 'The Impossibility of "Legal Transplants"', *Maastricht Journal of European and Comparative Law* 4 (1997), 111.

Menon, S., 'Transnational Commercial Law: Realities, Challenges and a Call for Meaningful Convergence', *Singapore Journal of Legal Studies* 2013 (2013), 231.

Menon, S., 'Response by Chief Justice Sundaresh Menon' (2013) Speech delivered at the Singapore Opening of Legal Year 2013 www.sal.org.sg/lists/speeches/dispform.aspx?id=112 accessed 1 January 2017.

Menon, S., 'The Somewhat Uncommon Law of Commerce', *Singapore Academy of Law Journal* 26 (2014), 23.

Menon, S., 'International Commercial Courts: Towards a Transnational System of Dispute Resolution' (2015) Opening Lecture for the DIFC Courts Lecture Series 2015.

Menon, S., 'The Transnational Protection of Private Rights: Issues, Challenges, and Possible Solutions', *Asian Journal of International Law* 5 (2015), 219.

Michaels, Ralf, '"One Size Can Fit All" – On the Mass Production of Legal Transplants' in Frankenberg, G. (ed.), *Order from Transfer: Comparative Constitutional Design and Legal Culture* (Edward Elgar, 2013).

Ministry of Law (Singapore), 'Government Welcomes Recommendations to Establish Singapore International Commercial Court' (2013) Press Release www.mlaw.gov.sg/news/press-releases/government-welcomes-recommendation-to-establish-sicc.html accessed 1 January 2017.

Ministry of Law (Singapore) 'Public Consultation on the Report of the Singapore International Commercial Court Committee' (2013) Public Consultation www.mlaw.gov.sg/news/press-releases/government-welcomes-recommendation-to-establish-sicc.html accessed 1 January 2017.

Seckelmann, M., 'Clotted History and Chemical Reactions – On the Possibility of Constitutional Transfer' in Frankenberg, G. (ed.), *Order from Transfer: Comparative Constitutional Design and Legal Culture* (Edward Elgar, 2013).

Shaffer, G., 'The Dimensions and Determinants of State Change' in Shaffer, G. (ed.), *Transnational Legal Ordering and State Change* (Cambridge University Press, 2012).

Shaffer, G., 'Transnational Legal Ordering and State Change' in Shaffer, G. (ed.), *Transnational Legal Ordering and State Change* (Cambridge University Press, 2012).

Sharar, Z. and Khulaifi, M. A. 'The Courts in Qatar Financial Centre and Dubai International Financial Centre: A Comparative Analysis', *Hong Kong Law Journal* 46 (2016), 529.

'SICC – Hearings & Judgments' www.sicc.gov.sg/hearingsjudgments.aspx?id=72 accessed 12 June 2017.

'SICC – Judges' www.sicc.gov.sg/judges.aspx?id=30 accessed 3 October 2016.

Silverstein G., 'Singapore: The Exception That Proves Rules Matter' in Ginsburg, T. and Moustafa, T. (eds.), *Rule by Law: The Politics of Courts in Authoritarian Regimes* (Cambridge University Press, 2008).

Singapore International Commercial Court, 'Singapore International Commercial Court Practice Directions' (2017).

Singapore International Commercial Court Committee, 'Report of the Singapore International Court Committee' (2013).

Smith, S. E., 'The Way We Do Things Back Home: Do Expatriate Judges Preferentially Cite the Jurisprudence of Their Home Countries?', *Oxford University Commonwealth Law Journal* 13 (2013), 331.

Supreme People's Court Monitor, 'SPC Reveals New Belt & Road-Related Initiatives' (*Supreme People's Court Monitor*, 7 October 2017) https://supremepeoplescourt monitor.com/2017/10/07/spc-reveals-new-belt-road-related-initiatives/ accessed 18 December 2017.

Teubner, G., 'Legal Irritants: Good Faith in British Law or How Unifying Law Ends up in New Divergences', *The Modern Law Review* 61 (1998), 11.

Thio, L.-A., 'Between Apology and Apogee, Autochthony: The "rule of Law" beyond the Rules of Law in Singapore', *Singapore Journal of Legal Studies* [2012], 269.

Twining W., 'Diffusion of Law: A Global Perspective', *The Journal of Legal Pluralism and Unofficial Law* 36 (2004), 1.

United Nations Commission on International Trade Law, 'UNCITRAL Arbitration Rules' (2013).

Watson, A., *Legal Transplants: An Approach to Comparative Law* 2nd edn (University of Georgia Press, 1993).

Whytock, C., 'Litigation, Arbitration, and the Transnational Shadow of Law', *Duke Journal of Comparative & International Law* 18 (2008), 449.

Wong, D. H., 'The Rise of the International Commercial Court: What Is It and Will It Work?', *Civil Justice Quarterly* 33 (2014), 205.

Yip M., 'Singapore International Commercial Court: A New Model for Transnational Commercial Litigation' in Ma, Y.-J. (ed.), *Chinese (Taiwan) Yearbook of International Law and Affairs*, vol. 32 (Brill, 2016).

Yip M., 'The Resolution of Disputes before the Singapore International Commercial Court', *International and Comparative Law Quarterly* [2016], 439.
Supreme Court of Judicature Act (Cap 322) 1969.
United Nations Convention on the Recognition and Enforcement of Foreign Arbitral Awards 38.

9

The Independent Lawyers' Association of Myanmar as a Legal Transplant: Local Challenges to the Idea of an Independent National Bar Association

Jonathan Liljeblad

I INTRODUCTION

The Independent Lawyers' Association of Myanmar (ILAM) was an outcome of a three-year programme by the International Bar Association (IBA) through its IBA Human Rights Initiative (hereafter IBAHRI). Lasting from 2014 to 2016, the IBAHRI programme in Myanmar sought to promote the idea of an independent legal profession, with ILAM being an attempt to provide an independent national bar association for Myanmar.[1] The IBAHRI sought to be an inclusive initiative encompassing state and non-state Myanmar legal actors, but it also provided international experts to engage Myanmar legal actors with alternative perspectives regarding the legal profession and the rule of law.[2] The IBAHRI programme in Myanmar falls within a framework of legal transplant theory, since the work of the IBAHRI essentially served to introduce IBA conceptions about an independent national bar association into a domestic Myanmar context.[3] As a result, the IBAHRI and ILAM

[1] International Bar Association, 'Myanmar, Capacity-Building 2014-2016' (International Bar Association 2015b) www.ibanet.org/Article/NewDetail.aspx?ArticleUid=B0DFF549-F0F3-4A90-83D5-40B902FEDBF9 accessed 8 April 2018.

[2] International Bar Association, 'Myanmar Lawyers Advance in Mission to Build a Representative National Bar Association' (International Bar Association 2014c) www.ibanet.org/Article/NewDetail.aspx?ArticleUid=2efce9cc-5ef9-4ddc-86e4-024648d54b93; S. Lwin, 'Lawyers Vow Greater Independence for New Bar Association', *Myanmar Times*, 18 January, 2016 (2016), available at: www.mmtimes.com/national-news/nay-pyi-taw/18513-lawyers-vow-greater-independence-for-new-bar-association.html; S. Lwin and P. T. Phyo, 'Independent Bar Association Aims to Usher in New Era', *Myanmar Times*, 21 January, 2016 (2016), available at: www.mmtimes.com/national-news/mandalay-upper-myanmar/18578-independent-bar-association-aims-to-usher-in-new-era.html).

[3] M. Crouch, 'The Layers of Legal Development in Myanmar' in M. Crouch and T. Lindsey (eds.), *Law, Society and Transition in Myanmar* (Hart Publishing, 2014); International Bar Association, 'The Rule of Law in Myanmar: Challenges and Prospects' (International Bar

represent an attempted transmission into Myanmar of ostensibly international standards for an independent national bar association held by the IBA.

Interpretation of ILAM as a case of a legal transplant involving the idea of an independent national bar association incurs questions as to the potential insights arising from ILAM's experiences for the notion of legal transplants. In particular, it raises questions about the difficulties associated with the formation of ILAM and what such issues indicate about the transplantation of legal institutions like an independent national bar association. Greater detail about the connections between the creation of ILAM and the conditions in Myanmar may provide greater understanding about the contextual challenges facing legal transplants and inform comparable efforts in other countries similar to Myanmar.

The following sections seek to provide such analysis. The discussion begins with an overview of legal transplant literature to note the major elements of theory, followed by brief background about the IBAHRI's programme from 2014 to 2016 that led to the formation of ILAM. The analysis then identifies the issues that challenged the creation of ILAM, organizing the issues as contextual factors representing elements of domestic structure and agents that constitute the conditions surrounding ILAM's creation. The analysis continues by drawing out implications for legal transplant theory before finishing with a conclusion that identifies directions for further studies in the future.

With respect to research method, the work of subsequent sections is part of a continuing research agenda following the ongoing development of ILAM. The discussion uses the results of field research conducted during 2014–17 and draws on observations taken from involvement in ILAM events and documents from the IBA, ILAM, Myanmar government ministries, and civil society organizations. The topic of reform in Myanmar's legal system is a sensitive topic with incendiary consequences between and among state and non-state actors. As a result, it is necessary to avoid disclosures of information that can be used to infer the identities of institutional and individual sources. To further protect sources, the discussion avoids interviews and tries to use documents available to the public.

Some note should be made about the loss of U Ko Ni, a Myanmar lawyer who was among the leaders advancing the creation of ILAM. U Ko Ni was assassinated in January 2017, and his loss inflicted a blow in the movement for

Association 2012a) www.ibanet.org/Document/Default.aspx?DocumentUid=DE0EE11D-9878–4685-A20F-9A0AAF6C3F3E); International Commission of Jurists, 'Right to Counsel: Independence of Lawyers in Myanmar' (International Commission of Jurists, 2013) www.icj.org/wp-content/uploads/2013/12/MYANMAR-Right-to-Counsel-electronic.pdf); N. Y. Kham, 'An Introduction to the Law and Judicial System of Myanmar' (National University of Singapore 2014) https://law.nus.edu.sg/cals/pdfs/wps/CALS-WPS-1402.pdf.

ILAM and rule of law in Myanmar. His loss demonstrates the dangers for efforts to reform Myanmar's legal system and underscores the risks for actors seeking to bring Myanmar into greater alignment with international standards for the rule of law.

II THEORY

The concept of legal transplants, in its basic form, refers to the adoption of foreign legal systems within a particular country.[4] The literature on legal transplants extends farther than the impasse between Alan Watson and Pierre Legrand raised by Andrew Harding.[5] John Cairns, in his review of the history of legal transplants, finds that the term 'transplants' in legal scholarship appeared as far back as Frederick P. Walton's 1927 speech to the International Academy of Comparative Law, and continued in various permutations through successive works in following decades by scholars such as R. W. Lee's study of Roman-Dutch law in European colonies, Hermann Mannheim's research on the propagation of the English jury system to continental Europe, and Henri Levy Ullman's investigation into the development of Turkey's legal system.[6] More general studies appeared in the works of John Beckstrom and Jean Rivero, each of whom dealt with the transmission of legal systems from one jurisdiction to another.[7]

The current state of the literature follows a spectrum of perspectives roughly demarcated between viewpoints that assert the existence of legal transplants versus those that see it as problematic. The former extreme is represented by Alan Watson, who sees a legal concept as independent of its context and so available for transfer from one location to another.[8] The latter is represented by Pierre Legrand, who believes that a legal idea is a unique product of its context and hence is not transferable to other locations.[9] Between the

[4] J. Cairns, 'Watson, Walton, and the History of Legal Transplants', *Georgia Journal of International and Comparative Law* 41 (2013), 687.

[5] See A. Harding, 'The Legal Transplants Debate: Getting beyond the Impasse', Chapter 1 in this Volume.

[6] Cairns (n. 4), 687, 694.

[7] M. Freedland, 'Otto Kahn-Freund (1900–1979)' in Jack Beatson and R. Zimmermann (eds.), *Jurists Uprooted: German-Speaking Émigré Lawyers in Twentieth-Century Britain* (Oxford University Press, 2004) 299, 311–12; J. Rivero, 'Les Phenomnenes d'imitation des modeles etrangers en droit administrative', *Pages de Doctrine* 2 (1980), 459; J. Beckstrom, 'Transplantation of Legal Systems', *American Journal of Comparative Law* 21 (1973), 557.

[8] A. Watson, *Legal Transplants: An Approach to Comparative Law* (University of Georgia, 1993).

[9] See Harding, 'The Legal Transplants Debate: Getting Beyond the Impasse', Chapter 1 in this Volume; W. Ewald, 'Comparative Jurisprudence (II): The Logic of Legal Transplants', *American Journal of Comparative Law* 43 (1995), 489.

positions of Watson and Legrand are a range of perspectives about the concept of legal transplants. For example, Anna Dolidze sees transplantation as occurring either horizontally between states or vertically between domestic and international levels.[10] John Gillespie frames transplantation as a discourse involving a structure of power relations and individual agency.[11] Jonathan Miller categorizes legal transplants into those that are cost-saving, where lawmakers save time and costs by using solutions from other jurisdictions; externally dictated, where foreign actors impose foreign legal models into a country; entrepreneurial, where domestic actors promote foreign legal ideas; or legitimacy-generating, where domestic actors associate themselves with prestigious foreign legal ideas to build legitimacy.[12]

Other scholars seek positions that bridge the positions of Watson and Legrand. For example, Otto Kahn-Freund divides legal transplants between mechanical legal institutions, which are insulated from culture and so – consistent with Watson – are easy to transfer from one context to another, versus organic legal institutions, which are culturally embedded and hence – in keeping with Legrand – are difficult to transfer across cultures.[13] Melissa Crouch and David Nelken see the idea of legal transplants as useful in describing the transfer of legal ideas so long as it is qualified by some consideration of context.[14] Gunther Teubner goes further in addressing the influence of context upon a legal transplant by formulating a dialectical approach that conceives of a legal transplant as a 'legal irritant' that incites change in a given context even as that same context reconstructs the meaning of the irritant.[15] Teubner goes beyond the Watson-Legrand dichotomy of integration or repulsion of legal ideas across cultures by seeing the idea of legal irritants as incurring unexpected consequences via an 'evolutionary

[10] A. Dolidze, 'Bridging Comparative and International Law: Amicus Curiae Participation as a Vertical Legal Transplant', *European Journal of International Law* 26 (2016), 851.

[11] J. Gillespie, 'Towards a Discursive Analysis of Legal Transfers into Developing East Asia', *International Legal Practitioner* 40 (2008), 683.

[12] J. Miller, 'A Typology of Legal Transplants: Using Sociology, Legal History, and Argentine Examples to Explain the Transplant Process', *American Journal of Comparative Law* 51 (2003), 839.

[13] Cairns (n. 4), 643–5; O. Kahn-Freund, 'On Uses and Misuses of Comparative Law' in O. Kahn-Freund, Selected Writings (Stevens, 1978): 298; G. Teubner, 'Legal Irritants: Good Faith in British Law or How Unifying Law Ends up in New Divergences', *Modern Law Review* 61 (1998), 11.

[14] M. Crouch, 'Asian Legal Transplants and Rule of Law Reform: National Human Rights Commission in Myanmar and Indonesia', *Hague Journal on the Rule of Law* 5 (2013), 146; D. Nelken, 'Legal Transplants and Beyond: Of Disciplines and Metaphors' in A. Harding and E. Örücü (eds.), *Comparative Law in the 21st Century* (Kluwer, 2002).

[15] Teubner (n. 13).

dynamic in which the external rule's meaning will be reconstructed and the internal context will undergo fundamental change'.[16] In offering a middle path between the Watson-LeGrand impasse, however, Teubner leaves uncertain the extent of the relationship between context and irritant, particularly in terms of the degree to which one affects the other? The following sections use the case of ILAM, seen as a legal transplant about the idea of an independent national bar association, to provide some additional detail about such a question.

III BACKGROUND

The Independent Lawyers' Association of Myanmar (ILAM) is a product of the International Bar Association (IBA) Human Rights Initiative (IBAHRI) that ran in Myanmar from 2014 to 2016. The IBAHRI followed prior IBA efforts in Myanmar, which in 2012 involved a fact-finding mission with attendant report and in 2013 encompassed a subsequent panel discussion and scoping mission to determine how the IBA could help reform Myanmar's legal profession.[17] In keeping with these activities, the IBAHRI was launched with the goals of 1) building support in Myanmar for a national bar association independent of the Myanmar state, 2) forming an independent national bar association as a legally registered entity, and 3) supporting reforms to Myanmar laws to allow an independent national bar association.[18]

The IBAHRI programme began in 2014 with a series of events conducted in partnership with the Myanmar Parliament's Committee on Law and Tranquility, which was led by its Chair Daw Aung San Suu Kyi.[19] In February 2014 the IBAHRI hosted a seminar that assembled international experts and various Myanmar stakeholders in the capital of Naypidaw to

[16] Teubner (n. 13), 12.

[17] International Bar Association, 'Myanmar/Burma Country Visit 2013' (International Bar Association 2013a), www.ibanet.org/Article/NewDetail.aspx?ArticleUid=7481efba-7855-4bd2-9af7-7cf71fe1ab43; International Bar Association, 'Panel Discussion—The Rule of Law in Myanmar: Challenges and Prospects' (International Bar Association 2013b) www.ibanet.org/Article/NewDetail.aspx?ArticleUid=c68828b3-9c10-48a7-a1c7-f5d394b63cc9; International Bar Association, 'The Rule of Law in Myanmar: Challenges and Prospects' (International Bar Association 2012a) www.ibanet.org/Document/Default.aspx?DocumentUid=DE0EE11D-9878-4685-A20F-9A0AAF6C3F3E; International Bar Association, 'Myanmar/Burma Fact-finding Mission' (International Bar Association 2012b) www.ibanet.org/Article/NewDetail.aspx?ArticleUid=DEBA1058-8D8D-47E3-B8DB-1BA2BA82E40E.

[18] International Bar Association (n. 1).

[19] International Bar Association, 'Myanmar: Major Legal Seminar on Bar Associations' Best Practices to be Hosted by IBAHRI' (International Bar Association 2014f) www.ibanet.org/Article/NewDetail.aspx?ArticleUid=ce33cd81-eb78-4209-9ca2-8a9338c17327.

discuss international standards for bar associations[20], with an accompanying report on the roles of bar associations, best practices for bar associations, different models for bar associations, and recommendations for the reform of Myanmar's legal profession.[21] Among the seminar outcomes was a statement to create an independent national bar association for Myanmar and form the requisite steering committee to lead the effort towards that goal.[22] Over the remainder of 2014 the Steering Committee, comprised of representatives from Myanmar's existing regional bar associations and lawyer groups, conducted three meetings to draft a constitution for an independent national bar association.[23] Concurrent to the Steering Committee meetings, in October 2014 the IBAHRI worked with Daw Aung San Suu Kyi's Committee on the Rule of Law and Tranquility to hold a workshop comparing laws regarding the legal profession in other countries and discussing their implications for reform of Myanmar laws consistent with international standards for the regulation of lawyers.[24]

In March 2015, the efforts of the Steering Committee led to a general assembly of stakeholders to endorse a draft constitution for an independent national bar association called ILAM, with initial elections for leadership posts in the same year.[25] In preparation for the elections, the IBAHRI held fifteen workshops in support of ILAM across the various states and administrative regions of Myanmar.[26] The elections were held in September 2015,[27] and in January 2016 ILAM subsequently held its

20 Ibid.; International Bar Association, 'Understanding Bar Associations and Their Roles and Responsibilities' International Bar Association 2014e) www.ibanet.org/Document/Default.aspx?DocumentUid=6a0a6d72-09ef-4976-8cec-df30c9674f05.

21 Ibid.; International Bar Association (n. 19).

22 International Bar Association, 'Myanmar's Legal Profession Moves to Establish a National Bar Association' (International Bar Association 2014d) www.ibanet.org/Article/NewDetail.aspx?ArticleUid=4670e898-428b-440d-b986-52b35593d40d.

23 International Bar Association, 'Myanmar Lawyers Advance in Mission to Build a Representative National Bar Association' (International Bar Association 2014c) www.ibanet.org/Article/NewDetail.aspx?ArticleUid=2efce9cc-5ef9-4dde-86e4-024648d54b93.

24 International Bar Association, 'Laws Regulating the Legal Profession: A Comparative Review from around the World' (International Bar Association 2014a) www.ibanet.org/Document/Default.aspx?DocumentUid=14490A0D-F6C4-4E12-AE48-A4D730D0CDE4; International Bar Association, 'Myanmar: IBAHRI Host Workshop on Laws Governing Legal Profession with Daw Aung San Suu Kyi' (International Bar Association 2014b) www.ibanet.org/Article/NewDetail.aspx?ArticleUid=5d4e7549-e00e-46ed-8c4c-2a0c421db55a.

25 International Bar Association, 'IBAHRI and Myanmar Lawyers Prepare for First Independent Lawyers' Association' (International Bar Association 2015a) www.ibanet.org/Article/NewDetail.aspx?ArticleUid=96554c4d-8391-4f10-9955-d5c1ba10f019.

26 Ibid.

27 Ibid.

inaugural meeting with the support of the IBA and Daw Aung San Suu Kyi.[28] At its first meeting, ILAM's Central Committee adopted its constitution, elected a Central Executive Committee, and set an agenda for committees and attendant action plans.[29] In November 2016, ILAM was officially registered as a legal entity in Myanmar in time for the close of the IBAHRI's three-year programme.[30]

IV FACTORS COMPLICATING FORMATION OF ILAM

Assessing the formation of ILAM against the IBAHRI's original three goals reveals arguably mixed results. The stated goals of the IBAHRI's programme from 2014 to 2016 were to 1) promote support for a nationwide bar association independent of the Myanmar state, 2) capitalize on the support by establishing an independent national bar association as a legally registered entity, and 3) advance reforms in Myanmar laws to allow such an entity to have authority over the legal profession.[31] With respect to these criteria there was a measure of progress: for the first criterion, the IBAHRI programme sought stakeholders from across Myanmar's various states and regions as well as from Myanmar government, and so ostensibly nurtured broad support for the idea of an independent national bar association; for the second criterion, the legal registration of ILAM effectively fulfilled the desire for an independent national bar association as a legal entity; and for the third criterion the involvement of Myanmar state representatives, both under the USDP-led government prior to the 2015 elections and the NLD-led government after the 2015 elections, indicate an acknowledgement of a need to reform Myanmar's laws on the legal profession.

A closer review of contextual factors, however, reveal issues that prevent ILAM from achieving the larger motive of the IBAHRI programme for a bar association that is independent and national. The issues characterize the operating space for ILAM as an organization, and their roles in defining the limits of ILAM can be understood by organizing them into issues that reflect structural constraints upon the work of ILAM and issues that reflect the

[28] International Bar Association, 'IBA President and Aung San Suu Kyi Open Inaugural Meeting of Myanmar's First National Independent Lawyers' Association' (International Bar Association 2016b) www.ibanet.org/Article/NewDetail.aspx?ArticleUid=67923557-0f67-403c-ad67-ff04adc4ac52.

[29] Ibid.

[30] Independent Lawyers' Association of Myanmar (ILAM) (Independent Lawyers' Association of Myanmar 2017) www.ilam.org.mm/en/pages/1.

[31] See above n. 18.

crowding of entities seeking to represent the legal profession. The two categories are addressed individually below.

V STRUCTURAL CONSTRAINTS ON LEGAL SPACE

To begin, the legal space available to ILAM is set by the constraints of Myanmar's laws on the legal profession. The current parameters for the legal profession under the Myanmar state follow the country's history from its time as colonial Burma under the British, through its post-independence decades under successive military regimes.[32] During the colonial era, the British divided the legal profession into pleaders and advocates, with pleaders being licensed to practice in civil and criminal matters in district and township courts and advocates being licensed to practice in all courts including the Supreme Court.[33] Pleaders were subject to the Legal Practitioners Act of 1879, which gave authority for regulation, licensing, and discipline to the High Court of British Burma,[34] and advocates were subject to the Bar Council Act of 1929, which placed authority over rules, licenses, and discipline in the High Court but made the High Court subject to the authority of the Bar Council.[35] In British Burma the Bar Council had fifteen members, with the Chair held by the Attorney General and the remaining seats filled by four nominees from the High Court and ten members elected by practising advocates.[36] This arrangement continued into post-independence through much of the military era until the Bar Council Act was amended in 1989 to have eleven members, with the Attorney General as Chair, Deputy Attorney General as Vice-Chair, the Director-General of the Attorney General's Office as Secretary, a Supreme Court Judge nominated by the Chief Justice, the Director-General of the Supreme Court, and six advocates chosen by the Supreme Court.[37] In Myanmar, the judicial system places the High Court at the administrative state or region level and the Supreme Court at the national level,[38] which means that the 1989 Amendment to the Bar Council Act increased the centralization of control over the legal profession by the national state.

The IBAHRI sought to accompany the formation of ILAM with a reform of the above legal framework, such that there would be an opportunity to place

32 See above n. 3.
33 Bar Council Act 1929; Courts Manual 1999; Legal Practitioners Act 1879; Kham (n. 3).
34 Legal Practitioners Act 1880, s. 6.
35 Bar Council Act 1929, s. 15; Courts Manual 1999, Part 1, ss. 1–2.
36 Bar Council Act 1929.
37 Bar Council Act Amendment 1989; Courts Manual 1999.
38 Kham (n. 3).

control over lawyers in an entity such as ILAM that functioned outside the Myanmar state. The support of Daw Aung San Suu Kyi and the cooperation of the Parliament's Committee on Law and Tranquility with the IBAHRI's programme indicated an acceptance of the idea of reform. The acceptance, however, did not translate into legislative action in time for the conclusion of the IBAHRI's agenda in Myanmar at the end of 2016, meaning that ILAM's powers were circumscribed by the status quo confines set by the 1989 Amendment to the Bar Council Act.

VI AGENTS IN LEGAL SPACE

The confinement of ILAM's powers under the 1989 Amendment to the Bar Council Act effectively set it in the same position held by other Myanmar bar associations and lawyer organizations in relation to the Myanmar state. The IBAHRI's three-year programme from 2014 to 2016 overlaid pre-existing efforts by endemic actors towards a national bar association independent of state control. For example, there were bar associations in Myanmar's administrative regions such as the Yangon Bar Association, the Mandalay Bar Association, and the Mon Bar Association.[39] In addition, prior to the IBA's missions in 2012 and 2013 to Myanmar, there were multiple domestic efforts to create national lawyer associations, with notable examples including the Myanmar Lawyers' Association (hereafter MLA, sometimes also called the Myanmar Lawyers' Network, or MLN) and the Myanmar Legal Aid Network (hereafter MLAN). Similar to the IBAHRI, both the MLA and MLAN held a goal of reforming Myanmar laws to enable a bar association with authority over lawyers independent of the state. The MLA had held its first meeting in June 2012 and the MLAN had garnered international support from the South East Asia Legal Aid Network to hold its own workshops throughout 2012.[40] As a result, ILAM was not unique in terms of being an association for lawyers in Myanmar. ILAM was distinguished from the endemic efforts in that it held a number of benefits relative to domestic lawyer organizations in terms of receiving legal registration from the Myanmar government and benefiting from the support of the IBA, but the persistence of Myanmar's laws on the legal profession meant that ILAM faced the same limitations on power that existed for other domestic lawyer organizations. As a result, despite the aspirations of the IBAHRI, ILAM came into being under laws that rendered just one among

39 International Bar Association (n. 3); International Commission of Jurists (n. 3).

40 N. Cheesman and K. Min San, 'Not Just Defending; Advocating for Law in Myanmar', *Wisconsin International Law Journal* 31 (2014), 718.

a slate of diverse organizations in Myanmar pursuing their respective agendas for the legal profession.

In a sense, the work of the IBAHRI could be interpreted as an intrusion into a domestic space of pre-existing actors. The IBAHRI, however, sought to ally itself with domestic actors by involving local stakeholders in its events.[41] In essence, the IBAHRI worked to subsume the efforts of pre-existing Myanmar bar associations and lawyer organizations within the IBAHRI agenda such that the IBAHRI served as a foreign impetus to local aspirations frustrated by a state that had stalled reforms of Myanmar laws over the legal profession. Despite the IBAHRI's efforts for inclusion, however, the creation of ILAM did not result in the dissolution of other bar associations or lawyer organizations, nor did it result in the merging of their disparate activities within ILAM's agenda. Instead, groups like the Yangon Bar Association, Mandalay Bar Association, or Mon Bar Association, MLA/MLN, or MLAN continued to maintain their operations in support of their respective interests.[42] Thus, the creation of ILAM did not resolve the disparate efforts of pre-existing actors but rather served as an addition to their number, creating uncertainty as to the position of ILAM vis-à-vis other lawyer organizations, the ability of ILAM to draw membership among lawyers facing a choice of lawyer organizations, and the conditions of competition versus cooperation among organizations with similar purposes operating in the same legal space prescribed by Myanmar laws.

VII PROSPECTS FOR ILAM AND IMPLICATIONS FOR LEGAL TRANSPLANT THEORY

The challenges posed by the structure and the agents of ILAM's environment have not dissipated since the inception of ILAM, with events proceeding at a pace resulting in marginal progress since the conclusion of the IBAHRI programme in 2016. ILAM has been engaged with the Attorney General's Office to reform the Bar Council laws, but as of May 2018 the work continues and legislation enabling greater independence for Myanmar's legal profession has not been introduced into Parliament.[43] In addition, based on the direction of the Bar Council amendment efforts, the objective seems to be to return to a composition of the Bar Council set by the Bar Council Act of 1929. If such an

41 Lwin (n. 2); Lwin and Phyo (n. 2).

42 Ibid.

43 A. Kyaw Min, 'Move to Amend Bar Law Gains Steam', *Myanmar Times*, 26 May 2018. Available at: www.mmtimes.com/news/move-amend-bar-law-gains-steam.html accessed 21 January 2019.

objective is realized, it would limit reforms to a return to a colonial-era structure wherein lawyers were allowed a measure of representation on the Bar Council but the state maintained a presence through a Chair held by the Attorney General and portion of seats held by judges.[44] In which case, the changes to the status quo would be limited since the legal profession would still be left short of aspirations for a legal profession fully independent from state authority. Similarly, there has been little change among the bar associations and lawyer organizations that pre-dated ILAM, with entities like the Yangon Bar Association, Mandalay Bar Association, MLN, MLAN, Myanmar Media Lawyers' Network, and other legal service organizations maintaining operations concurrent to the ILAM in terms of removing the country's lawyers from state control.[45] For its part, ILAM seeks to cooperate with these other lawyer associations.[46] Cooperation, however, implies a recognition of separate entities, and so indicates that ILAM accepts that it is one among multiple actors involved in the legal space regarding the issue of independence for Myanmar lawyers.

To the extent that the structure and the agents surrounding ILAM comprise the nature of its environment, ILAM is constrained by a context that offers limited prospects for achieving the aspiration of becoming an independent national bar association. The lack of change in Myanmar laws regarding the legal profession and the conduct of endemic legal actors means that the factors which stunted ILAM's creation appear set to continue as challenges to its future growth. Without further changes in context, ILAM will struggle to fulfill IBAHRI goals for it to serve as an independent national bar association: ILAM will not conform to the idea of a 'national' bar association in terms of a body with nationwide consensus to provide unitary representation for lawyers, and ILAM will not conform to the notion of an 'independent' bar association in terms of an entity with authority over lawyers outside the Myanmar state.

44 See n. 36.

45 See, e.g. the continued existence of offices and websites for the following: Mandalay Bar Association (2018), available at: www.mandalaydirectory.com/en/categories-index/mandalay-region/chan-aye-thar-zan/43-associations-clubs-societies/U00431677_000000000_mandalay-bar-association_40110 ; Myanmar Legal Aid Network (2014), available at: www.legalaidnetwork.org/ ; Myanmar Media Lawyers' Network (2018), available at: www.myanmarmedialawyers.org/ ; Yangon Bar Association (2018), available at: www.yangondirectory.com/en/categories-index/yangon-region/kyauktada/43-associations-clubs-societies/L52808_000000000_yangon-bar-association .

46 Independent Lawyers' Association of Myanmar. Our Objectives. Independent Lawyers' Association of Myanmar (2018). Available at: www.ilam.org.mm/pages/2.

The creation of ILAM poses implications for legal transplant theory. To begin, the experiences of ILAM demonstrates the ways in which context can complicate the process of transplantation despite the apparent acceptance and involvement of international and domestic actors for a foreign idea. The IBAHRI operated with the support of the Myanmar government, with both the Parliament's Committee on the Rule of Law and Tranquility and Daw Aung San Suu Kyi involved in IBAHRI events.[47] The IBAHRI also operated with the assistance of Myanmar civil society actors, with representatives from endemic bar associations and lawyer organizations participating in the IBAHRI's activities.[48] As much as the engagement with Myanmar state and society entities may have represented an acknowledgement of the IBAHRI work on behalf of the concept of an independent national bar association, it did not correlate into the installation of ILAM – or any other entity – as an expression of that concept. There was sufficient space for IBAHRI to further discussion on the former but not sufficient space to allow implementation of the latter. As a result, the ability of the IBAHRI to enable through ILAM to bring independence for Myanmar's legal profession is constrained by the space delimited by Myanmar's laws on the legal profession and the disposition of its current legal actors. The limitations facing ILAM demonstrate that the ability of a legal transplant to instigate transformative change can be restrained by contextual factors that impede the implementation of foreign ideas even as they allow discussion about them.

Second, the potential for domestic law and legal actors to delimit the scope of a legal transplant point indicate that the act of transplantation can incur a scale of work that goes beyond a simple introduction of a foreign idea. For ILAM to achieve the aspirations of an independent national bar association, the efforts supporting ILAM must extend to expanding the space within which ILAM operates. That is, the efforts supporting ILAM must be tied to concurrent efforts to 1) change Myanmar laws so that they allow the placement of lawyers under an authority separate from the state, and 2) rapprochement in relations with Myanmar legal actors, both the state as well as existing bar associations and lawyer organizations, that accept ILAM as the entity with authority over Myanmar lawyers. This means an integration of ILAM into a broader, comprehensive, and coordinated strategy to transplant a suite of associated ideas advancing reform of Myanmar's legal profession through transformation of both the structure and agents of Myanmar's context. To some degree, the IBAHRI sought to do this, with the events driving the

47 See above n. 19, n. 24, n. 28.

48 See above n. 20, n. 23, n. 25.

establishment of ILAM accompanied by IBAHRI activities to seek commitment of both state and civil society for an independent national bar association in the form of ILAM.[49] The conclusion of the IBAHRI programme in 2016, however, left these projects incomplete, with ILAM left unattended by changes in the state or civil society.[50] The experience of ILAM demonstrates that as much as a legal transplant can promote change within a given space of activity, the ability of a legal transplant to effect change expanding such a space calls for connection with allied transplants directed at bringing about transformation of contextual factors.

VIII CONCLUSION AND DIRECTIONS FOR FURTHER STUDY

As an example of a legal transplant, the experiences of ILAM are consistent with the work of Gunther Teubner in the sense of his sense of a 'legal irritant' that seeks to incite change in a context even as such a context reconstructs the meaning of the irritant. The formation of ILAM, to the extent that it began with IBAHRI intentions for an independent national bar association, was ostensibly an irritant introduced into the legal space of Myanmar. The above analysis, however, shows how the legal environment of Myanmar posed issues in structure and agents that essentially reconstructed IBAHRI intentions to render ILAM short of aspirations to be independent of the state or the national authority for Myanmar lawyers. The uncertain state of ILAM following the conclusion of the IBAHRI programme follows Teubner's expectation of an ongoing evolutionary dynamic. Moreover, with respect to the question posed at the outset of the analysis regarding the degree to which context and irritant affect each other, the experiences of ILAM present a case where Myanmar context seems to have had a more dominant effect in directing the IBAHRI's attempt to introduce the idea of an independent national bar association as an irritant.

The future of ILAM is not fixed, as the organization and Myanmar as a whole are in dynamic states of flux. The uncertainties of ILAM and Myanmar offer some directions for future research to extend the analysis of the preceding sections. ILAM, for its part, continues to evolve through an ongoing series of amendments, with one set of amendments occurring in December 2017 and another set of amendments occurring in July 2018. The transitory nature of ILAM is a reflection of its conditions, since in order to exist as a self-sufficient entity based on membership dues it must reach out to

49 See above n. 18, n. 19.

50 See above n. 43, n. 45, n. 46.

a population of lawyers with choices in terms of multiple bar associations or lawyer organizations. This means that ILAM must justify itself to Myanmar lawyers by differentiating the value of ILAM membership relative to entities such as the Yangon Bar Association, Myanmar Legal Aid Network, or others which are themselves attempting to differentiate their positions relative to each other. They are not necessarily mutually exclusive, but in a developing country discretionary funds and time are not always sufficient to allow a broad portion of legal professionals to pursue multiple affiliations. To a degree, ILAM distinguishes itself in being a national entity with foreign supporters, but this alone does not address other issues of potentially greater relevance for Myanmar lawyers such as skills training, knowledge building, or resource sharing, and so ILAM must seek to adjust its position as other bar associations and lawyer organizations work to place themselves in the constituency of Myanmar lawyers. The uncertainties posed by such conditions call for additional research to ascertain the relationship between ILAM versus Myanmar's other bar associations and lawyer organizations, with useful topics for study being the extent to which ILAM competes or cooperates with these other entities, the manner in which they are changing themselves to sustain survival or growth, the relative success such changes have brought for each, and what these types of experiences reveal about the nature of the legal profession in Myanmar.

ILAM's variability is accompanied by the fluid nature of Myanmar's transition. Larry Diamond, along with other scholars, observes that Myanmar is following a path with unresolved questions about the shift from authoritarian to democratic government, military to civilian leadership, closed to open economy, and fractured to coherent political union.[51] Within this transition various actors struggle to define their authority, creating a context of changing power relationships.[52] A potential implication arising from such conditions is that the disposition of the government with respect to the Myanmar legal profession may not remain fixed with the status quo, with the dynamic nature of Myanmar's transition leaving open the possibility that the state will follow

[51] M. Callahan, 'The Opening in Burma: The Generals Loosen Their Grip', *The Journal of Democracy* 23 (3) (2012), 120, 131; L. Diamond, 'The Need for a Political Pact', *The Journal of Democracy* 23 (4) (2012), 138, 149; R. Egreteau, 'Legislators in Myanmar's First "Post-Junta" National Parliament (2010-2015): A Sociological Analysis', *Journal of Current Southeast Asia Affairs* 33 (2014), 91, 124; B. Joseph, 'Political Transition in Burma: Four Scenarios in the Run-up to the 2015 Elections', *SAIS Review of International Affairs* 32 (2012), 137, 149.

[52] R. Horsey, 'Myanmar's Political Landscape Following the 2010 Elections', in N. Cheeseman, M. Skidmore, and T. Wilson (eds.), *Myanmar's Transition: Openings, Obstacles, and Opportunities* (ISEAS, 2012); M. Pedersen, 'Myanmar in 2014: "Tacking against the Wind"', *Southeast Asian Affairs* (2015), 223, 245.

through on the principle of independence for the legal profession and enact legislation that places Myanmar lawyers under authority of a non-state entity. The possibility of this type of legal reform calls for further research to assess the prospects for such an outcome and the optional means by which it may occur. It also calls for additional study regarding appropriate ways to achieve an independent legal profession relative to other priorities in Myanmar's transition, as well as identification of the ramifications arising from a more independent legal profession for Myanmar's legal system as a whole.

There is an additional direction for future study with respect to more general cross-country implications from the case of ILAM. The nature of the relationship between ILAM and the context of Myanmar laws and legal actors details nuances in the connection between legal transplants and context. At least in regards to the topics of bar associations and independence of lawyers, the experiences of ILAM suggest that there may be value in a cross-country comparison to gather more understanding as to the ways contextual factors challenge prospects for an independent legal profession. Such understanding would inform the efforts of developing countries undergoing transition in terms of recognizing the types of changes relevant for creating conditions supportive of aspirations for greater independence of lawyers. Such understanding would also improve the efforts of organizations such as the IBA, ICJ, and others that seek to advance the rule of law through the development of an independent legal profession.

IX BIBLIOGRAPHY

Cairns, J., 'Watson, Walton, and the History of Legal Transplants', *Georgia Journal of International and Comparative Law* 41 (2013), 637–96.

Callahan, M., 'The Opening in Burma: The Generals Loosen Their Grip', *The Journal of Democracy* 23 (4) (2012), 120–31.

Cheesman, N. and San, K. M., 'Not Just Defending; Advocating for Law in Myanmar', *Wisconsin International Law Journal* 31 (2014), 718–19.

Chen, J., 'Modernisation, Westernisation, and Globalisation: Legal Transplant in China' in Oliveira, J. C. and Cardinal, P. (eds.), *One Country, Two Systems, Three Legal Orders – Perspectives of Evolution* (Springer, 2009) 91.

Courts Manual of 1999 (1999) Myanmar Supreme Court. Available at: www.burmalibrary.org/docs14/Courts_Manual-ocr-en.pdf.

Crouch, M., 'The Layers of Legal Development in Myanmar', in Crouch, M. and Lindsey, T. (eds.), *Law, Society and Transition in Myanmar* (Hart Publishing, 2014).

Asian Legal Transplants and Rule of Law Reform: National Human Rights Commission in Myanmar and Indonesia. *Hague Journal on the Rule of Law* 5 (2013), 146–77.

Della Porta, D. and Tarrow, S. (eds.), *Transnational Protest and Global Activism* (Rowman and Littlefield, 2005).

Dezalay, Y. and Garth, B. 'The Import and Export of Law and Legal Institutions: International Strategies in National Palace Wars', in Nelken, D. and Feest, J. (eds.), *Adapting Legal Cultures* (Oxford University Press, 2001).

Diamond, Larry., 'The Need for a Political Pact', *Journal of Democracy* 23(4) (2012), 138–49.

Egreteau, R., 'Legislators in Myanmar's First "Post-Junta" National Parliament (2010–2015): A Sociological Analysis', *Journal of Southeast Asian Affairs* 33 (2) (2014), 91–124.

Dolidze, A., 'Bridging Comparative and International Law: *Amicus Curiae* Participation as a Vertical Legal Transplant', *European Journal of International Law* 26 (4) (2016), 851–80.

Gillespie, J., 'Towards a Discursive Analysis of Legal Transfers into Developing East Asia', *International Law and Politics* 40 (2008), 657–721.

Hamson, C. J., "The Istanbul Conference of 1955', *International and Comparative Law Quarterly* 5 (1956), 26.

Horsey, R., 'Myanmar's Political Landscape Following the 2010 Elections', in Cheeseman, N., Skidmore, M. and Wilson, T. (eds.), *Myanmar's Transition: Openings, Obstacles, and Opportunities* (Institute of Southeast Asian Studies, 2012).

Independent Lawyers' Association of Myanmar (2018) *Our Objectives*. Independent Lawyers' Association of Myanmar. Available at: www.ilam.org.mm/pages/2 accessed 21 January 2019.

International Bar Association (IBA) (2016a) *Myanmar Lawyers Attend Workshop Promoting Legal Ethics*. International Bar Association. Available at: www.ibanet.org/Document/Default.aspx?DocumentUid=14490A0D-F6C4-4E12-AE48-A4D730D0CDE4 accessed 21 January 2019.

International Bar Association (IBA) (2016b) *IBA President and Aung San Suu Kyi Open Inaugural Meeting of Myanmar's First National Independent Lawyers' Association*. International Bar Association. Available at: www.ibanet.org/Article/NewDetail.aspx?ArticleUid=67923557-0f67-403c-ad67-ff04adc4ac52 accessed 21 January 2019.

International Bar Association (IBA) (2015a) *IBAHRI and Myanmar Lawyers Prepare for First Independent Lawyers' Association Elections*. International Bar Association. Available at: www.ibanet.org/Article/NewDetail.aspx?ArticleUid=96554c4d-8391-4f10-9955-d5c1ba10f019 accessed 21 January 2019.

International Bar Association (IBA) (2015b) *Myanmar, Capacity-Building 2014–2016*. International Bar Association. Available at: www.ibanet.org/Article/NewDetail.aspx?ArticleUid=B0DFF549-F0F3-4A90-83D5-40B902FEDBF9 accessed 21 January 2019.

International Bar Association (IBA) (2014a) *Laws Regulating the Legal Profession: A Comparative Review from around the World*. International Bar Association. Available at: www.ibanet.org/Document/Default.aspx?DocumentUid=14490A0D-F6C4-4E12-AE48-A4D730D0CDE4 accessed 21 January 2019.

International Bar Association (IBA) (2014b) *Myanmar: IBAHRI Host Workshop on Laws Governing Legal Profession with Daw Aung San Suu Kyi*. International

Bar Association. Available at: www.ibanet.org/Article/NewDetail.aspx?ArticleUid =5d4e7549-e00e-46ed-8c4c-2a0c421db55a accessed 21 January 2019.

International Bar Association (IBA) (2014c) *Myanmar Lawyers Advance in Mission to Build a Representative National Bar Association*. International Bar Association. Available at: www.ibanet.org/Article/NewDetail.aspx?ArticleUid =2efce9cc-5ef9-4dde-86e4-024648d54b93 accessed 21 January 2019.

International Bar Association (IBA) (2014d) *Myanmar's Legal Profession Moves to Establish a National Bar Association*. International Bar Association. Available at: www.ibanet.org/Article/NewDetail.aspx?ArticleUid=4670e898-428b-440d-b986 -52b35593d40d accessed 21 January 2019.

International Bar Association (IBA) (2014e) *Understanding Bar Associations and Their Roles and Responsibilities*. International Bar Association. Available at: www .ibanet.org/Document/Default.aspx?DocumentUid=6a0a6d72-09ef-4976-8cec -df30c9674f05 accessed 21 January 2019.

International Bar Association (IBA) (2014 f) *Myanmar: Major Legal Seminar on Bar Associations' Best Practices to be Hosted by IBAHRI*. Available at: www.ibanet.org/ Article/NewDetail.aspx?ArticleUid=ce33cd81-eb78-4209-9ca2-8a9338c17327 accessed 21 January 2019.

International Bar Association (IBA) (2013a) *Myanmar/Burma Country Visit* 2013. International Bar Association. Available at: www.ibanet.org/Article/NewDetail .aspx?ArticleUid=7481efba-7855-4bd2-9af7-7cf71fe1ab43 accessed 21 January 2019.

International Bar Association (IBA) (2013b) *Panel Discussion—The Rule of Law in Myanmar: Challenges and Prospects*. International Bar Association. Available at: www.ibanet.org/Article/NewDetail.aspx?ArticleUid=c68828b3-9c10-48a7-a1c7-f5 d394b63cc9 accessed 21 January 2019.

International Bar Association (IBA) (2012a) *The Rule of Law in Myanmar: Challenges and Prospects*. International Bar Association. Available at: www.ibanet.org/Docu ment/Default.aspx?DocumentUid=DE0EE11D-9878–4685-A20F-9A0AAF6C3 F3E accessed 21 January 2019.

International Bar Association (IBA) (2012b) *Myanmar/Burma Fact-finding Mission*. International Bar Association. Available at: www.ibanet.org/Article/NewDetail .aspx?ArticleUid=DEBA1058-8D8D-47E3-B8DB-1BA2BA82E40E accessed 21 January 2019.

International Bar Association (IBA) (2011) *IBA International Principles on Conduct for the Legal Profession*. International Bar Association. Available at: www.ibanet.org/ Document/Default.aspx?DocumentUid=1730FC33-6D70-4469-9B9D-8A12 C319468C accessed 21 January 2019.

International Bar Association (IBA) (1990) *IBA Standards for the Independence of the Legal Profession*. International Bar Association. Available at: www.ibanet.org/Do cument/Default.aspx?DocumentUid=F68BBBA5-FD1F-426F-9AA5-48D26B5 E72E7 accessed 21 January 2019.

International Commission of Jurists (ICJ) (2013) *Right to Counsel: Independence of Lawyers in Myanmar. International Commission of Jurists*. Available at: www .icj.org/wp-content/uploads/2013/12/MYANMAR-Right-to-Counsel-electronic.pdf accessed 21 January 2019.

Independent Lawyers' Association of Myanmar (ILAM) (2017) Available at: www .ilam.org.mm/en/pages/1.

Joseph, B., 'Political Transition in Burma: Four Scenarios in the Run-up to the 2015 Elections' SAIS Review of International Affairs 32 (2) (2012), 137–49.

Kahn-Freund, O., 'On Uses and Misuses of Comparative Law', in Kahn-Freund, O. *Selected Writings* (Stevens, 1978).

Keck, M. and Sikkink, K. *Activists Beyond Borders* (Cornell University Press, 1998).

Khagram, S., Riker, J. and Sikkink, Kathryn *Restructuring World Politics: Transnational Social Movements, Networks, and Norms* (University of Minnesota Press, 2002).

Legal Practitioners Act of 1879 (1879) Myanmar Constitutional Tribunal. Available at: www.myanmarconstitutionaltribunal.org.mm/lawdatabase/sites/default/files/myanmar_code/2015/07/18–1879%20Legal%20Practitioners%20Act.pdf.

Legrand, P., 'The Impossibility of Legal Transplants', *The Maastricht Journal of Comparative Law* 4 (2) (1997), 111–24.

Lwin, S., 'Lawyers Vow Greater Independence for New Bar Association', *Myanmar Times* 18 January, 2016. Available at: www.mmtimes.com/national-news/nay-pyi-taw/18513-lawyers-vow-greater-independence-for-new-bar-association.html accessed 21 January 2019.

Lwin, S. and Phyo, P. T. (2016) 'Independent Bar Association Aims to Usher in New Era' Myanmar Times 21 January, 2016. Available at: www.mmtimes.com/national-news/mandalay-upper-myanmar/18578-independent-bar-association-aims-to-usher-in-new-era.html accessed 21 January 2019.

Mandalay Bar Association (2018) Available at: www.mandalaydirectory.com/en/categories-index/mandalay-region/chan-aye-thar-zan/43-associations-clubs-societies/U00431677_000000000_mandalay-bar-association_40110 accessed 21 January 2019.

Miller, J., 'A Typology of Legal Transplants: Using Sociology, Legal History, and Argentine Examples to Explain the Transplant Process', *American Journal of Comparative Law* 51 (2003), 839–86.

Min, A. K. (2018) 'Move to Amend Bar Law Gains Steam' *Myanmar Times*, 26 May, 2018. Available at: www.mmtimes.com/news/move-amend-bar-law-gains-steam.html accessed 21 January 2019.

Myanmar Legal Aid Network (2014) Available at: www.legalaidnetwork.org/ accessed 21 January 2019.

Myanmar Lawyers' Network (2018) Available at: www.facebook.com/myanmarlawyernetwork/ accessed 21 January 2019.

Myanmar Media Lawyers' Network (2018) Available at: www.myanmarmedialawyers.org/ accessed 21 January 2019.

Nicholson, P. and Gillespie, J., 'Interpreting Legal Transfers: The Implications for Law and Development' in Nicholson, P. and Gillespie, J. (eds.), *Law and Development and the Global Discourses of Legal Transfers* (Cambridge University Press, 2012).

Nelken, D., 'Legal Transplants and Beyond: Of Disciplines and Metaphors' in Harding, A. and Örücü, Esin (eds.), *Comparative Law in the 21st Century* (Kluwer, 2002).

Nicholson, P. and Low, S., 'Local Accounts of Rule of Law Aid: Implications for Donors', *Hague Journal on the Rule of Law* 5 (1) (2013), 1–43.

Pedersen, M., 'Myanmar in 2014: 'Tacking against the Wind', *Southeast Asian Affairs* (2015) 223–45.

Tarrow, S., *The New Transnational Activism* (Cambridge University Press, 2005).

Soe, T. N. (2013) 'Lawyers' Network to Register in Mandalay' *Myanmar Times 28 January, 2013*. Available at: www.mmtimes.com/national-news/mandalay-upper-myanmar/3919-lawyers-network-to-register-in-mandalay.html accessed 21 January 2019.

Teubner, G., 'Legal Irritants: Good Faith in British Law or How Unifying Law Ends up in New Divergences', *The Modern Law Review* 61 (1) (1998), 11–32.

Walton, F., 'The Historical School of Jurisprudence and Transplantations of Law', *Journal of Comparative Legislation and International Law* 9 (1927), 183.

Watley, B. A., 'Report on the Rome Conference 1950', *Journal of Comparative Legislation and International Law* 32 (1950), 91.

Watson, A., *Legal Transplants: An Approach to Comparative Law* (University of Georgia, 1993).

Wise, E., 'The Transplant of Legal Patterns', *American Journal of Comparative Law* 38 (Supplement) (1990), 1–22.

Yangon Bar Association (2018) Available at: www.yangondirectory.com/en/categories-index/yangon-region/kyauktada/43-associations-clubs-societies/L52808_000000000_yangon-bar-association accessed 21 January 2019.

PART III

10

Shark Sanctuaries as Vehicles for Transplanting Conservation Tools in Disparate Legal Jurisdictions

Erika Techera

I INTRODUCTION

Environmental law is of relatively recent origin having emerged as a genuine sub-field of law in the 1970s. Its evolution is top down, bottom up and transnational. International environmental law developed rapidly in the wake of the 1972 United Nations Conference on the Human Environment, leading to a proliferation of treaties that set standards and new frameworks for environmental legal protection and biodiversity conservation.[1] There is little doubt that this international environmental law has played a significant role in addressing global environmental problems by setting standards, assisting with capacity building, and providing a forum for discussion and sharing of ideas.[2] Nevertheless, national and sub-national legal responses to local environmental impacts and problems pre-existed international environmental law, but the environmental movement and public demand for action fuelled their expansion.[3] Transboundary environmental concerns have also led governments to adopt regional and transnational environmental law to achieve

[1] For an excellent summary of the development of international environmental law see: B. F. de Souza Dias and K. Garforth, 'Historical Perspectives on the Challenge of Biodiversity Conservation' in E. Morgera and J. Razzaque, *Biodiversity and Nature Protection Law* (Edward Elgar, 2017).

[2] See, e.g., the Convention on Biological Diversity opened for signature 5 June 1992, 1760 UNTS 79 (entered into force 29 December 1993); UN Framework Convention on Climate Change opened for signature 9 May 1992, 1771 UNTS 107 (entered into force 24 March 1994); and the Inter-Governmental Panel on Climate Change.

[3] Early laws can be found in many Indigenous and traditional communities including in the Pacific: R. E. Johannes, 'Traditional Marine Conservation Methods in Oceania and Their Demise', *Annual Review of Ecology and Systematics* 9 (1978), 349. In industrialized contexts, early influential laws included the US Clean Air Act 1970.

common goals.[4] It is therefore clear that environmental law has developed into a contemporary but substantive area of law, encompassing dozens of multilateral environmental agreements and myriad pieces of domestic legislation in every jurisdiction in the world.

A quick survey of this legal landscape reveals some striking features. First, many environmental problems such as climate change, biodiversity loss and pollution are global, leading to transplantations of law from the international level, and one jurisdiction to another, as states seek to implement their international obligations and address shared concerns. Where international instruments provide sufficient detail about obligations, domestic legislation is relatively well aligned as requirements are transposed even in quite diverse jurisdictions.[5] Where the international duties are less clear then domestic responses vary more,[6] and in the absence of any globally endorsed obligations, attempts to address environmental and natural resource challenges at the national level differ considerably.[7] Yet there are commonalities, in part because there is a finite range of regulatory options available.[8] Even where environmental problems are inherently local, ideas and legal tools have migrated between jurisdictions, translated into domestic law as states seek effective and efficient legal responses. Sometimes, model laws have assisted the horizontal transnational movement of environmental law but in most cases, there is no formal mechanism for the diffusion of legal provisions.[9]

4 See, e.g., R. Warner and S. Marsden, *Transboundary Environmental Governance: Inland, Coastal and Marine Perspectives* (Ashgate Publishing, 2013); and P. H. Sand, *Transnational Environmental Law: Lessons in Global Change* (Kluwer Law International, 1999).

5 An example is domestic laws implementing the Convention on International Trade in Endangered Species of Wild Fauna and Flora, opened for signature 3 March 1973, 993 UNTS 243 (entered into force 1 July 1975), which requires national authorities to be nominated and mandatory import and export permit regimes for listed wildlife.

6 Obligations to conserve biodiversity under the *Convention on Biological Diversity* (n 2) is one such area, with legal mechanisms including threatened species listing, more holistic ecosystem-based approaches, space-based protections, regulation of consumptive and non-consumptive activities, or combinations of these tools. Specific legal frameworks at the domestic level vary greatly.

7 Fisheries regulation is one such example, where legal frameworks include area-based, seasonal restrictions, permitting systems, gear restrictions, quotas and catch limits, differentiated regimes for subsistence, artisanal, commercial and foreign fishers, and market-based and trade measures.

8 As recognized by Andrew Harding, 'The Legal Transplants Debate: Getting beyond the Impasse?', Chapter 1 in this Volume.

9 There are examples of model law developments in the Pacific region: Secretariat of the Pacific Community, (2006) Guidelines for developing national legislation for the protection of traditional knowledge and expressions of culture based on the Pacific Model Law 2002, available at: www.wipo.int/edocs/lexdocs/laws/en/spc/spc001en.pdf accessed 7 September 2018.

In all situations legal transplants can be shown to exist as ideas, tools and provisions are 'borrowed' by law-makers faced with similar challenges.

Environmental law thus provides a fascinating lens through which to explore legal transplants and the vertical and horizontal movement of law across jurisdictional boundaries. This chapter focuses on the specific example of shark conservation and management and in particular the rapid creation of shark sanctuaries in Pacific Island states over the last decade. The plight of sharks has become increasingly well understood, and their rapid decline and role in maintaining ocean health is now beyond doubt.[10] Despite clear scientific consensus, there is no global treaty on sharks, and international legal measures extend across fisheries regulation, trade, and environmental instruments.[11] At the national level, similar fragmentation can be seen with shark fisheries remaining economically important in some countries and conservation dominating in others often driven by shark-based tourism. Domestic law and policy are also influenced by socio-cultural differences between nations; where some fear and others revere sharks.

A range of legal tools can be utilized to conserve and manage a species, including both area-based restrictions and species-based approaches. Sanctuaries are an area-based tool, one form of marine protected area (MPA), in which rules are established for a geographically defined space. As will be seen below, the adoption of sanctuaries to conserve and manage sharks has spread around the Pacific over the last ten years, with significant commitments to protect these species in large ocean areas. Although there is no specific convention on MPAs, international environmental law provides global endorsement and a mandate for their creation.[12] This has catalyzed global, national and regional action with the Pacific island nations demonstrating greater commitments than other areas of the world. These nations have made a disproportionate contribution to global targets through the creation of MPAs, many of which focus specifically on sharks. Given the declaration of these 'shark sanctuaries' closer examination of the laws that operationalize the commitments is warranted. In some cases there is clear evidence of transplantation of law, but in others quite disparate provisions have been adopted to achieve common aims; here it is the idea of shark

10 R. A. Myers, B. Worm, 'Rapid Worldwide Depletion of Predatory Fish Communities', *Nature* 423 (2003), 280; and R. A. Myers, J. K. Baum, T. D. Shepherd, S. P. Powers, C. H. Peterson, 'Cascading effects of the loss of apex predatory sharks from a coastal ocean', *Science* 315 (2007), 1846.

11 See E. Techera and N. Klein, *International Law of Sharks* (Brill, 2017).

12 Discussed further below.

sanctuaries and the conservation tool that has been transplanted rather than the rules themselves.

The sections that follow explore legal transplants and environmental law, the catalysis, emergence and diffusion of shark sanctuaries in the Pacific, and the laws across the various jurisdictions. The final sections critically analyze the developments and draw out some insights before making some conclusions and tentative recommendations for the future.

II LEGAL TRANSPLANTS AND THE EVOLUTION OF ENVIRONMENTAL LAW

The discourse on legal transplants is longstanding, dating back at least to the work of Montesquieu.[13] On the one hand are scholars who argue the 'impossibility of legal transplants', on the other side are those that point to clear evidence that they do occur. The differences in these viewpoints depends in part upon the definitions of both 'law' and 'transplant'. Those scholars that argue law cannot be transplanted tend to take a restricted view of the meanings of these words, finding that although rules may be similar, their local application is different and not, therefore, a true transplantation. Legrand, for example, quotes dictionary definitions of 'transplant' including to 'remove and reposition' and 'transport to another country'.[14] Watson takes a similar view of the movement and limits it to the normative element of law in defining legal transplants as the 'moving of a rule . . . from one country to another'.[15] On this basis it is said that 'rules cannot travel … [and] legal transplants are impossible.[16] Such an approach is overly narrow, limited to the mere words of the law regardless of their underlying principles, without any investigation of the social, cultural and political context. Although Legrand, for example, addresses this latter argument he finds that if rules include their local context, then a legal transplant could only exist where the articulation plus the interpretation of the rule is transported from one jurisdiction to another; which could hardly ever happen.[17]

[13] O. Kahn-Freund, 'The Uses and Misuses of Comparative Law', *Modern Law Review* 37 (1) (1974), 1.

[14] P. Legrand, 'The Impossibility of 'Legal Transplants', *Maastricht Journal of European and Comparative Law* 4 (1997), 111.

[15] A. Watson, *Legal Transplants* (University of Georgia Press, 1993) 21. See also A. Watson, 'Comparative Law and Legal Change', *Cambridge Law Journal* 37 (1978), 313.

[16] Legrand (n. 14), 114.

[17] Legrand (n. 14), 116–17.

Those scholars who believe that legal transplantation is possible focus less on the specific articulation of law, and instead accept that there is a limited number of legal tools; and where objectives are similar and the ideas aligned, then law can migrate with some tailoring for the local context. Kahn-Freund, for example, associates transplantation with surgical operations and this reference to living organisms is particularly relevant giving the evolving nature of law; legal tools and provisions that are 'borrowed' from one jurisdiction must be adjusted for the new context, and may not work in another and will be 'rejected'.[18] It is clear that legal transplants can encompass the choice to use law to address a problem, as well as the movement of specific rules from one jurisdiction to another, albeit with some adjustment, and because of their living nature they may continue to evolve further to meet local needs and enhance integration.

In considering the scope of 'law' involved in such transplantations, scholars such as Yang and Percival include principles[19] and Kahn-Freund goes further commenting that 'legal *ideas* are now moving freely around the world so as to influence legislation and pending law reform'.[20] For the purposes of this chapter the inclusion of principles and ideas is important because MPAs, and shark sanctuaries more particularly, are legal tools, but the normative provisions for their creation and management are often dissimilar. If ideas are included within the definition of law, then shark sanctuaries illustrate legal transplants.

It has been recognized that processes such as industrialization and globalization have resulted in some legal areas being virtually indistinguishable from each other, as the barriers to transplantation are removed.[21] Indeed it is clear that legal transplants occurred before these contemporary processes, and continue to do so as they persist. There is little doubt that the law in the Pacific island region has been the subject of transplantation, both formally through the forced reception of law from England, France, The Netherlands and other jurisdictions during colonial times, and since independence as 'homegrown law' develops.[22] Even before both of these developments, the

[18] O. Kahn-Freund, 'The Uses and Misuses of Comparative Law', *Modern Law Review* 37 (1) (1974), 1–27.

[19] T. Yang and R. V. Percival, 'The Emergence of Global Environmental Law', *Ecology Law Quarterly* 36 (3) (2009), 615–64.

[20] Kahn-Freund (n. 13) 10 (emphasis added). Affolder also refers to 'ideas', discussed further below: N. Affolder, 'Looking for Law in Unusual Places: Cross-Border Diffusion of Environmental Norms', *Transnational Environmental Law* (2018), 1–25.

[21] Kahn-Freund (n. 13) 9. There is little doubt that in the intervening four decades many remaining hurdles have been further removed.

[22] See further Chapter 2 'Transplant Shock: The Hazards of Introducing Statutes of General Application' by Jennifer Corrin in this Volume.

pattern of settlement across the region involved the movement of social groups who brought their cultures, customs and norms with them. Indigenous customary law remains a feature of many of these countries as well as received common and civil law. In developing new laws to address contemporary issues, inevitably 'new legal regimes … use concepts from prior legal regimes';[23] since it is easier to borrow from other jurisdictions than to invest in the development of an entirely new law.[24] Yet 'we cannot take for granted that rules or institutions are transplantable [and] any attempt to use a pattern of law outside the environment of its origin continues to entail the risk of rejection'.[25] This is not intended to dissuade legislators from legal transplants, rather to encourage exploration of the social, cultural and political context, as well as the legal jurisdiction.

It is also valuable to explore how environmental law scholars have analyzed legal transplants.[26] Some literature does address this sub-field, focusing on either horizontal diffusion of law across national boundaries,[27] or the multi-directional movements in the emerging area of global environmental law.[28] It is well accepted that many environmental problems transcend jurisdictional borders, lending themselves to transnational legal responses with varying degrees of commonality. Where contractual, rather than legislative, provisions are utilized to address environmental challenges 'boilerplate' language and 'standard forms' provide a vehicle for transplantation of environmental norms along with the legal tool.[29] Movements include horizontal transplants of provisions from one contract to the next, as well as movements from contract to legislation. Relevantly, Affolder reinforces that it is not only the legal content but also the 'idea of using contract to fill environmental regulatory

[23] J. B. Wiener, 'Something Borrowed for Something Blue: Legal Transplants and the Evolution of Global Environmental Law, *Ecology Law Quarterly* 27 (2001), 1295.

[24] Legrand (n. 14), 112.

[25] Kahn-Freund (n. 13), 27.

[26] Many scholars in the field tend to focus on other areas of law: Kahn-Freund (n. 13) refers to family law, labour law; and labour is also the focus in Anthony Forsyth, *The 'Transplantability' debate in comparative law and comparative labour law: Implications for Australian borrowing from European Labour Law* (Working Paper No. 38, Centre for Employment and Labour Relations Law, The University of Melbourne 2006).

[27] Affolder (n. 20), focusing on environmental contracts.

[28] See, e.g., Yang and Percival (n. 19), focusing on climate change and pollution. See also Wiener (n. 23), 1296 and K. Kern, H. Jörgens, H. and M. Jänicke, *The diffusion of environmental policy innovations: A contribution to the globalisation of environmental policy* (Discussion Papers, Wissenschaftszentrum Berlin für Sozialforschung, Forschungsschwerpunkt Technik – Arbeit – Umwelt, Abteilung Normbildung und Umwelt, 2001) http://nbn-resolving.de/urn:nbn:de:0168-ssoar-114964 accessed 13 September 2018.

[29] Affolder (n. 20).

gaps [that] is transplanted into new contexts'.[30] As will be explored in the sections that follow, this is analogous to the transplantation of the idea of shark sanctuaries being utilized to conserve and manage these marine species in the Pacific. Furthermore, she refers to the 'multiplier effect' where new arrangements repeat successful models from the past, including in the area of conservation.[31] Again this can be seen to be the case with Pacific shark sanctuaries which have grown in number exponentially. Therefore, the 'predicted impossibility of 'transplants' ... has not displaced the enthusiasm in practice of looking to such potential 'misfits' as contractual models'.[32]

Global environmental law recognizes the increasingly blurred boundaries between international and domestic law.[33] In essence, it encompasses international, transnational and domestic environmental law and involves multiple actors including governments, NGOs, corporations and networks. Scholars in this evolving field argue that a set of environmental law norms, principles and procedures are emerging, created by vertical and horizontal legal movements between systems: international legal norms moving downwards via implementation in domestic regimes, national environmental law feeding up to the international level, as well as transboundary transposition of law between jurisdictions. Therefore, proponents of global environmental law accept legal transplants occur, even where domestic cultures and traditions differ; indeed, transplantation with adaptation is one of the ways in which global environmental law is created.[34]

Evidence for global environmental law can easily be found in similar domestic provisions that implement international obligations,[35] and there are clear illustrations of horizontal transpositions.[36] It is the observation of vertical movement from the national to the international level that is particularly novel. Environmental impact assessment of development proposals is an example where statutory requirements originated in the domestic US context, were subsequently endorsed at the international level in the Rio

30 Ibid., 8 (emphasis added).
31 Ibid., 15.
32 Ibid., 13.
33 Yang and Percival (n. 19), 623.
34 The others are convergence, integration and harmonization: Yang and Percival (n. 19) 616–18.
35 See, e.g., domestic law implementing the Convention for the Protection of the Ozone Layer, opened for signature 22 March 1985, 26 ILM 1529 (entered into force 22 September 1988) and the Protocol on Substances that Deplete the Ozone Layer, opened for signature 16 September 1987, 26 ILM 154 (entered into force 1 January 1989).
36 The adoption of common domestic legal tools for environmental and natural resource management, such as protected areas and fishing licences, evidences horizontal movements between nations.

Declaration[37] and have been widely adopted in the majority of jurisdictions in the world.[38] Other examples include the 'vertical legal borrowing' of the precautionary principle from German law.[39]

As will be seen below, the rapid declaration of shark sanctuaries throughout the Pacific illustrates these patterns of movement. Firstly, vertical transplantation of the MPA tool to and from the global level, horizontal transposition of legal provisions from one jurisdiction to another, and transnational approaches through the creation of transboundary MPAs. In effect, in seeking to address the challenge of shark conservation and management, implement international law and cooperate across borders, national governments have borrowed and adapted legal tools, concepts and principles from other jurisdictions. There is no suggestion that a single 'best practice' harmonized legal framework would be appropriate, given that the specific legal history, culture, customs and natural environments are so different. Yet it is clear that the adoption of the 'sanctuary' tool for shark conservation and management has diffused throughout the region.

Scholars have explored legal transplantation of environmental law considerations in areas such as impact assessment, climate change, and pollution control but rarely species conservation.[40] This chapter contributes to this environmental law literature by critically analyzing the transplantation of legal tools for Pacific shark sanctuaries, and to the broader scholarship on the diffusion of ideas as legal transplants.

III PACIFIC ISLANDS, MARINE PROTECTED AREAS AND SHARKS

The study of MPAs in the Pacific is a highly appropriate vehicle through which to explore legal transplants in environmental law, in two key respects. First, the history of most of the Pacific islands involved initial settlement followed by waves of colonization and later independence. The majority are now legally pluralist, often involving customary law, common and/or civil law,

[37] Rio Declaration on Environment and Development, Report of the United Nations Conference on Environment and Development, (1992) UN Doc A/CONF.151/26 (14 June 1992).

[38] See Yang and Percival (n. 19), 627–30.

[39] Wiener (n. 23), 1305.

[40] For example, Yang and Percival (n. 19); and Wiener (n. 23). Affolder (n. 20) is an exception, exploring the Kiribati declaration of the Phoenix Islands Protected Area; yet even here the focus was on contractual arrangements rather than conservation tools.

and post-independence legal developments.[41] In other words, the history has involved legal transplants resulting in mixed legal systems involving diffusion of legal norms and tools from multiple sources. Furthermore, since independence these nations have actively adopted international laws including international environmental law. The challenge is now to implement their obligations in circumstances where they have limited financial, technical and legal resources. Legal transplantation, or at least the 'borrowing' of legal ideas, is an attractive option.

Second, MPAs are themselves transpositions of a conservation tool from a terrestrial to an oceanic environment. In western contexts, national parks, as area-based conservation tools, first emerged in the nineteenth century to protect habitats and spaces on land. It was not until the 1930s that such approaches began to be utilized in marine areas.[42] Since then MPAs have become a widely used conservation tool.[43] In the Pacific, Indigenous and traditional peoples had utilized a similar tool much earlier; closing areas of water to fishing, permanently or seasonally, in order to protect species and habitats.[44] Detailed customary rules controlled use of these *taboo, tabu* and *kapu* areas, in similar ways to MPA conservation tools.

MPAs now exist in almost all jurisdictions of the world in one form or another: as aquatic reserves, marine parks, or sanctuaries and as more traditional customary marine management areas. Although international law was not their origin, as demonstrated above, it has provided the catalyst for their expansion. Although a number of environmental law treaties provide for the designation of protected areas,[45] the scope of the1992 Convention on Biological Diversity (CBD) is the broadest. The CBD defined a protected

41 For example, Vanuatu has a mixed legal system involving customary law, French and British laws that remain in force as well as post-independence legislation: E. J. Techera, 'Protected Area Management in Vanuatu', *Macquarie Journal of International and Comparative Environmental Law* 2 (2) (2005), 107.

42 For a short history, see E. J. Techera, 'A Review of Marine Protected Area Legislation in Australia' in J. Fitzsimons and G. Wescott (eds.), *Big, Bold and Blue: Lessons from Australia's Marine Protected Areas* (CSIRO Publishing, 2016); and E. Techera, 'Marine Protected Areas: Contemporary Challenges and Developments' in D. Hussain and M. S. Karim (eds.), *International Marine Environmental Law and Policy* (Routledge, 2018).

43 For an interactive indication of MPAs globally see Protected Planet, *Marine Protected Areas* www.protectedplanet.net/marine accessed 11 September 2018.

44 Johannes (n. 3).

45 For example, Convention for the Protection of the World Cultural and Natural Heritage (Paris), opened for signature 16 November 1972, 1037 UNTS 151 (entered into force 17 December 1975); and Convention on Wetlands of International Importance especially as Waterfowl Habitat opened for signature 2 February 1971, 996 UNTS 245 (entered into force 21 December 1975).

area as a 'geographically defined area which is designated or regulated and managed to achieve specific conservation objectives'[46] and encourages *in situ* conservation utilising this tool.[47] In 2004, the CBD adopted the goal of fully conserving 10 per cent of coastal and marine areas by 2012.[48] Later, the date was extended to 2020 in the Aichi Targets,[49] and has been re-emphasized in Sustainable Development Goal 14.[50] This globally endorsed goal, in particular, has both triggered MPA declarations around the world and the setting of national MPA targets.[51]

The target does not mandate any specific law be used for the designation of an MPA; no model law has been developed and the obligation under the CBD remains vague in terms of the legal content of MPA designations. This is demonstrated by the adopted meaning of an MPA incorporating three key criteria:

> any *defined area* within or adjacent to the marine environment, together with its overlying waters and associated flora, fauna and historical and cultural features, which has been *reserved by legislation or other effective means*, including custom, with the effect that its marine and/or coastal biodiversity enjoys a *higher level of protection* than its surroundings.[52]

Some guidance has been provided by the International Union for Conservation of Nature, in terms of management categories and governance types, but not the nomenclature or the specific wording of legal provisions themselves.[53] This leaves wide open the available legal mechanisms by which MPAs can be established and operated, creating an environment for legal transplants and vertical as well as horizontal legal borrowing.

For the purposes of this chapter the interesting development is the contribution that Pacific shark sanctuaries are making to the global MPA target, and thereafter the array of legal provisions utilized to operationalize the

46 Art. 2.

47 Art. 8.

48 Convention on Biological Diversity, *COP 7 Decision VII/28*, Seventh Meeting of the Conference of the Parties to the Convention on Biological Diversity. See also S. Marinesque, D. M. Kaplan and L. D. Rodwell, 'Global Implementation of Marine Protected Areas: Is the Developing World Being Left Behind?', *Marine Policy* 36 (3) (2012), 727–37.

49 CBD, *Aichi Biodiversity Targets* www.cbd.int/sp/targets/ accessed 11 September 2018.

50 Sustainable Development Knowledge Platform, *Sustainable Development Goal 14* https://sustainabledevelopment.un.org/sdg14 accessed 11 September 2018.

51 Atlas of Marine Protection, *Global Marine Protection Agreements* www.mpatlas.org/progress/targets/accessed 11 September 2018.

52 Decision VII/5 of the CBD Conference of the Parties (emphasis added).

53 N. Dudley (ed.), *Guidelines for Applying Protected Area Management Categories* (IUCN, 2008).

commitments. It is estimated that 7.44 per cent of global oceans are currently protected as MPAs covering 26,945,395 km^2.[54] The total coverage of shark sanctuaries in the Pacific is 17,126,627 km^2;[55] over half the total MPA coverage in the world. This in itself is an interesting phenomenon as no other marine species is singled out in this way. There is no global regime for the protection of sharks, and although a small number of species are protected under international law there is no international mandate to protect sharks in this way.[56]

Before exploring the laws in detail, it is valuable to on some particular features of the Pacific island region, which predispose it to conserve sharks and follow similar patterns in doing so. First, many of these nations have cultural associations with sharks; they were often respected and believed to have spiritual powers,[57] and sometimes even revered as gods.[58] These beliefs are most clearly seen in relation to Polynesian and Micronesian cultures. Their prevalence across the region is suggestive of cultural diffusions, and perhaps then the protection of sharks through the mechanism of sanctuaries may be associated socio-legal transposition. Secondly, there is simultaneously a history of shark fishing in this region. This is demonstrated in part by the history of use of gear and methods such as shark hooks and shark calling,[59] and also by contemporary large-scale targeted fisheries in states such as the Cook Islands and Fiji. Finally, it is worth noting that this region is not one where shark attacks are prevalent. It is certainly the case that shark incidents have occurred but they are infrequent and less commonly fatal than in other jurisdictions such as South Africa, Australia or the USA.[60] The extent to which these factors have influenced the rapid adoption of shark sanctuaries is unclear; certainly these factors do not work against such

54 Protected Planet, *Protected areas coverage in 2018* www.protectedplanet.net/marine accessed 11 September 2018.

55 The Pew Charitable Trusts, *Shark sanctuaries around the world* www.pewtrusts.org/en/research-and-analysis/fact-sheets/2016/03/shark-sanctuaries-around-the-world accessed 11 September 2018.

56 Some species are protected under the *Convention on International Trade in Endangered Species* (n. 4) and the *Convention on the Conservation of Migratory Species of Wild Animals* opened for signature 23 June 1979 19 ILM 15 (entered into force 1 November 1983), as well as some Regional Fishery Management Organisation conservation management measures: Techera and Klein (n. 10).

57 D. Crawford, *Shark* (Reaktion Books, 2008).

58 This is the case in Hawai'i where sharks are '*aumakua*, but it was also the case in other parts of the Pacific: A. Dell'Apa, M. C. Smith, M. Y. Kaneshiro-Pineiro, 'The influence of Culture on the International Management of Shark Finning', *Environmental Management* 54 (2014), 151.

59 D. Owen, *Shark: In peril in the sea* (Allen and Unwin, 2009).

60 For an analysis see Shark Research Institute, *Global Shark Attack File*, www.sharkattackfile.net/incidentlog.htm accessed 11 September 2018.

declarations. Concern and focus on shark conservation can also be seen in the Pacific with the adoption of the Regional Plan of Action.[61]

Other relevant considerations include the very strong regional organisations that exist in the Pacific and the demonstration of regional responses to other environmental challenges[62] and model law frameworks.[63] However, these cooperative efforts would suggest that direct legal transplants would be more likely to occur because of the established pathways and collaborations in other areas. As will be demonstrated below, however, with only a few exceptions this is not the case. Rather than transplanting laws from one jurisdiction to another, it is the conservation goal and tool that has diffused throughout the region and operationalized via diverse legal instruments.

IV LEGAL FRAMEWORKS FOR SHARK SANCTUARIES IN THE PACIFIC

In the space of less than a decade, shark sanctuaries have been widely adopted in the Pacific region. Sixteen states and territories worldwide have now adopted shark sanctuaries covering their entire waters (the Territorial Sea and Exclusive Economic Zone (EEZ)[64]) and seven are in the Pacific region.[65] The seven jurisdictions include Palau, Cook Islands, Samoa, The Federated States of Micronesia, Kiribati, New Caledonia, French Polynesia.[66] In addition, Tokelau,[67] and Fiji[68] have also declared shark

[61] Mary Lack and Frank Meere (2009) *Pacific Islands Regional Plan of Action for Sharks: Guidance for Pacific Island Countries and Territories on the Conservation and Management of Sharks* SPC/FFA/SPREP, www.fao.org/3/a-br378e.pdf accessed 16 May 2018.

[62] For example, the Niue Treaty on Cooperation in Fisheries Surveillance and Law Enforcement in the South Pacific Region opened for signature, 9 July 1992, 32 ILM 136 (entered into force 20 May 1993).

[63] Secretariat of the Pacific Community (n. 6). See also E. Techera, 'Safeguarding Indigenous Bio-Cultural Heritage in the South Pacific Small Island States', *Policy Matters* 17 (2010), 29.

[64] Under the UN Convention on the Law of the Sea the territorial sea is defined as the first 12 nautical miles, and the EEZ covers 12 to 200 nautical miles, from the baseline (usually the low water mark): United Nations Convention on the Law of the Sea, opened for signature 10 December 1982, 1833 UNTS 3 (entered into force 16 November 1994), Arts. 3 and 57 respectively.

[65] For an analysis of all jurisdictions and their laws see C. Ward-Paige and B. Worm, 'Global Evaluation of Shark Sanctuaries', *Global Environmental Change* 47 (2017), 174.

[66] Atlas of Marine Protection, 'Shark Sanctuary' www.mpatlas.org/category/shark-sanctuary/ accessed 16 May 2018.

[67] An external territory of New Zealand.

[68] Fiji's shark sanctuary does not cover its entire waters but is significant.

sanctuaries. In addition, in 2011 agreement was reached between Palau, FSM and Marshall Islands to create a Micronesia Regional Shark Sanctuary.[69]

Despite the common use of the term 'sanctuary' there is no universal definition of what this means nor how it is to be operationalized. As will be seen below, the specific legal provisions sometimes utilize protected area management laws, but many are under fisheries law. In part, this may be explained by the different laws that existed prior to the declaration and therefore the limited legal frameworks available for inclusion of shark-based provisions. Furthermore, the specific conservation and management measures vary considerably in terms of the breadth of coverage of species and activities, as well as offences and penalties.

The legal provisions in the Cook Islands, Federated States of Micronesia, Kiribati, Marshall Islands, and Palau are examined here.[70] The sections that follow explore the domestic legal provisions in detail.

Palau was the first country in the world to close its entire EEZ to commercial shark fishing, which it did in 2009.[71] The Shark Haven Act prohibited the catching of or intentional fishing for sharks, with the exception that Palauan citizens (or wholly owned entities) could catch up to one shark a day, incidental to other fishing, provided it was landed whole, reported and not used for commercial purposes.[72] The Shark Haven Act also prohibited shark finning and chumming to attract sharks, possession, transfer, storage or trans-shipment of sharks or parts, and required that sharks incidentally caught as by-catch be released dead or alive. Fishing was broadly defined to include catching but also attempting to take or engaging in activity likely to result in the taking of a shark.[73] Placing or recovering a fish aggregating device is also prohibited.[74] Certain equipment was also restricted with steel leaders being prohibited.[75] A rebuttable presumption was created that anyone found with a shark or part had caught it in breach of these provisions. Penalties included fines up to

[69] The Pew Charitable Trust, *Pacific Islands Collaborate to Enforce World's First Regional Shark Sanctuary*, www.pewtrusts.org/en/research-and-analysis/articles/2016/04/21/pacific-islands-collaborate-to-enforce-worlds-first-regional-shark-sanctuary accessed 11 September 2018.

[70] Tokelau, New Caledonia and French Polynesia are not considered because they are external territories of other states and remain heavily influenced by this dependence.

[71] Shark Haven Act 2009. There was, however, an earlier law that recognized steel leaders as equipment that injured sharks and prohibited foreign fishing vessels from utilizing them in Palauan waters: Amendment to Title 27 of Palau National Code, Division 1, Chapter 1 (RPPL No. 6–36).

[72] Shark Haven Act 2009 amending Title 27 of the Palau National Code s. 181.

[73] Title 27 of the Palau National Code s. 102(i).

[74] Ibid.

[75] Title 27 of the Palau National Code s. 181(b).

$250,000 with separate offences in relation to each shark or part found.[76] This Act is critical for the purposes of this chapter, as it was the first in the region to take such bold steps to conserve and manage sharks. As will be seen in the paragraphs that follow, the pattern of fisheries laws restricting harvests, banning finning, prohibiting certain equipment and creating offences for breach has been followed elsewhere. Later the Marine Sanctuary Act 2015 strengthened these provisions banning all fishing for sharks, prohibiting fishing for any living resources within the sanctuary[77] and amending the Marine Protection Act 1994 prohibiting fishing or finning of sharks, requiring bycatch to be released and regulating export, trans-shipment or transport.[78] Penalties were also increased: between $500,000 and $1,000,000, with each shark constituting a separate offence.[79]

In the Marshall Islands, the Fisheries Act 1997 is the principal piece of legislation under which shark provisions are included. This instrument focuses on 'long term conservation and sustainable use of the fishery resources [... with] the objective of optimum utilization.' Under that legislation, targeted commercial fishing for sharks was prohibited.[80] Amendments introduced by Public Law No. 2011–63 ban shark fishing generally, finning, mutilating or injuring a shark.[81] Subsistence fishing is exempted (apart from the catching of protected species), and other authorized taking.[82] Any shark caught as bycatch must be released, dead or alive.[83] The taking, possession, sale, transfer, storage or trans-shipment of a shark or part is also prohibited.[84] The Act also prohibits the use of certain equipment including a trace wire.[85] Penalties include fines of $25,000-$200,000.[86]

In the Cook Islands the principal legislative instrument used was the Marine Resources Act 2005 which has the purpose of 'conservation, management and development of marine resources and related matters'; in essence it is fisheries legislation.[87] The specific instrument used to implement the shark

76 Title 27 of the Palau National Code s. 182.

77 Marine Sanctuary Act 2015 amending Title 27 of the Palau National Code s.181.

78 Marine Sanctuary Act 2015 amending the Marine Protection Act 1994 s. 1203, 1204 and 1209.

79 Title 27 of the Palau National Code s. 182(b).

80 Fisheries Act 1997 s. 229 (emphasis added).

81 Fisheries Act 1997 s. 229A(1).

82 Fisheries Act 1997 s. 229A(2). See also s. 229A(5).

83 Fisheries Act 1997 s. 229A(3).

84 Fisheries Act 1997 s. 229A(4).

85 Fisheries Act 1997 s. 229A(6).

86 Fisheries Act 1997 s. 230.

87 Notably sharks formerly featured as a targeted fishery under the Marine Resources (Longline Fishery) Regulations 2008 although finning was banned. Amendments in 2012 resulted in the adoption of the Marine Resources (Large Pelagic Longline Fishery and Quota Management

sanctuary is the Marine Resources (Shark Conservation) Regulations 2012. All sharks, rays and chimaera are included,[88] all of the Territorial Sea and EEZ is covered[89] and all commercial fishing of these species prohibited whether from a Cook Islands-registered or unregistered vessel.[90] The prohibited acts are set out in Regulation 5 and drafted broadly to outlaw the catch, capture, target or intentional fishing for sharks, as well as finning, mutilating, injuring, or chumming to attract sharks. Any shark accidentally caught must be released[91] and trading, selling, purchasing, bartering, receiving, possessing, transferring, storing or trans-shipping any shark part is banned.[92] Wire leaders and trace wires are prohibited.[93] These provisions are broad in scope and are supported by the penalty provisions: each shark or part constitutes a separate offence, and penalties range between $NZ100,000 and $NZ200,00.[94]

In the Federated States of Micronesia (FSM) shark provisions have also been included under fisheries law: Title 24 of the Code of the Federal States of Micronesia on Marine Resources. Three different amendments to Section 913 have been made. Public Law 18–108 (2014) bans shark finning (including the removal of shark fins on board a vessel) and makes it illegal to knowingly capture, possess, ship, transport, import, export, or sell any member of the *elasmobranchii* family.[95] In addition, the provision requires sharks caught as by-catch to be released if alive, or landed whole at a trans-shipment port if dead.[96] The possession of wire tracers or wire leaders is also prohibited.[97] Penalties range from $50,000 to $250,000 and any illegal fins seized will be incinerated.[98] Interestingly, evidence laws are also included: in addition to a rebuttable presumption that any shark or shark fin found on board a vessel was caught in the FSM EEZ,[99] tampering or destroying evidence including

System) Regulations 2016 that makes it clear sharks are no longer target species, and also refers to WCPFC measures aimed at reducing by-catch of silky and oceanic whitetip sharks.

88 Marine Resources (Shark Conservation) Regulations 2012 reg. 3.

89 Marine Resources (Shark Conservation) Regulations 2012 reg. 4.

90 Ibid.

91 Marine Resources (Shark Conservation) Regulations 2012 reg. 5(2).

92 Marine Resources (Shark Conservation) Regulations 2012 reg. 5(3) and (4).

93 Marine Resources (Shark Conservation) Regulations 2012 reg. 6.

94 Marine Resources (Shark Conservation) Regulations 2012 reg. 7.

95 Public Law No. 18–108 amending s. 913 of Title 24 of the Code of the Federated States of Micronesia on Marine Resources.

96 Title 24 of the Code of the Federated States of Micronesia on Marine Resources s. 913(4). The only exceptions are for scientific research.

97 Title 24 of the Code of the Federated States of Micronesia on Marine Resources s. 913(3).

98 Title 24 of the Code of the Federated States of Micronesia on Marine Resources s. 913(7) and (9).

99 Title 24 of the Code of the Federated States of Micronesia on Marine Resources s. 913(8).

a shark or fin is a separate offence with a penalty of $100,000 to $500,000.[100] Purse seine vessels were given an initial six-month moratorium on these provisions; Public Law 19–21 was subsequently passed in 2015 to make the entirety of Section 913 applicable to purse seine vessels.

Kiribati declared a shark sanctuary under the Shark Sanctuary Regulations 2015 pursuant to the Fisheries Act 2010. The Regulations specifically aim to conserve sharks[101] and 'protect the balance of the marine ecosystem' with reference to the national economy and shark-related tourism as well as Kiribati global reputation.[102] The Kiribati Shark Sanctuary is an area within which it is illegal to capture, kill, fish for, or fin a shark,[103] to offer for sale, sell, import or export,[104] or to possess (in person or on board a vessel) a shark or shark part.[105] The possession and use of wire traces is also banned.[106] Exceptions are provided for authorized use which is not limited to scientific research, and i-Kiribati people not engaged in commercial trade are permitted to catch a shark not warranting special protection.[107] Penalties are relatively low: $5,000 for an individual and up to $10,000 for a vessel.[108]

In Samoa, the Marine Wildlife Protection Regulations 2009 amend the Lands, Surveys and Environment Act 1989 to create a series of protections for sharks. Commercial fishing for sharks is prohibited, as is taking of a shark without intending to consume it, and landing a shark fin without the carcass.[109] By-catch is envisaged and subject to a licensing system; in the absence of approval it is an offence to retain a shark accidentally caught which was alive when landed, and if it dies before release failure to consume or otherwise use it.[110] Significantly, the Samoan legislation includes an exception: '[i]t shall not be an offence [...] if a shark is killed for the purpose of protecting human life'.[111]

100 Title 24 of the Code of the Federated States of Micronesia on Marine Resources s. 914.

101 Sharks are defined to include eight orders: Shark Sanctuary Regulations 2015 Reg 3.

102 Shark Sanctuary Regulations 2015 reg. 2.

103 Shark Sanctuary Regulations 2015 reg. 5.

104 Shark Sanctuary Regulations 2015 reg. 6(2).

105 Shark Sanctuary Regulations 2015 reg. 6(1) and (3).

106 Shark Sanctuary Regulations 2015 reg. 7. Foreign fishing vessels are exempt: reg. 8(3).

107 Shark Sanctuary Regulations 2015 reg. 8. See reg. 10 regarding limitations on authorized exceptions. Sharks warranting special protection are set out in Schedule 11 and include oceanic white tip, silky, whale, great white and basking sharks, all of which are afforded some protection under international law.

108 Shark Sanctuary Regulations 2015 reg. 9.

109 Marine Wildlife Protection Regulations 2009 reg. 11(2).

110 Ibid.

111 Marine Wildlife Protection Regulations 2009 reg. 11(3) (emphasis added).

In summary, some of the strongest shark conservation laws with the broadest scope are found in Palau, Cook Islands and FSM where all species are protected, in all waters and from a range of targeted and incidental catch. Palau, Marshall Islands and FSM have taken the further step of agreeing to establish the world's first regional shark sanctuary.[112] This will involve a transboundary MPA covering their respective adjoining EEZs covering 6.5 million km^2. This complements Pacific efforts to work collaboratively through the adoption of a Regional Plan of Action for Sharks, in response to the Food and Agriculture Organization (FAO) International Plan of Action.[113]

V ANALYSIS OF TRANSPLANTS AND OBSERVATIONS ON MIGRATIONS

The above section demonstrates that not only have the Pacific States adopted the 'idea' of shark sanctuaries, but the majority have utilized the common vehicle of fisheries legislation to operationalize their commitments. Surprisingly, protected area management law has not been an instrument of choice, so although these sanctuaries are considered as MPAs contributing to global goals, they are in essence, fishing bans across defined areas. The broad definition of protected areas within the CBD – a defined area, legal measures and higher protection within the area – permits such an approach.

The analysis also shows that the substantive provisions incorporating the prohibitions are alike in legal content covering species, areas and certain activities with punishments for breach. In order to demonstrate true transplantation of law, however, the legal drafting must be compared in further detail. A few examples identified below make it clear that a number of provisions have been drafted in almost identical terms, yet others differ considerably.

Looking firstly at the capture provisions, in the Cook Islands, for example, '[n]o person may catch, capture, target or otherwise intentionally engage in fishing [. . .] for any shark'.[114] This is in almost identical terms to the Marshall Islands wording: '[n]o person shall catch, capture or intentionally engage in fishing for shark'[115] This phraseology differs considerably from the Kiribati

[112] The Pew Charitable Trust, Pacific Islands Collaborate to Enforce World's First Regional Shark Sanctuary, www.pewtrusts.org/en/research-and-analysis/articles/2016/04/21/pacific-isla nds-collaborate-to-enforce-worlds-first-regional-shark-sanctuary accessed 11 September 2018.

[113] FAO, 'International Plan of Action for Conservation and Management of Sharks: Regional Shark Measures' www.fao.org/ipoa-sharks/regional-sharks-measures/en/ accessed 11 September 2018.

[114] Marine Resources (Shark Conservation) Regulations 2012 reg. 5(1) (emphasis added).

[115] Fisheries Act 1997 s. 229A(1) (emphasis added).

wording '[a] person must not [...] catch, capture or kill a shark';[116] yet the conservation goal is comparable.

In relation to by-catch, very similar wording is also used: in the Cook Islands 'if any shark is caught or captured, it must be immediately released, whether dead or alive [...]No shark, or any part of a shark, may be retained even if caught as bycatch.'[117] In the Marshall Islands the related provision reads: '[a]ny shark that is inadvertently caught or captured [...] shall be immediately released, whether the shark is dead or alive. No shark shall be retained even if caught as bycatch.'[118] This is very close to the Palauan wording: '[i]f any shark is inadvertently caught or captured, it shall be immediately released, whether dead or alive'.[119] Conversely, entirely different wording is used in FSM where

> [a]ll sharks caught by a fishing vessel shall be 4 either: (a) if still alive, immediately released back into the ocean. Fishing vessels must ensure that sharks are released whole, and that sharks are not unnecessarily harmed during the release process; or (b) if dead, landed at a transshipment port in the Federated States of Micronesia.[120]

This law was further amended in 2015 under Public Law 19–36 to allow sharks caught as by-catch if dead to be 'recorded in the daily catch report form for the vessel and discarded'.[121] In Samoa, a licensing system allows by-catch to be retained,[122] but in Kiribati no specific reference is made to by-catch at all.[123]

Again, rebuttable presumptions – that anyone found with a shark or part had caught it in breach of the provisions – are also similarly drafted. In the Cook Islands 'there is a rebuttable presumption that, if any shark or any part of a shark is found aboard a vessel, the shark or shark part was possessed or transferred in violation of this subsection.'[124] The Marshall Islands wording is almost identical: 'it shall be a rebuttable presumption that if any shark or any part of a shark is found aboard a vessel, the shark, or part of a shark, is deemed

116 Shark Sanctuary Regulations 2015 reg. 5(1)(a) (emphasis added).

117 Marine Resources (Shark Conservation) Regulations 2012 reg. 5(2) (emphasis added).

118 Fisheries Act 1997 s. 229A(3).

119 Title 27 of the Palau National Code s. 181(a).

120 Title 24 of the Code of the Federated States of Micronesia on Marine Resources s. 913(4) (emphasis added).

121 [121] Public Law 19-36 (2015).

122 Marine Wildlife Protection Regulations 2009 reg. 11(2)(d).

123 Although Shark Sanctuary Regulations 2015 reg. 5(2) notes that if charged with an offence, it is possible to argue in defence that the shark was caught inadvertently and immediately released.

124 Marine Resources (Shark Conservation) Regulations 2012 reg. 5(3).

possessed or transferred in violation of this subsection.'[125] The FSM legislation is also similar, but not identical: 'It shall be a rebuttable presumption that any sharks caught or shark fins possessed by a fishing vessel originated from the EEZ of the Federated States of Micronesia.'[126] The later Palauan legislation incorporates this wording but enhances it by extending the presumption to prohibited gear: 'it shall be a rebuttable presumption that any fish or steel leader found on board a fishing vessel [...] was taken, or retained, or used in violation of this chapter.'[127] This demonstrates not only the 'borrowing' of legal provisions but also the living nature of law and its continued adaptation to meet local needs.

In other respects, the provisions do differ. The Kiribati Shark Sanctuary Regulations 2015 is one of the only instruments to specifically refer to the establishment of a 'sanctuary' in its purposes.[128] There is relatively little alignment in terms of defining sharks and the species covered by the laws; some statutes offer no definition[129] and others include scientific names.[130] Shark parts are undefined in some statutes but specific in others: in Kiribati and shark part excludes the jaws and teeth allowing possession of these.[131] Another example is illustrated by exploring the scope of the laws. In the Cook Islands provisions are expansive and cover the act of catching, possession, trans-shipping, or otherwise dealing in sharks or their parts. There appear to be no loopholes and no exceptions. In Kiribati, no mention is made of trans-shipment. In the Marshall Islands subsistence fishing for sharks is excluded, and in Kiribati non-commercial fishing by an i-Kiribati person is excluded provided no 'shark warranting special protection' is caught.[132] Palau initially also permitted its citizens to catch one shark a day but this was subsequently removed by the Marine Sanctuary Act 2015.

Pacific shark sanctuaries demonstrate the implementation of international law to the extent that they contribute to the global MPA target. The laws that implement the commitments illustrate horizontal migrations – transnational law in the form of transboundary MPAs, as well as cross-border legal transplants. These legal transplants are not limited to the 'idea' of shark sanctuaries

[125] Fisheries Act 1997 s. 229A(4).

[126] Title 24 of the Code of the Federated States of Micronesia on Marine Resources s. 913(8).

[127] Title 27 of the Palau National Code s. 184(g) (emphasis added).

[128] Shark Sanctuary Regulations 2015 reg. 2(1).

[129] In the Marshall Islands for example.

[130] See e.g., Shark Sanctuary Regulations 2015 reg. 3(1) and FSM Public Law 18–108 [59].

[131] Ibid. Presumably as they are often sold or obtained as souvenirs. Teeth may be collected without harming a shark, but excluding jaws from the provisions would appear to be a loophole capable of resulting in harmful practices.

[132] Shark Sanctuary Regulations 2015 reg. 8(2).

and the 'pattern' of utilizing fisheries legislation as the vehicle. The analysis demonstrates strong similarities between legislative provisions, and in some circumstances, evidences significant 'borrowing' between jurisdictions supporting the conclusion that law has been transplanted.

VI CONCLUSION

The challenge of shark conservation and management is ripe for comprehensive solutions. Their plight is a global, transboundary and also a local issue that demands multi-jurisdictional responses. International law has a role to play but the lack of a coherent response at that level brings sharply into focus the need for transnational and regional multinational efforts. Simultaneously, national and sub-national efforts are needed to protect critical habitats and discrete communities of non-migratory species.

Law has an important role to play in this conservation effort. Although no global legal regime has emerged for the conservation and management of sharks, efforts at the international level have been significant albeit fragmented. National and regional efforts include both transboundary and domestic legal measures. Shark sanctuaries, as MPAs, can be an important conservation tool for these species, and also contribution to ocean health more broadly. The setting of a global target for MPAs has resulted in vertical transplantation of this tool into regional and national contexts. Yet little guidance is available to inform the content of laws that must be enacted in domestic jurisdictions. It is in this context that the Pacific shark sanctuaries have been analyzed, together with the legal provisions to support them.

This chapter has explored the development of shark sanctuaries as a regional phenomenon in the Pacific and examined whether the laws that support those MPAs demonstrate legal transplants. There is no doubt that the rapid adoption of shark sanctuaries over the last ten years demonstrates diffusion of ideas and transplantation of conservation tools; but this chapter has also shown that transposition of legal provisions also occurs across jurisdictional boundaries. Where once laws were transplanted by colonial powers, in the post-independence era the Pacific island nations appear to be comfortable adopting and adapting legal provisions to implement environmental commitments.

Therefore, the idea of creating shark sanctuaries provides a possible model for the transplantation of a conservation tool – via a common idea and commitment – with tailored national approaches that take account of jurisdictional differences but also with significant borrowing of legal provisions where appropriate. In this sense, the case study provides a potential way in which other environmental outcomes can be achieved across multiple jurisdictions via legal transplants.

Nevertheless, just as sharks must keeping swimming to stay alive, the living nature of law demands that it continues to evolve in response to emerging challenges. The pathways by which the idea, goals and tools of shark sanctuaries has migrated across the Pacific may serve the region well in operationalising legal provisions. The critical remaining challenge for shark conservation and management is ensuring effectiveness and enforcement of law[133] and here too legal transplants have a role to play.[134] The long history of legal transplants and migrations in the Pacific will, hopefully, ensure that diffusions of ideas continue to flourish, to ensure the ultimate aims of the shark sanctuaries are realized.

VII BIBLIOGRAPHY

Affolder, N., 'Looking for Law in Unusual Places: Cross-Border Diffusion of Environmental Norms' *Transnational Environmental Law* (2018) https://doi.org/10.1017/S2047102518000080, 1–25.

Atlas of Marine Protection, *Global Marine Protection Agreements* www.mpatlas.org/progress/targets/ accessed 11 September 2018.

Atlas of Marine Protection, *Shark Sanctuary*, www.mpatlas.org/category/shark-sanctuary/ accessed 16 May 2018.

Convention for the Protection of the Ozone Layer, opened for signature 22 March 1985, 26 ILM 1529 (entered into force 22 September 1988).

Convention for the Protection of the World Cultural and Natural Heritage (Paris), opened for signature 16 November 1972, 1037 UNTS 151 (entered into force 17 December 1975).

Convention on Biological Diversity, opened for signature 5 June 1992, 1760 UNTS 79 (entered into force 29 December 1993).

Convention on Biological Diversity, COP 7 Decision VII/28, Seventh Meeting of the Conference of the Parties to the Convention on Biological Diversity.

Convention on Biological Diversity, *Aichi Biodiversity Targets*, www.cbd.int/sp/targets/ accessed 11 September 2018.

Convention on International Trade in Endangered Species of Wild Fauna and Flora, opened for signature 3 March 1973, 993 UNTS 243 (entered into force 1 July 1975).

Convention on the Conservation of Migratory Species of Wild Animals opened for signature 23 June 1979 19 ILM 15 (entered into force 1 November 1983).

Convention on Wetlands of International Importance especially as Waterfowl Habitat opened for signature 2 February 1971 996 UNTS 245 (entered into force 21 December 1975).

133 L. N. K. Davidson, 'Shark Sanctuaries: Substance or Spin?', *Science* 338 (6114) (2012), 1538.

134 In relation to the role of global environmental law in this regard, see Yang and Percival (n. 19) 656.

Crawford, D., *Shark* (Reaktion Books, 2008).

Davidson, L. N. K., 'Shark Sanctuaries: Substance or Spin?', *Science* 338 (6114) (2012), 1538.

Dell'Apa, A., Chad Smith, M., and Kaneshiro-Pineiro, M. Y., 'The Influence of Culture on the International Management of Shark Finning', *Environmental Management* 54 (2014), 151.

Dudley, N. (ed.), *Guidelines for Applying Protected Area Management Categories* (IUCN, 2008).

FAO, 'International Plan of Action for Conservation and Management of Sharks: Regional Shark Measures' www.fao.org/ipoa-sharks/regional-sharks-measures/en/ accessed 11 September 2018.

Ferreira de Souza Dias, B., and Garforth, K., 'Historical perspectives on the challenge of biodiversity conservation' in Morgera, E. and Razzaque, J. *Biodiversity and Nature Protection Law* (Edward Elgar, 2017).

Forsyth, A., *The 'Transplantability' debate in comparative law and comparative labour law: Implications for Australian borrowing from European Labour Law* (Working Paper No. 38, Centre for Employment and Labour Relations Law, The University of Melbourne 2006).

Johannes, R. E., 'Traditional Marine Conservation Methods in Oceania and Their Demise', *Annual Review of Ecology and Systematics* 9 (1978), 349–64.

Techera, E. and Klein, N. *International Law of Sharks* (Brill, 2017).

Kahn-Freund, O., 'The uses and misuses of comparative law', *Modern Law Review* 37 (1) (1974), 1.

Kern, K., Jörgens, H., and Jänicke, M., The *diffusion of environmental policy innovations: A contribution to the globalisation of environmental policy* (Discussion Papers, Wissenschaftszentrum Berlin für Sozialforschung, Forschungsschwerpunkt Technik – Arbeit – Umwelt, Abteilung Normbildung und Umwelt, 2001) http://nbn-resolving.de/urn:nbn:de:0168-ssoar-114964 accessed 13 September 2018.

Legrand, P., 'The Impossibility of 'Legal Transplants', *Maastricht Journal of European and Comparative Law* 4 (1997), 111.

Marinesque, S., Kaplan D. M. and Rodwell, L. D., 'Global implementation of marine protected areas: Is the developing world being left behind?', *Marine Policy* 36 (3) (2012), 727.

Myers, R. A. and Worm, B., 'Rapid worldwide depletion of predatory fish communities', *Nature* 423 (2003), 280.

Myers, R. A., Baum, J. K., Shepherd, T. D., Powers, S. P. and Peterson, C. H., 'Cascading effects of the loss of apex predatory sharks from a coastal ocean', *Science* 315 (2007), 1846.

Niue Treaty on Cooperation in Fisheries Surveillance and Law Enforcement in the South Pacific Region opened for signature, 9 July 1992, 32 ILM 136 (entered into force 20 May 1993).

Owen, D., *Shark: In peril in the sea* (Allen and Unwin, 2009).

Protected Planet, *Marine Protected Areas* www.protectedplanet.net/marine accessed 11 September 2018.

Protected Planet, *Protected areas coverage in 2018* www.protectedplanet.net/marine accessed 11 September 2018.

Protocol on Substances that Deplete the Ozone Layer, opened for signature 16 September 1987, 26 ILM 154 (entered into force 1 January 1989).

Rio Declaration on Environment and Development (1992) UN Doc A/CONF.151/26 (14 June 1992).

Sand, P. H., *Transnational Environmental Law: Lessons in Global Change* (Kluwer Law International, 1999).

Secretariat of the Pacific Community (2006) *Guidelines for developing national legislation for the protection of traditional knowledge and expressions of culture based on the Pacific Model Law 2002* www.wipo.int/edocs/lexdocs/laws/en/spc/spc001en.pdf accessed 7 September 2018.

Shark Research Institute, *Global Shark Attack File* www.sharkattackfile.net/incidentlog.htm accessed 11 September 2018.

Sustainable Development Knowledge Platform, Sustainable *Development Goal 14* https://sustainabledevelopment.un.org/sdg14 accessed 11 September 2018.

Techera, E. J., 'A review of Marine Protected Area legislation in Australia' in Fitzsimons, J. and Wescott, G. (eds.), *Big, Bold and Blue: Lessons from Australia's Marine Protected Areas* (CSIRO Publishing, 2016).

Techera, E., 'Marine Protected Areas: contemporary challenges and developments' in Hussain, D. and Karim, M. S. (eds.), *International Marine Environmental Law and Policy* (Routledge, 2018).

Techera, E. J., 'Protected Area Management in Vanuatu', *Macquarie Journal of International and Comparative Environmental Law* 2 (2) (2005), 107.

Techera, E., 'Safeguarding Indigenous Bio-Cultural Heritage in the South Pacific Small Island States', *Policy Matters* 17 (2010), 29.

The Pew Charitable Trust, *Pacific Islands Collaborate to Enforce World's First Regional Shark Sanctuary* www.pewtrusts.org/en/research-and-analysis/articles/2016/04/21/pacific-islands-collaborate-to-enforce-worlds-first-regional-shark-sanctuary accessed 11 September 2018.

The Pew Charitable Trusts, *Shark sanctuaries around the world* www.pewtrusts.org/en/research-and-analysis/fact-sheets/2016/03/shark-sanctuaries-around-the-world accessed 11 September 2018.

UN Convention on the Law of the Sea, opened for signature 10 December 1982, 1833 UNTS 3 (entered into force 16 November 1994).

UN Framework Convention on Climate Change, opened for signature 9 May 1992, 1771 UNTS 107, art. 3 (1) (entered into force 24 March 1994)

Ward-Paige C. and Worm, B., 'Global evaluation of shark sanctuaries', *Global Environmental Change* 47 (2017), 174.

Warner, R. and Marsden, S., *Transboundary Environmental Governance: Inland, Coastal and Marine Perspectives* (Ashgate Publishing, 2013).

Watson, A., 'Comparative Law and Legal Change', *Cambridge Law Journal* 37 (1978), 313.

Watson, A., *Legal Transplants* (University of Georgia Press, 1993).

Wiener, J. B., 'Something Borrowed for Something Blue: Legal Transplants and the Evolution of Global Environmental Law', *Ecology Law Quarterly* 27 (2001), 1295.

Yang, T. and Percival, R. V., 'The Emergence of Global Environmental Law', *Ecology Law Quarterly* 36 (3) (2009), 615.

11

Global Norms; Local Resistance: Addressing Impunity in Japan and Beyond

Sophia O'Brien

I THE RISE OF THE ANTI-IMPUNITY NORM

This chapter analyses the nature of legal changes produced by the anti-impunity norm, an emerging doctrine in international law. As its name would suggest, the anti-impunity norm seeks to ensure that perpetrators of human rights violations and serious international crimes, such as genocide, crimes against humanity and war crimes, do not evade accountability for their actions. Relatedly, it also seeks to ensure that victims of rights violations and international crimes enjoy access to justice and suitable reparations, and that societies afflicted with impunity suitably recognize and memorialize past violations. As such, the anti-impunity norm is not only infused with key tenets of international human rights law, international humanitarian law, international criminal law, and transitional justice; it is a deeply political and moral agenda too.

The anti-impunity norm has emerged as a central element of the post-World War II international human rights agenda. Although its seeds were laid in post-war international military tribunals, it was not until the late 1980s and early 1990s that it gathered steam, when globalisation and geopolitical changes helped create the conditions for intensified interest and scrutiny in human rights around the world. Efforts to track and more effectively counter impunity –whether enjoyed by state agents,[1] private persons,[2] armed

[1] A particularly emblematic example is the case of *Filartiga* v. *Pena-Irala*, which played a 'path-breaking' role in the fight against impunity and the so-called 'justice cascade'. See *Filartiga* v. *Pena-Irala*, 630 F2d 876 (2d Cir 1980); E. Lutz and K. Sikkink, 'The Justice Cascade: The Evolution and Impact of Foreign Human Rights Trials in Latin America', *Chicago Journal of International Law* 2 (2001), 8–10.

[2] A key example in this regard is the attempt by Rwanda's international, national and neo-traditional justice systems to locate and prosecute the tens of thousands of Rwandan civilians who participated in the 1994 100-day genocide against Tutsis and moderate Hutus.

groups,[3] or heads of state[4]– became a significant human rights project in its own right in an overlapping, yet separate trajectory from the related field of transitional justice.[5] Its rise coalesced further with opportunities presented by dramatically increased numbers of states 'in transition',[6] the rising force and utility of international law, and a growing global appetite to confront historical prejudice and persecution.[7] Its crescendo could be said to be the establishment of the International Criminal Court; a permanent international tribunal dedicated to countering impunity through systematic judicialized accountability.[8]

The significant changes that the anti-impunity norm has heralded within the realm of international law – not least its role in the creation of the new field of international criminal law – have not yet pervaded state practice, however. Many states remain largely impervious to its demands and rhetoric.[9] This is the case for much of East Asia, South East Asia and Oceania, where factors such as underdevelopment, corruption and conflict have contributed to selective, partisan or unprofessional standards of law enforcement. A brief survey of Asian and Pacific nations reveals impunity around untrammelled human rights and governance disasters in North Korea[10] and Myanmar,[11] to be

3 An archetypal example is the establishment of the International Criminal Tribunal for the former Yugoslavia in 1993 and its trials for crimes including violations of international humanitarian law, crimes against humanity and genocide.

4 Particularly noteworthy efforts include attempts to locate, prosecute and punish Augusto Pinochet, Slobodan Milosevic, Hissène Habré and Jean Kambanda over the 1990s and 2000s. See G. Robertson, 'Ending Impunity: How International Criminal Law Can Put Tyrants on Trial', *Cornell International Law Journal* 38 (2005), 649; S. Freeland, 'A Prosecution Too Far? Reflections on the Accountability of Heads of State under International Criminal Law', *Victoria University of Wellington Law Review* 41 (2010), 179.

5 K. Engle, 'A Genealogy of the Criminal Turn in Human Rights' in K. Engle, Z. Miller and D. M. Davis (eds.), *Anti-Impunity and the Human Rights Agenda* (Cambridge University Press, 2016) 15–49; P. Arthur, 'How Transitions Reshaped Human Rights: A Conceptual History of Transitional Justice', *Human Rights Quarterly* 31 (2009), 321.

6 On the concept of 'transition', and of 'transitional justice', see Arthur, ibid., 321–67.

7 These dynamics have, in turn, been significantly fuelled by the impact of post-colonialism and critical race and gender studies and activism.

8 See P. Akhavan, 'Beyond Impunity: Can International Criminal Justice Prevent Future Atrocities?', *American Journal of International Law* 95 (2001), 7.

9 See D. McCargo, 'Transitional Justice and Its Discontents', *Journal of Democracy* 26 (2015), 5.

10 See United Nations Human Rights Council, 'Report of the Commission of Inquiry on Human Rights in the Democratic People's Republic of Korea' (2014) UN Doc A/HRC/25/63.

11 See, e.g., N. Cheesman, B. D'Costa and T. Haberkon, 'Anticipating the Struggle against Everyday Impunity in Myanmar through Accounts from Bangladesh and Thailand' *Asia and The Pacific Policy Studies* 3 (2016), 48; M. Zarni and N. Brinham, 'Reworking the Colonial-Era Indian Peril: Myanmar's State-Directed Persecution of Rohingyas and Other Muslims', *Brown*

indelibly linked to corruption in China[12] and still-entrenched in post-genocide Cambodia,[13] that it has again flared up in the Philippines[14] and remains endemic in parts of India and South Asia,[15] and continues to plague Indonesia[16] and its neighbours in the Pacific.[17]

Japan too, stands accused of tolerating impunity, albeit in relation to historical rather than contemporary crimes and rights violations. Its interaction with the anti-impunity norm over the last three decades is the central focus of this chapter. In particular, this chapter will consider Japan's war responsibility or war guilt[18] for crimes against the so-called 'comfort

Journal of World Affairs 24 (2017), 53; United Nations, 'Fact-Finding Mission on Myanmar: Concrete and Overwhelming Information Points to International Crimes' (*United Nations*, 12 March 2018) www.ohchr.org/EN/HRBodies/HRC/Pages/NewsDetail.aspx?NewsID=22794&LangID=E accessed 12 April 2018.

12 See B. Zhao, 'Land Expropriation, Protest, and Impunity in Rural China', *European Journal of Anthropology* 54 (2009), 97; R. Peerenboom, 'Assessing Human Rights in China: Why the Double Standard', *Cornell International Law Journal* 38 (2005), 71.

13 See W. Lambourne, 'Justice after Genocide: Impunity and the Extraordinary Chambers in the Courts of Cambodia', *Genocide Studies and Prevention: An International Journal* 8 (2014), 29.

14 See J. Bagas, 'Duterte and Donor Withdrawal', *Sur – International Journal on Human Rights* 26 (2017), 37; G. Boehringer, 'Duterte's Drug War: Violating Rights for a Quick Fix', *Alternative Law Journal* 42 (2017), 233.

15 See S. Kazi 'Rape, Impunity and Justice in Kashmir', *Socio-Legal Review* 10 (2014), 14; see too M. K. Sarkaria, 'Lessons from Punjab's Missing Girls: Toward a Global Feminist Perspective on Choice in Abortion [comments], *California Law Review* 97 (2009), 905; J. Kaur, 'A Judicial Blackout: Judicial Impunity for Disappearances in Punjab, India', *Harvard Human Rights Journal* 15 (2002), 269; E. Liddick, and J. Gagnon, 'Striving for Peace and Reconciliation in Sri Lanka: A Creative Solution to Conflict', *War Crimes, Genocide and Crimes against Humanity* 3 (2009), 39; S. Rajan, 'Domestication of International Criminal Law: International Crimes Tribunal of Bangladesh, A Case Study', *ISIL Year Book of International Humanitarian and Refugee Law* 12–13 (2013), 132.

16 See K. McGregor, 'Exposing Impunity: Memory and Human Rights Activism in Indonesia and Argentina', *Journal of Genocide Research* 19 (2017), 551; V. Hearman, 'Between Citizenship and Human Rights: The Struggle for Justice after Indonesia's 1965 Mass Violence,' *Citizenship Studies* 22 (2018), 175.

17 See B. Ottley, 'Legal Dissonance: The Interaction of Criminal Law and Customary Law in Papua New Guinea', *Asia Pacific Law Review* 24 (2016), 83; N. Dicker, 'Aiding Transitional Justice in Solomon Islands', *Buffalo Human Rights Law Review* 21 (2015), 77; N. Baird, 'The Role of International Non-Governmental Organisations in the Universal Periodic Review of Pacific Island States: Can Doing Good Be Done Better', *Melbourne Journal of International Law* 16 (2015), 550.

18 See Onuma Yasuaki on the Japanese term *senso sekinin*, which signifies certain responsibilities which Japan owes in relation to its conduct in World War II and in the course of its colonial rule over Taiwan and Korea in Onuma Y., 'Japanese War Guilt and Postwar Responsibilities of Japan', *Berkeley Journal of International Law* 20 (2003), 600.

women'[19] of World War II (hereafter WWII), which has been a defining impunity issue in East Asia since the early 1990s.

The women in question, drawn from diverse locations in the Asia-Pacific, included Korean, Chinese, Filipina, Taiwanese, Indonesian, Dutch, and Australian nationals, amongst others, and are estimated to have numbered in the hundreds of thousands.[20] After being recruited through force and deception, they were coerced into service in a network of military brothels, known as 'comfort stations', throughout the Asia-Pacific region. There, they were forced to provide sexual relief for Japanese troops in dangerous and degrading conditions; resulting in immense and devastating suffering.[21] This so-called 'comfort system' was justified as a means of boosting troop morale and preventing the rape of civilians,[22] but has since been described as a system

[19] Otherwise known in Korean as *jungshindae* (Women's Voluntary Labour Corps) or *ilbon'gu wianbu* (Japanese military comfort women), or in Japanese as *ianfu* (comfort women) or *jukun ianfu* (military comfort women). The women are also commonly referred to as 'military sexual slaves' in United Nations literature and Western research. This chapter will use the term 'comfort women' for consistency with much of the existing literature.

[20] Estimates of total numbers and population breakdowns are difficult to verify. It is commonly cited that around 200,000 women were 'recruited', while other sources suggest the number was closer to 400,000. See P. P. Qiu, S. Zhiliang and C. Lifei, *Chinese Comfort Women: Testimonies from Imperial Japan's Sex Slaves* (Oxford University Press, 2014).

[21] Testimonies indicate that many women were recruited by coercion and deception and were transported as if mere chattels to 'comfort stations' across the Asia-Pacific region. There, they were confined in squalid and restrictive conditions, and were forced to engage in sexual intercourse with a steady flow of patrons in an exploitative framework where rest, payment and basic amenities were rare. Depending on the time and place of station, they were made to service a steady stream of Japanese soldiers, officers and sometimes civilians, causing immense damage to their sexual and reproductive organs, and exposing them to venereal and other communicable diseases. Unwillingness to submit was often met with violence, reprisals or death. Of those who survived, legacies have included infertility and gynaecological problems; depressive illnesses; anxiety; relationship difficulties; ostracism and diminished prospects for marriage, employment and participation in community and civic life. Of those who survived until Japanese surrender, many were killed or abandoned at the end of the war. See, e.g., UNCHR, 'Final report submitted by Ms Gay J McDougall, Special Rapporteur' (22 June 1998) UN Doc E/CN.4/Sub.2/1998/13 [7] ('the McDougall Report').

[22] See, e.g., statement from Japan's War Ministry in 1940 that 'comfort stations' would 'heighten the men's morale, keep discipline and prevent crimes and sexual diseases' at Digital Museum: The Comfort Women Issue and the Asian Women's Fund, 'From a Memorandum sent by Tadaichi Kawahara, Adjutant in the Ministry of War, 'Measures to Enforce Military Discipline from the Experiences in the China Incident' (AWF) www.awf.or.jp/e1/facts-02.html accessed 20 December 2017.

of state-sanctioned rape and enslavement[23] which contravened laws in effect at the time.[24]

Local and foreign stakeholders have drawn on burgeoning anti-impunity sentiments over nearly three decades to call for action from Japanese lawmakers, including the commencement of prosecutions against surviving perpetrators of crimes against the 'comfort women', the institution of more generous reparations measures for survivors and their families, and reforms in public administration to promote governmental openness and access to justice.[25] Over time, these stakeholders have increasingly grounded their claims in legal argumentation; not just to call for the reform of Japanese laws and legal procedure, but also to insist that Japan is duty-bound to conform to obligations founded in international human rights and humanitarian law.[26]

[23] *Prosecutors and Peoples of Asia Pacific Region* v. *Hirohito; Prosecutors and Peoples of Asia Pacific Region* v. *Japan*, Summary of Findings and Preliminary Judgment, Women's International War Crimes Tribunal 2000 (12 December 2000) [91].

[24] Ibid [93]. Their Honours found, for example, that there was incontrovertible evidence that 'girls and women ... were taken either by abduction, conscription or coercion, or through deceptive means, and forcibly made part of the military sexual slavery system .... [and] subjected to continuous and sometimes gang rape and other forms of sexual violence and torture.' Ibid., [58]. This treatment gave rise to state responsibility and individual responsibility on the part of Emperor Hirohito for rape and sexual slavery as crimes against humanity.

[25] These have included United Nations human rights bodies, foreign governments and various civil society and victims' groups from the Asia-Pacific. See, e.g., statements made during the United Nations Human Rights Council Universal Periodic Review process, the UN Committee on the Elimination of Discrimination against Women, the UN Committee against Torture and the Human Rights Committee: UN Committee on the Elimination of Discrimination against Women, 'Concluding Observations on the Combined Seventh and Eighth Periodic Reports of Japan' (10 March 2016) UN Doc CEDAW/C/JPN/CO/7–8; UN Committee against Torture, 'Concluding Observations on the Second Periodic Report of Japan' (28 June 2013) UN Doc CAT/C/JPN/CO/2; UNHRC 'Consideration of Reports Submitted by States Parties under Article 40 of the Covenant : International Covenant On Civil and Political Rights: 6th Periodic Report of States Parties: Japan' (9 October 2012) UN Doc CCPR/C/JPN/6. See too J. Kingston, 'History Haunts Japan's Prime Minister Abe', *Asia-Pacific Journal* 13 (2015) and J. Landino, 'Ianfu: No Comment Yet for Korean Comfort Women and the Impact of House Resolution 121', *Cardozo Journal of Law and Gender* 15 (2009), 333; Cheah W. Ling, 'Walking the Long Road in Solidarity and Hope', *Harvard Human Rights Journal* 22 (2009), 99.

[26] Initially, the 'comfort women' focused on political claims to redress based on historical responsibility, but progressed to law and rights-based demands for an official, formal apology for past crimes; the requirement for fact-finding and truth-telling measures; the provision of reparations; memorialization and a commitment to educating future generations. A trend is also evident towards the provision of individualized apologies and reparations. See E. Hee-Seok Shin in 'The "Comfort Women" Reparation Movement: Between Universal Women's Human Right and Particular Anti-Colonial Nationalism', *Florida Journal of International Law* 28 (2016), 87; L. Hein, 'Savage Irony: The Imaginative Power of the 'Military Comfort Women' in the 1990s', *Gender and History* 11 (1999), 336, 347–8.

As this chapter will demonstrate, however, Japanese law-makers have largely rejected the legal basis of the anti-impunity norm, with the result that anti-impunity campaigns have not generated a significant programme of law reform. Nevertheless, the norm has infiltrated Japanese policy-making to a certain degree, generating elements of both resistance and concession. Rather than concluding that this case study is an instance of 'transplant failure', then, this chapter argues that it illustrates the limitations of transplant theory as an account for the complex interactions between municipal and international legal institutions and ideas.

II THE ANTI-IMPUNITY NORM: AN OVERVIEW

It is difficult to pinpoint the precise content of the anti-impunity norm. However, the term appears to refer to the general proposition that states must not tolerate or endorse the violation of human rights norms and serious international crimes. It is commonly interpreted to mean that states must at least carry out their due diligence obligations to investigate, prosecute and punish wrongdoers, and is justified on bases including the rule of law, the equality of all persons before the law, and the right of all persons to an effective remedy.[27] These foundations are not just moral but legal.[28] Impunity, for these purposes is commonly defined as:

> the impossibility, de jure or de facto, of bringing the perpetrators of violations to account – whether in criminal, civil, administrative or disciplinary proceedings – since they are not subject to any inquiry that might lead to their being accused, arrested, tried and, if found guilty, sentenced to appropriate penalties, and to making reparations to their victims.[29]

27 UNCHR (Sub-Commission), 'Question of the Impunity of Perpetrators of Violations of Human Rights (Civil and Political Rights): Final Report prepared by Mr L. Joinet, pursuant to Subcommission resolution 1995/35' (29 June 1996) UN Doc E/CN.4/Sub.2/1996/18 annex II 'Set of Principles for the Protection and Promotion of Human Rights through Action to Combat Impunity' ('Impunity Principles') 14–15.

28 See, e.g., Universal Declaration of Human Rights, which states that '[a]ll are equal before the law and are entitled without any discrimination to equal protection of the law.' Universal Declaration of Human Rights (adopted 10 December 1948 UNGA Res 217 A(III) (UDHR) art. 7. See too reiteration and extension of this principle in the ICCPR: International Covenant on Civil and Political Rights (adopted 16 December 1966, entered into force 23 March 1976) 999 UNTS 171 (ICCPR) art. 26; art. 14.1; See, e.g., UDHR art. 8, which states '[e]veryone has the right to an effective remedy by the competent national tribunals for acts violating the fundamental rights granted him by the constitution or by law': UDHR, ibid. See too ICCPR, ibid., art. 2.

29 UNHRC, 'Report of the Independent Expert [Diane Orentlicher] to Update the Set of Principles to Combat Impunity' UN Doc E/CN.4/2005/102/Add.1 (8 February 2005)

Efforts to articulate the core content and scope of the anti-impunity norm have culminated in an international instrument which is often referred to as the 'Impunity Principles'.[30] While they are 'not legal standards in the strict sense, but guiding principles',[31] the Impunity Principles nevertheless draw together authoritative statements of international human rights law, international humanitarian law, and international criminal law, including aspects of 'hard law' in the form of international treaty law;[32] legal principles which are said to have attained the status of customary international law, such as the duty to prosecute or extradite; judicial decisions of international tribunals;[33] and 'soft law' in the form of international declarations and similar instruments which seek to formulate international standards on the meaning of impunity and how practically to combat it.[34] Many of these standards are argued to be so widely accepted that they already enjoy the status of customary international law and, if so, are binding on all states regardless of whether states have voluntarily accepted them in international treaties or instruments – and if not, are en route to achieving this status.[35]

The Impunity Principles structure these duties into three core sets of rights: the right to justice;[36] the right to reparation;[37] and the right to know,[38] each of which contains detailed specifications for state practice. Most significant among these is the duty of states to investigate and take 'appropriate measures'

addendum 'Set of Principles for the Protection and Promotion of Human Rights through Action to Combat Impunity' ('Updated Principles') 6 [A].

30 The final and most widely cited iteration is often referred to as the 'Updated Principles'. See above (n. 29). For ease of reading, this chapter will refer simply to the 'Impunity Principles' and specify the version in footnotes.

31 Impunity Principles (n. 27) 11; Updated Principles (n. 29) 5.

32 Such as the International Convention on the Non-Applicability of Statutory Limitations to War Crimes and Crimes against Humanity (adopted 26 November 1968, entered into force 11 November 1970) 754 UNTS 73.

33 Notable cases include *Velázquez-Rodríguez* v. *Honduras*, wherein the Inter-American Court of Human Rights strongly articulated the duty incumbent on states to genuinely investigate human rights violations and to prevent impunity. *Velázquez-Rodríguez Case*, Inter-American Court of Human Rights Series C No. 4 (29 July 1988).

34 See, e.g., the Vienna Declaration and Programme of Action, which stressed, inter alia, the illegitimacy of national legislation that permitted impunity for grave violations of human rights. World Conference on Human Rights: Vienna Declaration and Programme of Action (adopted 25 June 1993) A/CONF.157/23.

35 See J. A. Hessbruegge, 'Justice Delayed, Not Denied: Statutory Limitations and Human Rights Crimes', *Georgetown Journal of International Law* 43 (2012), 335.

36 Updated Principles (n. 29) pt. IV.

37 Ibid., pt. V.

38 Ibid., pt. III.

with respect to perpetrators,[39] and, relatedly, the duty to refrain from adopting amnesty or clemency measures which prevent the prosecution and punishment of perpetrators of serious crimes under international law,[40] or which hinder victims' rights to reparation and to access information about violations.[41] In addition, the Impunity Principles impose restrictions on prescription – that is, the use of legal measures such as statutes of limitations or time bars to restrict legal proceedings against perpetrators or the state. They claim that rules on prescription cannot lawfully operate where no effective remedy is available; can never apply to crimes under international law that are considered 'imprescriptible',[42] and, even where operative, can never prevent victims' civil or administrative actions for reparations.[43]

These expectations represent nothing less than a paradigm shift in the protection of human rights, which have historically been responded to with amnesia or vengeance rather than accountability, and cover-ups rather than sober confrontation and reparation. Reversing these attitudes and practices is a complex and ambitious task for several reasons. Firstly, as a practical matter, the sheer magnitude of legal, political, and social change standards call upon states to undertake is immense. Impunity is a multi-dimensional problem, which tends to manifest in conjunction with a host of related phenomena, such as high levels of corruption, low respect for the rule of law, and pronounced levels of inequality.[44] Addressing impunity effectively, therefore, often necessarily requires a near-total transformation in the culture of societies' public administration, including their legal systems. Few states have both the appetite and capacity to carry this out.

Secondly, unpicking impunity is fraught with questions of 'societal fit'. It stands to reason that states which are hostile or ambivalent towards international human rights norms and their underlying premises of liberalism, dignity, individualism and equality are also more likely to resist core aspects

39 See Principle 19 (n. 29) which sets the expectation that states, inter alia: ' … shall undertake prompt, thorough, independent and impartial investigations of violations of human rights and international humanitarian law and take appropriate measures in respect of the perpetrators, particularly in the area of criminal justice, by ensuring that those responsible for serious crimes under international law are prosecuted, tried and duly punished … '.

40 Updated Principles (n. 29) Principle 24(a).

41 Ibid., Principle 24(b).

42 These are said to include war crimes and crimes against humanity and genocide. See Hessbruegge (n. 35) 335–85.

43 See Updated Principles (n. 29) Principle 23.

44 J. A. Le Clercq Ortega and G. R. S. Lara (eds.), *Global Impunity Index* (Fundación Universidad de las Américas Puebla, 2015) 32–8. See too H.-Y. Liu, *Law's Impunity* (Hart Publishing, 2015); M. M. Penrose, 'Impunity - Inertia, Inaction, and Invalidity: A Literature Review', *Boston University International Law Journal* 17 (1999), 273.

of the global anti-impunity agenda; even where they disapprove of impunity in the abstract. Thus, while it is entirely possible for such societies to abhor the violation of norms considered vital to the community, such an attitude is distinct from, and independent of, the international anti-impunity norm. This is because the anti-impunity norm is not reducible to the promotion of rule obedience. Rather, it also carries heavy normative baggage, being founded in a moralistic and rights-centred vision of what the relationship between citizen and state ought to entail. This inevitably colours states' attitudes and behaviour in relation to the norm.

III THE ANTI-IMPUNITY NORM: LEGAL TRANSPLANT?

As a mechanism of effecting legal and policy changes across jurisdictions the anti-impunity norm is an interesting case study of how legal ideas can travel in a globalized world. However, the norm sits uneasily under the conceptual umbrella of 'legal transplants': not only is it a product of public and international law and may therefore simply not be transplantable;[45] but it may neither be 'legal' nor a 'transplant', nor even a set of 'rules', depending on who you ask.[46]

Although the anti-impunity norm possesses what has been said to be the central character of a legal transplant; a propensity for movement,[47] its mechanics and the outcomes it seeks to produce are not strictly instances of 'the moving of a rule or a system of law from one country to another or from one people to another',[48] as Watson put it. Nor are they legal transplants in the precise sense that Harding proposes we adopt – that is, the export of law from empire to colony.[49]

The anti-impunity norm's legal character is also as ambiguous as its 'transplantability'. As part of a deeply political and moral project, it simply cannot be understood as one or more 'bare propositional statements' that can be seamlessly applied to novel impunity contexts.[50] However, this is not

45 See A. Dolidze, 'Bridging Comparative and International Law: Amicus Curiae Participation as a Vertical Legal Transplant', *European Journal of International Law* 26 (2015), 851.

46 Compare A. Watson, *Legal Transplants: An Approach to Comparative Law* 2nd edn (University of Georgia Press, 1993) and P. Legrand, 'The Impossibility of 'Legal Transplants', *Maastricht Journal of European and Comparative Law* 4 (1997), 111.

47 G. R. B. Galindo, 'Legal Transplants between Time and Space' in T. Duve (ed.), *Entanglements in Legal History: Conceptual Approaches* (Max Planck, 2014) 129.

48 Watson (n. 46) 21.

49 A. Harding, 'The Legal Transplants Debate: Getting beyond the Impasse?', Chapter 1 in this Volume.

50 See Watson (n. 46). Although, of course, Watson would probably agree – he apparently never intended for this framework to apply to public international law concepts.

necessarily evidence to support Legrand's claim that legal transplants are 'impossible'[51] – rather, what it demonstrates is the validity of a related claim by Legrand; that contemporary efforts to determine the impact of foreign legal ideas ought to transcend the 'rigid and jejune framework' of legal transplants;[52] a point echoed by Teubner,[53] Harding,[54] and others.[55]

The genesis and operationalization of the anti-impunity norm demonstrates a great degree of cross-institutional and cross-jurisdiction interaction; much of which is interesting precisely because it defies the transplant metaphor. The anti-impunity norm's amalgamation from a series of discrete international legal principles, for example, has depended not just on the emergence of certain legal rules in diverse legal institutions,[56] but their assembly into a conceptual composite by a transnational network of lawyers, scholars and activists, who have deliberately sought to borrow and build a body of rules capable of universal application in service of litigating human rights violations and serious international crimes.[57] Efforts in the field have been matched by the deliberative process of drafting the Impunity Principles over two decades, resulting in a detailed set of rules and guidelines that aggregated and reflected the state of international law on rights, remedies and reparations.[58] Doing so projected an apparent global consensus on the intolerability of impunity while also providing a blueprint on public administration and law enforcement for states in transition, largely on the basis of learnings from earlier experiments in transitional justice.

The transplant metaphor is further confounded by the anti-impunity norm's legal character. As has been canvassed earlier, advocates of the anti-impunity norm seek to entrench the norm and its sub-rules into municipal legal systems

[51] Legrand (n. 46).

[52] Ibid., 120.

[53] G. Teubner, 'Legal Irritants: Good Faith in British Law or How Unifying Law Ends Up in New Differences', *Modern Law Review* 61 (1998), 11.

[54] Harding (n. 49.).

[55] See, e.g., William Twining, 'Social Science and Diffusion of Law', *Journal of Law and Society* 32 (2005), 203; E. Örücü, 'Law as Transposition', *The International and Comparative Law Quarterly* 51 (2002), 205.

[56] Particularly significant is are decisions and findings of judicial and quasi-judicial bodies such as the Inter-American Court of Human Rights, the International Criminal Tribunals for the Former Yugoslavia and Rwanda, the United Nations' human rights treaty bodies, and of course the early work of the post-WWII international criminal tribunals.

[57] See Lutz and Sikkink (n. 1).

[58] T. van Boven, 'Basic Principles and Guidelines on the Right to a Remedy and Reparation for Victims of Gross Violations of International Human Rights Law and Serious Violations of International Humanitarian Law' (*United Nations Archive, Audiovisual Library of International Law*, 16 December 2005) http://legal.un.org/avl/ha/ga_60–147/ga_60–147.html accessed 22 November 2017.

on the basis of international legal obligation. However, as the Impunity Principles demonstrate, in their capacity as the leading embodiment of the norm's content, many of the standards that comprise the norm are neither fully aspirational nor fully binding as a matter of international treaty law. Rather, the central aspects of the norm are argued to be so widely accepted that they enjoy the status of customary international law.[59] If so, these rules effectively inhere in all states by virtue of both their unique character and the decentralized international legal order, and states are obliged to make them effective in whatever manner suits their circumstances. This commonality of obligation, however, is obviously far from a legal transplant; there being no obvious donor, and the 'transfer' being a matter of the imposition rather than the adoption of legal rules.

If, however, the rules that are central to the anti-impunity norm have not attained the rare status of customary international law, the position is different. The standards will be binding only on a select few; in the jurisdiction of origin, for example, or on those states that have voluntarily accepted the obligations by way of a simultaneously applicable international treaty. Although they cannot be imposed and enforced as a matter of international law, however, they are nevertheless capable of influencing cross-jurisdictional change in various fashions; whether that be properly described as 'transplantation'; 'borrowing', 'diffusion', or otherwise.

Relatedly, the introduction of the anti-impunity norm to novel settings further confounds the legal transplant metaphor insofar as determining or measuring 'success' or 'failure' is concerned – or indeed whether the introduction of the new norm has really been a 'transplant' or some other thing entirely. States differ vastly in their appetite and capacity to combat impunity, as well as in their disposition towards the proper means of doing so. Accordingly, no homogeneity of process or starting point; let alone outcome is discernible. These factors lend credence to Teubner's prediction that foreign norms act less as 'transplants' than as 'legal irritants' which unleash a unique and unpredictable set of events and outputs depending on the contexts and discourses they encounter.[60]

In further defiance of the transplant trope, many other legal reforms that the anti-impunity norm advocates for are not strictly legal 'rules' at all, but legal institutions, legal procedures, or what Harding calls the 'idea of a law'.[61] Some,

59 See, e.g., Hessbruegge (n. 35).

60 Teubner (n. 53). Teubner notably rues the sense that the lexicon of transplants is a 'misleading metaphor'; an apt observation here.

61 Harding (n .49) 6. See too Watson's claim that 'legal rules, in addition to being part of the social structure, also operate on the level of ideas', and that what is 'borrowed' is very often the

being products of international law, are intentionally framed in broad terms so as to be capable of adaption rather than repetition or mimesis. Others, such as the concept of judicial independence[62] or the reviewability of government action[63] are not novel or precise formulations, but form part of a global patchwork of general legal concepts, which may take different guises in different contexts.[64] Nevertheless, the 'un-ruly' status of much of the anti-impunity norm's content has not prevented it from effecting legal change in both international and municipal legal systems.[65] Whether or not we wish to use the term 'legal transplant' in relation to the forces of supply and demand for anti-impunity-inspired law reform appears to matter very little.

Harding rightly concludes in Chapter 1that comparativists' focus ought to be on when and how societies decide to accept and implement foreign legal solutions to tackle local problems,[66] and to contemplate the actual effects of legal change.[67] The following section of this chapter attempts to answer this call in relation to a seminal East Asian case study of impunity: Japan's interaction with the anti-impunity norm on the prickly terrain of its war responsibility for crimes against the Asian 'comfort women' of World War II.

IV JAPAN UNDER PRESSURE: EMERGENCE OF THE ANTI-IMPUNITY NORM

Since the early 1990s – more or less contemporaneously with the rise of the anti-impunity norm – and after nearly fifty years of silence and denial, the issue of whether the Japanese state and imperial military had systematically recruited young women into sexual servitude in the periods before and

idea, rather than simply the rule.' A. Watson, 'Comparative Law and Legal Change', *Cambridge Law Journal* 37 (1978), 315.

62 See Updated Principles (n. 29) Principles 30 and 36.

63 See, e.g., ibid., Principle 16.

64 Harding terms this 'global white noise of law'. Harding (n. 49) 6.

65 The Principles have been favourably cited by certain international criminal tribunals, human rights treaty bodies, and commissions of inquiry, and have informed the content of a fairly recent multilateral human rights treaty, the International Convention for the Protection of all Persons from Enforced Disappearance. See Van Boven (n. 58); International Center for Transitional Justice, 'Briefing Paper: Transitional Justice in the United Nations Human Rights Council' (*International Center for Transitional Justice*, 6 July 2011) www.ictj.org/publication/transitional-justice-united-nations-human-rights-council accessed 15 September 2017.

66 Harding (n. 49) 10; A Harding, 'Global Doctrine and Local Knowledge: Law in South East Asia', *International and Comparative Law Quarterly* 51 (2002), 35.

67 Harding (n. 49) 8.

during WWII became a defining issue on the international justice agenda.[68]

Of the Asian 'comfort women' who survived the war and were able to return home,[69] the cessation of hostilities marked the commencement of a long period of silence on this matter; derived from the shame felt by women themselves and foisted on them by their communities, and worsened by the poverty and low social status of many.[70] Not only did they return to the patriarchal societies that in many cases had contributed to their commodification,[71] but they returned to a political context marred by the lengthy and divisive Tokyo war crimes trials conducted by the International Military Tribunal for the Far East ('IMTFE'), which largely overlooked the systematic mistreatment of the 'comfort women'[72] and failed to generate a deep dialogue about Japan's war responsibility.[73] Japan's conclusion of post-war reparations treaties with Asian and Allied nations[74] further stifled any sense of impunity or responsibility towards war victims such as the 'comfort

[68] This was no accident; its case having been taken up by numerous intersectional justice advocates, including global feminist, anti-colonial, critical race, international relations and human rights activists and scholars. See M. P. Sonen, 'Healing Multidimensional Wounds of Injustice: Intersectionality and the Korean "Comfort Women"', *Berkeley La Raza Law Journal* 22 (2012), 269.

[69] Estimates suggest that only one quarter of the 'comfort women' survived their ordeals. See the McDougall Report (n. 21) [7]. See too UNCHR, 'Report of the Special Rapporteur on violence against women, its causes and consequences, Ms Radhika Coomaraswamy, in accordance with Commission on Human Rights resolution 1994/45: Report on the mission to the Democratic People's Republic of Korea, the Republic of Korea and Japan on the issue of military sexual slavery in wartime' (7 February 1996) UN Doc E/CN.4/1996/53/Add. 1/Corr. 1 'the Coomaraswamy Report').

[70] Ibid.

[71] C. S. Soh, *The Comfort Women: Sexual Violence and Postcolonial Memory in Korea and Japan* (University of Chicago Press, 2008) xvi.

[72] Although some evidence about the system's operation was adduced at the IMFTE, it was not a central or even significant focus of the trial. See U. Dolgopol, 'Crimes against the Comfort Women in the Tokyo Trial' in Y. Tanaka, T. L. H. McCormack, G. Simpson, *Beyond Victor's Justice? The Tokyo War Crimes Trial Revisited* (Brill, 2011) 243–4.

[73] See M. Futamura, *War Crimes Tribunals and Transitional Justice: The Tokyo Trial and the Nuremberg Legacy* (Routledge, 2007).

[74] See, e.g., Treaty of Peace between the Union of Burma and Japan (entered into force 16 April 1955) 251 UNTS 201, wherein Japan pledged, inter alia, to pay reparations equivalent to USD $20m to Myanmar over ten years; Reparations Agreement between Japan and the Philippines (entered into force 9 May 1956) 285 UNTS 3, wherein Japan pledged, inter alia, to pay reparations equivalent to USD $550m to the Philippines over twenty years; Treaty of Peace between Japan and the Republic of Indonesia (entered into force 15 April 1958) 324 UNTS 235 and Reparations Agreement 324 UNTS 247, wherein Japan pledged, inter alia, to pay reparations equivalent to USD $223.08m over twelve years to Indonesia; Treaty on Basic Relations between Japan and the Republic of Korea (entered into force 22 June 1965) 583 UNTS 44 and Agreement on the Settlement of Problems concerning Property and Claims and

women'; these instruments having been forged as a basis for finalizing liability for past wrongs rather than representing an initial or interim measure.[75]

It was not until the early 1990s that momentum gathered to do justice for the former 'comfort women', with numerous survivors' testimonies released publicly, lawsuits filed and evidence of state complicity revealed.[76] With various powerful reasons for this turn of events,[77] official denial became increasingly untenable.[78] After a brief official inquiry, the government conceded that the Japanese government had:

> been involved in the establishment of comfort stations, the control of those who recruited comfort women, the construction and reinforcement of comfort facilities, the management and surveillance of comfort stations, the hygiene maintenance in comfort stations and among comfort women, and the issuance of identification as well as other documents to those who were related to comfort stations.[79]

The Japanese government also extended its '. . . sincere apology and remorse to all those who have suffered indescribable hardship as so-called "wartime comfort women", irrespective of their nationality or place of birth.'[80] These sentiments were repeated in 1993, after another inquiry, when the government recognized that the Japanese military were involved in the establishment and management of the 'comfort stations' and the transfer of 'comfort women',

on Economic Co-Operation between Japan and the Republic of Korea (entered into force 18 December 1965) 583 UNTS 258 wherein Japan pledged, inter alia, to pay reparations equivalent to USD $300m over ten years and provide the equivalent of USD $200m in long-term and low-interest loans to South Korea.

75 See Treaty on Basic Relations between Japan and the Republic of Korea (n. 74) Art. II, stating that the instrument had the effect of settling claims between the parties 'completely and finally'.

76 However, the phenomenon was revealed many years earlier, most famously via Senda Kako's 1978 book *Jugun Ianfu* (San'Ichi Shobo, 1978).

77 Influential factors included rising forces of human rights law, international feminism, anti-colonialism and the rapid development of international criminal law jurisprudence, especially gendered, sexualized and race-based crimes, which all built momentum for transparency, accountability and justice. The timing of the revelation of key evidence – just before the visit of the South Korean Prime Minister – is also cited as a key catalyst, as is the death of Emperor Hirohito.

78 M. Kimura, *Unfolding the 'Comfort Women' Debates: Modernity, Violence, Women's Voices* (Springer, 2016) 5.

79 Ministry of Foreign Affairs, 'Statement by Chief Cabinet Secretary Koichi Kato on the Issue of the so-called "Wartime Comfort Women" from the Korean Peninsula' (*Japanese Government*, 1992) www.mofa.go.jp/policy/postwar/state9207.html accessed 11 September 2017.

80 Ministry of Foreign Affairs, 'Statement by Chief Cabinet Secretary Koichi Kato on the Issue of the so-called "Wartime Comfort Women" from the Korean Peninsula' (*Japanese Government*, 1992) www.mofa.go.jp/policy/postwar/state9207.html accessed 11 September 2017.

who were often 'recruited against their own will, through coaxing, coercion, etc.' by private actors as well as administrative and military personnel.[81] The Cabinet further resolved to 'face squarely the historical facts as described above instead of evading them'.[82]

Two years later, after fierce public campaigns and growing international pressure, the government announced its intention to found an entity to be known as the Asian Peace and Friendship Foundation for Women, which would undertake certain projects to atone for Japan's wartime treatment of the former 'comfort women'.[83] These included the Asian Women's Fund initiative, which would 'raise funds in the private sector as a means to enact the Japanese people's atonement',[84] and to complement state-run medical and other social welfare programmes[85] and efforts to collate relevant historical documents 'to serve as a lesson of history.'[86] Successive statements reiterated Japan's acknowledgement of its moral responsibility and the need for the Japanese people to atone for the 'comfort women's' suffering.[87]

Finally, in 2015, having faced continued pressure and scrutiny from domestic and transnational sources, including in the form of a prominent People's Tribunal – the Women's International War Crimes Tribunal on Japan's Military Sexual Slavery[88] – censure from United Nations human rights bodies,[89]

81 Ministry of Foreign Affairs, 'Statement by the Chief Cabinet Secretary Yohei Kono on the result of the study on the issue of "comfort women" ('Kono Statement')' (*Japanese Government*, 1993) www.mofa.go.jp/policy/women/fund/state9308.html accessed 11 September 2017.

82 Ibid.

83 Ministry of Foreign Affairs, 'Statement by the Chief Cabinet Secretary' (*Japanese Government*, 1995) www.mofa.go.jp/policy/women/fund/state9506.html accessed 11 September 2017.

84 Ibid.

85 Ibid.

86 Ibid.

87 See esp. Ministry of Foreign Affairs, 'Statement by Prime Minister Tomiichi Murayama on the occasion of the establishment of the "Asian Women's Fund"' (*Japanese Government*, 1995) www.mofa.go.jp/policy/women/fund/state9507.html accessed 11 September 2017; Digital Museum: The Comfort Women Issue and the Asian Women's Fund, 'Statement by Prime Minister Junichiro Koizumi on the 60th Anniversary of the End of the War' (*Asian Women's Fund*, 2005) www.awf.or.jp/e6/statement-36.html accessed 12 September 2017.

88 The Court was comprised of eminent jurists Carmen Argibay, Christine Chinkin, Willy Mutunga and Gabrielle Kirk McDonald. See Women's Caucus for Gender Justice, 'Re: Judgment of the Women's International War Crimes Tribunal 2000 for the Trial of Japanese Military Sexual Slavery, 'In the matter of the Prosecutors and the Peoples of the Asia-Pacific Region v. Emperor Hirohito et al. and the Government of Japan' (*Women's Caucus for Gender Justice*, 2000) www.iccwomen.org/wigjdraft1/Archives/oldWCGJ/tokyo/judgmentannounce.html. accessed 12 September 2017.

89 See above (n. 25).

foreign governments[90] and various regional and international civil society and victims' groups,[91] Japan restated its 'deep responsibility' and committed a considerable sum of government funds to compensate South Korean former 'comfort women' in a bid to conclude the matter once and for all.[92]

V HITS AND MISSES: JAPANESE ANTI-IMPUNITY PRACTICE IN CONTEXT

As the foregoing discussion illustrates, Japan has responded to demands for it to confront the responsibility owed by the authors and perpetrators of crimes against the former 'comfort women' with elements of concession. It has, over nearly three decades, taken steps to investigate and ascertain historical facts about the 'comfort system', and has acknowledged the state's complicity in, and responsibility for, the system. It has also offered various sincere and emotive statements of apology, and has implemented some compensation programmes for the former 'comfort women'.

Nevertheless, Japan continues to be criticized for its unwillingness to more fully conform to contemporary anti-impunity standards. Most obviously, Japan has evaded the 'right to justice'. It has refused to fully recognize any liability for crimes against the former 'comfort women' under international law,[93] and has

[90] Particularly prominent have been the efforts of South Korean and Chinese governments, but other states have also formally exhorted the Japanese government to provide full acknowledgement, acceptance and redress for the 'comfort women', including the United States of America; whose lower house passed House Resolution 121 in 2007, calling for recognition, redress and action, as did Canadian and European Union Parliaments, while the lower house of the Dutch Parliament did similarly in 2009. See analysis by Kingston (n. 25); Landino (n. 25); Cheah (n. 25).

[91] Key groups include the *Jeongdaehyeop* (Korean Council for Women Drafted for Military Sexual Slavery by Japan), the Dutch organization Foundation of Japanese Honorary Debts (*Stichting Japanese Ereschulden*), the Japanese Bar Association, the Indonesian Legal Aid Foundation (*Yayasan Lembaga Bantuan Hukum Indonesia*), the Asia Japan Women's Resource Centre and the Violence against Women in War Network. They have been supported by other prominent international NGOs such as Human Rights Watch and Amnesty International.

[92] Japan has pledged to establish a new foundation and provide a one-off transfer of funds that will enable projects designed to '[recover] the honour and dignity and healing the psychological wounds of all former comfort women'. South Korea in turn confirmed that this will resolve the issue 'finally and irreversibly'. See Ministry of Foreign Affairs, 'Announcement by Foreign Ministers of Japan and the Republic of Korea at the Joint Press Occasion' (*Japanese Government*, 28 December 2015) www.mofa.go.jp/a_o/na/kr/page4e_000364.html accessed 13 September 2017.

[93] McDougall Report (n. 21) [68]-[69]; U. Dolgopol and S. Paranjape, 'Comfort Women: An Unfinished Ordeal' (*International Commission of Jurists*, 1994) 198; R. Sakamoto, 'The Women's International War Crimes Tribunal on Japan's Military Sexual Slavery:

accordingly failed to take legal action in respect of surviving authors and perpetrators; whether via administrative or criminal means, through military discipline, or otherwise.[94] Rather than facing prosecution and punishment, perpetrators have continued to enjoy the largesse of the state in the form of military pensions,[95] giving the impression of both official remorselessness and tacit approval of wartime misconduct. This is set to continue indefinitely, with remaining perpetrators few and far between, and Japan unwilling to take what it calls 'retrospective action' against them.[96]

The inherent practical limitations of tackling the impunity of individual perpetrators, coupled with the illiberalness of collectively blaming Japanese society or values as a whole, has seen many former 'comfort women' and activist groups increasingly focus on the question of state responsibility.[97] This prospect was taken up with gusto by the Women's War Crime Tribunal, who established a strong basis for finding such responsibility exists under international law; further solidifying the rights to know, to justice and to reparations.[98] Despite compelling evidence that the Japanese state was intimately involved

A Legal and Feminist Approach to the 'Comfort Women' Issue', *New Zealand Journal of Asian Studies* 3 (2001), 49, 55–6. See too discussion below (n. 133) – (n. 135).

94 T. Etsuro, 'Proposals for Japan and the ROK to Resolve the "Comfort Women" Issue: Creating trust and peace in light of international law', *Asia Pacific Journal: Japan Focus* 1, 11 (2013), [10]-[12].

95 See P. Schmidt, 'Disabled Colonial Veterans of the Imperial Japanese Forces and the Right to Receive Social Welfare Benefits from Japan', *Sydney Law Review* 21 (1999), 240: ' . . . even those former servicemen and auxiliaries of the Imperial Forces, who had been tried and punished by postwar Allied military tribunals for war crimes, were included in the list of pension recipients after a reform of the Pension Law in 1953. Even though initially their payments had been somewhat reduced, they had again reached the general level by 1973.' Further, while certain high-ranking officials have been identified as being amongst the authors of the 'comfort system', they are made to posthumously bear the burden for the rest of the many anonymized ordinary wrongdoers, who go unidentified and unpunished. See, e.g., records of the Digital Museum: The Comfort Women Issue and the Asian Women's Fund (n. 22).

96 Japan's government has stated 'it is extremely difficult to investigate the facts of individual cases retrospectively, and therefore, the Government of Japan does not consider prosecuting and punishing perpetrators'. See Ministry of Foreign Affairs, 'Reply of the Government of Japan to the Letter Sent by the Special Rapporteur for Follow-up to Concluding Observations of the Human Rights Committee' (*Japanese Government*, 19 April 2016) www.mofa.go.jp/policy/human/cove_civil/index.html accessed 13 September 2017.

97 See Y. P. Hsu, '"Comfort Women' From Korea: Japan's World War II Sex Slaves and the Legitimacy of their Claims for Reparations', *Pacific Rim Law and Policy Journal* 2 (1993), 97; G. J. McDougall, 'Addressing State Responsibility for the Crime of Military Sexual Slavery during the Second World War: Further Attempts for Justice for the Comfort Women', *Korean Journal of International and Comparative Law* 1 (2013), 137.

98 See *Prosecutors and Peoples of Asia Pacific Region* v. *Hirohito; Prosecutors and Peoples of Asia Pacific Region* v. *Japan* (*Summary of Findings and Preliminary Judgment*) (n. 23).

in and knowledgeable about nearly every facet of the 'comfort system',[99] again, Japanese governments have remained staunchly opposed to the imposition of liability on this basis.[100]

An equally significant zone of resistance has been with respect to efforts by the former 'comfort women' and their supporters to have their cases heard in Japanese courts. They and their families have been left unable to pursue their claims for compensation and for the truth due to the expiry of statutory time limitations coupled with the government's legal arguments regarding, inter alia, the inapplicability of international rules stipulating the imprescriptibility of war crimes and crimes against humanity.[101] As with its reticence towards the commencement of prosecutions against perpetrators, Japan has evinced no intention of amending its civil laws and procedures in order to allow the remaining survivors to litigate their claims.[102]

It is also widely perceived that the survivors' quest to have their 'right to reparation' recognized has been delayed and denied; with the nature, quantum, allocation and sincerity of what has been offered by successive Japanese governments widely adjudged insufficient.[103] Japan's official recognition of the suffering of the former 'comfort women' did not initially lead to a state-funded compensation scheme: the Asian Women's Fund was mostly privately funded, leaving many survivors of the view that it inadequately acknowledged both their suffering and Japan's official guilt.[104] Further, formal apologies offered by the Prime Minister were viewed as personal rather than official,

99 See admission of the elements of control in the Kono Statement (n. 81).

100 See, e.g., statements by Japan in submissions to United Nations treaty bodies, esp. Committee on the Elimination of Discrimination against Women 'Consideration of reports submitted by States parties under Article 18 of the Convention, Seventh and eighth periodic reports of States parties due in 2014: Japan' (16 September 2014) UN Doc CEDAW/C/JPN/7–8 24–25.

101 See M. Igarashi, 'Post-War Compensation Cases, Japanese Courts and International Law', *Japanese Annual of International Law* 45 (2000), 45; Sigur Center for Asian Studies at the George Washington University, 'Korean Comfort Women v. Japan' (Memory and Reconciliation in the Asia-Pacific) https://memoryreconciliation.org/topics/comfort-women/comfort-women-korea/ accessed 13 September 2017.

102 Japan's unwillingness in this regard is, nevertheless, consistent with broad state practice in East and West, as considerable legal debate continues to cloud the question of whether statutory time limits for civil compensation are suppressed by the imprescriptability of criminal justice for international crimes. See A. Manirabona and J.-A. Wemmers, 'It Doesn't Go Away with Time: Victims' Need for Reparation Following Crimes against Humanity' in J.-A. Wemmers (ed.), *Reparation for Victims of Crimes against Humanity: the Healing Role of Reparation* (Routledge, 2014) 77–9.

103 See Landino (n. 25) 343–4; Shin (n. 26) 119–22; Cheah (n. 25).

104 Park Sonen (n. 68) 291; Ustinia Dolgopol, 'Cold Comfort', *Alternative Law Journal* 21 (1996), 156, 157.

and the programme was boycotted by many.[105] With only a brief period of operation, and the semblance of deflection of legal responsibility, it was considered by many as not, in substance, 'reparation'.[106]

Even the recent deal between Japan and South Korea, involving a commitment of one billion yen to a new foundation[107] established to support surviving Korean 'comfort women' and the families of deceased Korean 'comfort women',[108] has been interpreted as disingenuous in its implications for the third key pillar of the anti-impunity norm: the 'right to know'. This is because the deal is premised on South Korea's cessation of 'monument politics', which has been internationally embarrassing for Japan.[109] Thus, while has been the most comprehensive reparations measure yet, it has been construed as a 'cash for quiet' deal rather than an attempt at delivering the accountability, justice, openness and 'truth-telling' that is apparently so central to the anti-impunity norm. This is only emphasized by the limited scope of the deal: it appears that Japan has no intention of granting the many non-Korean former 'comfort women' commensurate reparations,[110] resulting in a racially discriminatory scheme which appears to be the product of political expedience rather than a commitment to international law and human rights norms.

Japanese governments appear to have also evaded the 'right to know' in various regards.

105 S. Wolfe, *The Politics of Reparations and Apologies* (Springer, 2013) 264.

106 See critiques made by scholars, NGOs and other interested parties, e.g. UN Committee against Torture (n. 25), Committee on the Elimination of Discrimination against Women (n. 25); the McDougall Report (n. 21). However, see contrary arguments by Onuma that, 'from a substantive perspective, the total amount of 3,200,000 to 5,000,000 yen provided to the victims was not an insubstantial amount in the Philippines, Taiwan, or Korea', Onuma (n. 18) 607.

107 Details of how the programme will operate are limited. However, it appears that the funds will be administered by the Korean government and will apparently be allocated on the basis of need. As with the Asian Women's Fund, funds will also be spent on medical and welfare services.

108 Subsequent statements indicate that 1 billion yen has been provided. See Ministry of Foreign Affairs, 'Japan-ROK Foreign Ministers' Telephone Talk' (*Japanese Government*, 12 August 2016) www.mofa.go.jp/a_o/na/kr/page4e_000490.html accessed 13 September 2017; The Mainichi, 'S. Korean foundation a vital bridge to solve "comfort women" issue', *The Mainichi*, 29 August 2016 http://mainichi.jp/english/articles/20160829/p2a/00m/0na/016000c#csidx54df400df19be84bb8e6ad12acf4533 accessed 13 September 2017.

109 See Ministry of Foreign Affairs (n. 92), where both governments stated that they 'have agreed to refrain from criticizing each other on this issue in the international community'.

110 See J. McCurry, 'Former Sex Slaves Reject Japan and South Korea's "Comfort Women" Accord', *The Guardian*, 26 January 2016 www.theguardian.com/world/2016/jan/26/former-sex-slaves-reject-japan-south-koreas-comfort-women-accord accessed 14 September 2017.

Subsequent administrations have failed to present all findings from their official inquiries and to remove legal obstacles to research, including the ongoing classification and secrecy of relevant military and ministerial documents.[111] This cultivated air of plausible deniability is often attributed to a liability-limiting impulse,[112] and has triggered questions about the sincerity of official statements of remorse,[113] especially when the effects have been to hinder the capacity of researchers to contest and resolve factual ambiguities, to stymie legal action by the former 'comfort women', and thus to create an ideal environment for counter-narratives and misinformation to proliferate.[114]

Japan has expressed positive intentions to 'face squarely the historical facts … instead of evading them', and to 'forever engrav[e] such issues in our memories through the study and teaching of history'.[115] However, its actual engagement with the so-called 'duty to preserve memory', a component of the 'right to know', has been thoroughly equivocal in the face of fierce domestic and international politicisation of its history. Even incontrovertible aspects of Japan's war history have given rise to allegations of revisionism and negationism from both the left and right wing,[116] which have been demonstrated in the 'textbook' and 'monuments' sagas of the 1990s and 2000s.

111 Governments have sought to prevent evidence arising from official inquiries from public release. See D. A. Schmidt, *Ianfu, the Comfort Women of the Japanese Imperial Army of the Pacific War: Broken Silence* (Edwin Mellen Press, 2000) 67. Japan also lacks freedom of information legislation; inhibiting researchers' access to primary sources. See N. Morris, 'Review: Yuki Tanaka – Japan's Comfort Women: Sexual Slavery and Prostitution during World War II and the US Occupation', *Intersections: Gender, History and Culture in the Asian Context* 9 (2003) http://intersections.anu.edu.au/issue9/morris_review.html.

112 See Cheah (n. 25) 63–108.

113 See Dolgopol (n. 104) 157.

114 Certain Japanese sources, for example, continue to insist that all 'comfort women' were consenting professional prostitutes over the age of 21, consistent with Japan's international obligations. See, e.g., Digital Museum: The Comfort Women Issue and the Asian Women's Fund (n. 22). Others point selectively to historical records to allege that certain [extremely rare] 'comfort women' were actually beneficiaries of the war, earning extraordinary sums of money in a time of great hardship, or that only a fraction of the numbers often alleged were recruited. Others insist that what occurred was simply prostitution; a dire yet banal occupation which many poor women reluctantly yet knowingly took part in as one of the few options open to them in desperate times. See, e.g., Hata I., 'No Organised or Forced Recruitment: Misconceptions about Comfort Women and the Japanese Military' (2007), Society for the Dissemination of Historical Fact, 5, 9; N. Tsutomu, 'Behind the Comfort Women Controversy: How Lies Became Truth' (2007) Society for Dissemination of Historical Fact, vi; all via www.sdh-fact.com/category/comfort-women/ accessed 5 October 2017. For the broader context and political dynamics, see G. Hicks, *Japan's War Memories: Amnesia or Concealment* (Ashgate, 1997).

115 Kono Statement (n. 81).

116 See Hicks (n. 114). It is also notable that there are few public museums and memorials commemorating comfort women or the suffering of women during WWII in Japan. Exceptions include the Women's Active Museum on War and Peace, which opened in

As part of their anti-impunity campaign, the former 'comfort women' seek explicit inclusion in historical texts; having effectively been censored for decades, and later, after a brief period of inclusion, been erased.[117] Despite their considerable transnational support base, however, their efforts have largely been blocked by methods including the official textbook review process.[118] Review bodies have been heavily influenced by conservatives, who oppose extensive official apologism and the dissemination of facts they consider unproven or inaccurate, as well as nationalists who seek to avoid compromizing national pride by portraying Japan' war conduct in a unique or negative light.[119] Endorsed texts have therefore typically sanitized or censored indisputable and more sensitive matters alike,[120] leaving younger generations largely unaware of the nation's past conduct.

The monuments saga has been another deeply contentious site of anti-impunity discourse. Japan's government strongly protests the erection of public monuments to the former 'comfort women' which have emerged in many locations around the world.[121] While the international community has largely received these as a measure of historical truth-telling and a demonstration of recognition and compassion for the former 'comfort women', Japan sees them on other terms: namely, as anti-Japanese propaganda; as incitements to racial hatred; and as unwarranted intrusions into Japan's internal or diplomatic affairs – in particular, its strained relations with South Korea.[122] These sentiments are forcefully argued by Japanese diaspora communities also, some of whom have resorted to legal measures to seek removal of monuments on the same grounds.[123]

2005, and the efforts by the Tokyo and the Osaka International Peace Center Museum, which notably ceased exhibiting items related to Japanese aggression after political pressure: P. Hein, 'Unresolved Comfort Women Issue: How Pragmatism Precludes Reconciliation', *The Korean Journal of International Studies* 14 (2016), 447.

117 See Coomaraswamy Report (n. 69); Soh (n. 71). The 'comfort system' was included in certain texts for a period of time before being edited out in subsequent years.

118 See Park Sonen (n. 68) 151–2.

119 See, e.g., M. Selden and Y. Nozaki, 'Japanese Textbook Controversies, Nationalism, and Historical Memory: Intra- and Inter-National Conflicts', *The Asia Pacific Journal – Japan Focus* 7 (2009).

120 Ibid.

121 These have sprung up in locations including the United States, the Philippines, China, Taiwan, Australia, Germany and, of course, South Korea, where the most famous monument is pointedly located opposite the Japanese embassy and has become a site for mass demonstrations by a public demanding recognition, apology and redress from Japan.

122 K. Mera, *Comfort Women not 'Sex Slaves': Rectifying the Myriad of Perspectives* (Xlibris, 2015).

123 See litigation history of *Koichi Mera and GAHT-US Corporation* v. *City of Glendale*, conducted variously in the US District Court of Los Angeles, the California State Superior Court and later the US Supreme Court from 2013 to 2017; Rhian Deutrom, 'Japanese 'Comfort Women's' Memorial in 18C Complaint', *The Australian*,

VI INTERPRETING JAPANESE PATTERNS OF RESISTANCE AND CONCESSION

Japan's reluctance to embrace the anti-impunity norm is commonly attributed to bad faith and the exigencies of surging nationalism. However, other factors are clearly at play. Japan's oscillation between resistance and concession can also be interpreted as a conflict of norm-sets: the anti-impunity norm's universal and moralistic human rights standards, its preference for individual accountability and victim-centricity on one hand, and Japanese approaches to law and politics which favour sovereign power, formalism, stability and the centrality of extra-legal institutions on the other. Thus, while the social context in question is receptive to a certain conception of human rights and the rule of law, it does not accept that the anti-impunity norm's standards are necessarily correct, applicable or binding as a matter of law.

Accordingly, Japan has tended to interpret international human rights standards strictly and conservatively, providing a basis for law-makers and courts to read down norms which it considers to be uncertain or unsettled. This has been evident in its responses to questions of the legality of statutory time limits in instruments such as the Japanese Code of Criminal Procedure. While repealing or amending these limits would allow the former 'comfort women' to obtain redress from domestic courts,[124] Japan has insisted on their legality. This interpretation of its international obligations is a 'minimalistic' one:[125] having rejected both the opportunity to accede to the Convention on the Non-Applicability of Statutory Limitations to War Crimes and Crimes against Humanity of 1968 and the proposition that the imprescriptibility principle has attained the status of customary international law,[126] Japan contends it is not bound by the rule unless and until it voluntarily assumes

15 December 2016 www.theaustralian.com.au/national-affairs/war-womens-memorial-in-18c-complaint/news-story/f4a13f4a10fede4b1c19c96e403679aa accessed 14 September 2017.

124 Ibid.

125 On this tendency, see P. Alston, 'Transplanting Foreign Norms: Human Rights and Other International Legal Norms in Japan', *European Journal of International Law* 10 (1999), 627–8: 'Japan is a notably conservative participant in international legal and policy debates . . . [i]ts reticence goes not only to its own record, both historically and currently, but also to effort to develop the system of accountability of governments in general.'

126 Given that Japanese law recognizes customary international law as part of the law of Japan, with some sources finding that it can prevail over both statute and the Constitution, a cautious approach is not surprising. Japanese jurisprudence demands that rules of customary international law be precisely defined in order to be directly applied domestically, which has militated against expansive readings of customary norms. See Y. Iwasawa, International Law in the Japanese Legal Order: Recent Developments, *American Society of International Law Proceedings* 91 (1997), 302.

the obligations via accession to the 1968 Convention.[127] While this vexes many human rights lawyers, it is nevertheless supported by broad state practice, and challenges the proposition that the norm has crystallized as custom.[128]

Japanese legal minimalism has also been the basis for resistance towards the duty to prosecute and punish perpetrators of crimes against the former 'comfort women'. Again, Japanese legal arguments deny the existence of a binding conventional or customary international obligation to do so to justify their inaction in this regard.[129] While this is a much weaker argument in the face of considerable scholarship pointing to this duty as a recognized feature of international law,[130] Japan's position is partly supported by evidence that the scope of the duty remains unsettled,[131] as does the question of whether it forms a necessary or desirable element in the *victims*' right to justice.[132]

Japan's interpretation of the substantive content of international law is also, consistently, conservative. Japan has long argued, for example, that rape was not specifically prohibited under either the Hague Convention IV of 1907 or customary international law in force during WWII; that the 'comfort women' were not 'enslaved' within the legal meaning of the term; and at any rate, that prohibitions against slavery had not crystallized as a binding norm of customary international law by WWII.[133] Further, it has argued against the notion of an individual right to reparation which is said to arise from violations of the laws of war that were considered to be effect during WWII and directly applicable in Japan pursuant to Japanese constitutional law.[134] It contends further that, as the policy basis of the law of crimes against humanity is the

[127] See Igarashi (n. 101) 55–75.

[128] See Hessbruegge (n. 35) 335.

[129] See S. R. Lee, 'Comforting the Comfort Women: Who Can Make Japan Pay?', *University of Pennsylvania Journal of Economics and Law* 24 (2003), 509.

[130] See A. Orakhelashvili, 'Between Impunity and Accountability for Serious International Crimes: Legal and Policy Approaches', *Netherlands International Law Review* 55 (2009), 217. To Orakhelashvili, ' . . . arguing that there is no duty to prosecute means arguing that there is the legal position admitting impunity.'

[131] See M. Scharf, 'From the eXile Files: An Essay on Trading Justice for Peace', *Washington and Lee Law Review* 63 (2006), 342–9; M. Scharf, 'The Letter of the Law: The Scope of the International Legal Obligation to Prosecute Human Rights Crimes', *Law and Contemporary Problems* 53 (1996), 60; A. Seibert-Fohr. *Prosecuting Serious Human Rights Violations* (Oxford University Press, 2009) 279. See too M. du Plessis and J. Ford, 'Transitional Justice: A Future Truth Commission for Zimbabwe?', *International and Comparative Law Quarterly* 58 (2009), 87, 109–10.

[132] Seibert-Fohr (n. 131) 279.

[133] See B. Say, 'Ripe for Justice: A New UN Tool to Strengthen the Position of the "Comfort Women" and to Corner Japan into Its Reparation Responsibility', *Pennsylvania State International Law Review* 23 (2004), 953; The McDougall Report (n. 21).

[134] Igarashi (n. 101) 55–75; Say (n. 133).

international criminal responsibility of wrongdoers, it cannot form the basis of state responsibility to compensate.[135]

Most of these arguments are refuted by many international legal scholars[136] but have largely prevailed in efforts by the 'comfort women', with the effect that, even where the claims of the former 'comfort women' are accepted as true,[137] the Japanese courts have been incapable of offering the relief sought. This has allowed Japan to 'have its cake and eat it too' to a certain degree; to demonstrate its sympathy for the 'comfort women' through the provision of qualified apologies and compensation measures, but to insist that these have been granted on other bases than legal duty.

Japan's unwillingness to cede to the more fulsome interpretations of international law that proponents of the anti-impunity norm seek to advance is not just illustrative of its law-makers' hostility towards, or potentially even ignorance of international law at times.[138] It also reflects Japanese attitudes about the role of law as a mechanism of social ordering. Japan's adherence to a form of the *Rechtsstaat* principle, one which is closer to the idea of rule by law than the rule of law,[139] for example, deeply colours modern Japanese conceptions of rights and governance; operating less as a principle attuned to the protection of individuals' rights and liberties, but rather, as a means of favouring consistent legality, certainty and rule-obedience.[140] This orientation is inclined towards

135 Ibid.

136 Nevertheless, see Zwanenburg: '[p]ractice outside of the context of conventional regimes appears to indicate that there is no individual procedural right to claim a remedy for human rights violations', and that extant case law and state practice 'suggests that there is no right under IHL to an individual claim for a remedy'. M. Zwanenburg, 'The Van Boven / Bassiouni Principles: An Appraisal', *Netherlands Quarterly of Human Rights* 24 (2006), 641, 655, 660.

137 Ibid. This is posed as the exception, as questions of historical and factual veracity have consistently blighted the women's redress claims and become a point of considerable political debate.

138 See Igarashi's discussion of the potential for Japanese judges to have misunderstood certain international law principles in the 'comfort system' debate (n. 101) 78–9. See too Alston (n. 125) 631, noting that 'Japanese courts consistently reject international human rights-based arguments, are systematically averse to reliance upon international norms which they use at best as a form of icing upon the cake, very rarely find violations of international norms, and consistently assume those norms provide no greater protection than the bill of rights in the Constitution.'

139 N. Urabe, 'Rule of Law and Due Process: A Comparative View of the United States and Japan', *Law and Contemporary Problems* 53 (1990), 69.

140 This may also be expressed in terms of judicial attitudes. L. Repeta argues, for example, that 'modern Japanese judges tend to hold an extremely broad view of administrative discretion and a rather limited view of their own authority to order change. This combination means that fundamental human rights as enforced by Japanese courts can be rendered "merely illusory"': 'The International Covenant on Civil and Political Rights and Human Rights', *Law in Japan* 20 (1987), 1 as quoted in P. Schmidt (n. 95) 246.

formalism over naturalism;[141] and both statutory time limitations and positivist-cum-contractarian philosophies of international law[142] align with this worldview. Further, unlike in the West, in Japan, law's domain is limited; law bearing no intrinsic or necessary moral content;[143] morality instead defined and secured by extra-legal institutions.[144] Grafting the universal and transcendental moral standards that undergird the anti-impunity norm into Japanese law and society is therefore not just a question of amending the content of Japanese laws, but also the worldview within which law operates.

Japan's relative imperviousness to the anti-impunity norm is in many regards a context-specific one which is partly explained by the temporal – and thus socio-legal – disjunct between the past violations and present calls for justice; with the crimes in question long-since ended, seemingly dealt with by post-war treaties, and demonstrably replaced with a commitment to pacifism and the rule of law. This is highlighted by the fact that while Japan considers it anathema to apply contemporary standards to the past, it has nevertheless demonstrated its commitment to combating contemporary and future impunity by acceding to the jurisdiction of the International Criminal Court and contributing generously to its operating budget.[145]

Contemporary Japanese law-makers appear to view the application of anti-impunity measures to the question of responsibility for the 'comfort system' as impractical and unnecessary in these circumstances, if not unreasonable. Commencing prosecutions of surviving perpetrators, for example, would be

[141] This is also consistent with the Japanese conception of 'situation-based morality'; which avoids transcendental moral principles. See T. Se and R. Karatsu, 'A Conception of Human Rights Based on Japanese Culture: Promoting Cross-Cultural Debates', *Journal of Human Rights* 3 (2004), 283.

[142] On contract theory and its utility in facilitating international cooperation without endangering sovereign equality through the illegitimate coercion of unwilling states, see, e.g., J. Goldsmith and D. Levinson, 'Law for States: International Law, Constitutional Law, Public Law', *Harvard Law Review* 122 (2009), 1–74. See too Knop and Riles on the policy purposes of statutes of limitations: K. Knop and A. Riles, 'Space, Time, and Historical Injustice: A Feminist Conflict-of-Laws Approach to the Comfort Women Agreement', *Cornell Law Review* 102 (2017), 853, 915.

[143] K. Port, 'The Impact of Human Rights Law in Japan', *Stanford Journal of International Law* 28 (1991), 140, 166.

[144] Ibid.; J. Haley, *Authority without Power: Law and the Japanese Paradox* (Oxford University Press, 1991) 13–14.

[145] Japan is one of the largest financial contributors to the Court. See Assembly of States Parties to the ICC, 'Statement by Ambassador Motohide Yoshikawa, at the thirteenth session of the ASP to the Rome Statute of the International Criminal Court' (*Assembly of States Parties*, 11 December 2014) https://asp.icc-cpi.int/iccdocs/asp_docs/ASP13/GenDeba/ICC-ASP13-GenDeba-Japan-ENG.pdf accessed 2 October 2017.

chiefly symbolic; would be hampered by lack of evidence;[146] would run contrary to longstanding penological approaches[147] and approaches to human rights law;[148] and may not be strictly necessary if Japanese legal arguments are correct.[149]

The perception that it is too late in the day, too costly and too dramatic a change for too little reward also appears to inform Japanese resistance towards more generous, individualized reparations measures. Japanese practice with respect to post-war compensation has been restricted by practical necessity, with only a very limited category of war victims eligible for compensation – namely, those who could prove they had suffered serious injuries caused by the atomic blasts. Further, their compensation has been limited to pensions and medical aid rather than individualized lump sum payments.[150] Radically changing the basis and method for compensating war victims in these circumstances remains highly unlikely; especially in light of the impetus it could generate for broader access to compensation by other victims of rights violations.

The political climate that the anti-impunity norm has been unleashed within is a particularly compelling explanation for Japanese resistance to the norm. This climate is characterized by the 'smoldering discontent and grievance held by many ordinary people in Japan'[151] about international demands for admissions of responsibility,[152] which has generated fatigue and cynicism amongst the public, and clouded sympathy for the former 'comfort women'.[153]

[146] Although see *Prosecutors and Peoples of Asia Pacific Region* v. *Hirohito; Prosecutors and Peoples of Asia Pacific Region* v. *Japan* (*Summary of Findings and Preliminary Judgment*) (n. 23).

[147] Japan's criminal justice system, for example, is known for its distinctive focus on offender reintegration and rehabilitation; extra-curial settlements and 'leniency' in charging, adjudication and sentencing. See C. Banks and J. Baker, *Comparative, International, and Global Justice: Perspectives from Criminology and Criminal Justice* (SAGE, 2015); R. J. Terrill, World Criminal Justice Systems: A Comparative Survey (Routledge, 2015) 215–84; D. T. Johnson, *The Japanese Way of Justice: Prosecuting Crime in Japan* (Oxford University Press, 2001).

[148] Port (n. 143) 166.

[149] On this possibility, see Seibert-Fohr (n. 131) 285. See too D. Orentlicher, '"Settling Accounts" Revisited: Reconciling Global Norms with Local Agency', *International Journal of Transitional Justice* 1 (2007), 19, arguing that the duty to prosecute need not entail prosecuting *every* person who bears criminal responsibility, but should focus on those most culpable.

[150] Dolgopol and Paranjape (n. 93) 197.

[151] Onuma (n. 18) 602.

[152] Ibid., 601–2.

[153] N. Odanaka, 'From Responsibility to Compassion: Lessons from the Controversy over 'Comfort Women in Japan', *Journal of Japanese Law* 31 (2011), 49; Shin (n. 26) 101; Hein (n. 116) 451–2. See too K. Gustafsson, 'The 'History Problem' in Sino-Japanese Relations: What's the Problem?' (E-International Relations, 31 October 2016) www.e-ir.info/2016/10/31/the-history-problem-in-sino-japanese-relations-whats-the-problem/, citing recent Japanese

These factors have favoured official inertia, as has the risk of electoral backlash from demands that today's Japanese both symbolically renounce the past and literally pay for it, by funding reparations, accountability and truth-telling measures.[154]

Relatedly, the sense that the rise of anti-impunity discourse is but another front by which regional diplomatic tussles can be fought[155] has further undermined Japanese perceptions of the legitimacy and utility of the norm. These sentiments are intertwined with the lingering resentment that Japan continues to feel in relation to its treatment at the IMFTE, a genesis moment for the norm. It is hard to escape the sense that Japan sees the anti-impunity norm as a continuation of what it perceived the Tokyo Trials to be: vengeful international politics masquerading as international law.[156]

Japanese gender norms provide a further clue to the relatively low priority accorded to fighting impunity for crimes against the former 'comfort women'. While Japanese attitudes to human rights norms in general, and women's rights in particular, became remarkably liberal from the 1990s onwards,[157] discrimination against women is still widespread,[158] and responses to rape and sexual crimes against women still cast shame and blame on victims and

opinion polls which indicate that issues relating to 'reparations from Japan for WWII, comfort women, and forced labour' were considered 'history issues in need of resolution' by 25.7 per cent of respondents in 2013, 23.6 per cent in 2014, 23.2 per cent in 2015 and 35 per cent in 2016; while the related question of whether '[t]he lack of apology for the historical events by Japan' was a history issue in need of resolution has attracted only single-digit support in the same period. When contrasted with earlier polls, these demonstrate a higher degree of satisfaction (or perhaps fatigue) amongst respondents than in the 1990s, where polls indicated a wider degree of support for compensating the 'comfort women' and apologizing for Japan's wartime conduct. See too P. A. Seaton, *Japan's Contested War Memories: The 'Memory Rifts' in Historical* (Routledge, 2007) 196.

154 These must ordinarily be funded via taxation or borrowing; both of which ultimately impose costs onto citizens.

155 See Onuma (n. 18) 600–20; n. 101) 87–158; Odanaka (n. 153) 49–60; H. Donghua, 'The Tokyo Trials and Japanese Revisionism: Political Maneuver or Criminal Justice', *China Legal Science Journal* 3 (2015), 71–93.

156 See S. Chesterman, 'International Criminal Law with Asian Characteristics?', *Columbia Journal of Asian Law* 27 (2013), 142, 143.

157 Among other measures, it has acceded to the Convention against the Elimination of all Forms of Discrimination against Women (entered into force 3 September 1981) 1249 UNTS 13, and has subsequently implemented a suite of national laws to foster gender equality. See J. Chan, *Gender and Human Rights Politics in Japan: Global Norms and Domestic Networks* (Stanford University Press, 2004).

158 See Committee on the Elimination of Discrimination against Women, 'Concluding observations on the combined seventh and eighth periodic reports of Japan' (10 March 2016) UN Doc CEDAW/C/JPN/CO/7–8. See too Y. Hayashi, 'Implementation of the Convention on the Elimination of All Forms of Discrimination against Women in Japan', *Journal of East Asian and International Law* 6 (2013), 341.

minimize, trivialize or excuse these forms of violence.[159] Further, women's voices and experiences remain largely unheard in political life; which has been described as 'hegemonically masculine'.[160] These factors have suppressed demand within Japan to conform to the anti-impunity norm on this issue, which is notably not just a human rights issue in the abstract, but a women's human rights one at that; and one largely intended to benefit foreigners at the perceived expense of Japanese men and the Japanese nation; the two being inseparable.

VII JAPANESE ANTI-IMPUNITY INTERACTIONS BEYOND THE TRANSPLANT TROPE

For the reasons explored earlier in this chapter, the processes by which the anti-impunity norm has been formed and operationalized are not well explained by the metaphor of legal transplants. Likewise, Japanese responses to the anti-impunity norm cannot simply be explained away as 'transplant failure' or norm rejection when a range of more complex interactions are observable in its statements and behaviour.

As has previously been canvassed, Japanese practice is notable for its admixture of resistance and concession to the anti-impunity norm. Although it has apparently rejected specific international legal rules, such as the imprescriptibility principle, this has not precluded its apparent acceptance of the notion that impunity is inconsistent with fundamental human rights norms and should be addressed; albeit within the limits of the prevailing socio-legal traditions and the political climate. These attitudinal changes have been coupled with increasingly generous apologies and compensation measures, and appear to be causally linked to the anti-impunity campaigns waged against Japan in recent decades. How these changes ought to be understood, rather than whether they are changes that answer the description of a 'legal transplant', is the important question.

As a transformative legal norm, the anti-impunity norm needs to be understood from a broader vantage. This is because, as Harding alludes, the point of the new ideas is not to find the best societal fit, but to change existing

159 J. Dussich, Y. Fujiwara and A. Sagisaka, 'Decisions Not to Report Sexual Assault in Japan', *International Journal of Offender Therapy and Comparative Criminology* 45 (2001), 35–40; C. Burns, *Sexual Violence and the Law in Japan* (Routledge, 2005).

160 E. Dalton, *Women and Politics in Contemporary Japan* (Routledge, 2015). See too K. Iwanaga, 'Women's Political Representation in Japan' in K. Iwanaga (ed.), *Women's Political Participation and Representation in Asia: Obstacles and Challenges* (NIAS Press, 2008) 101–29.

behaviours and attitudes.[161] Merry's anthropological framework on the capacity of human rights norms to become 'vernacularised' in new contexts examines this further. Merry explains that new norms can be translated within context.[162] However, the essential dilemma that the introduction of new ideas such as the anti-impunity norm face is that while they need to be capable of a degree of resonance with local practices in order to travel, too much resonance generates an echo chamber rather than transformation.[163] Accordingly, vernacularization occurs along a continuum, from outright rejection to 'replication', and to 'hybridisation'; depending on the degree to which local ideas and practices are incorporated.[164] 'Subversion' is also possible where key referents are retained, but the new norm's content and structure are significantly altered.[165]

International human rights lawyers may well perceive Japanese responses to the anti-impunity norm as outright rejection. However, in key regards, Japan has not remained immune from the norm's influence. Rather, its approach to the anti-impunity norm could be described as subversive: While the norm resonates in a high-level sense and has generated a call to action, it has not produced a fundamental transformation. Demands for key legal changes have been unsuccessful; and policy-makers have been unwilling to conceive of the former 'comfort women's' suffering in the vocabulary of international law.[166] However, a distinctly Japanese mode of confronting and addressing this historical impunity has emerged, which is characterized by an ethos of atonement and which is rooted in the suggestion of collective social and moral responsibility rather than the legal responsibility of the state and individuals; its endpoint the resolution of the conflict rather than a fundamental transformation in public administration. This need not be essentialized on the basis of Japanese culture, but has provided a means for Japan to acknowledge and confront its war responsibility without sacrificing core interests and socio-legal traditions.

161 See Harding (n. 49) 7.

162 See S. E. Merry, *Human Rights and Gender Violence: Translating International Law into Local Justice* (Chicago University Press, 2006).

163 S. Merry and P. Levitt, 'Vernacularization on the Ground: Local Uses of Global Women's Rights in Peru, China, India and the United States', *Global Networks* 9 (2009), 441, 456.

164 S. E. Merry, 'Transnational Human Rights and Local Activism', *American Anthropologist* 108 (1) (2006), 44.

165 Ibid.

166 Successive governments have notably refused to adopt legal descriptors of the women as 'sex slaves' or their treatment as 'torture' or 'crimes against humanity' on the basis of legal arguments elaborated earlier in this chapter.

Interpreting Japanese interaction with the international anti-impunity norm as a subversive form of vernacularization may be another way of expressing Teubner's prediction of the results of introducing new norms, or 'legal irritants' to novel contexts.[167] In the case of Japan, the introduced legal ideas cannot easily be evaluated in terms of success or failure, because their introduction has caused a unique and unpredictable set of events. They have fundamentally disrupted anterior policy arrangements and discourses, helping to erode Japanese reticence to acknowledge its wrongdoing. In the process, however, the meaning of 'impunity' and its counterpart, 'anti-impunity', have been challenged and reconstructed anew; albeit in ways that are inconsistent with Western understandings of the essential content of the norm.

The social, political and legal conditions into which the anti-impunity norm has been introduced in Japan are also a far cry from those in one of the most acclaimed case studies of the anti-impunity norm's triumph: the so-called 'justice cascade' in Latin America. Lutz and Sikkink claim that the surge in human rights litigation in Latin America throughout the 1980s and 1990s was partly due to key intermediaries:

> small groups of activist lawyers who pioneered the strategies, developed the legal arguments, often recruited the plaintiffs and/or witnesses, marshaled the evidence, and persevered through years of legal challenges.[168]

Not only was this transnational justice network persistent, however, they were active within a broader context of a profound regional human rights norms shift, which saw key human rights norms gain popular, political, and legal support.[169]

The differences between the Japanese and Latin American examples are significant. For one, while the former 'comfort women' have been supported by a powerful network of transnational activists, they have had fewer powerful intermediaries within Japan supporting and propelling their calls for change.[170] Rather, they have been subject to indifference, critique and, at

167 Teubner (n. 53).

168 Lutz and Sikkink (n. 1) 2.

169 Ibid.

170 This may also reflect differences in the norms being violated, the identities of victims, and the power dynamics that these respective quests for justice have represented. While the Latin American case study has archetypically conceptualized the victim as the protagonist in a masculinized power struggle against political repression, the former 'comfort women' have been understood within discourses of virtue, honour and shame; and victims have been alienated from society rather than created into heroes to be avenged. See too arguments by Park Sonen (n. 68) regarding the intersection of gender, race and class, which have hindered victims' pursuit of justice.

times, humiliation by nationalist groups, historians and politicians who have sought to minimize official war responsibility.[171] Likewise, while Japan has endorsed certain aspects of international human rights law, and has sought conformity with certain Western norms,[172] it has done so selectively; seeking to ensure that social norms and modes of law-making are preserved so far as possible,[173] and has done so on a reactionary basis, as a 'rule taker' rather than a 'rule maker'.[174]

Perhaps more importantly, in contrast with the Latin American case, there has been no fundamental human rights norm cascade in East Asia; no rapid shift towards a consensus about the legitimacy of human rights norms or the need for regional action to generate compliance with those norms.[175] Unlike Latin America, Japan's regional context is one of great social and political diversity. Instrumentally, regional human rights agreements are modest; reflecting this diversity but also inhibiting interstate cooperation and coordination.[176] Institutionally, there are no regional human rights tribunals to hold states to account. By practice, Asian nations are more insular, the least likely of all regions to have engaged with global anti-impunity institutions,[177] and remain demonstrably committed to the use of amnesties rather than

[171] Particularly noteworthy are statements by current Prime Minister Shinzo Abe, who has previously, in an official capacity, highlighted the role of independent contractors who enslaved women in the 'comfort system' and downplayed as indirect the involvement of the Japanese government. See Landino (n. 25) 349. See too justificatory comments such as those by former Mayor of Osaka Hashimoto Toru, who stated in 2013 'for soldiers who risked their lives . . . if you wanted them to get some rest, a comfort woman system was necessary': cited in Y. Tanaka, '"Comfort Women Bashing" and Japan's Social Formation' in M. Lewis (ed.), *'History Wars' and Reconciliation in Japan and Korea: The Roles of Historians,* Artists *and Activists* (Springer, 2016) 170.

[172] See D. Nelken, 'Signaling Conformity: Changing Norms in Japan and China', *Michigan Journal of International Law* 27 (2006), 933, 935, 967.

[173] Port (n. 143) 140–71; Alston (n. 125) 631, noting that 'Japanese courts consistently reject international human rights-based arguments, are systematically averse to reliance upon international norms which they use at best as a form of icing upon the cake, very rarely find violations of international norms, and consistently assume those norms provide no greater protection than the bill of rights in the Constitution.'

[174] See S. Chesterman, 'Asia's Ambivalence about International Law and Institutions: Past, Present and Futures', *European Journal of International* Law 27 (2016), 950.

[175] See A. D. Ba, C. C. Kuik and S. Sudo, *Institutionalizing East Asia: Mapping and Reconfiguring Regional Cooperation* (Routledge, 2016); R. Jeffery and H. J. Kim (eds.), *Transitional Justice in the Asia-Pacific* (Cambridge University Press, 2014); H. Kim 'Missed Opportunities in the Judicialisation of International Criminal Law? Asian States in the Emergence and Spread of the Rome Statute System to Punish Atrocity Crimes', *Netherlands Quarterly of Human Rights* 35 (2017), 246.

[176] Ibid.

[177] Chesterman (n. 156) 131, 139; Kim (n. 175).

measures that promote individual criminal accountability.[178] The absence of these relevant forms of external pressure and consensus helps to explain survivors' and activists' inability to persuade Japanese policy-makers that the case for justice, rights and reparations for the former 'comfort women' and their families outweighs prevailing interests.

VIII CONCLUSIONS

The anti-impunity norm is a radically ambitious human rights norm. It seeks to intervene in state practice so as to transform the content, method, and, at times, the role of law to achieve a vision of justice and legality founded on universal human rights concepts. Among other things, it calls for states to reject impunity by ensuring that perpetrators of rights violations and serious international crimes are subject to appropriate prosecution and punishment, that victims receive appropriate reparations, and that the history of rights violations is preserved rather than obliterated. It is not reducible to a single rule, but is an amalgam of key propositions in international human rights, humanitarian and criminal law, and is grounded in the moral conviction that impunity is universally abhorrent and intolerable, and must be combatted.

As the case study demonstrates, successive post-war Japanese governments have deeply contested the legal boundaries and applicability of the anti-impunity norm and the rules it seeks to advance in relation to the 'comfort system' issue. While this has been, in part, an expedient response to domestic and international political imperatives, it is also emblematic of the high barriers to the norm's vernacularization produced by Japan's socio-legal context. These have seen Japan fashion a response to impunity on its own terms.

This case study also demonstrates that the interactions generated by the anti-impunity norm defy the framework of 'legal transplants'. A broader vantage demonstrates that the norm's influence may be subtle and subversive, demonstrating elements of resistance, concession and refashioning. Evaluating influence in zero-sum terms of 'success' or 'failure' can conceal the fact that in the 'real world of legal diffusion', to quote Twining,[179] the internalization of foreign legal norms is a highly contingent and dynamic process which will vary depending on factors including how high the new society's barriers to vernacularization are and the extent of local and regional appetite for the new norm.

178 Ibid.

179 W. Twining, 'Diffusion of Law: A Global Perspective' in W. Twining, *General Jurisprudence: Understanding Law from a Global Perspective* (Cambridge University Press, 2004).

IX BIBLIOGRAPHY

Akhavan, P., 'Beyond Impunity: Can International Criminal Justice Prevent Future Atrocities?', *American Journal of International Law* 95 (2001), 7.

Alston, P., 'Transplanting Foreign Norms: Human Rights and Other International Legal Norms in Japan', *European Journal of International Law* 10 (1999), 627.

Arthur, P., 'How Transitions Reshaped Human Rights: A Conceptual History of Transitional Justice', *Human Rights Quarterly* 31 (2009), 321.

Ba, A., Kuik C. C. and Sueo S., *Institutionalizing East Asia: Mapping and Reconfiguring Regional Cooperation* (Routledge, 2016).

Bagas, J., 'Duterte and Donor Withdrawal', *Sur – International Journal on Human Rights* 26 (2017), 37.

Baird, N., 'The Role of International Non-Governmental Organisations in the Universal Periodic Review of Pacific Island States: Can Doing Good Be Done Better', *Melbourne Journal of International Law* 16 (2015), 550.

Banks, C. and Baker, J. *Comparative, International, and Global Justice: Perspectives from Criminology and Criminal Justice* (SAGE, 2015).

Boehringer, G., 'Duterte's Drug War: Violating Rights for a Quick Fix', *Alternative Law Journal* 42 (2017), 233.

Burns, C., *Sexual Violence and the Law in Japan* (Routledge, 2005).

Chan, J., *Gender and Human Rights Politics in Japan: Global Norms and Domestic Networks* (Stanford University Press, 2004).

Cheah W., 'Walking the Long Road in Solidarity and Hope', *Harvard Human Rights Journal* 22 (2009), 99.

Cheesman, N., D'Costa, B. and Haberkon, T. 'Anticipating the Struggle against Everyday Impunity in Myanmar through Accounts from Bangladesh and Thailand', *Asia and The Pacific Policy Studies* 3 (2016), 48.

Chesterman, S., 'International Criminal Law with Asian Characteristics?', *Columbia Journal of Asian Law* 27 (2013), 142.

'Asia's Ambivalence about International Law and Institutions: Past, Present and Futures', *European Journal of International Law* 27 (2016), 950.

Dalton, E., *Women and Politics in Contemporary Japan* (Routledge, 2015).

Deutrom, Rhian, 'Japanese 'Comfort Women's' Memorial In 18 C Complaint', *The Australian*, 15 December 2016 www.theaustralian.com.au/national-affairs/war-womens-memorial-in-18 c-complaint/news-story/f4a13f4a10fede4b1c19c96e403679aa accessed 14 September 2017.

Dicker, N., 'Aiding Transitional Justice in Solomon Islands', *Buffalo Human Rights Law Review* 21 (2015), 77.

Digital Museum: The Comfort Women Issue and the Asian Women's Fund, 'From a Memorandum sent by Tadaichi Kawahara, Adjutant in the Ministry of War, "Measures to Enforce Military Discipline from the Experiences in the China Incident' www.awf.or.jp/e1/facts-02.html accessed 20 December 2017.

'Statement by Prime Minister Junichiro Koizumi on the 60th Anniversary of the End of the War' (Asian Women's Fund, 2005) www.awf.or.jp/e6/statement-36.html accessed 12 September 2017.

Dolgopol, U., 'Cold Comfort', *Alternative Law Journal* 21 (1996), 156.

'Crimes against the Comfort Women in the Tokyo Trial' in Tanaka, Y., L. H. McCormack, T., Simpson, G., *Beyond Victor's Justice? The Tokyo War Crimes Trial Revisited* (BRILL, 2011).

and Paranjape S, 'Comfort Women: An Unfinished Ordeal' (Report, International Commission of Jurists, 1994) 197 http://icj.wpengine.netdna-cdn.com/wp-content/uploads/1994/01/Japan-comfort-women-fact-finding-report-1994-eng.pdf accessed 21 January 2019.

Dolidze, A., 'Bridging Comparative and International Law: Amicus Curiae Participation as a Vertical Legal Transplant', *European Journal of International Law* 26 (2015), 851.

Donghua, H., 'The Tokyo Trials and Japanese Revisionism: Political Maneuver or Criminal Justice', *China Legal Science Journal* 3 (2015), 71.

du Plessis, M. and Ford, J. 'Transitional Justice: A Future Truth Commission for Zimbabwe?', *International and Comparative Law Quarterly* 58 (2009), 87.

Dussich J., Fujiwara, Y. and Sagisaka, A. 'Decisions Not to Report Sexual Assault in Japan', *International Journal of Offender Therapy and Comparative Criminology* 45 (2001), 35.

Engle, K., 'A Genealogy of the Criminal Turn in Human Rights' in Engle, K., Miller, Z. and Davis, D. M. (eds.), *Anti-Impunity and the Human Rights Agenda* (Cambridge University Press, 2016).

Freeland, S., 'A Prosecution Too Far? Reflections on the Accountability of Heads of State under International Criminal Law', *Victoria University of Wellington Law Review* 41 (2010), 179.

Futamura, M., *War Crimes Tribunals and Transitional Justice: The Tokyo Trial and the Nuremberg Legacy* (Routledge, 2007).

Galindo, G., 'Legal Transplants between Time and Space' in Thomas Duve (ed.), *Entanglements in Legal History: Conceptual Approaches* (Max Planck, 2014).

Goldsmith J. and Levinson, D., 'Law for States: International Law, Constitutional Law, Public Law', *Harvard Law Review* 122 (2009), 1.

Gustafsson, K., 'The 'History Problem' in Sino-Japanese Relations: What's the Problem?' (E-International Relations, 31 October 2016) www.e-ir.info/2016/10/31/the-history-problem-in-sino-japanese-relations-whats-the-problem/ accessed 21 January 2018.

Haley, J., *Authority without Power: Law and the Japanese Paradox* (Oxford University Press, 1991).

Harding, A., 'Global Doctrine and Local Knowledge: Law in South East Asia', *International and Comparative Law Quarterly* 51 (2002),35.

Hata I., 'No Organised or Forced Recruitment: Misconceptions about Comfort Women and the Japanese Military' (Society for the Dissemination of Historical Fact, 2007) www.sdh-fact.com/category/comfort-women/ accessed 5 October 2017.

Hayashi, Y., 'Implementation of the Convention on the Elimination of All Forms of Discrimination against Women in Japan', *Journal of East Asian and International Law* 6 (2013), 341.

Hearman, V., 'Between Citizenship and Human Rights: The Struggle for Justice after Indonesia's 1965 Mass Violence', *Citizenship Studies* 22 (2018), 175.

Hee-Seok Shin, E., 'The "Comfort Women" Reparation Movement: Between Universal Women's Human Right and Particular Anti-Colonial Nationalism', *Florida Journal of International Law* 28 (2016), 87.

Hein, L., 'Savage Irony: The Imaginative Power of the 'Military Comfort Women' in the 1990s', *Gender and History* 11 (1999), 336.

Hein, P., 'Unresolved Comfort Women Issue: How Pragmatism Precludes Reconciliation', *The Korean Journal of International Studies* 14 (2016), 447.

Hessbruegge, J., 'Justice Delayed, Not Denied: Statutory Limitations and Human Rights Crimes', *Georgetown Journal of International Law* 43 (2012), 335.

Hicks, G., *Japan's War Memories: Amnesia or Concealment* (Ashgate, 1997).

Igarashi, M., 'Post-War Compensation Cases, Japanese Courts and International Law', *Japanese Annual of International Law* 45 (2000), 45.

International Center for Transitional Justice, 'Briefing Paper: Transitional Justice in the United Nations Human Rights Council' (*International Center for Transitional Justice*, 6 July 2011) www.ictj.org/publication/transitional-justice-united-nations-human-rights-council accessed 15 September 2017.

Iwanaga, K., 'Women's Political Representation in Japan' in Iwanaga, K. (ed.), *Women's Political Participation and Representation in Asia: Obstacles and Challenges* (NIAS Press, 2008).

Iwasawa, Y., 'International Law in the Japanese Legal Order: Recent Developments', *American Society of International Law Proceedings* 91 (1997), 302.

Jeffery R. and Kim, H. (eds.), *Transitional Justice in the Asia-Pacific* (Cambridge University Press, 2014).

Johnson, D., *The Japanese Way of Justice: Prosecuting Crime in Japan* (Oxford University Press, 2001).

Kaur, J., 'A Judicial Blackout: Judicial Impunity for Disappearances in Punjab, India', *Harvard Human Rights Journal* 15 (2002), 269.

Kaur Sarkaria, M., 'Lessons from Punjab's Missing Girls: Toward a Global Feminist Perspective on Choice in Abortion [comments]', *California Law Review* 97 (2009), 905.

Kazi, S., 'Rape, Impunity and Justice in Kashmir', *Socio-Legal Review* 10 (2014), 14.

Kim, H., 'Missed Opportunities in the Judicialisation of International Criminal Law? Asian States in the Emergence and Spread of the Rome Statute System to Punish Atrocity Crimes', *Netherlands Quarterly of Human Rights* 35 (2017), 246.

Kimura, M., *Unfolding the 'Comfort Women' Debates: Modernity, Violence, Women's Voices* (Springer, 2016).

Kingston, J., 'History Haunts Japan's Prime Minister Abe', *Asia-Pacific Journal* 13 (2015).

Knop, K. and Riles, A., 'Space, Time, and Historical Injustice: A Feminist Conflict-of-Laws Approach to the Comfort Women Agreement', *Cornell Law Review* 102 (2017), 853.

Lambourne, W., 'Justice after Genocide: Impunity and the Extraordinary Chambers in the Courts of Cambodia', *Genocide Studies and Prevention: An International Journal* 8 (2014), 29.

Landino, J., 'Ianfu: No Comment Yet for Korean Comfort Women and the Impact of House Resolution 121', *Cardozo Journal of Law and Gender* 15 (2009), 333.

Le Clercq Ortega J. and Sánchez Lara, G. (eds.), *Global Impunity Index* (Fundación Universidad de las Américas Puebla, 2015).

Lee, S., 'Comforting the Comfort Women: Who Can Make Japan Pay?', *University of Pennsylvania Journal of Economics and Law* 24 (2003), 509.

Legrand, P., 'The Impossibility of 'Legal Transplants', *Maastricht Journal of European and Comparative Law* 4 (1997), 111.

Liddick E. and Gagnon, J. 'Striving for Peace and Reconciliation in Sri Lanka: A Creative Solution to Conflict', *War Crimes, Genocide and Crimes against Humanity* 3 (2009), 39.

Liu, H., *Law's Impunity* (Hart Publishing, 2015).

Lutz, E. and Sikkink, K. 'The Justice Cascade: The Evolution and Impact of Foreign Human Rights Trials in Latin America', *Chicago Journal of International Law* 2 (2001), 8.

Manirabona A. and Wemmers, J.-A. 'It Doesn't Go Away with Time: Victims' Need for Reparation Following Crimes against Humanity' in Wemmers, J.-A. (ed.), *Reparation for Victims of Crimes against Humanity: the Healing Role of Reparation* (Routledge, 2014), 77.

McCargo, D., 'Transitional Justice and Its Discontents', *Journal of Democracy* 26 (2015), 5.

McCurry, J., 'Former Sex Slaves Reject Japan and South Korea's "Comfort Women" Accord' *The Guardian*, 26 January 2016 www.theguardian.com/world/2016/jan/26/former-sex-slaves-reject-japan-south-koreas-comfort-women-accord accessed 14 September 2017.

McDougall, G., 'Addressing State Responsibility for the Crime of Military Sexual Slavery during the Second World War: Further Attempts for Justice for the Comfort Women', *Korean Journal of International and Comparative* Law 1 (2013), 137.

McGregor, K., 'Exposing Impunity: Memory and Human Rights Activism in Indonesia and Argentina', *Journal of Genocide Research* 19 (2017), 551.

Mera, K., *Comfort Women not 'Sex Slaves': Rectifying the Myriad of Perspectives* (Xlibris, 2015).

Merry, S., *Human Rights and Gender Violence: Translating International Law into Local Justice* (Chicago University Press, 2006).

'Transnational Human Rights and Local Activism', *American Anthropologist* 108 (1) (2006), 44.

and Levitt, P. 'Vernacularization on the Ground: Local Uses of Global Women's Rights in Peru, China, India and the United States', *Global Networks* 9 (2009), 441.

Morris, N., 'Review: Yuki Tanaka – Japan's Comfort Women: Sexual Slavery and Prostitution during World War II and the US Occupation', *Intersections: Gender, History and Culture in the Asian Context* 9 (2003) http://intersections.anu.edu.au/issue9/morris_review.html accessed 21 January 2019.

Nelken, D., 'Signaling Conformity: Changing Norms in Japan and China', *Michigan Journal of International Law* 27 (2006), 933.

Odanaka, N., 'From Responsibility to Compassion: Lessons from the Controversy over 'Comfort Women in Japan', *Journal of Japanese Law* 31 (2011), 49.

Onuma, Y., 'Japanese War Guilt and Postwar Responsibilities of Japan', *Berkeley Journal of International Law* 20 (2003), 600.

Orakhelashvili, A., 'Between Impunity and Accountability for Serious International Crimes: Legal and Policy Approaches', *Netherlands International Law Review* 55 (2009), 217.

Orentlicher, D., "Settling Accounts' Revisited: Reconciling Global Norms with Local Agency', *International Journal of Transitional Justice* 1 (2007),19.

Örücü, E., 'Law as Transposition', *The International and Comparative Law Quarterly* 51 (2002), 205.

Ottley, B., 'Legal Dissonance: The Interaction of Criminal Law and Customary Law in Papua New Guinea', *Asia Pacific Law Review* 24 (2016), 83.

Park Hsu, Y., "Comfort Women' From Korea: Japan's World War II Sex Slaves and the Legitimacy of Their Claims for Reparations', *Pacific Rim Law and Policy Journal* 2 (1993), 97.

Park Sonen, M., 'Healing Multidimensional Wounds of Injustice: Intersectionality and the Korean "Comfort Women"', *Berkeley La Raza Law Journal* 22 (2012), 269.

Peerenboom, R., 'Assessing Human Rights in China: Why the Double Standard', *Cornell International Law Journal* 38 (2005), 71.

Penrose, M., 'Impunity- Inertia, Inaction, and Invalidity: A Literature Review', *Boston University International Law Journal* 17 (1999), 273.

Port, K., 'The Impact of Human Rights Law in Japan', *Stanford Journal of International Law* 28 (1991), 140.

Qiu P., Zhiliang, S. and Lifei, C., *Chinese Comfort Women: Testimonies from Imperial Japan's Sex Slaves* (Oxford University Press, 2014).

Robertson C., 'Ending Impunity: How International Criminal Law Can Put Tyrants on Trial', *Cornell International Law Journal* 38 (2005), 649.

Rajan, S., 'Domestication of International Criminal Law: International Crimes Tribunal of Bangladesh, A Case Study', *ISIL Year Book of International Humanitarian and Refugee Law* 12–13 (2013), 132.

Sakamoto, R., 'The Women's International War Crimes Tribunal on Japan's Military Sexual Slavery: A Legal and Feminist Approach to the 'Comfort Women' Issue', *New Zealand Journal of Asian Studies* 3 (2001), 49.

Say, B., 'Ripe for Justice: A New UN Tool to Strengthen the Position of the "Comfort Women" and to Corner Japan into Its Reparation Responsibility', *Pennsylvania State International Law Review* 23 (2004), 953.

Scharf, M., 'From the eXile Files: An Essay on Trading Justice for Peace', *Washington and Lee Law Review* 63 (2006), 342.

'The Letter of the Law: The Scope of the International Legal Obligation to Prosecute Human Rights Crimes', *Law and Contemporary Problems* 53 (1996), 60.

Schmidt D., *Ianfu, the Comfort Women of the Japanese Imperial Army of the Pacific War: Broken Silence* (Edwin Mellen Press, 2000).

Schmidt P., 'Disabled Colonial Veterans of the Imperial Japanese Forces and the Right to Receive Social Welfare Benefits from Japan', *Sydney Law Review* 21 (1999), 240.

Se, T. and Karatsu, R. 'A Conception of Human Rights Based on Japanese Culture: Promoting Cross-Cultural Debates', *Journal of Human Rights* 3 (2004), 283.

Seaton, P., *Japan's Contested War Memories: The 'Memory Rifts' in Historical* (Routledge, 2007).

Seibert-Fohr, A., *Prosecuting Serious Human Rights Violations* (Oxford University Press, 2009).

Selden M. and Yoshiko, N., 'Japanese Textbook Controversies, Nationalism, and Historical Memory: Intra- and Inter-National Conflicts', *The Asia Pacific Journal – Japan Focus* 7 (2009).

Senda, K., *Jugun Ianfu* (San'Ichi Shobo, 1978).
Sigur Center for Asian Studies at the George Washington University, 'Korean Comfort Women v. Japan' (Memory and Reconciliation in the Asia-Pacific) https://memoryreconciliation.org/topics/comfort-women/comfort-women-korea/ accessed 13 September 2017.
Soh, S., *The Comfort Women: Sexual Violence and Postcolonial Memory in Korea and Japan* (University of Chicago Press, 2008).
Tanaka, Y., "Comfort Women Bashing' and Japan's Social Formation' in Lewis, M. (ed.), *'History Wars' and Reconciliation in Japan and Korea: The Roles of Historians, Artists and Activists* (Springer, 2016).
Terrill, R., *World Criminal Justice Systems: A Comparative Survey* (Routledge, 2015).
Teubner G., 'Legal Irritants: Good Faith in British Law or How Unifying Law Ends Up in New Differences', *Modern Law Review* 61 (1998), 11.
Totsuka E., 'Proposals for Japan and the ROK to Resolve the "Comfort Women" Issue: Creating trust and peace in light of international law', *Asia Pacific Journal: Japan Focus* 11 (2013), 1.
The Mainichi, 'S. Korean Foundation a Vital Bridge to Solve 'Comfort Women' Issue', *The Mainichi*, 29 August 2016 http://mainichi.jp/english/articles/20160829/p2a/00m/0na/016000 c#csidx54df400df19be84bb8e6ad12acf4533 accessed 13 September 2017.
Tsutomu, N., 'Behind The Comfort Women Controversy: How Lies Became Truth' (2007) Society for Dissemination of Historical Fact, www.sdh-fact.com/category/comfort-women/ accessed 5 October 2017.
Twining, W., 'Diffusion of Law: A Global Perspective' in Twining, W. *General Jurisprudence: Understanding Law from a Global Perspective* (Cambridge University Press, 2004).
'Social Science and Diffusion of Law', *Journal of Law and Society* 32 (2005), 203.
Urabe, N., 'Rule of Law and Due Process: A Comparative View of the United States and Japan', *Law and Contemporary Problems* 53 (1990), 69.
van Boven, T., 'Basic Principles and Guidelines on the Right to a Remedy and Reparation for Victims of Gross Violations of International Human Rights Law and Serious Violations of International Humanitarian Law' (*United Nations Archive, Audiovisual Library of International Law*, 16 December 2005) http://legal.un.org/avl/ha/ga_60–147/ga_60–147.html accessed 22 November 2017.
Watson, A., 'Comparative Law and Legal Change', *Cambridge Law Journal* 37 (1978), 315.
Legal Transplants: An Approach to Comparative Law 2nd edn (University of Georgia Press, 1993).
Wolfe, S., *The Politics of Reparations and Apologies* (Springer, 2013).
Women's Caucus for Gender Justice, 'Re: Judgment of the Women's International War Crimes Tribunal 2000 for the Trial of Japanese Military Sexual Slavery, 'In the matter of the Prosecutors and the Peoples of the Asia-Pacific Region v. Emperor Hirohito et al. and the Government of Japan' (Women's Caucus for Gender Justice, 2000) www.iccwomen.org/wigjdraft1/Archives/oldWCGJ/tokyo/judgment announce.html accessed 12 September 2017.
Zarni M. and Brinham, N. 'Reworking the Colonial-Era Indian Peril: Myanmar's State-Directed Persecution of Rohingyas and Other Muslims', *Brown Journal of World Affairs* 24 (2017), 53.

Zhao, B., 'Land Expropriation, Protest, and Impunity in Rural China', *European Journal of Anthropology* 54 (2009), 97.
Zwanenburg, M., 'The Van Boven / Bassiouni Principles: An Appraisal', *Netherlands Quarterly of Human Rights* 24 (2006), 641.

CASES

Filartiga v. *Pena-Irala*, 630 F2d 876 (2d Cir 1980).
Koichi Mera and GAHT-US Corporation v. *City of Glendale* (9th Cir 2016).
Prosecutors and Peoples of Asia Pacific Region v. *Hirohito; Prosecutors and Peoples of Asia Pacific Region* v. *Japan*, Summary of Findings and Preliminary Judgment, Women's International War Crimes Tribunal 2000 (12 December 2000).

INTERNATIONAL TREATIES AND INSTRUMENTS

Agreement on the Settlement of Problems concerning Property and Claims and on Economic Co-Operation between Japan and the Republic of Korea (entered into force 18 December 1965) 583 UNTS 258.
Convention against the Elimination of all Forms of Discrimination against Women (entered into force 3 September 1981) 1249 UNTS 13.
International Convention for the Protection of all Persons from Enforced Disappearance (opened for signature 6 February 2007, entered into force 23 December 2010) 2716 UNTS 3.
International Convention on the Non-Applicability of Statutory Limitations to War Crimes and Crimes against Humanity (adopted 26 November 1968, entered into force 11 November 1970) 754 UNTS 73.
International Covenant on Civil and Political Rights (adopted 16 December 1966, entered into force 23 March 1976) 999 UNTS 171.
Reparations Agreement between Japan and the Philippines (entered into force 9 May 1956) 285 UNTS 3.
Treaty of Peace between Japan and the Republic of Indonesia (entered into force 15 April 1958) 324 UNTS 235 and Reparations Agreement 324 UNTS 247.
Treaty of Peace between the Union of Burma and Japan (entered into force 16 April 1955) 251 UNTS 201.
Treaty on Basic Relations between Japan and the Republic of Korea (entered into force 22 June 1965) 583 UNTS 44.
UNCHR (Sub-Commission), 'Question of the Impunity of Perpetrators of Violations of Human Rights (Civil and Political Rights): Final Report prepared by Mr L Joinet, pursuant to Subcommission resolution 1995/35' (29 June 1996) UN Doc E/CN.4/Sub.2/1996/18 annex II 'Set of Principles for The Protection and Promotion of Human Rights through Action to Combat Impunity'.
UNHRC, 'Report of the Independent Expert [Diane Orentlicher] to Update the Set of Principles to Combat Impunity' UN Doc E/CN.4/2005/102/Add.1 (8 February 2005) addendum 'Set of Principles for the Protection and Promotion of Human Rights through Action to Combat Impunity'.

Universal Declaration of Human Rights (adopted 10 December 1948) UNGA Res 217 A(III).
World Conference on Human Rights: Vienna Declaration and Programme of Action (adopted 25 June 1993) A/CONF.157/23.

JAPANESE GOVERNMENT SOURCES

Ministry of Foreign Affairs, 'Statement by Chief Cabinet Secretary Koichi Kato on the Issue of the so-called "Wartime Comfort Women" from the Korean Peninsula' (*Japanese Government*, 6 July 1992) www.mofa.go.jp/policy/postwar/state9207.html accessed 11 September 2017.
'Statement by the Chief Cabinet Secretary Yohei Kono on the result of the study on the issue of "comfort women" ('Kono Statement')' (*Japanese Government*, 4 August 1993) www.mofa.go.jp/policy/women/fund/state9308.html accessed 11 September 2017.
'Statement by Prime Minister Tomiichi Murayama on the occasion of the establishment of the "Asian Women's Fund"' (*Japanese Government*, July 1995) www.mofa.go.jp/policy/women/fund/state9507.html accessed 11 September 2017.
'Statement by the Chief Cabinet Secretary' (*Japanese Government*, 14 June 1995) www.mofa.go.jp/policy/women/fund/state9506.html accessed 11 September 2017.
'Announcement by Foreign Ministers of Japan and the Republic of Korea at the Joint Press Occasion' (*Japanese Government*, 28 December 2015) www.mofa.go.jp/a_o/na/kr/page4e_000364.html accessed 13 September 2017.
'Reply of the Government of Japan to the Letter Sent by the Special Rapporteur for Follow-up to Concluding Observations of the Human Rights Committee' (*Japanese Government*, 19 April 2016) www.mofa.go.jp/policy/human/cove_civil/index.html accessed 13 September 2017.
'Japan-ROK Foreign Ministers' Telephone Talk' (*Japanese Government*, 12 August 2016) www.mofa.go.jp/a_o/na/kr/page4e_000490.html accessed 13 September 2017.

NON-GOVERNMENTAL AND UNITED NATIONS SOURCES

Assembly of States Parties to the ICC, 'Statement by Ambassador Motohide Yoshikawa, at the thirteenth session of the ASP to the Rome Statute of the International Criminal Court' (*Assembly of States Parties*, 11 December 2014) https://asp.icc-cpi.int/iccdocs/asp_docs/ASP13/GenDeba/ICC- ASP13-GenDeba-Japan-ENG.pdf accessed 2 October 2017.
UN Committee against Torture, 'Concluding Observations on the Second Periodic Report of Japan' (28 June 2013) UN Doc CAT/C/JPN/CO/2.
UNHRC 'Consideration of Reports Submitted By States Parties under Article 40 of the Covenant : International Covenant on Civil and Political Rights: 6th Periodic Report of States Parties: Japan' (9 October 2012) UN Doc CCPR/C/JPN/6.
UN Committee on the Elimination of Discrimination against Women, 'Report of the Committee on the Elimination of Discrimination against Women' (12 April 1994) UN Doc A/49/38.

'Consideration of reports submitted by States parties under article 18 of the Convention, Seventh and eighth periodic reports of States parties due in 2014: Japan' (16 September 2014) UN Doc CEDAW/C/JPN/7–8.

Concluding Observations on the Combined Seventh and Eighth Periodic Reports of Japan' (10 March 2016) UN Doc CEDAW/C/JPN/CO/7–8.

UNCHR, 'Report of the Special Rapporteur on violence against women, its causes and consequences, Ms Radhika Coomaraswamy, in accordance with Commission on Human Rights resolution 1994/45: Report on the mission to the Democratic People's Republic of Korea, the Republic of Korea and Japan on the issue of military sexual slavery in wartime' (7 February 1996) UN Doc E/CN.4/1996/53/ Add. 1/Corr. 1.

'Final report submitted by Ms Gay J McDougall, Special Rapporteur' (22 June 1998) UN Doc E/CN.4/Sub.2/1998/13.

'Report of the Commission of Inquiry on Human Rights in the Democratic People's Republic of Korea' (2014) UN Doc A/HRC/25/63.United Nations, 'Fact-Finding Mission on Myanmar: Concrete and Overwhelming Information Points to International Crimes' (*United Nations*, 12 March 2018) www.ohchr.org/EN/ HRBodies/HRC/Pages/NewsDetail.aspx?NewsID=22794&LangID=E accessed 12 April 2018.

12

Legal Transplants, Temporary Migration Projects and Special Rights

Tiziana Torresi

I INTRODUCTION

In this chapter I analyze and discuss a specific kind of temporary migration pattern that I have identified using the term 'temporary migration projects'.[1] This is a kind of temporary migration which, inscribed within an overall life plan, is defined by the intention to return to the home country after specific aims and goals are achieved. Migrants engaged in temporary migration projects, given their plans and goals, do not seek involvement, and, indeed, avoid investment in the receiving society. This is the case even when they are not constrained by temporary migration visas, for example if they are EU citizens that migrate within the European Union. The life of the migrants engaged in these projects remains centred in the home country, where the migrants' objectives and plans are meant to come to fruition.

Temporary migration projects, while rational, sensible, and legitimate, as a consequence of their specific characteristics, place the migrants in a position which engages in them in a condition of vulnerability. As such they raise

[1] The notion of temporary migration projects, and the analysis of the normative issues they raise, has been developed elsewhere in a longstanding collaboration with Valeria Ottonelli and together, we have developed and discussed the idea of temporary migration projects over a series of articles. See, e.g., V. Ottonelli and T. Torresi 'Temporary migration projects and children's education', *Notizie di Politeia* (2010); V. Ottonelli and T. Torresi, 'Inclusivist Egalitarian Liberalism and Temporary Migration: A Dilemma', *Journal of Political Philosophy* 20 (2012), 202; V. Ottonelli and T. Torresi, 'When Is Migration Voluntary?', *International Migration Review* 47 (2013), 783; V. Ottonelli and T. Torresi, 'Temporary migration projects and voting rights', *Critical Review of International Social and Political Philosophy* 17 (2014), 580; V. Ottonelli and T. Torresi 'Temporary Migration, Identity and Allegiance' in F. Jenkins, M. Nolan, K. Rubinstein, *Allegiance and Identity in a Globalised World* (Cambridge University Press, 2014), V. Ottonelli and T. Torresi 'Temporary Migration and the Shortcomings of Citizenship' in C. Sonia Solé, T. Parella, and S. N. S. Martí (eds.), *Impact of Circular Migration on Human, Political and Civil Rights* (Springer, 2016).

specific normative questions. I argue that neither the traditional notion of liberal national citizenship, nor more flexible notions such as post-national citizenship, can accommodate the life plans and address the specific vulnerabilities of this special category of migrants. Addressing these specific needs and plans means instituting a set of special rights meant to protect the migrants and facilitate their unorthodox life plans.

While my analysis is in some ways steeped in, and has in the past concentrated on. examples drawn from, the context of the European Union; in this chapter, I instead consider whether similar patterns of migration in the context of the Asia-Pacific are amenable to being accommodated through similar institutional arrangements to the ones I have previously suggested are necessary and appropriate in the European context.[2] I frame this discussion within the debate around legal transplants, and argue that there are no obvious obstacles to the adoption of a regime of special rights for migrants engaged in temporary migration projects in the Asia-Pacific. The chapter develops as follows. In section I, I describe temporary migration projects and their specific phenomenology. Section II is dedicated to explaining why access to citizenship, often considered the ideal solution to addressing migrants' vulnerability, is insufficient in the case of these particular migration projects. I also advance there the case for a regime of special rights. Section III is instead dedicated to a review of the debate around legal transplants, I argue there that the idea for a regime of special rights I propose is transferable to, and would represent a good fit for, the region. The final section concludes the argument.

II TEMPORARY MIGRATION PROJECTS

Discussions about temporary migration often tend to concentrate on temporary migration *programmes*, and particularly on their problematic institutional design, their unfavourable consequences for migrants and, therefore, their questionable justifiability.[3] This means scholarship in this area often concentrates on states and sometimes supranational institutions such as the EU, as defining and shaping temporary migration. Migrants, on the other hand, are often portrayed as somewhat passive recipients of the programmes, whose choices are shaped by the institutional constraints that are imposed on them. In particular, temporary migration has been considered to represent

2 Ottonelli and Torresi, 'Temporary Migration and the Shortcomings of Citizenship' (n. 1).

3 See e.g., P. T. Lenard and C. Straehle (eds.), *Legislated Inequality: Temporary Labour Migration in Canada* (McGill-Queen's Press, 2012); S. Castles, 'Guestworkers in Europe: A Resurrection?', *International Migration Review* 40 (2006), 741.

always a second-best choice, dictated by the lack of opportunities for permanent migration.[4]

Commentators often assume that temporary migration is invariably a first step in a long-term strategy towards permanent settlement, or that temporary migration will eventually result in permanent settlement despite migrants' own initial plans and states stated policy objectives of preventing permanent settlement. Temporary migration programs are in fact often designed with the specific intent of preventing permanent settlement, which is often assumed to be what the migrants' "really" want; "there's nothing as permanent as a temporary migrant" is a belief commonly expressed in this regard.[5] These beliefs even shape methodology, and scholars have remarked how most of the empirical literature on return migration concentrates on the return of labour-aged migrants as a "failed" migration, marginalizing the fact that many returns before retirement age are actually planned.[6]

Of course, institutions do constrain and shape people's behaviours and choices in significant ways, and it is also obviously true that many more people desire to migrate to a new country permanently then there are opportunities to do so, so that temporary migration often is a second-best choice. However, this 'methodological statism' as we might call it, often obscures migrants' own understanding, motivations, and aims in choosing, planning and shaping their own migration experience, including temporary migration as a first preference. Exclusive focus on institutional constraints often leads to misunderstanding some aspects of migratory experiences and therefore also leads, in some cases and for some migrants, to inappropriate or incomplete normative analysis and problematic policy responses. To partially correct this focus, in

4 See Graeme Hugo, 'International migration and development in Asia' (2007) 8th International Conference of the Asia Pacific Migration Research Network, Fuzhou, China 25–29 May 2007. Graeme Hugo, in his work on migration to Australia, has instead raised the generally ignored question of how many times permanent settlement is used in the absence of a temporary visas. In other words, commentators often assume that migrants pursue temporary migration visas because they lack access to regular permanent migration, but the question of how many apply for permanent migration but would have instead applied under a temporary visa category had it been available is rarely raised, see G. Hugo, 'A New Paradigm of International Migration: Implications for Migration Policy and Planning in Australia' (2004) *Information and Research Services Parliamentary Library* 84.

5 Hugo (n. 4). There are of course exceptions, temporary visas for the highly skilled often offer opportunities for permanent settlement (see M. Czaika (ed.), *High-Skilled Migration: Drivers and Policies* (Oxford University Press, 2018)).

6 V. Junge, J. R. Diez and L. Schätzl, 'Determinants and Consequences of Internal Return Migration in Thailand and Vietnam', *World Development* 71 (2015), 94; K. B. Newbold, 'Counting Migrants and Migrations: Comparing Lifetime and Fixed-Interval Return and Onward Migration', *Economic Geography* 77 (2001), 23.

this paper, I want to concentrate instead on temporary migration *projects* placing therefore the emphasis on the migrants' own agency in choosing temporary migration as part of their life plans.[7]

By *temporary migration projects*, I mean a particular sub-set of return migration with specific characteristics. Return migrants are not an homogenous group, and therefore these characteristics are not present in all cases, thus my analysis is not meant to apply in all instances of temporary migration. Temporary migration projects are defined by the project of return to the home country after a period of residence in the host country that may be more or less prolonged, but that results in return before the migrants' retirement age. The presence in the host country is motivated by a desire to advance specific projects back home and never intended to lead to a permanent move and settlement in the host country.

The phenomenology of these migratory experiences is, of course, diverse. Migrants' projects are shaped by the specific and diverse social contexts in which they take place, as well as by the characteristics of individual migrants themselves, such as their gender, age, cultural origin, and circumstances specific to each individual and their family. However, here, and in previous work, I have attempted to delineate an ideal-typical sketch of the migrants who engage in temporary migration projects. This sketching is possible because this kind of migration involves specific behavioural patterns that are consequent to the rationale of the migration project itself: migrants engaged in temporary migration projects move to achieve specific goals connected with their life in their home country (e.g. building a house, financing children's education, starting a business).[8] They live and work in the host society in order

[7] Emphasizing choice of course raises the issue of the voluntariness of migration. Nothing of what I say here is meant to deny that much migration, both temporary and permanent, is forced migration, nor that often return migration or cyclical forms of migration would not be the first choice of migrants if permanent settlement was an option. I have described in some detail which conditions need to be met for a migration project to be considered voluntary in an article co-authored with Valeria Ottonelli (See Ottonelli and Torresi 'When Is Migration Voluntary?' n. 1): there we list non-coercion; sufficiently good options and opportunities in the home country at the time the decision to migrate is made; exit options once the migratory project is underway; and appropriate information as conditions that need to be met for a migratory project to be considered voluntary. A central point we make in our work is that, given the above conditions, migratory projects are to be considered voluntary even when they happen against background conditions of injustice, as is after all the case for most projects and life plans devised by individuals.

[8] For example, about half of Turkish returnees who had migrated to Germany became active as entrepreneurs upon return using capital acquired abroad (B. Aleman-Castilla, 'The returns to temporary migration to the United States: Evidence from the Mexican urban employment survey' Centre for Economic Performance, London School of Economics and Political Science, 2007). Agunias reports similar findings also for return migrants in Southern Italy,

to advance an overall life plan and long-term goals that will be realised at a future time and in a different social space to the host country. Advancing their overall plans back home means, for these migrants, bracketing many essential components of their life while abroad. For these migrants, migration does not represent a transferring of their whole life to a new social setting with a concomitant process of settlement and integration. It is, in some senses, not a migration in the general and accepted sense at all. This idea is well expressed by the comment that migrants engaged in this kind of migration 'travel, but do not migrate'.[9]

The characteristics for this group I have identified are as follows. Older and more skilled migrants are significantly represented, even though both the migrants' ages and skill levels vary. In many cases, migrants engaged in temporary migration projects move on their own, leaving children, spouses and relatives in the home country.[10] In line with their projects' rationale, migrants engaged in temporary migration projects adopt specific economic strategies: they tend to maximize participation in the labour force when measured per household,[11] they work on average for longer than non-

Colombia, Mexico, Portugal, Somaliland, Egypt, Ghana and Jamaica (D. R. Agunias, 'From a Zero-Sum to a win-win Scenario', *Literature Review on Circular Migration*, Washington, DC: Migration Policy Institute, 2006)). The situation is comparable in Asia: for returnees to China the accumulation of human capital while abroad proves as important as the accumulation of resources; East Javanese women report fulfilling basic family needs as the main motivation for migration (N. Heyzer and V. Wee 'Domestic Workers in Transient Overseas Employment: Who Benefits, Who Profits', *Canadian Woman Studies* 15 (1995) 98), in general, the main reason for temporary labour migration in Indonesia is reported to be increased income, a significant part of which is used to invest in productive activity to improve the wellbeing of migrants' family members (G. Hugo, 'Effects of International Migration on the Family in Indonesia', *Asian and Pacific Migration Journal* 11 (2002), 13).

9 M. Morokvasic, 'Transnational Mobility and Gender: A View from Post-Wall Europe' in M. Morokvasic, U. Erel and K. Shinozaki (eds.), *Crossing Borders and Shifting Boundaries* (Wiesbaden, VS Verlag für Sozialwissenschaften, 2003), 101.

10 E. Castagnone, M. Eve, R. Petrillo, F. Piperno 'Madri Migranti: Le Migrazioni di Cura dalla Romania e dall'Ucraina in Italia: Percorsi e Impatto sui Paesi di Origine' (CESPI, 2007); A. Leogrande, Uomini e Caporali: *Viaggio tra i Nuovi Schiavi nelle Campagne del Sud* (Feltrinelli Editore, 2016); R. S. Parreñas, 'Women, Migration and Domestic Work', *Región Y Sociedad* 15 (2001); Aleman-Castilla n. 8; C. Dustmann, 'Return Migration: The European Experience', *Economic Policy* 11 (1996), 213; O. Galor and O. Stark 'Migrants' Savings, the Probability of Return Migration and Migrants' Performance', *International Economic Review* (1990), 463; T. K. Bauer and M. G. Sinning. 'The Savings Behavior of Temporary and Permanent Migrants in Germany', *Journal of Population Economics* 24 (2011) 421; I. Gang and T. K. Bauer 'Temporary Migrants from Egypt: How Long Do They Stay Abroad?' IZA Discussion paper series, No. 3, Institute for the Study of Labor (IZA, Bonn, 1998); D. Catania, D. Recchia, M. Simoni, G. Zucca 'Il welfare fatto in casa' Indagine nazionale sui collaboratori domestici stranieri che lavorano a sostegno delle famiglie italiane (2007).

11 Aleman-Castilla (n. 8); Dustmann (n. 10).

migrants and for longer hours than they would in their home country.[12] The kinds of jobs they accept are also different; temporary migrants tend to accept less attractive and lower paid jobs than permanent migrants – the infamous 3D (dirty, dangerous and difficult) jobs – and their earnings also tend to be lower than those of nationals. This difference between migrants engaged in temporary migration projects and both permanent migrants and citizens is understandable: given their overall life plans and the aim of their migration, temporary migrants have an incentive to accept jobs that, despite being very poorly paid in the context of the host economy, still allow savings which would be impossible in the home country and therefore serve the migrants' ends.[13]

One example of this migratory experiences is found in the patterns of circular migration to Southern Europe developed by Romanian women since the early 2000s.[14] This migratory flow was characterized by short term or 'shuttle' circular migration that exploited the opportunity the migrants had to travel as tourists for up to three months. These migrants developed a form of shared employment as care workers through a turnover system by which they would be replaced, at the expiration of their visa, by other members of their family or sometimes close friends. This allows the migrants to spend significant periods of time back home with their family – the majority of them have one or more children at home – while maintaining a temporary job abroad, which would be periodically resumed for another three-month shift.[15] As with most migrants in this category, the jobs the women perform are very tiring physically and psychologically and often underpaid. Especially when they work as live-in domestics or caregivers, their work conditions are such that it would be impossible to sustain them on a permanent basis, so that it is the sharing of the positions that makes holding the jobs feasible.[16] This pattern also fits in with the migrants general plan and aims which are not to pursue a permanent settlement in the host country.[17] This can be understood by considering the destination of the migrants' remittances and savings earned: the purposes they most frequently serve are building a house in the home

12 Aleman-Castilla (n. 8); Dustmann (n. 10).

13 Leogrande (n. 10).

14 Ottonelli and Torresi, 'Temporary Migration and the Shortcomings of Citizenship' (n. 1).

15 Morokvasic (n. 9).

16 M. Alexandru, 'Migration and Social Mobility: A New Perspective on Status Inconsistency', *The Romanian Journal of European Studies* 5 (2007) 153; C. M. Uccellini 'Outsiders after Accession: The Case of Romanian Migrants in Italy, 1989–2009', *Political Perspectives* 4 (2010), 70.

17 See Castagnone *et al.* (n. 10). Similar motivations are given by Ukrainian women immigrated to Italy.

country, paying for the higher education of their children, or helping them to start a new family.[18] Female circular migration still persists as a central trend of migration from Romania even after the 2007 accession to the EU, and the consequent lifting on all bans on the circulation and the employment of Romanian domestic and care workers.[19]

The saving strategies and remittances patterns of migrants engaged in temporary migration projects are also specific. They generally involve a higher rate of savings when compared to permanent migrants and native citizens, as well as higher remittances when compared to permanent migrants.[20] Their aim to maximize savings also means that they often choose cheap housing, sometimes living in dramatically sub-standard conditions.[21] In the case of circular Romanian migrant care workers, we see high rates of co-residency and shared accommodation.[22] Consumption is also limited while in the host country and deferred until the time of return.[23]

Migrants engaged in temporary migration projects also adopt a specific social strategy which is also consequential to the overall rationale of their project. The centre of their lives remains their home country and their engagement with the host country reflects this fact. They therefore limit their civic, social, and political participation in the host society.[24] They do not participate in the political life of the receiving country, not even in relation to advancing their own social and economic conditions there.[25] Socially, they invest little time in building stable relationships in the host

18 Castagnone *et al.* (n 10); P. Cingolani and F. Piperno, "Il Prossimo Anno a Casa'. Radicamento, Rientro e Percorsi Translocali: Il Caso delle Reti Migratorie Marginea-Torino e Focsani-Roma' Rome: CeSPI-FIERI (2005).

19 European Commission, Directorate-General for Economic and Financial Affairs (2009).

20 Galor and Stark (n. 10); Bauer and Sinning (n. 10).

21 Leogrande (n. 10).

22 T. Caponio, 'Documenti, Lavoro, Casa: Percorsi di Integrazione non Lineari di Donne Filippine, Marocchine e Rumene in Italia' (2009) STAMPA 85; G. Fullin and V. Vercelloni, 'Dentro la Trappola. Percezioni e Immagini del Lavoro Domestico e di Cura nei Percorsi delle Donne Immigrate' *Polis* 22 (2009) 427.

23 N. P. Glytsos, 'Remitting Behaviour of "Temporary" and "Permanent" Migrants: The Case of Greeks in Germany and Australia', *Labour* 11 (1997), 409.

24 G. Fouron, 'Haitian immigrants in the United States' 205–50 in B. S. A. Yeoh, M. W. Charney and T. C. Kiong (eds.), *Approaching Transnationalisms* (Springer, 2003); T. Hammar, *Democracy and the Nation State* (Aldershot, 1990).

25 S. K. Ramakrishnan and T. J. Espenshade 'Immigrant Incorporation and Political Participation in the United States', *International Migration Review* 35 (2001), 870; M. A Stoll and J. S. Wong 'Immigration and Civic Participation in a Multiracial and Multiethnic Context', *International Migration Review* 41 (2007), 880. This is of course not generalizable to all migrants, some groups have engaged in political mobilization which is often steeped in, and particular to, the migrants' experience, such as for example when migrants use transnational networks and diasporas for their political activism (See e.g., P. Boccagni, J.-M. Lafleur and P. Levitt 'Transnational Politics

community.[26] It is however the very temporary nature of these migration projects and the social displacement they create that makes it psychologically and socially possible for the migrants to accept low-status, difficult and underpaid jobs and a life of sacrificed consumption and limited social interaction. These conditions could hardly be considered acceptable at home or indeed within the context of a permanent migration project.[27] But for migrants engaged in temporary migration projects the social bases of their self-esteem and self-respect are centred around a different social space, that of their home country, making their condition in the host country tolerable as it is separated from the home space and instrumental to their overall plans.[28]

It is hardly surprising, then, that despite their rationality and legitimacy, this type of migratory projects result in the *vulnerability* and *marginality* of the migrants involved in them. This is due to several of their characteristics. First, temporary migration projects are very risky, with significant probability of failure. Migrants may fail to successfully achieve their aims and may therefore not manage to return due to the lack of the necessary resources, to the breakdown of the connection with their original community, often including their closest family relations,[29] but also to the lack of institutional support that these migrants face in carrying out their plans of investments and return.

Second, this can then mean, for some migrants, a lack of *exit options*, i.e. the high risk of becoming 'trapped' in this kind of condition without being able to carry out their original plan of return but also without leading to proper settlement and integration in the host community, which was after all never intended in the first place.

Third, migrants engaged in temporary migration projects, given their specific mode of interaction with the host society and their overall aims, end up acquiring a lesser status and a marginal position within the receiving society. Their social isolation and their lack of investment in the political networks that

as Cultural Circulation: Toward a Conceptual Understanding of Migrant Political Participation on the Move', *Mobilities* 11 (2016) 444.

26 Glytsos (n. 23).

27 Parreñas (n. 10); Leogrande (n 10)

28 Ottonelli and Torresi 'Inclusivist Egalitarian Liberalism and Temporary Migration: A Dilemma' (n. 1); Ottonelli and Torresi 'Temporary Migration and the Shortcomings of Citizenship' (n. 1).

29 A. Sayad *La Double Absence: Des Illusions de l'émigré aux Souffrances de l'immigré* (Seuil, 2000); J.-P. Cassarino 'Theorising Return Migration: The Conceptual Approach to Return Migrants Revisited' (2004), http://cadmus.eui.eu/bitstream/handle/1814/2744/04_02.pdf;sequence=1 accessed 3 October 2018.

are an essential precondition for the effective enjoyment of the legal protections provided to local workers, make these migrants vulnerable and marginal even when better living and working conditions and full inclusion are formally accessible, as is the case for European Union citizens in EU host countries, such as Romanian shuttle migrants discussed above.[30]

III THE LIMITATIONS OF CITIZENSHIP AND THE CASE FOR SPECIAL RIGHTS

In previous work, I have suggested that the solution to accommodating, recognizing and facilitating temporary migration projects – and therefore mitigating migrants' vulnerability – should come from the development and institution – in addition to conventional citizenship rights – of a new set of special rights.[31] The argument for special rights is grounded in the recognition that access to citizenship rights is not adequate to accommodate the life plans of these migrants nor sufficient to address their vulnerabilities.

Of course, the concept of 'citizenship' itself is, like many others in political philosophy, a highly contested one; there isn't one single notion of citizenship, but rather various competing interpretations with varying normative implications.[32] Historians of ideas insist that even these existing interpretations are often artificially neat, and obscure the permanent tensions within the concept and the practice of citizenship itself.[33] However, a traditional, national liberal understanding of citizenship – such as that found for example in the work of authors such as Michael Walzer and David Miller[34]– entails for migrants, once they are admitted, a process of full integration and commitment to their new polity, including, to a degree, to the sharing of the national culture. On the part of the political community, a commitment to full equality for new members is also required. Migrants, in this model, once admitted are presumed to be on the road to citizenship and on becoming fully fledged members of their political community with the same rights and

[30] Leogrande (n. 10).

[31] Ottonelli and Torresi 'Inclusivist Egalitarian Liberalism and Temporary Migration: A Dilemma' (n. 1); Ottonelli and Torresi 'When Is Migration Voluntary?' (n. 1); Ottonelli and Torresi 'Temporary Migration Projects and Voting Rights' (n. 1); Ottonelli and Torresi 'Temporary Migration, Identity and Allegiance' (n. 1); Ottonelli and Torresi Temporary Migration and the Shortcomings of Citizenship' (n. 1).

[32] D. Miller *Citizenship and National Identity* (Polity Press, 2000).

[33] P. Magnette *Citizenship: The History of an Idea* (ECPR Press, 2005).

[34] Miller (n. 32); M. Walzer *Spheres of Justice: A Defense of Pluralism and Justice* (Basic, 1983).

responsibilities as native citizens.[35] Similar understandings are also, in general, held by citizens of liberal democracies and reflected in public debates on migrant integration.[36] But this model of incorporation, with its insistence on social cohesion, allegiance to the polity, and cultural integration is unsuited to migrants engaged in temporary migration projects who simply do not possess such commitment to the host society.[37]

However, more flexible understandings of membership, such as post-national citizenship, where migrants' incorporation in the host community is grounded on the migrants' personhood and human rights rather than on solid conceptions of national citizenship,[38] also fail to suit migrants engaged in temporary migration projects. Granting access to these forms of membership, given the characteristics of temporary migration projects, would mean establishing purely formal equality between citizens and immigrants. The effectiveness of civil, social, and political rights is, in fact, grounded on a set of economic and social preconditions, on networks and connections, knowledge of the host society's functionings, of its language and laws, as well as on practices of political mobilization and activism that are simply not present in the case of these migrants. Developing these capacities and connections is not part of the migrants' life plan, and it would entail diverting precious energies from their migration projects, that are already very taxing and demanding. Therefore, access to citizenship is not sufficient for accommodating these migrants' life plans, although access to citizenship remains crucially

35 It is indeed also because of the logic of this conception of membership and incorporation that temporary migration programmes are often considered very problematic, see e.g. Walzer (n. 34).

36 The expectations of exclusive allegiance of citizens to their state and how these should extend to migrants who naturalize are highlighted in public debates in liberal democracies around, for example, the issue of dual citizenship (See e.g. T. Brøndsted Sejersen, '"I Vow to Thee My Countries" – The Expansion of Dual Citizenship in the 21st Century', *International Migration Review* 42 (2008), 523), while the degree to which migrants should take on the national culture and identity remain amongst the most heated issues in the public debates of many liberal democracies, and are, in fact, according to some commentators becoming more intense and polarized (See, e.g., W. Kymlicka, 'The Rise and Fall of Multiculturalism? New Debates on Inclusion and Accommodation in Diverse Societies', *International Social Science Journal* 61 (2010), 97).

37 See Ottonelli and Torresi 'Temporary Migration, Identity and Allegiance' (n. 1), in which we argue there that the migrants' lack of allegiance to the receiving country is not normatively problematic. This is because the relationship between the migrants and their host society does not represent a form of exploitation on the part of the migrants since it is mutually beneficial. In fact, as I also have indicated here, it is the migrants engaged in these projects who often find themselves in a condition of vulnerability and therefore potentially open to exploitation and abuse.

38 Y. N. Soysal *Limits of Citizenship: Migrants and Postnational Membership in Europe* (University of Chicago Press, 1994).

important for those migrants initially engaged in temporary migration projects who may nevertheless decide to settle permanently. To reiterate, recognising the limitation of the conventional citizenship protections for these migrants, and arguing for special rights does not imply that the duty to provide temporary migrants with protections should be given up, but quite the opposite: special rights are intended to set up the institutional conditions in which these protections can be effectively guaranteed and enforced.

Of course, given the variety in the phenomenology of these migration experiences and the diversity in the host countries own economic, social, political, and institutional characteristics – as well as the presence or absence of regional migration governance structures – the specific measures and policies to be enacted to provide migrants with appropriate protections would need to vary and be adapted to different circumstances.

But, given the general characteristics of the migratory experiences I have described and their specific risks, and considering the goal the regime of special rights is meant to achieve, i.e. to protect temporary migrants from the vulnerability of their position, it is possible to provide a general sketch of the function and nature of these special rights.

In particular, there are two specific goals that the special rights ought to achieve: first, making migrants' plans reasonably feasible, mitigating the high risks they entail and protecting the migrants from the negative effects of the failure of their project to return. Second, the regime of special rights ought to aim at providing temporary migrants a substantive exit option at any stage in their migration project, to avoid the painful conditions of suspension that may derive from being trapped in the host country as consequence of a failed plan of return.

The special rights regime may include provisions in a number of different areas. In terms of social provisions, when these are present in the host country, temporary migrants could be granted pension and social security benefit portability. Benefits sometimes provided to families – e.g. rebates or subsidies for child care or special provisions for the care of elderly and sick relatives, such as special leave – could be altered to take into consideration that the migrants' families are likely to be back home. In particular, the care of left behind children has been identified as an area of concern.[39] Migrants could

[39] L. A. Hoang, T. Lam, B. S. A. Yeoh and E. Graham, 'Transnational Migration, Changing Care Arrangements and Left-behind Children's Responses in South-East Asia', *Children's Geographies* 13 (2015), 263; L. Baldassar and L. Merla (eds.), *Transnational Families, Migration and the Circulation of Care: Understanding Mobility and Absence in Family Life* (Routledge, 2013); R. S. Parreñas, *Children of Global Migration: Transnational Families and Gendered Woes* (Stanford University Press, 2005); A. Gheaus, 'Care Drain: Who Should

be allowed to divert part of their income taxes and social security payments to private health insurance, or other forms of social guarantee could be devized that would mean that the migrants could use them in their home countries.[40]

Within the labour market, temporary migrants would benefit from being free from some of the restrictions that follow from their visa status if they have migrated through a temporary migration programme. Temporary migrants who travel under temporary migration programmes are often tied to their employer, are allowed in the country for limited periods of time, and often are prohibited from travelling repeatedly to the host country for further work, or can do so only under specific conditions.[41] Being able not only to change jobs but also to return for further employment freely would provide temporary migrants with significant protections against abuse and exploitation during their employment, and with the capacity to plan properly and reach their savings goals.

In terms of freedom of movement, another freedom often curtailed by temporary migration programmes,[42] legal provisions could be arranged to make frequent visits to the home countries possible in order to protect

Provide for the Children Left Behind?', *Critical Review of International Social and Political Philosophy* 16 (2013), 1.

40 An added complication here is that sending countries may not have social security systems that the benefits may be incorporated into (See C. Brickenstein, 'Social Protection of Foreign Seasonal Workers: From State to Best Practice', *Comparative Migration Studies* 3 (2015), 2).

41 Castles (n. 3); K. Strauss and S. McGrath 'Temporary Migration, Precarious Employment and Unfree Labour Relations: Exploring the "Continuum of Exploitation" in Canada's Temporary Foreign Worker Program', *Geoforum* 78 (2017), 199; P. T. Lenard, 'Why Temporary Labour Migration Is Not a Satisfactory Alternative to Permanent Migration', *Journal of International Political Theory* 8 (2012), 172; J.P. Walsh, 'Watchful Citizens: Immigration Control, Surveillance and Societal Participation', *Social & Legal Studies* 23 (2014), 237.

42 S. Castles and D. Ozkul, 'Circular Migration: Triple Win, or a New Label for Temporary Migration?' in G. Battistella (ed.), *Global and Asian Perspectives on International Migration* (Springer, 2014); H. De Haas, 'International Migration, Remittances and Development: Myths and Facts', *Third World Quarterly* 26 (2005) 1269. Migrants' mobility can also be affected within the host country, where sometimes employers themselves limit migrants' freedom to move (See, e.g., E. Reid-Musson, 'Grown Close to Home: Migrant Farmworker (Im) Mobilities and Unfreedom on Canadian Family Farms', *Annals of the American Association of Geographers* 107 (2017), 716), these effects, and a series of other serious abuses are particularly common in Gulf Cooperation Council (GCC) countries, a situation which many scholars attribute to the *Kafala* system. The Kafala system was set up by the GCC countries in the 1950s and used especially from the 1970s onwards. Under the system, a migrant worker needs to be sponsored by a citizen or government agency to obtain an entry visa and residence permit. This gives employers significant power over migrant workers, which often results in limitations of the migrants' freedoms and abuse, especially for domestic workers whose lack of visibility, as employees within the household, makes them particularly vulnerable (see H. E. Murray, 'Hope for Reform Springs Eternal: How the Sponsorship System, Domestic

migrants from the risk of becoming alienated form their family and community back home and in order to keep ties to the sending society alive in general; such alienation may otherwise contribute to the failure of the migrant's project of return. The continued sustenance of social relations in the home country is, of course, also important for the degree of success migrants experience upon return, with some evidence pointing to the importance of migrants' family and social networks also for their economic, and in particular for their entrepreneurial success.[43]

Special policies and programmes could also be established to facilitate the post-return resettlement of temporary migrants. For example, we know that returnees, because of the human, social and financial capital gained overseas, often become entrepreneurs upon their return. They are more likely than non-migrants to own their own businesses or to be self-employed then they are to be employees.[44] The establishment of these enterprises could be facilitated by appropriate support, and infrastructure and institution-building in the home countries.[45]

These measures, would have, according to some analyses, the added benefit of a positive impact on development. It is often in fact the lack of such provisions that limits migration's capacity to enhance development.[46]

Laws and Traditional Customs Fail to Protect Migrant Domestic Workers in GCC Countries', *Cornell International Law Journal* 45 (2013), 461; R. Kanchana, 'Is the Kafala Tradition to Blame for the Exploitative Work Conditions in the Arab-Gulf Countries?' in M. Chowdhury and S. I. Rajan (eds.), *South Asian Migration in the Gulf* (Palgrave Macmillan, 2018); M. Johnson and C. Wilcke, 'Caged in and Breaking Loose: Intimate Labor, the State, and Migrant Domestic Workers in Saudi Arabia and Other Arab Countries' in S. L. Friedman and P. Mahdavi (eds.), *Migrant Encounters: Intimate Labor, The State and Mobility across Asia* (University of Pennsylvania Press, 2015)).

43 S. Pruthi, 'Social Ties and Venture Creation by Returnee Entrepreneurs', *International Business Review* 23 (2014), 1139.

44 F. Marchetta, 'Return Migration and the Survival of Entrepreneurial Activities in Egypt', *World Development* 40 (2012), 1999; J. Wahba and Y. Zenou 'Out of Sight, Out of Mind: Migration, Entrepreneurship and Social Capital,' *Regional Science and Urban Economics* 42 (2012), 890; B. McCormick and J. Wahba 'Overseas Work Experience, Savings and Entrepreneurship amongst Return Migrants to LDCs', *Scottish Journal of Political Economy* 48 (2001), 164; S. Démurger and H. Xu, 'Return migrants: The Rise of New Entrepreneurs in Rural China', *World Development* 39 (2011), 1847; C. Mahe, 'Occupational Choice of Return Migrants: Is There a 'Jack-of-all-trades' Effect?', United Nations University-Maastricht Economic and Social Research Institute on Innovation and Technology (39 (2017), MERIT); J. Maria Hagan and J. Wassink 'New Skills, New Jobs: Return Migration, Skill Transfers, and Business Formation in Mexico', *Social Problems* 63 (2016), 513.

45 O. ZhangSun, Z. XinZhi, W. RunQun, L. Feng, S. AiGuo and W. XingLin 'Typical Survey and Research on Returning-Home Migrant Workers' Entrepreneurship in Jiangxi Province under Post-Financial Crisis', *Asian Agricultural Research* 2 (2010), 34.

46 De Haas (n. 42).

Temporary and circular migration have been, in the last decade, promoted by international organizations, such as the International Organization for Migration and the European Union, and other advocates as a 'win-win-win' migration policy, a triple-win capable of benefiting economically both sending and receiving countries; as well as providing better access to labour markets for migrant workers.[47] Despite concerns with a number of possible negative effects and potential for exacerbating already problematic inequalities between countries – because of phenomena such as brain drain and care drain – the benefits of economic and social remittances have convinced many of the potentially significant benefits of migration as a powerful means of development, while others remain unconvinced.[48] It is of course impossible to do justice to such a complex debate in the short space I have here, however, it seems to me that Graeme Hugo is right when he observes that there exists empirical evidence to substantiate both sides of the debate, and that, positive or negative outcomes of temporary and circular migration on development will depend on the specific contextual circumstances of specific migration flows. Therefore, the most productive question to ask is under what circumstances, and with the aid of which policies can a positive outcome be reached both for migrants and the sending societies?[49] The suggestion here is that policies aimed at accommodating migrants' plans, given that these plans often tend to include goals that are conducive to good development outcomes, is one such policy.

To this end, for example, policies facilitating safe and efficient money transfers could be established to accommodate migrants plans and further development goals. But another positive effect on development is the direct impact of returnees, both in term of their returning with increased human capital and their entrepreneurial activities. Thus, implementing strategies for successful reinvestment of human and financial capital gained overseas would

[47] For a discussion see, e.g., C. Woodruff and R. Zenteno 'Migration Networks and Microenterprises in Mexico', *Journal of Development Economics* 82 (2007), 509. Of course, scholars have also expressed concerns about the burden these policies place on temporary migrants and the potentially exploitative nature of temporary migration programmes, in particular, see Castles and Ozkul (n. 42); Lenard and Straehle (n. 3), amongst many.

[48] R. H. Adams Jr and J. Page, 'Do International Migration and Remittances Reduce Poverty in Developing Countries?', *World Development* 33 (2005), 1645; P. Giuliano and M. Ruiz-Arranz 'Remittances, Financial Development, and Growth', *Journal of Development Economics* 90 (2009), 144; P. Fajnzylber and H. J. López 'Close to Home: The Development Impact of Remittances in Latin America', (2007) AGRIS; De Haas (n 42); D. Ratha and W. Shaw, South-South Migration and Remittances (The World Bank, 2007): http://citeseerx.ist.psu.edu/viewdoc/download?doi=10.1.1.576.4220&rep=rep1&type=pdf accessed on 3 October 2018.

[49] G. Hugo 'Best Practice in Temporary Labour Migration for Development: A Perspective from Asia and the Pacific', *International Migration* 47 (2009), 23.

be in the interest of both the migrants and the sending society as a whole. In fact, there is evidence that entrepreneurial activities initiated by returnees have a better chance of longevity then activities initiated by non-migrants,[50] and also of being more profitable.[51]

It should be clear from the above description, then, that the institution of these special rights would often require extensive cooperation between the migrants' host countries and their countries of origin. This cooperation may be achieved, depending on the specific circumstances and on the content of the right or policy at hand, through bilateral, multilateral and even global agreements, and there might be an important role to be played in their implementation by international, regional and supranational institutions as well.

IV MIGRATION GOVERNANCE IN THE ASIA-PACIFIC AND THE POSSIBILITY OF 'TRANSPLANTS'

My analysis of the specific characteristics of temporary migration projects is not geographically bounded in the sense that it draws on research on a variety of migration flows, with examples of this pattern of migration in the experience of migrants coming from various parts of the world. In this sense, it is clear that the particular migratory experiences I identified, temporary migration projects, are undertaken by migrants from – and are happening in – many, if not all, regions of the world. This is perhaps not surprising and indeed explicable if we consider global determinants of migration patterns. Despite differences in circumstances specific to each migration pattern and institutional setting, there are drivers of migration, dependant in part on global economic integration, that help explain global migration patterns. Stephen Castles lists the following as some of global migration's drivers: 'neo-liberal globalisation and social transformation; inequality; state security and human security; technology; labour demand; demographic changes; politics; law and governance; the social dynamics of migration; and the role of people who make their living by facilitating migration (sometimes called "the migration industry")'.[52] Graeme Hugo refers to differentials in the 3Ds – demography, development, and democracy – as explaining migratory flows.[53] Similar patterns of migration

50 Marchetta (n. 44).

51 Woodruff and Zenteno (n. 47).

52 S. Castles, 'The Forces Driving Global Migration', *Journal of Intercultural Studies* 34 (2013), 124.

53 Hugo (n. 4). Note: Hugo refers to differentials in migration flows. The term '3Ds' should be distinguished from the classification of migration jobs: 3D (dirty, dangerous and difficult).

drivers in different regions, often shaped by common global determinants, will produce similar migratory flows.

However, my analysis here is grounded in liberal political thought and often based on analysis of liberal democratic practices in relation to citizenship, to migrants' incorporation, to migration in general and temporary migration in particular, especially in the European Union context. The models of liberal national and post-national citizenship I have discussed are both associated with Western liberal political norms, discourses and practices. The most articulate discussion of post-national citizenship and migration is in fact to be found in the work of Yasemin Soysal,[54] and Soysal's research is a comparative sociological analysis of the modes of integration of migrants within different Western liberal democracies, specifically European states.

In fact, if we consider 'post-nationalism' to be the 'reflexive transformation' of the conception of membership in liberal democracies which switches the emphasis away from traditional understandings of sovereignty and citizenship towards a conception of shared sovereignty between different loci of authority – local, national and supranational – corresponding also to a, new and multi-layered conception of membership,[55] then European Union citizenship itself possesses many of the (relevant) attributes of post-national citizenship, e.g. it being multi-layered and void of a definite cultural content, at least a solid one, and arguably, even of a strong sense of identification of the citizens with the Union's political institutions. There is a question, then, to be explored more explicitly about the applicability of my analysis in a different context to that of the EU. Would a similar regime of rights for migrants engaged in temporary migration projects be equally appropriate – and necessary – for the Asia-Pacific? Can the idea for a regime of special rights developed on the basis of an analysis steeped in one context be transferred to a new one?[56]

The migration governance in the Asia-Pacific is of course in some ways different from that of the European Union. Migration governance in the region is characterized by the lack of significantly integrated regional legislation to govern migration, although recent literature has underlined how a regional dimension of migration governance is emerging.[57] Migration

54 Soysal (n. 38).

55 G. Delanty *Citizenship in a Global Age* (Open University Press, 2000).

56 There is of course a deeper philosophical question about the universal validity of liberal values, but this is not the question I am addressing here.

57 J. Elias, 'Governing Domestic Worker Migration in Southeast Asia: Public–Private Partnerships, Regulatory Grey Zones and the Household', *Journal of Contemporary Asia* 48 (2018) 278; J. Ramji-Nogales, 'Under the Canopy: Migration Governance in Southeast Asia', *UCLA Journal of International Law and Foreign Affairs* 21 (2017), 10.

flows are governed principally through bilateral agreements, non-binding Memoranda of Understanding,[58] and also through state partnership with private sector actors.[59] Bilateral agreements are often characterized by unequal bargaining power between sending and receiving countries and often ineffectual in protecting migrants' rights.[60] Could the idea of a special regime of rights for migrants engaged in temporary migration programmes make sense in this context?[61]

One way of considering this question is through the idea of legal transplants. Legal transplants are defined as the movement of laws and legal institutions between states.[62] Despite being central to the study of comparative and international law, the debate around legal transplants has reached what Andrew Harding describes, in his opening chapter in this Volume, as an impasse centred around a number of binaries, one of which is the very possibility of legal transplants. The issue at the core of the debate in this sense is whether law is a mirror of society, and reflects the dynamics, however differently identified by different theorists, of that society.[63] If this were true, law being steeped in a society's own language, culture and institutional structure, legal transplants ought to be impossible, and law should emerge form society's own workings. However, as Harding points out, transplants happen all the time, and in fact, in Asia, legal transplantation is the 'primary mode of legal change'.[64]

Harding suggests two ideas in resolving this impasse that allow me to address the question at hand in this chapter, these are the notions that first, what is being transplanted in legal transplants is an *idea* of a law, stripped of its 'institutional and interpretative' baggage, and second, that while this explains in what sense legal transplants can happen we are nevertheless left with the issue of 'fit', that is how well the transplanted idea of law will fit in the society that receives it.

58 S. Rother, 'Labour Migration in Southeast Asia: In Search of Regional Governance' in A. D. Ba and M. Beeson (eds.), *Contemporary Southeast Asia: The Politics of Change, Contestation, and Adaptation* (Palgrave, 2018); Elias (n. 57).

59 Elias (n. 57).

60 Rother (n. 58); Elias (n. 57).

61 Of course, some of the needed regimes of cooperation may need to be across regions, which may, in some instances, present additional difficulties but the analysis of these cases should not necessarily be fundamentally different.

62 J. M. Miller, 'A Typology of Legal Transplants: Using Sociology, Legal History and Argentine Examples to Explain the Transplant Process', *American Journal of Comparative Law* 51 (2003), 839.

63 W. Ewald, 'Comparative Jurisprudence: The Logic of Legal Transplants', *American Journal of Comparative Law* 43 (1995), 489.

64 Harding, Chapter 1 in this Volume.

What I have suggested in my analysis is indeed an idea for a new regime of special rights for a particular category of temporary migrants. On Harding's reading, the fact that this idea is based on an analysis that is grounded, in ways I have described, in one specific context ought to be no obstacle to its adoption in a different context. However, what remains open is the question of 'fit'. It seems to me, however, that there are good reasons to believe that a regime of special rights of the sort I am proposing would be a good fit for the Asia-Pacific for a number of reasons that I suggest below.

As I have argued, similar patterns of migration and the presence of migrants engaged in temporary migration projects indicates the presence of similar needs and vulnerabilities that ought to be addressed. Moreover, there are incentives for states to adopt this kind of legislative approach. Some countries in the region have invested in migration as a development strategy and have therefore a stake in the continued sustainability of this model.[65] These countries have also, at times, shown their willingness to attempt to protect their citizens abroad. For example, Indonesia, Pakistan, Bangladesh, India, the Philippines, and Nepal have all decided on moratoria or bans for their migrants to travel to certain countries in reaction to cases of migrant abuse.[66] They also therefore have an incentive in pursuing the kind of agreements that I have suggested are necessary to accommodate and protect those of their migrants who are engaged in temporary migration projects. Of course, power inequalities between states remains, however, maintaining their supply of labour, ensuring continued circular and temporary migration by avoiding migrants becoming trapped despite their intention to return home,[67] and development dividends that are positive for the region as a whole, may represent incentives for the receiving countries to cooperate as well.[68]

However, people's life plans are flexible and revisable, therefore a migration plan that began as oriented to return may change into a desire or need for permanent settlement. From the perspective of effectively accommodating changes in the migratory projects of migrants – from

65 See e.g., M. S. Solomon, 'State-led Migration, Democratic Legitimacy, and Deterritorialization: The Philippines' Labour Export Model', *European Journal of East Asian Studies* 8 (2009), 275.

66 Murray (n. 42).

67 There is evidence, for example, that policies aimed at increasing policing of borders and control over migrants actually increases the probability of migrants remaining permanently, sometimes irregularly (see Hugo (n. 4); D. S. Massey, K. A. Pren and J. Durand 'Why Border Enforcement Backfired', *American Journal of Sociology* 121 (2016), 1557).

68 Scholars have suggested that regional security as well may benefit by the institution of circular migration programs (see H. Ware 'Melanesian Seasonal Migration as a Potential Contribution to Security', *Global Change Peace and Security* 19 (2007), 221).

return to settlement – and of the protection of migrants' rights, lack of access to permanent residency and citizenship is problematic, and such lack of access remains unfortunately a characteristic of migration in the Asia-Pacific.[69]

My analysis centred on the idea that special rights *in addition* to access to citizenship was needed to accommodate the life plans of migrants engaged in temporary migration projects, I have argued that a regime of special rights of this sort would be appropriate in the Asia-Pacific region, too, and there are no obvious obstacles to its 'transplant' to the region. Arguably, however, citizenship law represents a more complicated case. Citizenship law defines the parameters of a society's membership and is, therefore, closely connected with national identity, culture and values.[70] Liberal nationalist theorists have argued for the right of communities to shape their membership as part of their right to national self-determination, for example Michael Walzer, who defined membership as the primary good we distribute to one another.[71] States' practices of immigrant incorporation also vary, and even though scholars have underlined how tensions and incoherencies within states make the identification of neat national models of incorporation difficult,[72] differences in the modes of incorporation of states have nevertheless been identified. Soysal's own sociological analysis of the modes of integration of migrants identified such difference, while also underlying common trajectories, and these differing patterns have been identified by other scholars as well.[73] The transplant of more inclusive citizenship models, and models of regional membership akin to EU citizenship may therefore face greater obstacles. One can hope that states will each develop pathways of inclusion for migrants in accordance to their own understanding of membership and incorporation.

69 G. Hugo, 'Migration in the Asia-Pacific Region' Geneva: Global Commission on International Migration, 2005; it is important to note that this remains an issue for third-country immigrants in the EU context as well, even when it is not an issue for EU citizens migrating within the EU, and it is a characteristics of temporary migration programmes in other regions, too, see Lenard (n. 41).

70 And it is often at the time of deciding a migrant's access to citizenship that national identity, culture, and values are reasserted by states (see, e.g., E. Kofman, 'Citizenship, Migration and the Reassertion of National Identity', *Citizenship Studies* 9 (2005) 453).

71 Walzer (n. 34).

72 G. P. Freeman, 'Immigrant Incorporation in Western Democracies', *International Migration Review* 38 (2004), 945.

73 Soysal (n. 38); E. A. Chung, 'Workers or Residents? Diverging Patterns of Immigrant Incorporation in Korea and Japan', *Pacific Affairs* 83 (2010), 696; A. M. Messina, 'Asylum, Residency and Citizenship Policies and Models of Migrant Incorporation' *Migration and Health in the European Union* (Open University Press, 2011).

V CONCLUSION

In this chapter, I argued that temporary migration projects – while rational, sensible, and legitimate – as a consequence of their specific characteristics, place the migrants that engage in them in a condition of vulnerability. Neither the traditional notion of liberal national citizenship, nor more flexible notions such as post-national citizenship, can accommodate the life plans and address the specific vulnerabilities of this special category of migrants. Addressing these specific needs and plans means instituting a set of special rights meant to protect the migrants and facilitate their unorthodox life plans. I considered whether similar patterns of migration in the context of the Asia-Pacific are amenable to being accommodated through similar institutional arrangements in the EU. I framed this discussion within the debate around legal transplants, and argued that there are no obvious obstacles to the adoption of a regime of special rights for migrants engaged in temporary migration projects in the Asia Pacific.

VI BIBLIOGRAPHY

Adams Jr, R. H. and Page, J, 'Do International Migration and Remittances Reduce Poverty in Developing Countries?', *World Development* 33 (2005), 1645.

Aleman-Castilla, B., 'The Returns to Temporary Migration to the United States: Evidence from the Mexican Urban Employment Survey' Centre for Economic Performance, London School of Economics and Political Science, 2007.

Alexandru, M., 'Migration and Social Mobility: A New Perspective on Status Inconsistency', *Romanian Journal of European Studies* 5 (2007),153.

Anh Hoang, Lam, L. T. Brenda, S. Yeoh, A. and Graham, E., 'Transnational Migration, Changing Care Arrangements and Left-behind Children's Responses in South-East Asia', *Children's Geographies* 13 (2015), 263.

Agunias, D. R., 'From a Zero-Sum to a Win-Win Scenario', *Literature Review on Circular Migration* (Washington, DC: Migration Policy Institute, 2006).

Baldassar L. and Merla, L. (eds.), *Transnational Families, Migration and the Circulation of Care: Understanding Mobility and Absence in Family Life* (Routledge, 2013).

Bauer, T. K. and Sinning, M. G., 'The Savings Behavior of Temporary and Permanent Migrants in Germany', *Journal of Population Economics* 24 (2011), 421.

Boccagni, P., Lafleur, J. and Levitt, P., 'Transnational Politics as Cultural Circulation: Toward a Conceptual Understanding of Migrant Political Participation on the Move', *Mobilities* 11 (2016), 444.

Brickenstein, C., 'Social Protection of Foreign Seasonal Workers: From State to Best Practice', *Comparative Migration Studies* 3 (2015), 2.

Brøndsted Sejersen, T. '"I Vow to Thee My Countries"– The Expansion of Dual Citizenship in the 21st Century', *International Migration Review* 42 (2008), 523.

Caponio, T., 'Documenti, Lavoro, Casa: Percorsi di Integrazione non Lineari di Donne Filippine, Marocchine e Rumene in Italia' STAMPA 85 (2009).

Cassarino, J., 'Theorising Return Migration: The Conceptual Approach to Return Migrants Revisited' (2004) http://cadmus.eui.eu/bitstream/handle/1814/2744/04_02.pdf;sequence=1

Castagnone, E., Petrillo, M., Piperno, E., Flavia, R., 'Madri Migranti: le migrazioni di cura dalla Romania e dall'Ucraina in Italia: percorsi e impatto sui paesi di origine' (CESPI,2007).

Castles, S., 'Guestworkers in Europe: A Resurrection?', *International Migration Review* 40 (2006), 741.

'The Forces Driving Global Migration', *Journal of Intercultural Studies* 34 (2013), 140.

Castles S. and Ozkul, D., 'Circular Migration: Triple Win, or a New Label for Temporary Migration?' in Battistella, G. (ed.), *Global and Asian Perspectives on International Migration* (Springer, 2014).

Danilo C., Recchia D., Simoni M., Zucca G., 'Il Welfare Fatto in Casa' Indagine Nazionale sui Collaboratori Domestici Stranieri che Lavorano a Sostegno delle Famiglie Italiane' (2007).

Chung, E. A., 'Workers or Residents? Diverging Patterns of Immigrant Incorporation in Korea and Japan', *Pacific Affairs* 83 (2010), 696.

Cingolani, P. and Piperno, F. 'Il Prossimo Anno a Casa'. Radicamento, Rientro e Percorsi Translocali: Il Caso delle Reti Migratorie Marginea-Torino e Focsani-Roma' (Rome: CeSPI-FIERI, 2005).

Czaika, M. (ed.), *High-Skilled Migration: Drivers and Policies* (Oxford University Press, 2018).

De Haas, H., 'International Migration, Remittances and Development: Myths and Facts', *Third World Quarterly* 26 (2005), 1269.

Démurger, S. and Xu, H. 'Return Migrants: The Rise of New Entrepreneurs in Rural China', *World Development* 39 (2011), 1847.

Delanty, G. *Citizenship in a Global Age* (Buckingham: Open University Press, 2000).

Dustmann, C. 'Return Migration: The European Experience', *Economic Policy* 11 (1996), 213.

European Commission, Directorate-General for Economic and Financial Affairs (2009).

Elias, J., 'Governing Domestic Worker Migration in Southeast Asia: Public–Private Partnerships, Regulatory Grey Zones and the Household', *Journal of Contemporary Asia* 48 (2018), 278.

Ewald, W., 'Comparative Jurisprudence: The Logic of Legal Transplants', *American Journal of Comparative Law* 43 (1995), 489.

Fajnzylber, P. and López, H. J., 'Close to Home: The Development Impact of Remittances in Latin America' (AGRIS, 2007).

Fouron, G., 'Haitian Immigrants in the United States' in Yeoh, B. S. A. Lai, K. P. Y., Charney, M. W., and Kiong, T. C. (eds.), *Approaching Transnationalisms* (Springer, 2003).

Freeman, G. P., 'Immigrant Incorporation in Western Democracies', *International Migration Review* 38 (2004), 945.

Fullin, G. and Vercelloni, V., 'Dentro la Trappola. Percezioni e Immagini del Lavoro Domestico e di Cura nei Percorsi delle Donne Immigrate', *Polis* 22 (2009), 427.

Galor, O. and Stark, O. 'Migrants' Savings, the Probability of Return Migration and Migrants' Performance', *International Economic Review* (1990), 463.

Gang, I. and Bauer, T. K. 'Temporary Migrants from Egypt: How Long Do They Stay Abroad?' IZA Discussion paper series, No. 3, Institute for the Study of Labor (Bonn: IZA, 1998).

Gheaus, A., 'Care Drain: Who Should Provide for the Children Left Behind?', *Critical Review of International Social and Political Philosophy* 16 (2013), 1.

Giuliano, P. and Ruiz-Arranz, M. 'Remittances, Financial Development, and Growth', *Journal of Development Economics* 90 (2009), 144.

Glytsos, N. P., 'Remitting Behaviour of "Temporary" and "Permanent" Migrants: The Case of Greeks in Germany and Australia', *Labour* 11 (1997), 40.

Hammar, T., *Democracy and the Nation State* (Aldershot, 1990).

Heyzer, N. and Wee, V., 'Domestic Workers in Transient Overseas Employment: Who Benefits, Who Profits', *Canadian Woman Studies* 15 (1995), 98.

Hugo, G., 'Effects of International Migration on the Family in Indonesia', *Asian and Pacific Migration Journal* 11 (2002), 13.

'A New Paradigm of International Migration: Implications for Migration Policy and Planning in Australia', *Information and Research Services Parliamentary Library* (2004), 84.

'Migration in the Asia-Pacific Region' (Geneva: Global Commission on International Migration, 2005)

'International migration and development in Asia' 8th International Conference of the Asia Pacific Migration Research Network, Fuzhou, China 25–29 May 2007 (2007).

'Best Practice in Temporary Labour Migration for Development: A Perspective from Asia and the Pacific', *International Migration* 47 (2009), 23.

Johnson M. and Wilcke, C., 'Caged in and Breaking Loose: Intimate Labor, the State, and Migrant Domestic Workers in Saudi Arabia and Other Arab Countries' in Friedman S. and Mahdavi, P. (eds.), *Migrant Encounters: Intimate Labor, The State and Mobility across Asia* (University of Pennsylvania Press, 2015).

Junge, V., Revilla Diez J. and Schätzl, L., 'Determinants and Consequences of Internal Return Migration in Thailand and Vietnam', *World Development* 71 (2015), 94.

Kanchana, R., 'Is the Kafala Tradition to Blame for the Exploitative Work Conditions in the Arab-Gulf Countries?' in Chowdhury, M. and Rajan, S. I. (eds.), *South Asian Migration in the Gulf* (Palgrave Macmillan, 2018).

Karthick Ramakrishnan, S. and Espenshade T. J., 'Immigrant Incorporation and Political Participation in the United States', *International Migration Review* 35 (2001), 870.

Kofman, E., 'Citizenship, Migration and the Reassertion of National Identity', *Citizenship Studies* 9 (2005), 453.

Kymlicka, W., 'The Rise and Fall of Multiculturalism? New Debates on Inclusion and Accommodation in Diverse Societies', *International Social Science Journal* 61 (2010).

Lenard, P. T., 'Why Temporary Labour Migration Is Not a Satisfactory Alternative to Permanent Migration', *Journal of International Political Theory* 8 (2012), 172.

Lenard, P. T. and Straehle, C. (eds.), *Legislated Inequality: Temporary Labour Migration in Canada* (McGill-Queen's Press, 2012).

Leogrande, A., *Uomini e Caporali: Viaggio tra i Nuovi Schiavi nelle Campagne del Sud* (Feltrinelli Editore, 2016).

Mahe, C., 'Occupational Choice of Return Migrants: Is There a 'Jack-of-all-trades' Effect?', United Nations University-Maastricht Economic and Social Research Institute on Innovation and Technology (MERIT) 39 (2017).

Magnette P., *Citizenship: The History of an Idea* (ECPR Press, 2005).

Marchetta, F., 'Return Migration and the Survival of Entrepreneurial Activities in Egypt', *World Development* 40 (2012), 1999.

Maria Hagan, and Wassink J. 'New skills, New Jobs: Return Migration, Skill Transfers, and Business Formation in Mexico', *Social Problems* 63 (2016), 513.

Massey, D. S., Pren, K. A. and Durand, J. 'Why Border Enforcement Backfired', *American Journal of Sociology* 121 (2016), 1557.

McCormick, B. and Wahba, J. 'Overseas Work Experience, Savings and Entrepreneurship amongst Return Migrants to LDCs', *Scottish Journal of Political Economy* 48 (2001), 164.

Messina, A. M., *Asylum, Residency and Citizenship Policies and Models of Migrant Incorporation' Migration and Health in the European Union* (Open University Press, 2011).

Miller D., *Citizenship and National Identity* (Polity Press, 2000).

Miller, J. M., 'A Typology of Legal Transplants: Using Sociology, Legal History and Argentine Examples to Explain the Transplant Process', *American Journal of Comparative Law* 51 (2003), 839.

Morokvasic, M., 'Transnational Mobility and Gender: A View from Post-Wall Europe' in Mirjana Morokvasic, Umut Erel and Kyoko Shinozaki (eds.), *Crossing Borders and Shifting Boundaries* (VS Verlag für Sozialwissenschaften, 2003), 101.

Murray, H. E., 'Hope for Reform Springs Eternal: How the Sponsorship System, Domestic Laws and Traditional Customs Fail to Protect Migrant Domestic Workers in GCC Countries', *Cornell International Law Journal* 45 (2013), 461.

Newbold, B. K., 'Counting Migrants and Migrations: Comparing Lifetime and Fixed-Interval Return and Onward Migration', *Economic Geography* 77 (2001), 23.

Ottonelli, V. and Torresi, T. 'Temporary Migration Projects and Children's Education' *Notizie di Politeia* (2010).

'Inclusivist Egalitarian Liberalism and Temporary Migration: A Dilemma', *Journal of Political Philosophy* 20 (2012), 202.

'When Is Migration Voluntary?', *International Migration Review* 47 (2013), 783.

'Temporary Migration Projects and Voting Rights', *Critical Review of International Social and Political Philosophy* 17 (2014), 580.

'Temporary Migration, Identity and Allegiance' in Fiona Jenkins, Mark Nolan and Kim Rubinstein (eds.), *Allegiance and Identity in a Globalised World* (Cambridge University Press, 2014).

'Temporary Migration and the Shortcomings of Citizenship' in Carlota Solé, Sonia Parella, Sonja Nita and Teresa Sordé Martí (eds.), *Impact of Circular Migration on Human, Political and Civil Rights* (Springer, 2016).

Parreñas, R. S., 'Women, Migration and Domestic Work', *Región Y Sociedad* (2001) 15.

Children of Global Migration: Transnational Families and Gendered Woes (Stanford University Press, 2005).

Pruthi, S., 'Social Ties and Venture Creation by Returnee Entrepreneurs', *International Business Review* 23 (2014), 1139.

Ramji-Nogales, J., 'Under the Canopy: Migration Governance in Southeast Asia', *UCLA Journal of International Law and Foreign Affairs* 21 (2017), 10.

Ratha, D. and Shaw, W., South-South Migration and Remittances, The World Bank (2007) http://citeseerx.ist.psu.edu/viewdoc/download?doi=10.1.1.576.4220&rep=rep1&type=pdf.

Reid-Musson, E., 'Grown Close to Home: Migrant Farmworker (Im)mobilities and Unfreedom on Canadian Family Farms', *Annals of the American Association of Geographers* 107 (2017), 716.

Rother, S. 'Labour Migration in Southeast Asia: In Search of Regional Governance' in Ba, A. D. and Beeson, M. (eds.), *Contemporary Southeast Asia: The Politics of Change, Contestation, and Adaptation* (Palgrave, 2018).

Sayad, A., *La double Absence: Des Illusions de l'émigré aux Souffrances de l'immigré* (Seuil, 2000).

Solomon, M. S., 'State-led Migration, Democratic Legitimacy, and Deterritorialization: The Philippines' Labour Export Model', *European Journal of East Asian Studies* 8 (2009), 275.

Soysal, N. Y., *Limits of Citizenship: Migrants and Postnational Membership in Europe* (University of Chicago Press, 1994).

Strauss K. and McGrath, S. 'Temporary Migration, Precarious Employment and Unfree Labour Relations: Exploring the 'Continuum of Exploitation' in Canada's Temporary Foreign Worker Program', *Geoforum* 78 (2017), 199.

Stoll M. A. and J. S. Wong 'Immigration and Civic Participation in a Multiracial and Multiethnic Context', *International Migration Review* 41 (2007), 880.

Uccellini, C. M., 'Outsiders after Accession: The Case of Romanian Migrants in Italy, 1989–2009', *Political Perspectives* 4 (2010), 70.

Wahba, J. and Zenou, Y., 'Out of Sight, Out of Mind: Migration, Entrepreneurship and Social Capital', *Regional Science and Urban Economics* 42 (2012), 890.

Walzer M., *Spheres of Justice: A Defense of Pluralism and Justice* (Basic, 1983).

Ware H., 'Melanesian Seasonal Migration as a Potential Contribution to Security', *Global Change Peace and Security* 19 (2007), 221.

Woodruff C. and Zenteno, R., 'Migration Networks and Microenterprises in Mexico', *Journal of Development Economics* 82 (2007), 509.

ZhangSun, O. XinZhi, Z., RunQun, W., Feng, L., AiGuo, S. and XingLin, W., 'Typical Survey and Research on Returning-Home Migrant Workers' Entrepreneurship in Jiangxi Province under Post-Financial crisis', *Asian Agricultural Research* 2 (2010), 34.

Conclusion

Vito Breda

This collection of essays has provided an overview of a series of *Legal Transplants in East Asia and Oceania*. The transplants of foreign law into these regions has been directly linked to a modernization process aimed at improving national economic efficiency and, albeit to a lesser extent, increasing political and administrative accountability. A series of brief summaries of each of the collection's contributions and an analysis of the relation between each of the chapters, which I hope I delivered with equanimity, is in the introduction of this book and does not need to be reproduced here. What is worth mentioning in this final essay is, perhaps, that *Legal Transplants in East Asia and Oceania* intended to show the distinctive connection between multifaced policies aimed at stimulating national economies and the East Asian conception of a transparent and efficient market economy.

These types of legal transplants are distinctive from the ones that, in Europe, abetted the great national codification processes and were imposed historically by colonial powers. The legal reforms, for instance, that in successive waves inspired the Prussian, the French and the Italian codification processes, were perceived as part of the Enlightenment movement and claimed, at least in theory, universal normative values. In the collection of essays included in this book, there is little evidence of an intention to implement universal values in East Asia and Oceania. Even in those instances in which legal transplants were designed to implement policies that have global ramifications (such as the protection of the marine environment or the regulation of the flow of human capital in Torresi's essay), legal reforms in East Asia and Oceania tend to be specifically designed to meet the requirements of distinctive cultures.

Legal transplants in East Asia, Harding explains, must 'fit' a distinctive culture. Kaino's analysis of the past and present influence of Bentham into the Japanese legal system also supports the claim that foreign legal concepts are practically, rather than ideologically, assessed. In other words, this collection of essays shows that there is, within the margin of reasonableness, no intent to develop a cosmopolitan legal system. One of the side effects of this pragmatic rather than theoretical understanding of foreign-inspired legal reforms is that much of the debate over the nature and pragmatic plausibility of legal transplants appears hollow. This point is made in the opening chapter of this book by Harding and it has been confirmed, directly or indirectly, by most of the essays collected in this book.

A corollary of the East Asia and Oceania pragmatism is a tendency to strip transplanted institutions from cultural perceptions and doctrinal analyses. Harding refers to the transplant of English and Welsh trust law into the Chinese legal system as one example in which a receiving legal system tried to re-design legal concepts that have been part of donor legal traditions for centuries. The final result, in Harding's narrative, is a Frankenstein-like English–Chinese trust law. Gray's analysis of the migration of the concept of good faith in Australian contract law is another example of an attempt to transplant one of the most articulated and historically entrenched concepts in civil law traditions. Gray's highly articulated analysis and Harding's series of examples would be, if they were to be considered as individual analyses, mere anecdotal narratives. However, as part of a collection of essays and combined with the rest of the contribution, these analyses show a tendency to free alien institutions from their doctrinal, historical, and jurisprudential burdens. The resulting transplanted institutions might look like the result of a mismanaged cultural extrapolation.

However, the multifarious aims of legal transplants are not to recreate a cultural artefact; these are attempts to achieve a change of conduct. The result of the process might be difficult to predict. The Frankenstein English–Chinese trust might not be as functional as expected by Chinese legal scholars, yet, modern legal systems are extremely complex; therefore, anticipating in a scientific way the role that a new institution might have in a large country such as China would require the assessment of a mindboggling number of variables. Again, the aim of this collection was not to provide an ideal model that a successful legal transplant ought to follow. It is reasonable to argue that suggesting a model for legal transplants in highly diversified regions in East Asia would be a quixotic endeavour.

A dysfunctional legal transplant – and in Harding's chapter there is a hint of dismay regarding the state of the current literature – might be described as a social-engineering experiment that did not deliver the expected results. The consideration of the costs and the potential benefits that foreign-inspired legal reforms might have is one of the reasons that might expedite or reduce the speed of legal transplants. Australian legislative institutions and judges, when tasked with the assessment of potential legal transplants, have been particularly cautious. The level of restraint manifested in the Australian jurisprudence was noted by Lee, Campbell and Gray in this book. A predilection to walk slowly on the path of innovation is also manifested in the implementation of UNIDROIT Principles of International Commercial Contracts and the Convention on Contracts for the International Sale of Goods. Viven-Wilksch noted, for instance, that the implementation of these international devices aimed at increasing trade and facilitating multinational cooperation had not been absorbed into the Australian legal system in the way that would reasonably be expected by modern mercantile economies. On a general level, the Australian legal system, by way of comparison to other liberal democracies, tends to be conservative. For instance, the doctrine of human rights, by way of comparison to its effects in all European legal systems (the UK, Canada, and New Zealand) has made little headway in Australia. Analyses, such as those proposed by Viven-Wilksch, Gray and Lee, show that conservative attitudes are not limited to the protection of rights and minorities, but are a general feature of the Australian legal system.

Such a claim might be sustained only via a comparative perspective. Institutions are rules that have been imbedded into a legal culture for a period of time exactly because they are perceived as having value for the stakeholders. It is common for communities that hold those institutions as valuable, Fukuyama explains, to be conservative. However, the series of essays in this collection show that Australian judges tend to be, compared to other legal systems, less inclined to innovate. The comparative reluctance to change is evident in areas such as commercial law.

Singapore's mercantile economy, for instance, appears to have a level of institutional adaptiveness that might be perceived as unique in the East Asian and Oceania regions and therefore at first sight, a comparison between Australia and Singapore might appear unhelpful. Recall that the scope of the collection is not to compare legal transplants; rather, it is to show, within the limit of reasonableness associated with any comparative analysis, the connection between national aspirations, foreign-inspired reforms and a legal culture.

The process of balancing the connection between these three elements has, and still is, been conducive to a gamut of legal reforms in East Asia and Oceania. However, the protection of the environment is comparatively the area of law in which the combination of national aspirations, foreign-inspired reforms and a legal culture produced a larger variation in legal transplants. This distinctive flexibility is reported in Techera. In her chapter, she points out the cultural connection that exists between East Asian and Oceania nations with the marine environment. That connection is manifested in a series of adroit foreign-inspired legal reforms.

It could be argued that I, and the rest of the contributors, looked at the correlation between national aspirations, the adoption of foreign law, and culture with *rose-tinted glasses*. For instance, fishing and cultural eating habits that depleted the shark population contributed to the alignment of a negative perception of East Asian and Oceania environmental policies. It could be also suggested that the project has edited the collection (or indeed selected the contributors) in a way that appears to give relevance to a selection of legal transplants.

Legal transplants can be a cheap window-dressing exercise that small countries with limited resources do to facilitate trade, to obtain international recognition or to request financial support from, for instance, the World Bank. These transplants are part of state-promoted simulation strategies which are, sometimes, imposed on small states that seek to increase their trade opportunities in a globalized market. A few of these foreign-inspired reforms do take place in legal systems that are corrupt. Plebendalism, that is, the assumption that state resources should be distributed to political supporters; and amoral familism, that is, a combination of nepotism and the allocation of public resources that hinders political enemies, are reported as hindering factors in the development of East Asian and Oceania's political system. However, the collection of essays in this book reported little evidence of the impact on these political pathologies. Again, there are indications, based on an international survey; some East Asian and Oceania political systems are committed, just as the colonizers were, to harvesting public resources to support their own fiefdoms. However, it is also reasonable to suggest, firstly, that mimicked foreign reforms tend to deliver transient prizes. Secondly, these processes are often found in modern legal systems. Fukuyama uses, for instance, the example of Italy and Greece to explain the implications of large-scale corruption in national economies.

The aim of this collection was, in short, not to compare the effect of amoral practices in a geographical area or to become part of a saturnalia of the process of legal modernization in East Asia and Oceania. This collection of essays has, instead, provided the reader with new knowledge of the effect of the migration of legal ideas into East Asian and Oceania's legal systems. These new modern transplants are, in theory, distinguishable from the Eurocentric policies that were imposed using brutal imperial institutions. Modern legal transplants in East Asia and Oceania are, instead, a manifestation of multiple social-engineering endeavours managed by receiving legal systems. The book shows the benefits and a few of the shortcomings that foreign-inspired legal reforms have had in these geographical areas.

Index

For EU product safety concerns, contact us at Calle de José Abascal, 56–1°,
28003 Madrid, Spain or eugpsr@cambridge.org.

www.ingramcontent.com/pod-product-compliance
Lightning Source LLC
LaVergne TN
LVHW052032200926
848481LV00005B/1654
* 9 7 8 1 0 0 9 0 0 1 8 3 0 *